D1453446

Pierre's Hole!

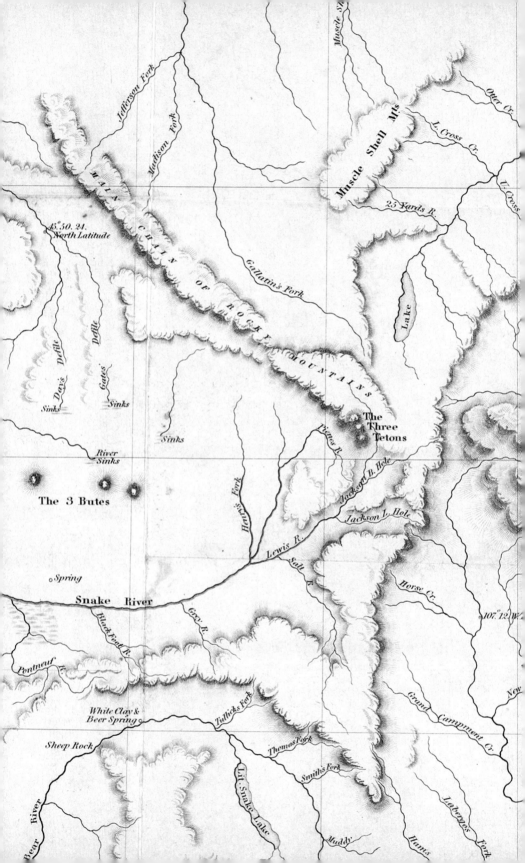

Pierre's Hole!

THE FUR TRADE HISTORY OF TETON VALLEY, IDAHO

by Jim Hardee

MUSEUM OF THE MOUNTAIN MAN
SUBLETTE COUNTY HISTORICAL SOCIETY

Pierre's Hole: The Fur Trade History of Teton Valley, Idaho
by Jim Hardee

Published by the Sublette County Historical Society
P.O. Box 909
Pinedale, WY 82941
http://MMMuseum.com

Printed in the United States of America.

ISBN-13: 978-0-9768113-6-7
ISBN-10: 0-9768113-6-7

*Frontispiece illustration: Detail of the map included in Washington
Irving's 1837 book,* The Adventures of Captain Bonneville, USA.
Museum of the Mountain Man, Pinedale, Wyoming.

Book and cover design by Sommers Studio
http://sommstudio.com

To my dad, who instilled in me a
love for the outdoors and taught me
so much about living off the land.

CONTENTS

List of Color Plates

ACKNOWLEDGMENTS

Such a book would not be possible without assistance. Many people from all over the country and various walks of life lent their support to this project. Grateful appreciation is extended to Mark Kelly and Carol Kuhn, who reviewed the initial manuscript and offered invaluable suggestions to improve the work. They also convincingly argued for altering the documentary style, leading to a far better resource for future users. Jim Auld provided key insights that raised the level of the story. Thanks also to Scott Walker, whose consultation made a remarkable difference in several conclusions drawn within these pages. The extraordinary diligence of Isabel Waddell improved the book's technical aspects and readability. Allen Hall's paper, "Snake River, Crossroads of the Fur Trade," was a boon to this author. Mike Powell and Richard Ashburn provided valuable input from a local perspective. Bruce Belason looked over the history presented and offered meticulous observations that truly improved the writing. The staff at the Teton County Museum in Driggs, Idaho, was especially helpful, allowing unfettered access to the files and stacks in the museum's research library. Deep appreciation is extended to Laurie Hartwig, Angie Thomas, and the rest of the staff at the Museum of the Mountain Man, who put so much time and effort into this project, along with Pinedale, Wyoming's Clint Gilchrist, who did a fabulous job on the maps, and Sue Sommers, whose design skills are unsurpassed. Finally, a heartfelt thank you is extended to the Sublette County Historical Society Board of Directors, the Sublette County Museum Board, and the Sublette County Commissioners, whose commitment to expanding fur trade history made such a partnership possible.

INTRODUCTION

Once the scene of so much fur trade activity, Teton Valley, Idaho, deserves an accurate version of its past. Updating the available information about the fur trade and its relationship to Pierre's Hole, as Teton Valley was known in the early 1800s, is overdue. An account of trapper adventures, hardships, depredations and struggles which brings new insight and analysis to the early history of the Teton Basin is essential in preserving an accurate record of the region. The legends, stories, and misinformation promulgated over the past near-century need review and correction. Here, then, is a fresh look at events from 1807 to 1840 which shaped the development of the valley that rests in the morning shadows of the Tetons – Pierre's Hole!

Named after Iroquois trapper Pierre Tevanitagon *(ti van' u ti gun)*, Pierre's Hole lies on the southeastern edge of the state of Idaho, where it borders western Wyoming. The Teton Basin once abounded in beaver sought by the mountaineers and traders of the first half of the nineteenth century. Beaver fur was in such high demand by the fashion industry in Europe and America that, for a brief and volatile period, tempting profits could be made by well-connected entrepreneurs with good timing. Luxurious beaver fur was converted to felt by hat makers, then used to create the stylish accessories so popular in New York, Boston, London, and Paris – virtually all of the world's major cities. Native Americans were side-stepped in the interest of advancing the fur trade.

This book examines that early period in Pierre's Hole. It explains the origins of many place names in use today, locations often christened by mountain men. It tells of the indigenous people in the valley, the Shoshone, and their life prior to Euro-American contact. Background on Pierre Tevanitagon provides a look at the man and his relationship to the region, as well as his involvement in the fur trade. Details of the period 1807 through 1840 suggest the role Teton Valley played, not just in early Idaho history, but in the story of America's West. Where possible, excerpts from the journals,

1

diaries and letters of men who were there tell the story from their point of view. Their spelling and use of punctuation is left intact, conveying a bit of the character of these men and their times.

At an elevation of 6,200 feet above sea level, Pierre's Hole is home to roughly 8,500 people today.[1] The valley is about thirty miles long and varies in width from around fifteen miles through its central portion to roughly eight or ten miles at either end. Population centers include the hamlet of Tetonia at the north end; the governmental seat of Teton County – Driggs – is located in the middle; Victor lies to the south. Wyoming's western border cuts the eastern edge of the valley and claims the town of Alta. Montana also has a Teton County, as does Wyoming, the county seat of which is Jackson.

The snow-capped Teton Range of the Rocky Mountains towering on the east and the evergreen-shrouded Big Hole Mountains on the west cradle the placid meanders of the Teton River which flow nearly the entire length of the basin. To the south lies the Palisades backcountry, while the north end of the valley slopes gently upward through rolling hills that seldom obstruct the vista of the lordly Tetons.

The jagged Teton Range contrasts sharply with the pasturelands and rolling fields of grain and potatoes cultivated on the valley floor. Along its many creeks, modern methods of irrigation have affected the riparian wetlands associated with Teton Valley's floodplain, making these areas drier than during the fur trade days. Additionally, throughout the West, early settlers who raised livestock and crops put a lot of time and energy into clearing willow thickets or straightening and cleaning out stream channels which included removing what beaver were still to be found.

The end of what climatologists call the "Little Ice Age" occurred around 1850, so the climate of the early- to mid-nineteenth century, when the events in this book took place, was colder and wetter in general than today. Chillier temperatures, more snow, and greater snow accumulations at lower elevations all resulted in a wetter landscape. While the high elevation snows were probably not melting as much as they do now, snowfall at lower elevations was still subject to seasonal warm weather and thus melted. That type of snowmelt probably did a better job than mountain runoff of remaining in the valley, recharging the groundwater and creating marshy, boggy meadows in Pierre's Hole.[2]

Dr. Robert Van Kirk, a water resource researcher who has completed several projects in and around the Teton Valley region, said:

If you accounted for increased recharge from a wetter climate (both in the stream channels and on the valley floor), increased retention of runoff in floodplains, and perhaps much more inflow from the mountains to the south and west of the valley, you could make a solid, quantitative case that water tables, especially in the southwest corner of the valley, were higher during the fur trade era than today. I mention the mountains south and west of the valley, because under the current climate, the vast majority of water in the valley comes from the Teton Range. The east side of the Big Hole Mountains is in a precipitation shadow and contributes very little to the overall water budget in the valley. A very slight shift in storm tracks and precipitation patterns could greatly increase precipitation there, and more than overall averages, such a difference between now and the "Little Ice Age" could easily account for large differences in precipitation and hence runoff from the Big Holes. Resulting differences in groundwater tables would be especially large during the summer and at locations where streams converged (this is definitely the case in the southwest corner of the valley). During the period of wetter and colder climate, runoff would have lasted much later into the summer than it does now, perhaps even being halted by re-freezing at higher elevations rather than by exhaustion of the snowpack. So, put all that together, and I would accept that water tables in the valley could have been as high or higher during the fur trade era than now.[3]

Thus, the Teton Basin was wetter during the days of the trapper, and readers of journals and diaries should keep this in mind.

Pierre's Hole is a rapidly growing, busy region today. The town of Driggs frequently winds up on the top of lists identifying the best places to live in the nation.[4] A haven for winter and summer sports, the mountains and rivers of Teton Valley attract thousands of visitors each year. A sturdy few stay permanently. The population of

Pierre's Hole today is a diverse mix of pioneer families and recently immigrated residents from every region, culture and background imaginable – much like the variety of trappers who descended on the basin nearly two hundred years ago.

Pursuit of profitable pelts brought multi-ethnic peoples – American, British, French, German, a variety of Native Americans and many others – into Teton Valley in the early 1800s. What had long been an active seasonal hunting and gathering ground for many indigenous peoples became the scene of extensive trapper activity. While beaver swarmed the swamps and streams, prosperity in hides was one of few successful businesses in an untamed land of romance and adventure. It was a heroic life for hardy mountaineers who ventured into what was, for them, a trackless wilderness. The stories of these men are told in the pages ahead.

Beginning with the return of Meriwether Lewis and William Clark to St. Louis, Missouri, from across the Rocky Mountains in 1806, reports of abundant fur bearing mammals in that region triggered an escalation in trapping interests. One of the first to capitalize on the new information was Manuel Lisa, who organized a fur trade company in 1807 and headed up the Missouri River.[5] Lisa was joined by John Colter, who had been with Lewis and Clark's Corps of Discovery. Andrew Henry, another early fortune-hunter, established a winter post in 1810 on what would become known as Henry's Fork of the Snake River, the Tetons beckoning in the distance.

Some of Henry's men undoubtedly trapped beaver in Pierre's Hole; evidence of a camp is still located on Conant Creek at the north edge of the Hole.[6] The following year, Wilson Price Hunt, leader of the Pacific Fur Company, brought an expedition through the valley on the way to Astoria, in modern Oregon.[7] From 1818 to 1823, the Northwest and Hudson's Bay Company's annual Snake Country Expeditions routinely sent fur hunters to this part of the country hoping to leave with their packs full of beaver skins.[8]

These mountaineers include many names familiar to fur trade historians, including Jedediah Smith, David Jackson, William Sublette, Andrew Drips, Lucien Fontenelle and Joseph Meek. For these trappers, the ultimate fur trade event was the annual rendezvous, where they sold their pelts and bartered for the upcoming year's supplies. Celebrating life in the Rocky Mountains with their brethren, these gatherings occurred in various locations throughout the West – twice in Pierre's Hole. The grandest of them all was the 1832 assembly in Teton Valley. More Indians than trappers attended that particular trade fair. More than 300 mountain men are estimated to have congregated with 120 lodges of Nez Perce Indians and eighty lodges of Flatheads. Together, they traded, competed and frolicked after a hard year toiling in the icy beaver streams of the Shining Mountains, as the Rockies were often called.

Old timers, free trappers, and new competitors from across the country, including Nathaniel J. Wyeth of Massachusetts, and Fort Smith partners Bean and Sinclair, flocked to the 1832 rendezvous at Pierre's Hole hoping to reap rich rewards. This rendezvous also saw the famous "Battle of Pierre's Hole," a dramatic skirmish between trappers and their Indian allies against hostile Gros Ventres, later recounted by numerous trappers in first-hand, and often conflicting, journal entries.

Trapping continued in and around Pierre's Hole until the downturn in demand for Rocky Mountain furs made it less fruitful to stay in the mountains. Trapping expeditions came to Pierre's Hole as late as 1840. That year also saw Father Pierre Jean De Smet in the valley, on his way to start Jesuit missions among the Indians of the Pacific Northwest.[9] A new phase of western expansion had begun.

Well after the heyday of the fur trade was over, in the 1860s, a trapper did settle in the area. He was the Englishman Richard Leigh, more commonly known as "Beaver Dick."[10] Leigh was followed by horse thieves, cattle rustlers, sheep herders and miners. Eventually more settlers discovered the valley, and a Mormon community founded in the late 1880s was one of the first to blossom.

While many journals, memoirs and letters tell of fur trade events in the valley, few modern historians have attempted a comprehensive history of this region that includes the fur trade period. Benjamin W. Driggs wrote *The History of Teton Valley* in 1926, compiling the fur trade portions based to a large degree on oral history.[11] A veritable archive of new information has come to light since its publication. Besides being out-of-print and difficult to obtain, the early story of Pierre's Hole as told by B. W. Driggs is inaccurate.

Subsequent historians of the fur trade in Teton Valley have relied on B. W. Driggs too much. Noted historian Nolie Mumey attempted to chronicle valley history twenty years later, but depended too heavily on B. W. Driggs, making his book, *The Teton Mountains,* nearly as problematic. An edited version of Driggs' book was printed in 1970, annotated by Louis Clement and Harold Forbush, but did little to correct the errors. Margaret Sanborn wrote *The Grand Tetons* in 1978 but, while including information on several trappers, covered the area's fur trade aspects with a broad brush, underutilizing many trapper journals and diaries that could have been accessed.[12]

Pierre's Hole oral history, based on the memories of those who arrived in the valley long after the fur trade, often fails to withstand serious investigation. Historical markers within the valley are poorly located and provide a disappointing, sometimes faulty narrative. Local historical displays are debatable, often presenting regional lore as fact. Such inaccuracies are refuted and corrected in this book.

Here then is gathered in one place the full story of Teton Valley's early history. From the return of Lewis and Clark's expedition of 1804-1806 through the last rendezvous in 1840, the saga of the fur trade in Pierre's Hole is portrayed.

The Teton Range, looking east from the uplands on the north end of Pierre's Hole. The Teton River runs across the bottom of the photo; trees across the center delineate Leigh Creek. JIM HARDEE PHOTO

1

THE MOUNTAINS

The geographic borders of Teton Basin are the mountains and foothills of southeast Idaho and the extreme western edge of Wyoming (see maps, color plates 1 and 2). Rolling hills rise gently on the valley's northern perimeter, undulating ever higher but never becoming truly mountainous. The Snake River Range, including the Big Holes and the Palisades backcountry, along with the Teton Range form the boundaries of Pierre's Hole to the west, south, and east, respectively. The Snake River Range begins where the Tetons end – a tangled web of ridges, streams, aspen thickets and meadows, rising out of the Snake River Plain. On the west, the Big Holes gain in elevation, culminating with Piney Peak topping out at 9,019 feet, the highest point in the Big Hole group.

To the south, Highway 31 separates the Palisades region from the Big Holes portion of the Snake River Range. Today's Pine Creek Pass, at roughly 6,800 feet in elevation, provides access to the southwest corner of Pierre's Hole through the Palisades from Swan Valley. Many trapping parties used this route in the early 1800s though it was apparently never named. Pine Creek Pass may at one time have been called Piney Pass, at least as late as the 1920s. B. W. Driggs also insisted Nathaniel Wyeth exited Pierre's Hole "over what is now called Piney Pass" in 1834.[1] No trapper journal names Piney Pass or Pine Creek Pass but in more recent times, Piney Pass has been designated as a gap just south of Garns Mountain, high up in the Big Holes. About eight miles to the southeast, Highway 31 traverses Pine Creek Pass going from Teton Valley into Swan Valley. The two should not be confused.

From the floor of Pierre's Hole, looking east, most viewers cannot help but be awed by the beauty of the granite spires reaching into cerulean skies – the Tetons. The mountains are in nearby Wyoming but were included as a part of the Idaho Territory until 1868. Snowmelt from the peaks contributes to the Teton Basin watershed. These mountains are veritable symbols of the early history of the fur trade as well as that of Idaho itself.

Geologically speaking, the Teton uplift is relatively young, two to ten million years old. This is in contrast to nearby Rocky Mountain ranges formed some fifty-five to sixty-five million years earlier. The ice age played an integral part in sculpting slopes where glaciers rest year-round in the deep recesses of hidden canyons. The Tetons continue to grow today at the snail-like pace of about one inch every one hundred years. The largest peak on the range, Grand Teton, stands at 13,772 feet above sea level.[2] Without a doubt, the Tetons offer some of the most picturesque mountain scenery in Wyoming/Idaho – perhaps in the entire country.

The range, protected as Grand Teton National Park by President Calvin Coolidge in 1929, encompasses an area of approximately 150 square miles.[3] The peaks rise almost vertically, some reaching over seven thousand feet from the floor of Pierre's Hole. These mountains make up a short spur of the Continental Divide, running south about forty-five miles from the boundary of Yellowstone National Park to Teton Pass. At an elevation of 8,431 feet, today's Teton Pass allows travelers to depart Pierre's Hole and enter Jackson Hole to the east along Idaho Highway 33/Wyoming Highway 22.

Three sides of Pierre's Hole are surrounded by the Targhee National Forest. The name Targhee refers to a Bannock chief, instrumental in numerous peace negotiations for his people, who was later killed by the Crow in the early 1870s.[4] The Bridger-Teton National Forest includes a portion of the valley as well. The name Bridger refers to trapper Jim Bridger, who will appear repeatedly in the pages ahead. The bulk of the Tetons' west slope beyond the borders of Grand Teton National Park was designated by a 1984 act of Congress as the Jedediah Smith Wilderness Area. Smith was another trapper who played a prominent role in the fur trade annals of Teton Valley.[5]

The valley was once under water, as evidenced by various sea shells and terraces suggesting an ancient shore line. These waters cut through the lava bed and drained into the Columbia River then on to the Pacific Ocean. During the Middle Archaic Period, about 5000 to 3000 B.P., Paleo-Indians entered Pierre's Hole along trails that still traverse the mountainsides.[6] These people built rough "forts" from flat stones laid in a circular formation, apparently to denote a route of travel. B. W. Driggs described one of these circles, still extant at the time he wrote the valley's history in 1926. Early settlers reported the fort was located on Bald Hill, south of Fox Canyon, with walls five to six feet high.[7]

On the west slope of the Tetons, the Shoshone found rock which geologists call "steatite." It is more commonly known as soapstone, and from this material they fashioned practical items such as cups and bowls for cooking and eating. While gathering this useful stone, they ventured into Pierre's Hole, Jackson Hole and the Yellowstone Country to hunt, fish, and harvest seeds, berries and other plant materials. Today, the area around Teton Pass and south near Mosquito Pass is the source for the majority of pre-contact obsidian artifacts recovered in the region of Grand Teton National Park. Obsidian flakes from this area have been found as far away as the Carolinas.[8]

Crossing the Tetons

Archeologists believe early people who moved off the plains and into the mountains frequently entered Jackson Hole from the south, but eleven primary routes into that valley have been identified. Of these, three originated in Pierre's Hole and crossed the mountains. The northernmost corridor passed through today's Conant Pass. Two options from the south included a path through Philips Canyon by way of the pass of the same name, and one over Mosquito Pass. Trail Creek, on the Jackson side, rising up to and over Teton Pass, does not appear to have been frequented as often.[9]

Trails followed by early trappers and settlers navigating through Pierre's Hole essentially followed these same Indian-made paths. Starting up the Moose Creek drainage, travelers climbed the ridge between Moose and Trail creeks, and then crossed over to the Trail Creek drainage near modern Teton Pass. From that gap, Trail Creek flows east toward the neighboring valley, beginning with an initial segment of remarkably steep terrain. On the Jackson Hole side, Trail Creek was known as Pass Creek. Settlers used this trail into the late 1880s.

An apparently well-used option for crossing the Teton Range went up Moose Creek to Mesquite Creek, hit Coal Creek and crossed to Mail Cabin Creek, then over Mosquito Pass and down that stream. This seems to have been the preferred course for east-bound travelers. Trappers used this extensively between 1820 and 1840. Segments of this trail provided access to Jackson Hole and Swan, Star, or Teton valleys.[10]

Today, Idaho State Highway 33 follows Trail Creek and becomes Wyoming State Highway 22 after crossing the state line. The road ascends 2400 feet in elevation in about six miles – it remains a steep pass even in modern times.

Naming the Tetons

Native Americans had a different name for the Tetons. A diary entry by trapper Osborne Russell declared the Shoshone called the range "the Hoary-headed Fathers."[11] Historian Merrill J. Mattes says other nations also referred to these peaks as "The Three Brothers," or as "Tee Win-at," meaning "The Pinnacles." Another source indicates the Blackfoot may have called this range the "Ghost Robbers."[12]

Most people believe the name *les Trois Tetons* was given to these mountains by French trappers in the early 1800s. Tom Sun, a French-Canadian living in Wyoming in its pioneer days, purportedly knew many frontiersmen and reported this foreign moniker to Nolie Mumey who wrote it as fact in his manuscript.[13]

However, during Donald Mackenzie's 1818-1820 Northwest Company (NWC) trapping excursions into the Snake River Plains region, French Canadians or Iroquois Indians who were a part of his brigade named a different landmark *les Trois Tetons*.[14] This title translates from French into English as The Three Teats or Breasts. Apparently, those randy Northwest Company trappers, too long separated from their female counterparts, imagined certain protruding anatomical features. (A teen-aged visitor to Teton Valley has recently asserted it is the sky in the gaps between the peaks, not the mountains themselves, that forms the engrossing appendages at which the trappers gaped.)

Interestingly, an inspection of early journals and maps indicates the name may not have referred to the modern Tetons at all. Rather, the Three Tetons seem to be the name originally given to what are now known as the Three Buttes on the Snake River Plain, just over twenty miles east of modern Arco, Idaho. Only later was the name transferred to today's Tetons. This case is well made in an interesting booklet by Bruce H. Blevins, *A.K.A. the Tetons*.[15] Blevins records additional names for the Tetons that crop up in early diaries and maps including Pilot Knobs, Pilot Knob Mountain, Pilot Bute, Les Trois Tetons, 3 Paps, Three Paps, 3 Tops, 3 Guides, Pilot Knobes, 3 Peaks, The Three Tetons, Teton Range and, simply, Tetons.[16]

Donald Mackenzie was with Wilson Price Hunt in 1811 when Hunt named today's Tetons the "Pilot Knobs." Mackenzie continued to use "Pilot Knobs" in his later reports to Alexander Ross as Factor at Fort Nez Perces. Ross, whose book was published in 1855, called the current Three Buttes on the Snake River "The Trois Tetons." In a clarifying footnote, Ross indicated the Pilot Knobs "are now generally known as the Three Paps, or Tetons."[17]

The Pilot Knobs was a fitting name for these mountains. The great altitude of these peaks made the Grand Teton famous in fur trade history as a landmark. Surrounding topography is such that its summit is visible at amazing distances in nearly every direction. Its

View of the Tetons from the Big Holes looking across Pierre's Hole, as Robert Stuart may have seen them in 1812. The road at left roughly parallels Pack Saddle Creek; the band of vegetation across the middle of the basin marks the course of the Teton River. JIM HARDEE PHOTO

appearance from wherever viewed is striking and unmistakable. The remarkable prominence of this peak and its ease of identification from other mountains made it useful to early trappers. A beacon to the mountaineers, its different aspects when seen from various directions enabled travelers to tell their position at once.

One of the first maps to properly mark the Tetons was created in 1821 by Chevalie Lapie, a Frenchman, on which they are labeled "Pilotes Knobs."[18] Until the mid-1830s, these pinnacles were rather consistently referred to as The Pilot Knobs. In 1831, trapper Warren A. Ferris began keeping a journal and in 1836, drew a map, both of which reference the Tetons as they are known today.[19] The 1834 map of British cartographer John Arrowsmith is the first published document to show the Tetons in their current location. He uses the name "3 Paps or Tetons" to indicate the mountain range.[20]

The word "Teton" in reference to the mountain range appeared in literature for the first time in 1836. The term debuted in Washington Irving's book, *Astoria, or Anecdotes of an Enterprise Beyond*

12

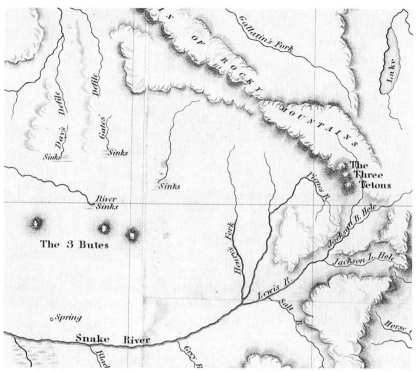

Detail of the map included in Washington Irving's 1837 book, The
Adventures of Captain Bonneville, USA. MUSEUM OF THE MOUNTAIN MAN, PINEDALE,
WYOMING

the Rocky Mountains, relating the adventures of Wilson Price Hunt
and the Pacific Fur Company's expeditions to the west coast.[21]
Another of Irving's books, *The Adventures of Captain Bonneville,
U.S.A.,* describes Bonneville's explorations in the Rockies and was
published in 1837. It included the first map showing the Tetons and
the Buttes, respectively, in the same locations as modern maps.[22]

The buttes, on the other hand, are documented on a map
by William Kittson as early as 1825, and are labeled as the *Trois
Boutes*. Kittson had accompanied the trapping party led by
Mackenzie in 1818 but traveled with Peter Skene Ogden on this
1825 expedition.[23] Beginning in 1837, some derivative of Three
Buttes is used for the mounds rising from the Snake River Plain
on virtually all published maps up to modern times. The buttes
are now individually called East Butte, Middle Butte, and Big
Southern Butte, or, as a group, Three Buttes.

An illustration from John Charles Fremont's Report of 1843-1844 depicts the American Falls on the Snake River, with the Three Buttes in the background.
COURTESY OF THE BENEDICTINE COLLEGE LIBRARY, ATCHISON, KANSAS

Despite various attempts to change it, the name "Tetons" has stuck when referring to the peaks visible to the east from Pierre's Hole. The United States Geological Survey itself tried to rename the Tetons in 1872. Some wanted to name the highest peak in the range Mt. Hayden, after Dr. Ferdinand V. Hayden, who had conducted several mapping expeditions of the region.[24] Failing to gain recognition, the suggestion was dropped. Certainly, in modern days, the popularity of "Tetons" has not sagged.

2
THE SHOSHONE: FIRST PEOPLE IN THE VALLEY

For thousands of years, Pierre's Hole was familiar ground to indigenous peoples of the Snake River Plains. Indians are believed to have called Pierre's Hole the "Broad Valley." B. W. Driggs claimed the name was interpreted by John Colter, an early trapper, but no existing record confirms this.[1] Notable aboriginal inhabitants in the valley included at various times Blackfoot, Crow, Flathead, and Nez Perce people; however, the area was the primary tribal territory of the Shoshone. The Bannock, descendants of Uto-Aztecan stock like the Shoshone, were often found in the ranges of the Teton Basin as well.[2]

The Name

This is not intended to be an in-depth history of the Shoshone people; however their background is worth including because they play a prominent role in numerous fur trade accounts. "Shoshone" has also been spelled "Shoshoni" in modern times.[3] Fur trade diaries spell it in nearly every phonetic combination imaginable. Some modern writers report the meaning of the word "shoshone" has been lost even to the Indians themselves. Others indicate "shoshone" means "The Valley People."[4] Fur trader Alexander Ross, who pursued beaver riches in the West from 1810 until 1825, reports "they all go by the general appellation of Sho-sho-nes, or Snakes. The word sho-sho-ne means in the Snake language 'Inland.'"[5]

French traders sometime after 1668 reported hearing about Indians on the Plains whose name in sign language was a snake-like movement of the hand.[6] This was taken to mean "snake," thus these tribes were called Gens du Serpent, which translates from French to English as "Snake People." Others say when French trappers came into contact with the Shoshone, around 1742, the Indians with whom they traveled were frightened off by the "Snakes," as they called them. This sobriquet came about because, so it is told, the Shoshone painted snakes on sticks to scare their Plains enemies.[7]

However, the hand gesture may well have been meant to indicate grass waving in the wind or grass being woven, in and out, into an early form of lodging used by these people. Some writers claim the sinuous motion indicated the tribe was from the place where salmon spawn. Either way, it did not take much for trappers to simply call them "Snakes" so this designation is frequently seen in the journals and diaries of trappers, traders and explorers.[8]

Fur trade documents use Snake and Shoshone interchangeably. In the chapters ahead, where journal entries are frequently used, it will be noticed that some record-keeping trappers seem unable to make up their minds, switching back and forth between the two. Shortly after 1880, this nation came to be known primarily by their linguistic name, Shoshone.

The Territory

Alexander Ross described what he believed to be the Shoshone tribal lands:

The country, then, that the other Snake tribes claim as their own and over which they roam is very extensive. It is bounded on the east by the Rocky Mountains, on the south by the Spanish waters [the Colorado River drainage]. On the Pacific or west side by an imaginary line beginning at the west end or spur of the Blue Mountains behind Fort Nez Perces and running parallel with the ocean to the height of land beyond the Umpqua River, in about north Lat. 41. This line never approaches within one hundred and fifty miles of the Pacific. And on the north by another line running due east from the said spur of the Blue Mountains and crossing the great south branch or Lewis [Snake] River at the narrows, till it strikes the Rocky Mountains two hundred miles north of the Stone Pilot Knobs [the Teton range], or the place hereafter called the 'Valley of Troubles' [the southern end of the Bitterroot Valley]. The Snake country therefore contains an area, on a rough calculation, of about 150,000 square miles. For Indian country it may be called thickly inhabited, and may contain 36,000 souls or nearly one person to every four miles square.[9]

Tribal Lifestyle

There are several divisions of the Shoshone nation. The tribal group closest to Pierre's Hole was the Sheep-eaters. Other bands were familiarly known by their primary diet – Root-eaters, Salmon-eaters or Buffalo-eaters. While they, naturally, had names for their bands in their own tongue, these names were more commonly used by non-Indians. Lewis and Clark met the Lemhi band, Salmon-eaters, in Idaho's panhandle far to the north of Pierre's Hole, during the Corps of Discovery's early exploration of the West. Ethnological information regarding this tribe in the journals of Lewis and Clark is the first written description of the Shoshone lifestyle.[10]

Essentially, the people of this nation spent their lives in the endless task of securing food. Edible plants and game were in relatively short supply in the semi-arid regions where they lived, so most bands were constantly on the move. Diet consisted of seeds, roots, insects, birds, small game such as rabbits, and occasionally, larger game animals when available. Lewis and Clark recorded,

In this loose and wandering life they suffer the extremes of want; for two thirds of the year they are forced to live in the mountains, passing whole weeks without meat, and with nothing to eat but a few fish and roots.[11]

Desire for meat brought native hunters into the Teton Basin. Wild game abounded in the vicinity of Pierre's Hole and Shoshone territory, making it prime hunting ground. Buffalo, beaver, elk, deer, antelope, bear, fox, wolverine, badger and martin could all be found here. An admirable combination of mountains, valleys, semi-desert country and numerous streams made Teton Valley a choice seasonal habitat. Coyotes and jack rabbits were unknown in those early times, according to early settler accounts.[12]

Most conditions were favorable for Indian habitation but although the Shoshone were fond of this region, harsh winters kept them from living here year round. The vicinity of the Menan Buttes and Market Lake, just west of Teton Valley, was a favorite camping ground. "Menan" is a Shoshone term meaning "many waters," presumably due to their location at the confluence of the Henry's Fork and Snake River.[13] Here the Shoshone and Blackfoot tribes would come for annual buffalo hunts, slaying hundreds of bison with bows and arrows. A map published by Albert Gallatin in 1836, titled "Map of the Indian Tribes of North America about 1600 A.D. along the Atlantic; & about 1800 A.D. westwardly," clearly shows how close traditional tribal boundaries were between nations (see detail on facing page).

As winter progressed, it was not uncommon for food supplies to run short or be depleted altogether. The nature of hunter-gatherer life in a harsh climate is precarious; starvation was not unusual. This is attested by Lewis and Clark describing the condition of Sacagawea's people when the expedition encountered them in late August 1805.[14] Ethnologists believe it was this hunger that pushed the Shoshone from the Great Basin into the Rocky Mountains early in the sixteenth century.

The hard winters in Teton Valley, with fierce winds and heavy snow, persuaded Shoshone clans to winter elsewhere. During the remaining seasons, however, these Indians hunted abundant big game in Pierre's Hole. Bighorn sheep roamed the mountains. The rivers and lakes held fish. Growing on the slopes, along the streams and in the woods were serviceberries, currants, thimbleberries, huckleberries and chokecherries to be harvested by the basket load.

By 1730 the Shoshone had become one of the most important tribes on the Plains. Their "number was large and their territory was vast."[15] Pierre's Hole was well within the tribal boundaries.

While the exact date of acquisition is unknown, the Shoshone were well-mounted on Spanish horses by the late 1600s or early 1700s, giving them a clear advantage over many other tribes. These animals were obtained primarily from the Comanche in the Southwest who raided Spanish settlements in New Mexico.[16] Being one of the first tribes to acquire horses the Shoshone nation gained strength and influence. Mounted Shoshone warriors ranged as far north as the Saskatchewan River in modern Alberta, Canada, and as far east as the Black Hills of present South Dakota.[17] They could ride into an enemy village, wreak havoc, and gallop off again before their foe could string a bow. Horses made it easier to pursue large game, such as buffalo or elk, in greater numbers. Tribal hunters could travel greater distances to trade, sometimes as far south as Mexico.

As they followed the buffalo herds, the Shoshone adopted a plethora of Plains Indian clothing styles as well as the hide tipi for

A detail of Map of the Indian Tribes of North America, *published by Albert Gallatin in 1836, shows the Pierre's Hole region. The "3 Peaks" in the center are the Tetons.* LIBRARY OF CONGRESS, GEOGRAPHY AND MAP DIVISION

19

This group of Shoshone men on horseback was photographed sometime between 1880 and 1910. COLLECTION OF THE DENVER PUBLIC LIBRARY, WESTERN HISTORY COLLECTION, X-32287

their primary dwelling. Even though they assimilated many aspects of Plains culture, they never became typical Plains Indians but showed influence from three definite cultures – Basin, Plateau and Plains.[18]

In 1781, the Shoshone people were afflicted with a smallpox epidemic. Then, around the time of Lewis and Clark, other tribes, particularly the Blackfoot, obtained guns from French and British traders more quickly than did the Shoshone. Between sickness and advances in weaponry, the balance of power shifted from the speed and mobility of the horse to the destructive power of firearms. By the beginning of the 1800s, the once-powerful Shoshone had been driven entirely from the Plains into the mountains and had lost many of their horses as well.[19]

Not entirely safe even in the mountains, a great number of Shoshone were pushed out onto the Plateau region west of the Continental Divide, where they were subject to enemy raids and abductions. The well-known capture of Shoshone maiden Sacagawea by the Hidatsa is one example. Her brother, Chief Cameahwait, told Meriwether Lewis if his people had had guns, they would not have been "compelled to hide ourselves in these mountains and live on roots and berries as the bear do." Such was their condition when the Corps of Discovery encountered them.[20]

Gradually, Northern Paiute Indians also found their way onto the Snake River Plains. These peoples eventually joined the Shoshone to form a united band. By the time Euro-American fur traders reached Snake River country, these Paiutes were known as Bannock Indians. Over the years, the Bannock merged with the Shoshone, through intermarriage and close association, developing so solid a relationship as to be legally known as Shoshone-Bannock since 1936.[21]

Fur Trade Interaction

Many trappers record interactions with Shoshone bands in the vicinity of Pierre's Hole. Their dealings were typically positive, but not always so. In many instances, the Shoshone helped ensure the survival of the mountaineers, sharing food, shelter or information that allowed the newcomers to succeed in their endeavors. Shoshone men such as Washakie and Togwotee were noted as being predominantly friendly toward these Euro-Americans. Togwotee was the person for whom the former Wind River Pass was renamed in 1873 by Captain William Jones, U.S. Corps of Engineers.[22]

Many Shoshone lands were rich in beaver. Small creeks which in modern times have become irrigation canals once abounded with beaver. In late 1810, fur trappers began to trickle into the heart of Shoshone country, willing to face unfriendly Indians and the winters of Pierre's Hole on the chance of a rich harvest of pelts. Initially organized by Donald Mackenzie for the Northwest Company, the first Snake Country Expeditions traveled through Shoshone country on an annual migratory cycle. After merging with NWC, the Hudson's Bay Company (HBC) continued annual expeditions under various leaders.[23] The goal of this new effort was to wipe out the region's fur-bearing animals, making a "fur desert" barrier to discourage competing American trappers. The HBC wanted to keep the Americans from moving closer to the Pacific Northwest.[24] Encounters between trappers and the local people were common, and exposure to the trappers' Euro-American culture was constant.

The Shoshone were increasingly influenced by Euro-American beaver men from 1816 through the mid 1820s. After that, the influx of non-Indians surged to a steady stream. St. Louis-based traders/trappers entered their territory in 1824, and persisted throughout the next few decades.[25]

As early as 1818, a group of Iroquois trappers traveling under Mackenzie joined a Shoshone band in the Boise, Idaho, area, introducing an Iroquois strain into the local population's gene pool. Scottish and French Canadian trappers are recorded as having Shoshone wives and families during this period. This genetic blending was amplified by the introduction of St. Louis-based mountain men a few years later.[26]

Although strong worldwide demand for beaver fur was the underpinning of the fur trade enterprise, a trapper's success in many ways depended upon amicable relations with his Indian hosts. There was give and take between Indians in an arms race with neighbors, constantly at the mercy of the traditional hunter-gatherer mode, yet anxious to obtain the more secure lifestyle that trade goods offered – and trappers anxious to keep their scalps and eke out profits. The annual rendezvous system developed by William H. Ashley swelled Shoshone desire for European goods and provided more opportunities for Indian/trapper interaction. John Wyeth noted in 1832:

> *We were surprised to find the Indians in the vicinity of the mountains and all around Pierre's Valley, and the Black-foot tribe, and the Shoshonees, or Snake-tribe, so well provided with muskets, powder and ball, woolen cloth and many other articles, until we were informed that Mr. Mackenzie, an established and wealthy Indian trader, had long supplied them with every article they desired.[27]*

When Nathaniel Wyeth built Fort Hall within Shoshone boundaries in 1834, Indian demand increased, dramatically altering the native environment as mountain men continued to pour into their homelands. Rather than subsistence hunting, many Shoshone converted to market-driven harvests, combing their locales for beaver and other sellable furs.

This proved to be a brief interlude. By the mid 1830s, not enough beaver were left in Rocky Mountain streams to maintain a strong commercial fur business. By around 1839, declining prices for beaver pelts in eastern markets had virtually shut down the fur trade for the Shoshone. But during the period of fur trade influences, according to University of Utah history professor Brigham D. Madsen, the Shoshone had "emerged with an improved way of life that still preserved most of their traditional values and provided a few appropriate conveniences to give them an easier existence."[28]

From this fur trade interface, the Shoshone learned Euro-American cultural habits and enjoyed access to guns, ironware, and other beneficial technologies. Ethnologist Sven Liljebald said, "It was a time of prosperity and mutual amity between Indians and whites."[29] Unfortunately, white migration over the Oregon and California Trails would introduce another quite different and less positive consequence, but that story, less related to the fur trade, is for another time and another story teller.

The Gallatin map already mentioned delineates the Shoshone territory as inclusive of Pierre's Hole. The same can be said for a map presented to Colonel D. D. Mitchell, drawn by Father Jean Pierre De Smet in 1851 (see following page). Both of these maps show the proximity of Crow and Blackfoot land to Pierre's Hole.

The Snake River

Stories persist that today's Snake River was named for its twisting "snaky" course. In fact, the Snake River was named around 1812 for the Snake Indians who lived along its shores.[30] William Clark named the upper reaches of the water course Lewis River for his expedition co-leader, Meriwether Lewis. That same upper flow appeared in a few diaries as the Nez Perce River. American trappers tended to refer to the main channel as the Lewis River or Lewis Fork. Wilson Price Hunt of the 1811 Astorian party also reported it as Mad River.[31] The streams draining Pierre's Hole flow into Teton River, once called Pierre's Fork, and wind up in the Snake River, pouring westward to the Columbia and into the Pacific Ocean.

French Canadian trappers had their own name for the waterway, calling it *la maudite riviere enrage*, meaning the accursed mad river.[32] The Indians called it by several names, often depending on the tribe, or on the section of the river referred to. Some of these

This segment of Pierre Jean De Smet's 1851 map of the upper Great Plains and Rocky Mountains locates Shoshone or Snake territory near the Three Buttes and the Tetons, which are both indicated with clustered trios of large dots at center left and center. Numerous landmarks, such as Fort Hall, Colter's Hell, and Devil's Gate are marked in tiny notations.

names included Kimooenem, Shoshone, Sahaptin, and Chopunnish rivers. Yam-pah-pa, the name of a root that grew along its bank, was bestowed on the water course by some, and Po-og-way, meaning river road, was given to it by others. Various spellings for all of these variations exist in the historical record.[33]

One final note regarding Indian tribes – the Teton Lakota Indians, an important division of the Sioux Nation, should not be confused with the indigenous peoples who lived around Pierre's Hole. This Siouan name is a corruption of the Lakota words *t'inta t'unwan* meaning "dwellers of the prairie." These Tetons lived near the Missouri River, in sections of modern North and South Dakota. They are one of several bands of the Sioux Nation, being the western-most of the Lakota division. Lewis and Clark mentioned them frequently in the journals of their 1804-1806 expedition.[34] Notable Teton men who appear in the history of the American West include Sitting Bull, Crazy Horse, Red Cloud and Black Elk.

This name confusion caused B. W. Driggs to surmise that George Catlin was in Pierre's Hole prior to 1832, painting portraits of Native Americans.[35] In truth, Catlin made repeated reference to the Teton River, but it is the water course of the Teton Sioux, found in what is today North Dakota, not the Teton River of Pierre's Hole. There is no record Catlin ever traveled to Teton Valley, Idaho.

Speaking of artists, B. W. Driggs also alleged the painter John Mix Stanley was in Pierre's Hole in 1835 with trapper Joe Meek whom he used as a model for the painting *The Trapper's Last Shot*.[36] Meek's biographer placed the date Meeks met Stanley as 1837. In reality, Stanley was not in the West until 1846, did not become acquainted with Meek until 1847, and did not paint "The Trapper's Last Shot." This particular canvas was created by William T. Ranney in 1850.[37] Neither Stanley nor Ranney was in Pierre's Hole during the fur trade era.

3

The "Hole" Story

In the jargon of beaver-seeking fur traders and trappers who ventured into the Rockies, a low-lying valley surrounded by high mountains was commonly called a "hole." Today, several of these valleys retain names from the early 1800s. For example, many trappers traveled through the Big Hole in what is now southwestern Montana during the fur trade era.[1] Also in Montana, the Burnt Hole, along the Madison River, crops up repeatedly in fur trade journals. Jean-Baptiste Chalifoux, also known as Baptiste Brown, was in northwest Colorado as early as 1820, when he discovered a valley of the Green River which became Brown's Hole. Gardner's Hole, in Yellowstone National Park, was named for trapper Johnson Gardner. Ross's Hole, in Montana, was named for Alexander Ross, and Ogden's Hole on the eastern slope of the Wasatch Range near Huntsville, Utah, was named for Peter Skene Ogden. Both of these latter landmarks commemorate HBC brigade leaders.

To the immediate east of Pierre's Hole is the well known Jackson Hole, originally called Jackson's Hole. The possessive form was dropped over the years. Since it is such a close neighbor to Pierre's Hole, this is a good place to clear up some of the fallacies surrounding the naming of Jackson Hole. That the valley was named after trapper David Jackson is a given. Many writers assert that the hole was one of his favorite spots and he spent a lot of time there. Some say one of Jackson's partners, William Sublette, named the valley in 1829. However, such statements cannot be proven by the fur trade's written history because records of such events do not exist.

Joseph Meek, whose rather fanciful biography was written by Mrs. Frances F. Victor in 1870, recalled that in March 1829:

Sublette led his company up the valley of the Wind River, across the mountains, and on to the very head-waters of the Lewis or Snake River. Here he fell in with Jackson, in the valley of Lewis Lake, called Jackson's Hole, and remained on the borders of this lake for some time.[2]

Warren A. Ferris, a trapper with the American Fur Company, kept a journal during his time in the Rockies. Portions of it were published in a newspaper, the *Western Literary Messenger*, of Buffalo, New York in 1843. Ferris wrote in July 1832:

> *We set out on the 2d and reached the head of Pierre's Hole on the 3d. On the 4th we crossed the mountain, and descended into a large prairie valley, called Jackson's Big Hole. It lies due east of the Trois Tetons ... The Hole is surrounded by lofty mountains, and receives its name from one of the firm of Smith, Sublett and Jackson.*[3]

In 1826, Jedediah Smith, David Jackson and William Sublette bought out the fur business formerly operated by Smith and William H. Ashley, known simply as Ashley and Smith.[4] This new company, the Smith, Jackson and Sublette Fur Company (SJS), was the "firm" of which Ferris spoke. From these two passages, it is clear that the valley was indeed named after David Jackson. Originally it was called "Jackson's Big Hole" to differentiate it from "Jackson's Little Hole" about thirty miles farther south and east, near the modern town of Bondurant, Wyoming. Meek also reported Jackson was often called "Davey" so the valley could easily have been known as Davey's Hole.[5]

However, neither an 1829 christening, nor that it was named by William Sublette, can be proven through existing historical documents. Respected historian Merrill J. Mattes says the legend of Sublette naming the valley has been inferred from the Meek passage cited above.[6] Meek's is the first recorded use of the name "Jackson's Hole" and the map drawn by Ferris is the first map upon which the name shows, but the exact time and place it was bestowed will likely never be known.

Meek's biography was written in 1870, over forty years after he trekked into the valley. Meek or his biographer might have used the name for the valley as it was called in 1870 rather than as it was known in 1829. For example, the name "Humboldt" was used by Victor for a river known then as "Ogden's" or "Mary's," the Humboldt title not having been applied until well after 1840. Ferris, however, drew his map and wrote in the 1830s, and thus is more dependable for pinpointing a provable date for the christening of the valley.

Jackson Hole may well have been so named because it was one of David Jackson's preferred stomping grounds, but this cannot be proven in the historical record either. It was Harvey E. Tobie, writing in 1938 for the Oregon Historical Society, who first identified Jackson Hole as "[Jackson's] favorite place of operation."[7] No primary source confirms this but many of these "holes" were named for the trappers who seemed to frequent them so it can be inferred Jackson likely traveled to, trapped and possibly enjoyed his time in this valley on multiple occasions.

Another misleading notion about Jackson Hole is that some of the annual fur trade rendezvous were held in that valley. This is simply untrue. Not one of the yearly Rocky Mountain rendezvous, between their inception in 1825 and the final assembly in 1840, was held in Jackson Hole. Nevertheless, it was an important historic crossroads for trappers traveling in the Rockies and it was common for brigades to meet there before traveling on to other destinations. In that sense, mountaineers did "rendezvous" in Jackson Hole.[8]

Grey's Hole is another nearby valley that relates to this story. An expansive vale, roughly eighty miles south of Pierre's Hole, Grey's Hole was named after an Iroquois man active in the fur trade. Ignace Hatchiorauquasha was, fortunately, more commonly known as John Grey to those who spoke English. It is believed he explored that tranquil basin while trapping with Mackenzie between 1818 and 1820.[9]

One of Grey's several Iroquois associates was Pierre Tevanitagon, from whom Pierre's Hole takes its name. Located north of Grey's Hole and west of Jackson's Hole, Pierre's Hole became a strategic center for the fur trade in the northern Rocky Mountains. Reportedly, Pierre liked to trap in this valley though it is not clear who discovered it. B. W. Driggs wrote of:

> *Vieux Pierre, an Iroquois Indian trapper, who in his search for beaver found his way, along with some companion hunters, into this valley in 1818, and revealed its existence to the Hudson Bay Company.*[10]

This 1818 date was accepted by Mumey, though no period document is found to confirm it. Exactly when the valley was dubbed "Pierre's Hole" is not recorded. Though it definitely bears the name by 1832, it was likely called that much earlier. The Teton River was originally referred to as Pierre's River or Fork, and is identified as such on many early maps, some as late as the 1890s.

Fur trade historian Hiram M. Chittenden, in his definitive work *A History of the Fur Trade of the American West*, stated:

> *The Teton or Pierre river drains the western slope of the Teton mountains. It rises in Teton Pass, and flows slightly west of north for about thirty miles, when it turns due west and flows into Henry Fork of Snake River. It was that portion of the valley that lay along the northerly course of the stream to which the name Pierre's Hole applied.*[11]

However, most journals and diaries made no distinction about certain parts of the basin being Pierre's Hole, so Chittenden's remark may be set aside. Some writers think Pierre Tevanitagon named the valley after himself, though this is never stated in primary documents either. An early history of Wyoming by Charles G. Coutant included:

> *The name "Pierre's Hole" is derived from an incident that occurred in the early part of the century. A party of Iroquois hunters in the employ of the Hudson Bay Company wandered into that locality and were there attacked by a fierce band of Blackfeet. Many were killed on both sides and the chief of the Iroquois, Pierre, was among the slain. He was a noted man among the Indian tribes and a firm friend to the whites. In consequence of the death of this chieftain in this valley his name was given to the locality. It is now called Teton Basin.*[12]

Regrettably, there is no factual basis for Coutant's tale. At least one diary indicated the valley "receives its name from an Iroquois chieftain, who first discovered it," which only adds to the confusion.[13]

One trapper account used the French language to identify the valley. Such was the case with Charles Larpenteur, who wrote from the Green River rendezvous site in 1833,

> *The day we reached the rendezvous, Mr. Campbell, with ten men, started to raise a beaver cache at a place called by the French Trou á Pierre, which means Peter's Hole.*[14]

An interesting comment about this particular passage is found in a footnote written by historian Elliot Coues in 1898 when he edited Larpenteur's journal for publication. Coues penned, "I have not elsewhere found Trou á Pierre translated 'Peter's Hole' – always Pierre or Pierre's Hole, the name it still bears." Apparently unknown to Coues, Father Pierre Jean De Smet also used "Peter's Valley" rather than "Pierre's" in a letter to the Reverend Father Roothan in 1841.[15]

Coues also wrote that, "'Pierre's Hole' will be found marked on various maps, but the name seems to be lapsing of late years, like that of Pierre's river for the Teton."[16] An echo of Coues is evident in Nolie Mumey's statement, "After 1888, the main settlers in Pierre's Hole were Mormons, who called this region 'The Valley of the Tetons.'"[17] Thus, by the time Larpenteur's journal went to press, the original name of the valley was "lapsing" to the point that, in modern times, few people remember Teton Basin had once been known as Pierre's Hole.

Fortunately, the Idaho Transportation Department maintains a roadside marker on Highway 33 in Teton Valley that reminds travelers that this once was Pierre's Hole. While the wording on the sign is debatable, it is at least a remembrance of Old Pierre. That marker reads:

Teton Valley was known originally as Pierre's Hole. Rich in beaver, it was a favorite stomping ground for British and American fur traders and trappers between 1819-40. "Old Pierre" Tevanitagon, an Iroquois Indian fur trapper for the Hudson's Bay Co., gave his name to this beaver-rich valley. Pierre's Hole was the scene of the annual rendezvous of mountain men and suppliers – The Great Rocky Mountain Fair – in 1832. That wild party ended in a free-for-all battle with the Gros Ventre Indians, which the trappers and their Indian friends won. The valley was permanently settled in 1882.[18]

4
PIERRE TEVANITAGON

To write the biography of Pierre Tevanitagon, for whom Pierre's Hole is named, is a difficult task, for hardly anything is known about the man's early life. Fragments can be gleaned of his later years from documents and journals written by others, but no diary ascribed to Tevanitagon has yet been found. His name shows up in the historical record in a variety of spellings. He can be traced as Tontavantogan, Tontantogan, Tivanitagon, Tevanitogans, le Grand Pierre, Old Pierre, Vieux Pierre, Peter and, simply, Pierre. Sometimes he is referred to as "The Iroquois chief," or as simply, "The Iroquois." Consequently, tracking him is a tricky prospect.

Many modern authors create their own spellings for this Iroquois name, apparently without reference to historical documents. B. W. Driggs evidently believed Pierre's first name was "Vieux," which is merely a French adjective meaning "old." Unfortunately, Mumey and many other writers followed this lead.[1]

In the late 1770s, Iroquois from upstate New York moved westward to Ontario, Canada, driven from their homeland by General John Sullivan's campaign.[2] Many joined the ranks of the Canadian fur trade, becoming a key factor in the success of the business. Most Iroquois were already skilled canoe men, familiar with the waters of the western Great Lakes. These Eastern Indians entered the fur trade as *voyageurs*, a name given to those hired to operate the countless boats taking supplies and furs into and out of interior fur posts. This watercraft experience was in high demand and a surprising number of Iroquois enlisted as *engages*, the hired hands of the fur companies.

As fur bearing animals were trapped to scarcity, the adept Canadian Iroquois moved farther west. Author Washington Irving attested to the qualifications of these Iroquois in his book, *The Adventures of Captain Bonneville, U.S.A.*, regaling the story of Benjamin Bonneville's exploits. Writing about a party of Iroquois who joined Bonneville's camp, Irving said they "made themselves useful in a variety of ways, being excellent trappers and first-rate woodsmen."[3]

Many Iroquois who came west are unidentifiable because, as freemen, they were not always given a contract, which kept many names off of the records. For those who did make the historical registers, European trappers gave up trying to spell Iroquois last names and instead would list their last name as Iroquois, like "Pierre Iroquois," or butcher the name so badly that they were unrecognizable. Some Iroquois changed their names to French sounding names, in response to being frequently misunderstood. In addition, many Iroquois called themselves "Canadians" confusing them with other groups coming from Canada. For these reasons, it is hard to trace them through primary documents.[4]

Among those migrating to the Rocky Mountains was Pierre Tevanitagon, whose surname is likely related to his given Iroquois name. Pierre's date and place of birth are unknown. Moreover, nothing is available about his early life until his first appearance in fur trade records. Given that he is often differentiated from other Iroquois as "old," it may be assumed he was more advanced in years than the bulk of his fellow beaver-trapping tribesmen. Journal writers often portray Pierre as irascible and unreliable, yet he participates in numerous trapping expeditions. He is apparently valued by Iroquois tribesmen but seems an unwilling leader, a role for which he exhibits limited capacity.

Pierre first appears on a roster of NWC *voyageurs*. In November 1804, he was based at Fort Kiministiqua. This post, soon to be renamed Fort William, was the company's headquarters, on the Canadian shores of Lake Superior. The list was compiled as part of the agreement drawn up when the NWC absorbed the XY Company in that year.[5]

When the NWC decided to attack the beaver populations of the Snake River Country, only the best of the Iroquois were assigned to the project. Pierre was in that category, so he may have come to the Pacific Northwest as early as 1809.[6]

Certainly by 1816, Pierre was serving in the brigade led by Donald Mackenzie which has been mentioned previously, and which will be discussed more thoroughly in the chapters ahead.[7] Pierre spent the next twelve years as a leader among the Iroquois trappers who accompanied him westward, often referred to as their "chief" in fur trade diaries.

The Pacific Northwest was predominantly unexplored by non-indigenous peoples at the time. For the Iroquois, adjusting to Euro-American ways of life in this new environment was problematic. These Indians approached hunting buffalo, for example, with what historian Theodore Karamanski called "an unfortunate mixture of bravado and imprudence, with the inevitable result of one man injured and another killed." Similar consequences followed an encounter with a grizzly bear.[8]

On at least one occasion, Pierre got himself in trouble by failing to observe the Company's prohibition against private deals with local Indians. Not long after reaching new trapping grounds on the Columbia River drainages, Pierre had found himself in serious difficulty during a horse trade with the Nez Perce. He approached his boss for an advance of goods to consummate the trade. Mackenzie, annoyed by Pierre's disregard for the rules, settled the matter post-haste. He stopped the negotiations, bought the horse himself, then in his anger drew his belt pistol and shot it dead – a supposed lesson to the Iroquois about misconduct. Pierre and his Indian brethren resented Mackenzie for his act, and, according to trapper Alexander Ross, "meditated the destruction of their leader."[9]

Pierre's group decided it would rather trap on its own than be tied so closely to Mackenzie. The brigade leader was not terribly happy about the situation but there was little he could do to prevent it. Since the Iroquois were technically free men, supplied on contract by the Company, they were allowed to trap independently throughout the winter of 1818-1819. The party spent the majority of that time around modern Boise, Idaho, plying its trade in the tributaries of the Snake River. But it is not beyond the limits of credibility to imagine the men trapped as far east as the Teton Basin.

According to B. W. Driggs, this was when Pierre may have first entered Teton Valley. Driggs wrote a detailed account of Pierre trapping in the basin for about two months. The information attributed to Pierre, however, came from Alexander Ross and pertained to the 1824 excursion, which had nothing to do with Teton Valley.[10]

Much to Mackenzie's chagrin, Pierre and his Iroquois got themselves into hot water again. Ross, a close associate of Mackenzie, left a written record of events. He reported the Iroquois seemed to spend more time chasing Indian women than trapping beaver in the Boise River. Trading for assorted female favors, they squandered most of their tools and equipment by the time they rejoined the Company brigade in the summer of 1819.[11]

Despite Mackenzie's negative feelings toward Tevanitagon, the following season thirteen Iroquois were again trapping independently under the leadership of Old Pierre. Fortunately, this time they had a little better luck, trapping 669 beaver. But misfortune seemed to follow them. They were forced to dig a cache and leave their pelts buried in the Snake Country for nearly two years before anyone could retrieve them.[12] What caused them to leave these pelts behind was not recorded.

In 1821, the NWC merged with the HBC. Pierre now found himself wading streams for the large British conglomerate. After a brief season of inactivity, Michael Bourdon assumed command of the Snake Country brigade. Pierre Tevanitagon and his Iroquois were an integral, though hard to manage, part of Bourdon's new assignment.

In the fall of 1822, Bourdon led his men from Spokane House, northwest of modern Spokane, Washington, south to the region around the Bear River, traveling by way of Pierre's Hole. This is the first record of Pierre actually being in Teton Valley, but, as mentioned, it is likely he had been there before. Pierre's two sons are listed on the roster at Spokane House so they may have been with the brigade as well.[13]

A major defection of the Iroquois to competing American fur companies occurred in 1822, but Pierre remained true to his HBC employer. In 1823, Finan MacDonald took charge of the Snake Country brigade, pushing the trappers beyond Bear Lake and into the valley of the Green River. The brigade traversed Pierre's Hole during this expedition in one direction or the other, trapping as they went. MacDonald refused to take the brigade out in 1824, having had his fill of Blackfoot attacks. The party had been accosted by hostile Indians on the Lemhi River and again on Henry's Fork, and that was enough for MacDonald.[14]

Shortly after leaving Flathead House, on Clark's Fork of the Columbia River, near present Thompson Falls, Montana, Pierre also expressed a reluctance to trap that season, though more for economic reasons than for fear of hostile attack. His complaint was that:

> *The price allowed for their fur was so small in proportion to the exorbinate advance on goods sold to them, they would never be able to pay their debts much less make money and would not risk their lives any more in the Snake country.*[15]

Nevertheless, a new brigade leader, the prolific reporter Alexander Ross, was able to convince Tevanitagon to accompany the party. Pierre served as spokesman for his brethren, making several appeals to management. When he held out for currency payable in Quebec or even sterling, Ross had to relent, promising accounts would not be paid in company script.

Mid-March found the brigade stuck in camp in the upper Bitterroots due to heavy snowfall. They were in what would become Ross's Hole. Ross described the miserable state of affairs:

> *This morning sent off forty men with shovels and fifty horses to beat the road. Weather bad with snow and drift, they returned to camp. The crust is eight inches thick lying under two feet of snow. Owing to crust the horses made no headway. There are now eight miles of the road made, oft the prospect is gloomy, people undecided whether to continue or turn back.*[16]

Three weeks later, little progress had been made. Pierre was the only man in camp willing to work on clearing the snow-packed road so they could leave the valley. On the evening of April 10, John Grey had constructed a fiddle, another man a drum, and a concert ensued. Taking advantage of their good humor, Ross got everyone's consent to work on the road and the next day, the final mile was opened.[17]

Rather than retrace the route of the previous two years, Pierre suggested a trek west from Lemhi Pass through the Salmon River Mountains, returning to familiar territory in the Boise River area. Along the way, the Iroquois chief exhibited leadership ability when a band of eight trappers got separated from the main party. Pierre organized a group of twenty men and was successful in finding the lost trappers. At one point, they crossed trails with a Blackfoot raiding party but rather than fight Pierre's experienced troop, the enemy warriors fled.

Whether from loyalty or sympathy, Old Pierre occasionally displayed support for his Iroquois kinsman. In late spring 1824, fresh tracks of a warring Blackfoot band caused high anxiety within the brigade. Ross issued explicit orders for keeping the horse herd together and close to camp. One morning, twenty-four of the Iroquois mounts were strolling and feeding at large among the hills. A warning from the commander was apparently not motivation enough because the next morning, six horses assigned to a man named Martin were once again turned out unfettered, to feed.

Incensed by such blatant disregard for orders, Ross confiscated all of Martin's horses and when camp broke the following dawn, Martin and his family were left sitting by the fire. Other Iroquois lent him horses for the day so he was able to travel with the brigade. That evening, Tevanitagon led a small delegation to lobby on behalf of Martin. Ross noted in his record that

> *after giving me every assurance that they would all take care of their horses in the future and observe the regulations of the camp, I delivered Martin's horses up to him again; this was what I wanted, and the example had for a long time afterwards a good effect.*[18]

Such events seemed to have bolstered Tevanitagon's confidence. Upon hearing where Ross wanted to take the brigade, Pierre and his Iroquois petitioned to break off from the main party to trap on their own. Pierre made his case to Ross, saying, "We have already been through [that] country ... and have trapped in that quarter for two years in succession."[19] Like Mackenzie before him, Ross was powerless to prevent them from leaving, and they separated from the main party on June 12.

Pierre led his small band southeast while Ross continued west, toward the Boise River. Tevanitagon took his Iroquois down Henry's Fork, through Pierre's Hole and over Pine Creek Pass into Swan Valley. They trapped along the left bank of the Snake River as far as the Blackfoot and Portneuf rivers. Again, Pierre's group tended to pass their time with local Indians, neglecting their traps, much like the routine of 1818.

On the Portneuf River, the Iroquois camped with a band of Shoshone and Bannock Indians under a chief named The Horse.

Everyone got along fine until news reached the encampment that some of Ross's men had stolen several Snake horses far to the west. On hearing this, The Horse seized all of the livestock and most of the furs belonging to Pierre and his men. In the ensuing fracas, a Shoshone leader was killed and the Iroquois barely escaped.[20]

Now "pillaged and destitute," in mid-September 1824 Pierre and his party wandered along, trapping pretty much at random. Near today's Blackfoot, Idaho, they met up with a brigade of St. Louis-based trappers led by Jedediah Smith, an "Ashley man." Andrew Henry, of whom more will be told later, and William H. Ashley had started their own fur company, moving into the Rockies to collect beaver skins. Smith and other subsequently famous mountain men were part of this outfit.

Smith traded Pierre a few horses and some equipment in exchange for the 105 beaver skins in their possession. Smith then offered to escort the edgy Iroquois to their planned meeting with Ross at the Three Buttes on the Snake River Plain. Upon rejoining the HBC crew on October 14, Pierre introduced the Americans to Ross who was none too pleased to find that the Iroquois had no pelts to show, and that moreover, here was new competition in the Rocky Mountains. Even more upsetting to the HBC commander, Smith invited himself to accompany Ross back to the HBC post at Flathead House.[21]

In late December of that year, when the Snake Country Expedition again set out from Flathead House, Smith and his men tagged along with the HBC crew, now under the command of Peter Skene Ogden. Having the Americans along suited Ogden no better than it had Ross. Pierre Tevanitagon and the Iroquois plodded south as well. Since wives of HBC trappers often accompanied their husbands, Pierre's mate was likely with him, even though official HBC policy indicated families were not permitted on the expeditions.[22]

A roster made by brigade leader Ogden noted that Pierre had six of the brigade's 268 horses assigned to him. He is the only man logged as having twelve traps; of the sixty-one men the vast majority possessed only six or eight. Pierre also carried two guns, while all but one other man carried only a single firearm.[23]

Like his predecessors, Ogden faced the slapdash Iroquois approach to trapping. Back on the Portneuf again in April 1825, Pierre and some others had horses stolen near the same spot where they had trouble with The Horse the preceding summer. Pierre's horses were stolen more than once on trapping excursions, leading one to question the care he provided his stock. Giving his mounts, in Ogden's words, "full liberty all night" only increased the chances of loss or theft.[24]

This brigade stayed in the field throughout the winter and in May 1826 Ogden camped on what would become known as the Malade River, *malade* being the French word for "sick." Today, this stream near Sun Valley, Idaho, is called the Wood River. Beaver on this stream ate the highly poisonous wild hemlock growing in abundance along the banks with apparently no ill affect. However, men who ate the meat of these creatures became violently sick. Several of Ogden's trappers were debilitated by throbbing, aching heads and limbs; one "suffered excruciating pains and at times almost despaired of his life."[25]

One afternoon, Pierre fell senseless at his traps. He endeavored to reach the camp but could not manage the effort. Ogden's men, sent to search for the old Iroquois, found him lying on the plains, unable to move. The unique remedy for the malady, as administered by Ogden, was a little pepper and gunpowder mixed with water. He was as good as new in no time.[26]

Several days later, Ogden's HBC party was camped in Ogden's Hole, directly south of today's Cache Valley, Utah. While there, Johnson Gardner, another Ashley man, stirred up one of the first international incidents of the Rocky Mountain fur trade.[27] Gardner, presuming they were all in Oregon Territory, informed the Iroquois they were on United States soil, where, Gardner extolled, men were free to choose employers and could desert the British company. Ogden rightfully asserted that Oregon was jointly occupied by Great Britain and thus, the men were still bound to their contracts.

An intense argument erupted over claim to the territory. A battle nearly ensued when Gardner convinced Pierre, John Grey and about a dozen of their brethren to walk out on Ogden and join forces with the Americans, taking HBC property with them when they left. This event took place on the Weber River at what came to be called "Deserter's Point." Incidentally, both Gardner and Ogden were wrong regarding which country held dominion over the region. At that time it still belonged to Mexico.

During the squabble, several tents came down as Ogden gathered what beaver skins he could, even from the belongings of men who were absent. But Ogden was not fast enough and the deserters succeeded in absconding with many of those pelts as well. Just how the HBC leadership viewed Pierre is revealed by Ogden's clerk, William Kittson:

> *A scuffle took place between Old Pierre and Mr. Ogden regarding the horses lent by that Gentleman to the old villain, who was supported by all the Americans and 13 of our scamps of Freemen.*[28]

Banking on the American's promise of fair treatment and better prices for his fur, Pierre went along with John Weber's brigade of Ashley men. He showed up a few months later at Ashley's 1825 rendezvous on Henry's Fork of the Green River, the first of these renowned events that would take place over the next fifteen years. Ashley's accounts indicate Pierre bought plenty of supplies, but also arranged for an array of goods to be delivered to him and his men the following summer at the 1826 fur fair to be held in Willow Valley, now Cache Valley, Utah.[29]

An examination of Ashley's business accounts indicates Pierre sold 100 beaver skins at the 1825 rendezvous. The old Iroquois appears to have done nearly twice as well as most of the other trappers. Although the records are somewhat difficult to decipher, they suggest that Pierre put those twelve HBC traps he brought from the Flathead post to good use. Purchases recorded in Ashley's 1825 accounts for Tevanitagon were as follows:

3 Beads – 5	15 00
8 knives	12
1 Coffee & Sugar	6
4 Lead	4
[2?] powder & Lead	[14?]
Flints	2
Bag	2

Though not totaled on the ledger page, Pierre's acquisitions came to at least fifty-five dollars. The amount he earned for his skins was probably three dollars per hide, the going rate in most of Ashley's ledgers. While beaver was often priced by the pound, the price recorded for most of the trappers at the 1825 rendezvous appeared to be by the hide. Assuming this is correct, Pierre had about three hundred dollars to spend. Subtracting the items purchased leaves Tevanitagon with $245 to pay for the order he placed for next year's rendezvous. Traders were happy to provide credit to trappers, indebting the mountaineers to the fur company for the coming year's catch. There is a good possibility Ashley was looking forward to having the Iroquois sell any impending beaver harvest to his firm only.

Pierre's request for those future supplies was also recorded in Ashley's accounts. For some items, Ashley appeared willing to contract at a future price, but pricing on most articles was omitted. Whether Pierre contemplated going into business for himself or was acting as a general agent for his tribesmen cannot be determined. The requested items are listed on the facing page.

This list provides an example of the equipment Pierre deemed necessary to advance a trapping career. Many of these are common trade goods, used to gain the trust and cooperation of Indians whom the trappers would encounter. These same items would also keep wives happier while on the trail. This sort of "foofuraw," in the trapper's lingo, was at times as important as the tools of their trade.

Tevanitagon continued to trap with Ashley's men, making enough money from his furs to pay off some of the outstanding debt still showing on the HBC books when he met up with Ogden in April 1826. Ogden expressed a degree of surprise when several of the Iroquois made payments to their accounts.[30]

After Pierre's defection in the Gardner incident, the HBC revamped its pricing structure to better compete with Ashley. Ogden noted in his 1826 journal that Pierre and his fellow deserters were "already tired of the New Masters" and predicted they would return to the Flathead post in the fall.[31] However, Pierre stayed with Ashley's company, participating in the 1826 rendezvous in Willow Valley, where it can only be presumed that his order was delivered.

Pierre Tevanitagon's request for future supplies
from William Ashley, 1825

Scatcheneele [cochineal?]

Silk sewing

small beads white

very small needles

alum fine Cloth

Sugar & Coffee

files for traps

gimblets vices

Small red green & Blue beads

Flour sugar & Coffee

Small Kettles

Earrings

large chisels 2 doz.

Blanketts - - - $9

Powder - - - - 1 50

Lead - - - - - 1 -

Sugar - - - - - 1 -

Coffee - - - - 2 -

Tobacco - - - 1 50

Knives 75

alls -

gun Locks first quality

flints c 5 100 Rifles

Blue cloth $5 yd

Scarlett 6

Slay bells

Ribband assorted

Pencils lead

Pen Knife

Gallon Rum

flour – 30 pounds

flour - 1 lb

Pepper 1 [75?]

Kettles assorted

Bridles

vermillion

Spurs – guns

[S?]

Flannel red green yellow

Rusha sheeting

Soap worsted webbing

combs assorted

small thin bar iron

Trap springs

double bit Bridle per Mr
[John] Gray

3 doz Serscinlges –

Saddle for Mr Gray

hats- Gardner & Gray

Black silk HKs

Tomhawks

axes – chisels – 3/8 Inches Thick

pipes – 2 ½ wide socket

Spending another year with the American company, Pierre joined Robert Campbell's brigade after the 1827 rendezvous at the south end of Bear Lake, then called Sweet Lake to differentiate it from Salt Lake. The Campbell brigade traveled to the waters of the Upper Missouri River for the fall hunt. The trappers were repeatedly harassed by Blackfoot war parties. Reaching Red Rock Creek, near the head of Jefferson River in southwest Montana, they met yet another party of enemy warriors. Campbell reported the trappers knew trouble was brewing when their adversary constructed a makeshift breastwork. Early the next morning, the trappers set off for the Snake River. The Blackfoot followed and soon attacked the brigade. In a later dictation about this fight, Campbell said, "Old Pierre, the chief of our Iroquois, was killed. He had advanced too far."[32]

In a letter to Senator Thomas Hart Benton, Ashley provided more details of the skirmish:

> *P. Tontavantogan was killed by a party of Blackfoot Indians, who advanced near to where about 25 of our hunters were encamped, and proposed trading with them: Some difficulty arose – the Indians fired upon the whites, shot this man dead, and wounded another; took one horse and about one hundred and fifty pounds of beaver fur.*[33]

A letter sent to William Clark recapping events in the Rockies between 1826 and 1829 includes a list of mountaineers working for the Smith, Jackson and Sublette Fur Company who lost their lives. "Pierre Irrequois, by the Blackfeet," is the only entry for 1827.[34] Ogden's 1828 journal included:

> *They had a skirmish with the Black Feet, and old Pierre the Iroquois chief who deserted from me four years ago was killed and cut into pieces. Three Black Feet were also killed.*[35]

Apparently, the corpse of the old Iroquois was mutilated by the Blackfoot, because Campbell added, "We found a portion of old Pierre's remains – a portion of his feet – in the Blackfoot village – after they left."[36] Exactly how they identified these body parts as Pierre's was not disclosed. Perhaps Pierre's wife, who may have been with the brigade, knew her husband's feet well enough to spot them.

On his death in 1827, the ledgers of Smith, Jackson and Sublette showed a debt owed by Pierre in the amount of twenty-four dollars. It looks as though his widow continued on with the brigade, because three years later she was at the 1830 rendezvous on Wind River. Thomas Fitzpatrick, acting as the company's official spokesperson, presented Pierre's widow with a note for $783.14. It is not clear what caused this financial turnaround; perhaps she was a gifted trapper. Madame Tevanitagon took the note to the States the following year and endorsed it to the firm of Fontenelle and Drips at Liberty, Missouri.[37]

When Ogden learned of the death of Old Pierre from some Americans who visited his camp in February 1828, he wrote in his journal, "The ... man owes a considerable debt to the concern, but as we have a mortgage on his property in Canada I am in hopes we will recover it."[38] Tevanitagon's widow possessed enough economic acumen to pay off the amount owed to Pierre's former British employer, the HBC, clearing the note to own the property.

Robert Campbell dictated his fur trade experiences to William Fayel in 1870. More than forty years had elapsed since these events were chronicled. Thus, Campbell made comments that have tripped some modern authors when he claimed, "The eventful valley in which Pierre met his fate, has perpetuated his name as 'Pierre's Hole.'"[39]

Another trapper, who had written a more contemporaneous journal, told a different story regarding the original name of Teton Valley. Warren Ferris noted that Pierre's Hole, "receives its name from an Iroquois chieftain, who first discovered it; and was killed in 1827, on the source of the Jefferson River."[40] A map drawn by Ferris marks "Pierre's Fork" on the Jefferson, but that name has been changed to Red Rock Creek.

Ironically, Washington Irving mentions Pierre in conjunction with a party of Iroquois who visited Bonneville on Salmon River during the autumn of 1832:

In the course of the autumn, four Iroquois hunters, driven by the snow from their hunting grounds, made an appearance at the cantonment. They were kindly welcomed, being excellent trappers, and first-rate woodsmen. They were the remnants of a party of Iroquois hunters that came from Canada into these mountain regions many years previously, in the employ of

Hudson's Bay Company. They were led by a brave chieftain, named Pierre, who fell by the hands of the Blackfeet, and gave his name to the fated valley of Pierre's Hole.[41]

This statement has been misinterpreted by some historians to suggest Pierre dropped in on Bonneville's camp. Clearly, this visitation was several years after Pierre died at the hands of the Blackfoot, and Irving is stating that the party of Iroquois was the remainder of Pierre's group.

Some of the events in the life of Pierre Tevanitagon will be revisited in the chapters ahead in more detail. At the risk of repetition, this chapter stands alone as a complete biography of the somewhat obscure trapper for whom Teton Valley was named during the Rocky Mountain fur trade era.

5
JOHN COLTER AND PIERRE'S HOLE: 1807-1808

The men attached to the Corps of Discovery, better known as the Lewis and Clark Expedition, were the first non-native visitors to what is now the state of Idaho who can be authenticated in the historical record. On August 12, 1805, a reconnaissance party consisting of Meriwether Lewis, John Shields, George Drouillard and Hugh McNeal crossed the boundary of the modern state and shortly thereafter met a band of Lemhi Shoshone who generously prepared a salmon dinner for the Americans.

During their sojourn with the Lemhi, the captains gleaned vital information regarding the land around them, but there is no indication they learned anything at all about the Tetons or the "Broad Valley," as Indians called Pierre's Hole. The closest the expedition came to Teton Valley was approximately 175 miles to the north, near Tendoy, Idaho.[1]

Many historians credit the Euro-American "discovery" of Pierre's Hole to John Colter in 1807-1808. The historical record provides enough contradictions, however, to cast significant doubt on that claim. This chapter will examine the evidence, pro and con, for acknowledging John Colter as the first non-indigenous person to enter Teton Valley.

Colter was a member of the Lewis and Clark Expedition that left St. Louis in May 1804, returning in September 1806. Captain William Clark lauded the efforts of Colter on the journey, proclaiming him of invaluable aid to the success of the venture.

On the return trip, in the vicinity of the Mandan villages in present day North Dakota, the party met Forrest Hancock and Joseph Dickson as they traveled up the Missouri River, paddling their canoe for beaver country. Colter requested leave to accompany these two trappers, returning to the territory from which the expedition had so recently come. The captains granted permission and Clark wrote in that day's journal entry, "we were disposed to be of service to any one of our party who had performed their duty as well as Colter had done, we agreed to allow him the privilege."

In August 1806, Colter left the Corps of Discovery to trap with his two new partners.[2]

For the next nine months or so, little is known of Colter's exact whereabouts. The party is believed to have trapped the waters of the Yellowstone River. In late spring 1807, Colter was alone in a dugout canoe, once again paddling his way down the Missouri River toward St. Louis. Near the mouth of the Platte River, Colter met a large party of over forty men in two keelboats, under the command of Manuel Lisa.

In partnership with Pierre Menard and William Morrison of Kaskaskia, Illinois, Lisa had targeted the fur resources of the Upper Missouri country for an invasion of trappers. Lisa must have been ecstatic to learn Colter was familiar with the area to which they were headed. What incentive Lisa proffered is unknown, but Colter agreed to join Lisa's crew even though he had been in the wilds for over three years. Again, Colter wound his way back up the Missouri, then onto the Yellowstone River.

Among the crew, Colter found former companions of the Lewis and Clark Expedition: George Drouillard, John Potts, John Collins and Peter Weiser. Some documents suggest expedition members Richard Windsor and Jean-Baptiste LePage may also have accompanied Lisa.[3] Other trappers enlisted with this crew who appear in the pages ahead included Edward Rose, John Dougherty and the inseparable Kentucky trio of Edward Robinson, John Hoback and Jacob Reznor.

Robinson, Hoback and Resnor played a central role in the earliest years of the Rocky Mountain fur trade. Hoback's name appears at times in fur trade records as Hobaugh, Hobough, Hubbough and Hauberk. Variants of Reznor's name include Rexner, Rizner, Reesner, Regnier, Reasoner, and Reesoner. The three Kentuckians seem inseparably linked and are generally considered to have been together even when only one of the names is mentioned in the historical record. Washington Irving described them as

> *three Kentucky hunters, of the true "dreadnought" stamp.*
> *Their names were Edward Robinson, John Hoback, and Jacob*
> *Rizner. Robinson was a veteran backwoodsman, sixty-six years*
> *of age. He had been one of the first settlers of Kentucky, and*
> *engaged in many of the conflicts of the Indians on 'the Bloody*

Ground.' In one of these battles he had been scalped, and he still wore a handkerchief bound round his head to protect the part. These men had passed several years in the upper wilderness.[4]

By late October or early November 1807, Lisa's party had reached the mouth of the Big Horn River and constructed a crude fort. This establishment has been called by several names but was written as "Fort Remon" by Lisa after his firstborn son.[5] In reality, it was a modest log structure of two rooms and a loft. From this camp, emissaries Colter, Drouillard, Weiser and Rose were sent out separately to attract business. They were dispatched to the south and west to inform the Indians of the new trading post where furs could be exchanged for European goods.

In this early foray, Weiser may have been the first non-Indian to view the Teton Mountains. Indications are that Weiser, taking a different route from Rose and Drouillard, reversed William Clark's 1806 return route along the Yellowstone River. Accompanied by Jean-Baptiste Champlain, he appears to have revisited Three Forks,

The site of Fort Remon lies at the mouth of the Big Horn River. The confluence of the Yellowstone and Big Horn rivers is in the distance, the Yellowstone entering from the left. The fort site would have been slightly to the right of center, along the dirt road that runs across the middle of the scene.
TODD GLOVER PHOTO

ascended the Madison River to the south, and turned out onto the plains of the Snake River.[6]

On Clark's 1810 manuscript map and the one published in 1814, there is a curious watercourse marked "Wiser's River" which appears in the vicinity of modern Island Park, Idaho. In 1810, Reuben Lewis wrote a letter to his famous brother Meriwether, stating

> *Mr. Shamplain tels me that the martin abound in the mountains dividing the Spanish River ... the rout by the middle fork on Madison's River is almost without mountains it is about 5 or 6 days travel to an illigable plan for a fort on that River where the Beavers from the account of Peter Wyzor, is as abundant as in our part of this Country.*[7]

It is evident from this report and the location of "Wiser's River" that these two men were in the neighborhood of Henry's Fork of the Snake River while on the Lisa-assigned trek in 1807-1808.

Fort Remon was built in the land of the Apsáalooke nation. Their name translates to "children of the large-beaked bird." This bird, apparently now extinct, was described by Thomas H. Leforge as "a peculiar kind of fork-tailed bird resembling the blue jay or magpie." The term was misinterpreted by Euro-Americans to mean "Crow."[8]

Colter's assignment was to recruit the Crow people, who were anticipated to be friendly, to come trade at Fort Remon. He left the fort in the fall of 1807 but it is not certain when he returned. He may have come back to Fort Remon and then ventured out again in the early months of the new year or he may have been on the trail until the spring of 1808. The length of Colter's journey is tied up with his potential visit to Pierre's Hole.

The only evidence of Colter's trek in the written historical record is hearsay. In 1811, Manuel Lisa told Henry Brackenridge the story, who then repeated it in 1817. According to Brackenridge's third-hand report,

> *This man, with a pack of thirty pounds weight, his gun and some ammunition, went upwards of five hundred miles to the Crow nation; gave them some information, and proceeded from them to several other tribes. On his return, a party of Indians in whose company he happened to be was attacked, and he was lamed by a severe wound in the leg; notwithstanding which,*

he returned to the establishment, entirely alone and without assistance, several hundred miles.[9]

It is on this supposed solitary trip that Colter may have entered Pierre's Hole, though he left no record telling of this. Several contemporaries recited stories he told, or talked of maps he supposedly drew, but no first-hand testimony from Colter has been found to confirm his presence in Teton Basin. Enough circumstantial evidence exists, however, to allow historians a reasonable degree of confidence that Colter likely passed time in the region.

There is much deliberation about the actual route Colter took because so few details are known.[10] Given that Colter was looking for Indians, it seems logical he followed virtually any well-traveled trail he crossed, hoping it led to a village. Crow people he met along the way undoubtedly aided in plotting his course. Yet, aside from the slim clues provided by Brackenridge, some markings on a map drawn by William Clark are about all there is to go on.

In 1810, Clark produced a map of his own earlier route across the West with the Corps of Discovery. Clark later added to this master map of America's West, updating it with information received from Zebulon Pike, Ramsay Crooks, George Drouillard, John Colter and others upon their return from the frontier (see page 50). This master map became the basis for the map accompanying the first issue of the Lewis and Clark Journals. The master map was given to editor Nicholas Biddle, who assigned cartographer Samuel Lewis (no relation to Meriwether Lewis) to redraw it (see page 51). Samuel Lewis's creation was passed to Samuel Harrison, who produced a copper plate engraving from which multiples of Clark's map were printed (see page 52). This final map was first published in 1814 in Paul Allen's *History of the Expedition Under the Command of Lewis and Clark*.[11]

Variations between the master map and the published map abound. Because Clark later added data to his master map, Wilson P. Hunt's 1811 route appears but is not on the map first published by Biddle. Oddly, both maps lack specifics in regions where Clark possessed the details to accurately portray the area. For example, George Drouillard drew a map for Clark in 1808 containing precise topography of the Big Horn Basin but this was never transferred to the master map.

This detail of William Clark's 1810 map blurs Colter's 1807 route with the track of the Astorian party. At the "Gap," (large arrow) it is not clear where the trail goes, but it appears to turn north, passing between Lake Biddle and a range of mountains. Note "peaks" (small arrow) where the Tetons should be.

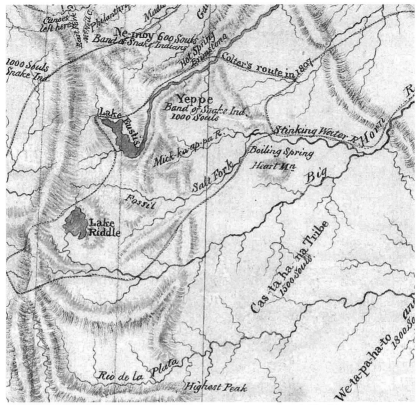

A detail of cartographer Samuel Lewis' interpretation of Clark's master map clearly shows Colter's route crossing into Pierre's Hole. Note Lake Biddle is now "Riddle," perhaps a more appropriate name. RG 77: CIVIL WORKS MAP FILE #US529

A circular track bearing the legend "Colters Route in 1807" appears on the Clark maps. On the 1810 master map, Colter's track melds with that of Hunt's Astorian party. At the "Gap," probably Teton Pass, the dotted line indicating Colter's trail does not clearly cross into present day Idaho. Instead, it appears to turn north, passing between a range of mountains and Lake Biddle. This is easier to see by tracing the route westward from Eustis Lake. Conversely, on the 1814 version, Colter's trail undoubtedly crosses into Teton Valley, turns north, and then crosses east, back into Jackson Hole in the vicinity of Conant Pass.

To Colter biographer Burton Harris, this dotted line on the 1814 rendering "establishes incontrovertibly that Colter did cross the Tetons."[12] Yet, the discrepancies between this 1810 map

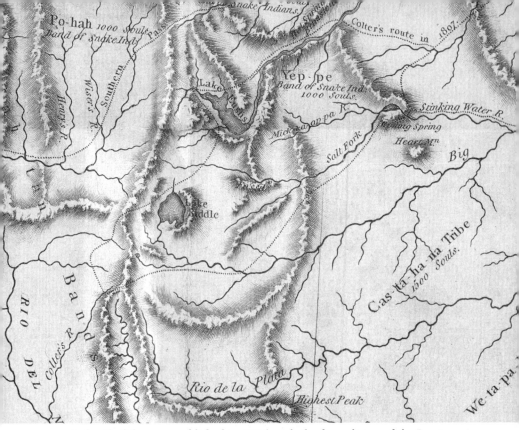

A detail of the map published in 1814 with the first edition of the Lewis and Clark Journals shows "Colter's Route of 1807" as drawn by William Clark and prepared by engraver Samuel Harrison. YALE COLLECTION OF WESTERN AMERICANA, BEINECKE RARE BOOK AND MANUSCRIPT LIBRARY, #ZC10814LE

and the 1814 published version cannot be adequately explained. Furthermore, the landmarks drawn on both of Clark's maps often hold little resemblance to geographic reality, making it difficult to determine a specific route.

Colter is believed to have met with Clark when he returned to St. Louis. It is not known whether Colter described the route or drew a rough map for Clark, but neither a journal nor a map attributed to Colter is known to exist. Nor have any notes of this meeting, made by either man, been found. Still, Clark's maps are the primary documentary evidence for John Colter being the first Euro-American to enter Pierre's Hole.

The published map had been redrawn from the original by the cartographer, and this version would again have been redrawn by the engraver, which may explain why it is so different from Clark's hand-drawn master map. Clark's 1810 version is therefore a more reliable representation of what Colter told him. Dr. John L. Allen, Emeritus Professor of Geography at the University of Wyoming, sums it up:

> It is not at all unusual for people who copy (or, in the early 19th century, engrave) maps for publication to make errors. In using maps as evidence, it is always best to use the original rather than the published version. Thus, Clark's manuscript is the only reliable source of data from this early period – the map published with the Biddle History of the Expedition ... can simply be discounted as a reliable source.[13]

Unfortunately, the topographical inaccuracies and imprecise scale of both maps make it literally impossible to identify Colter's route with absolute certainty.

A map produced by Belgian cartographer Phillippe Marie Vandermaelen in 1827 unmistakably used Clark's master map as a resource (see page 54). This map, titled *Amèrica Septentrionale No. 39. Partie des Ètats Unis,* depicts much of today's Idaho and western Montana, but also included "Colter's Route in 1807." The dotted line clearly does not cross the Teton Range into Pierre's Hole.[14]

The differences of opinion about the precise route revolve largely around the identification of lakes Biddle and Eustis, and the true location of the "Boiling Spring" and "Hot Brimstone Spring" on the maps. The names Biddle and Eustis were bestowed on these bodies of water by William Clark in honor of Nicholas Biddle, first editor of the Lewis and Clark journals, and William Eustis, Secretary of War under President James Madison.[15] Eustis Lake is now called Yellowstone Lake; Lake Biddle is generally considered to represent Jackson Lake. Some historians have declared Lake Biddle to be Brooks Lake. If so, this negates a Colter visit to Pierre's Hole. Without a doubt, Clark's drawing of Lake Biddle appears to be the headwaters of the Wind/Big Horn River; that is Brook's Lake. However, the size and position of the lake on Clark's map does not resemble its actual topographical placement.[16]

The 1836 journal of trapper Warren Ferris remarks on the sources of the Wind/Big Horn River in a way that may help interpret Clark's sketch. Ferris believes these rivers head from Jackson

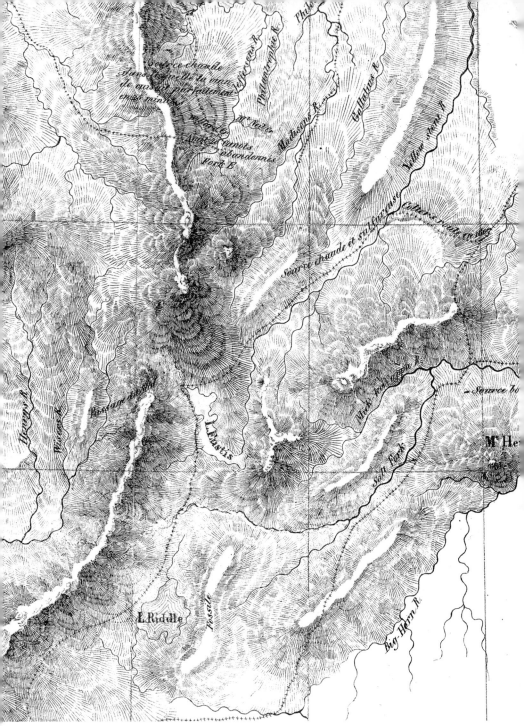

This detail of Vandermaelen's 1827 map clearly shows that "Colter's Route 1807" does not cross the Teton Range into Pierre's Hole. Although based on the same William Clark map as the Samuel Lewis version, it displays a different interpretation. DAVID RUMSEY MAP COLLECTION, WWW.DAVIDRUMSEY.COM

54

Lake, and denies Brooks Lake is their source:

> *The waters of this river, in the head of the Hole, expand into a lake of considerable magnitude, which I believe is identical with one attached to the Big Horn River, on the maps of the United States, for I have never heard of any lake on the sources of that river, although our trappers have explored every spring source of it.*[17]

Many qualified historians have tried, to no avail, to make sense of Clark's map. Stallo Vinton, Colter's first biographer, believed Colter crossed Union Pass, and then made his way into Jackson Hole via Fish Creek and the Gros Ventre River. According to Vinton, Colter left Jackson Hole via Teton Pass, traveled north through Pierre's Hole, returned to the northern end of Jackson Hole via Conant Pass, and moved into the Yellowstone Region.[18]

Alternative theories have Colter entering Jackson Hole and simply traveling north along the eastern shore of Jackson Lake. By contrast, J. Neilson Barry concluded Colter crossed Two Ocean Pass and traveled northwest into Yellowstone, bypassing Jackson Hole altogether. This would not be surprising as no trading Indians were then known to live in the interior of the Yellowstone region. Another of Colter's biographers, Burton Harris, believed Colter crossed Togwotee Pass into Jackson Hole, traveled south, and left via Teton Pass. Harris speculated Colter may have laid low to avoid Indians, fled south back across Teton Pass, and then traveled north past Jackson Lake into Yellowstone.[19] At least the idea of crossing Togwotee Pass fits well with Colter's later claim to having found a road over which wagons could travel during this trek.

Though Colter's 1807 path can only be conjectured, the generally established track, according to historian Merrill Mattes, is that Colter

> *ascended the Bighorn, followed up the Shoshone River to near present Cody, went south along the foot of the Absaroka Mountains, up Wind River to Union Pass, into Jackson Hole (and possibly across Teton Pass into Pierre's Hole), thence north along the west shore of Yellowstone Lake and northeast to the crossing of the Yellowstone near Tower Falls, thence up the Lamar River and Soda Butte Creek, back across the Absarokas,*

thence south to the Shoshone River, and back to Lisa's fort by way of Clark's Fork and Pryor's Fork.[20]

Even Mattes avoids committing to the Teton Valley portion of the route, though Colter could certainly have at least seen the Tetons from some points along the trail through Union Pass.

Other evidence helps establish parts of Colter's route but does not clear the mist. The Missouri History Museum possesses a manuscript map drawn by William Clark in 1808. Another Lewis and Clark veteran, George Drouillard, provided information for this map of the Big Horn country, which shows Colter definitely reached the boiling springs near present Cody, Wyoming.

If Colter really saw the Tetons, those mountains should have impressed him enough to make it on the map. Certainly almost every other early traveler in their proximity was struck by the majestic nature of this landmark. Scratched into the concentrated mountain range drawn to the west of Lake Biddle is the word "peaks," which is as close as Clark's master map comes to identifying these pinnacles. The Tetons are certainly more remarkable than Heart Mountain, which does get drawn in its proper place.

There is no Snake River shown on either of Clark's maps, calling into question whether Colter saw it. To climb through any pass from the eastern base of the Tetons near where Clark shows his route, he would have had to ford the Snake River somewhere in Jackson Hole. The fast moving waters of this river seldom freeze near the trails crossing the range. Colter would not have forgotten the bone-chilling, icy waters of such a winter crossing. With no mention of crossing a major river such as the Snake, known to be a tributary of the Columbia River, it is conceivable Colter never thought he crossed the Continental Divide to the Pacific drainage.

Many have wondered why Colter would continue to trek west at all. Merlin K. Potts, former Chief Naturalist at Grand Teton National Park, remarked:

From the broad valley of [Jackson] Hole the route northward up the Snake River into the Yellowstone was to any eye an easy one. The terrain sloped gently, there were no mountain walls to scale or circle, nothing to indicate any obstacle of consequence. Indeed, many notable historical scholars have opposed the

Teton Pass theory, asserting that [Colter] did avoid the Tetons by moving northward. He would certainly have fulfilled Lisa's orders to contact nearby Indian tribes by the time he had reached Jackson Hole.[21]

Moreover, if Colter were truly looking for the Crow, the west side of the Tetons was known to be Shoshone land. He would have learned that from the Apsáalooke people whom he met along the way. Even if he had wanted to revisit the Shoshones he had met with Lewis and Clark, he would have learned from the Crow that the Shoshone did not winter in Pierre's Hole but were usually camped to the southwest. The Crow were well aware of the winter ranges of neighboring tribes in order to steer clear and guard against attack.

Manuel Lisa had heard a rumor that twenty-two days travel from their location at Fort Remon on the Big Horn would bring them to the "Spanish settlements," presumably located on the Green River. Other hearsay included reports of Spanish traders in the mountains, thus it is possible Colter was instructed to investigate that information as well.[22] This might clarify why the large river on the west side of the "Gap" is labeled as the Rio del Norte rather than the Snake, further confirming Colter's assumption that he had not reached a feeder stream for the Pacific but that he was in a region drained by the Colorado River.

But if Colter made his final westward push after traveling the twenty-two days supposedly necessary to reach Spanish lands, it placed him only a little over three weeks into his round trip from Fort Remon. A trek of 500 miles, as defended by Brackenridge, adds up easier if Colter indeed bypassed Teton Valley.

To complicate matters a bit further, in August 2008, Dr. Allen introduced new information from a digitally enhanced version of Clark's manuscript map.[23] From these images, argued Dr. Allen, it is clear Colter never crossed the Continental Divide. He asserted Colter followed up the Wind River to its source – Lake Biddle on Clark's map, Brooks Lake on modern maps – then traveled north, skirting Lake Yellowstone. This means Colter did not enter Jackson Hole, did not go to Pierre's Hole and could have missed seeing the Tetons altogether.

Incidentally, the term "Colter's Hell" in trapper days specifically referred to an area Colter described near the forks of the Shoshone, or Stinking Water River. This was close to, but definitely outside of the region that became Yellowstone National Park. There is no contemporary evidence the name was applied to the area of today's Park at all, by trappers or the public, until after 1872. Joe Meek and Jim Bridger were fur men of that period who were intimately familiar with the area. Both men made a clear distinction between the two locales and regarded only the Shoshone River thermal district as Colter's Hell. In short, Yellowstone National Park is definitely not Colter's Hell.[24]

The actual dates of Colter's departure and return to Fort Remon are not recorded. Lisa's company arrived at the Big Horn in late October or early November 1807. Many historians believe Colter did not leave until the fort's construction was complete, marking late November as his departure time. Yet Lisa could have sent Colter out while the post was being built. A person can move quickly with only a thirty pound pack and a rifle.[25] If the trek covered 500 miles the trip could be made in less than two months at an average rate of only ten miles per day. George Drouillard drew a pencil map of his own travels that gave thirty miles a day as an average distance of travel. If Colter maintained a similar pace, 500 miles could be covered in seventeen days. Allowing for extra days to visit villages or get stuck in a storm or two, Colter could still have been back at the fort in time for Christmas.

The Crow people were a mounted tribe, proud of their enormous horse herds. They were also notorious horse thieves, having stolen from William Clark on his return trip in 1806.[26] If it is assumed Colter started on foot, there is no reason to think he completed his entire journey without bartering for a horse somewhere along the way. In fact, he would likely remain on foot only if he knew his journey consisted mainly of steep areas that a horse could not traverse. On horseback, the length of time necessary to cover 500 miles is reduced even more.

Further, he may not have made the entire trip alone. Colter could easily have been accompanied by a Crow guide from any village he visited. This would not only have shortened his trip, but would explain why he seemed to never flounder in his directions.

In fact, historian John C. Ewers claims Colter was sent with two Crow guides.[27]

Winter travelers of the time apparently figured on about thirty pounds of equipment per man. Jim Beckwourth described in his memoirs an express to St. Louis he and Moses "Black" Harris made in the winter of 1825-1826:

The following morning we prepared for departure. Each man loading himself with twenty-five pounds of provisions, besides a blanket, rifle and ammunition each, we started on our journey.[28]

Beckwourth points out he was loaded with items he would require for a winter trek, not trade goods. This raises the possibility Colter packed no merchandise at all and was merely announcing the grand opening of a new store in the region.

Carrying a small pack might indicate Colter brought efficient wool blankets rather than a heavy, impractical buffalo robe. One thick winter hide could easily account for at least half of the pack's total thirty pounds, leaving little room for trade goods. A robe wet from a stream crossing or winter weather would have been much heavier, and hard to dry. This calls into question the accuracy of John Clymer's vision of those events in his painting *John Colter Visits the Crow – 1807*, magnificent scene though it is (see color plate 4).

Colter had experienced several winters in the Rockies and would have been prepared. While at Fort Mandan during the winter of 1804-1805, Colter experienced 40 degree below zero weather in early January. At that time, Clark recorded, "a man Came in who had also Stayed out without fire, and verry thinly Clothed, this man was not the least injured."[29] A person thus acclimatized becomes inured to the cold to a large degree.

It is likely the trade goods he carried were less for trading than for exhibition – salesman's samples, more or less. The display of merchandise was meant to entice Indians to bring their beaver skins to the fort. Doling out a few trinkets would not impress prospective customers very much, especially having to ration his meager supply, not knowing exactly how many villages he might encounter. On the other hand, demonstrating the miraculous steel kettle or iron blade would have a greater impact, much like the magnets, air rifle and magnifying glasses Lewis and Clark used as they crossed the continent a few years prior.

With winter fast approaching, there would be no time for sightseeing. The terrain would only get harder to cross when covered with snow. Henry Brackenridge reported that Colter told him "a loaded wagon would find no obstruction in passing" the route he took, suggesting that at least portions of his trail were adequately devoid of snow so as to make such a declaration.[30] A mild winter would give Colter fewer troubles in the mountain passes.

However, Dr. Allen indicates that the winter of 1807-1808 was one of the more severe on record.[31] If true, given Colter's experience, he would not have attempted to cross Teton Pass at this time, and would not have described the route as appropriate for a loaded wagon. Game animals would have been driven to lower elevations and crossing the Teton Range might have recreated his near-starvation trip across the Bitterroot Mountains with Lewis and Clark.

Snowshoes might have been carried, traded for, or constructed along the way. While on the Lewis and Clark expedition, Colter likely witnessed several snowshoes styles as Lewis recorded in April 1806, "I observe snowshoes in all the lodges of the natives above the Columbean vally."[32] It would not have been beyond his woods lore to make snowshoes, however rudimentary, should he find it necessary.

Regardless of when Colter returned to Fort Remon, he was back on the trail again in the spring and participated in a battle described by Thomas James. Though never named in any fur trade record, this fight has been dubbed "the Battle of the Flats" by some writers of Pierre's Hole history and B. W. Driggs claims the encounter occurred in Teton Valley on the plain between Leigh Creek and Teton Creek.[33] But the real story was recounted by Colter, personally, to Thomas James in 1809, as they traveled past the site – in present day Montana – where the conflict had actually occurred.

In his autobiography *Three Years Among the Indians and Mexicans*, James described accompanying Colter as they descended from what is now Bozeman Pass onto the Gallatin River, near the Three Forks of the Missouri. James reported they

> *passed a battlefield of the Indians, where the skulls and bones were lying around on the ground in vast numbers. The battle which had caused this terrible slaughter took place in 1808,*

the year but one before, between the Blackfeet to the number of fifteen hundred on the one side, and the Flatheads and Crows, numbering together about eight hundred, on the other. Colter was in the battle on the side of the latter, and was wounded in the leg, and thus disabled from standing. He crawled to a small thicket and there loaded and fired while sitting on the ground. The Blackfeet engaged at first with about five hundred Flatheads, whom they attacked in great fury. The noise, shouts, and firing brought a reinforcement of Crows to the Flatheads, who were fighting with great spirit and defending the ground manfully. The Blackfeet, who are the Arabs of this region, were at length repulsed, but retired in perfect order and could hardly be said to have been defeated ... at the time of this well-fought battle Colter was leading them [Flatheads] to Manuel's fort to trade with the Americans.[34]

Oddly, neither Clark map shows Colter's route going anywhere near the Gallatin River where this fight allegedly occurred which may mean his trek did not extend into 1808. Presuming the battle occurred on a journey that stretched into the following year, two questions beg to be asked: if Colter was recruiting Crow customers for Lisa's trading post, why does Thomas James indicate it was Flatheads being led to Fort Remon; and why was Colter alone when he returned to the fort from this trek, as Brackenridge said?

The Colter Stone: Evidence or Monkey Wrench?

An artifact of debatable provenance may or may not provide other evidence that Colter was the first Euro-American to enjoy the beauty of Pierre's Hole. In 1931, William Beard and his son were clearing timber from their land five and a half miles east of Tetonia, Idaho, when they unearthed from beneath eighteen inches of soil a shaped and inscribed stone. The property was located between North and South Leigh Creeks, just over the modern Wyoming state line, on the north side of today's South Leigh Canyon Road. The stone was a block of rhyolite lava measuring thirteen inches high, eight inches wide, and four inches thick. It had been worked into the shape of a crude human head. One side bore the inscription "John Coulter," the other, "1808."

Beard placed the stone on his porch, where it sat for almost two years. A. C. Lyon, a neighbor, learned of the stone and traded a pair of used boots for it. In turn, Lyon donated it to Grand Teton National Park in 1934. Today, the "Colter Stone" rests in the Teton Valley Museum in Driggs, Idaho, on loan from the Colter Bay Museum in Grand Teton National Park.

There are plausible reasons to believe the stone is genuine. In 1931, when the stone was uncovered, Colter's tale was fairly unknown. The Beard family apparently had no idea who Colter was, nor did they try to make any money off their treasure. Geologist Fritiof Fryxell, Grand Teton National Park's first naturalist, concluded the inscriptions, prior to being embedded in the soil, had been exposed to weathering consistent with the 1808 date. The inscription and facial features, in Fryxell's opinion, were every bit as weathered as the stone's other surfaces, indicating no one had recently touched up an older rock. Fryxell also located a ledge of rhyolite not far from Beard's field that was similar to the composition of the Colter Stone, convincing him no one had carved the stone somewhere else and relocated it in the valley. Moreover, the stone had been discovered buried deeply in the soil. Had it been intended as a gag, whoever put it there had greatly reduced the chance that it would ever be found. Thus, Fryxell ruled out a hoax by the Beard family or by someone else planting the artifact on their land.[35]

The authenticity of the stone is complicated by other arguments, however, such as whether Colter was even literate and able to carve his name. The U.S. Army had no literacy requirement for new recruits when Colter enlisted. However, Colter's signature appears on several documents, and three books are listed in his estate at the time of his death, suggesting he could indeed read and write.[36]

John Colter's signature appears on a promissory note to John G. Comegys dated December 12, 1810. MISSOURI HISTORY MUSEUM, ST. LOUIS

A photo of the Colter Stone included in Nolie Mumey's 1947 book, The Teton Mountains, *shows that the inscription reads "John Coulter."*

U.S. DEPARTMENT OF THE INTERIOR, GRAND TETON NATIONAL PARK

One wonders if Colter had kept track of dates enough to know that the 1807 winter had become 1808.

Yet, doubts about the authenticity of the Colter Stone persist. In recent years, writer W. C. Lawrence alleged Lyon planted the stone to curry favor with the National Park Service in order to secure a horse concession at Jenny Lake.[37] But this is an unlikely motive because Lyon had acquired that concession in 1929; the stone was discovered in 1931.[38]

Comparisons with other inscriptions believed to be from Colter's hand might be helpful. A stone found on the site of Fort Remon possesses minor similarities between the two etchings, particularly in the letter "O," but there is no way to authenticate it. There is evidence to suggest, however, that Colter was at Fort Remon in 1810.[39]

More worrisome is evidence that the original inscription has been tampered with since its discovery. A comparison between the

Colter is alleged to have made this inscription on a rock at Fort Remon.
KENNETH F. ROAHEN, PHOTOGRAPHER, BIG HORN COUNTY HISTORICAL MUSEUM, HARDIN, MONTANA

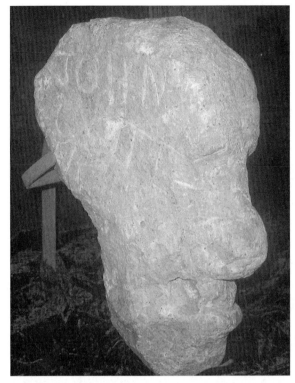

These two modern images of the Colter Stone show disturbing alterations when compared with the photo taken in 1947, shown on page 63. Note the gouge between the letters "L" and "T," and the way the last name has been hyphenated, which does not appear in Mumey's 1947 book.

BRUCE BELASON PHOTOS

circa 1947 Mumey photo of the Colter Stone and a modern snapshot exhibits alteration of the rock's inscription. A close look at early photos of the deteriorating carving reveal the letters, "C-O-U-L-T-E-R" erratically spaced.

This is not the spelling Colter used when he signed various extant documents.[40] Newer photos, however, show the inscription as "COLTER." A distinct gouge in the rhyolite converts the "U" in the Mumey photo to an "L." The earlier "R" has been replaced by an "E," while an "R" has appeared in a third line of carving. This alteration clearly indicates someone wants the Colter Stone to be more than it truly is.

The Colter Stone is probably not authentic and the most likely culprits are pranksters with the 1872 Hayden Geological Surveys. Dr. Allen mentions a sergeant with Hayden who liked to salt areas with assorted "artifacts." The Colter Stone is one of six such stones found within a 25-mile radius in Teton Basin.[41] Two are clearly frauds, both bearing the legend "Clark 1805."

Lewis and Clark did not pass anywhere near the Pierre's Hole region. One of these "Clark" stones was found on the farm of M. B. Yeaman in Swan Valley in 1911. A similar stone was found about five miles away. John Hailey, secretary of the Idaho Historical Society at the time, innocently conjectured that Clark had given the stones to Indians who must have carried them as far as the Snake River.[42]

Another question is whether a suspect Hayden Survey prankster could have known or guessed the correct dates of Colter's journey, given that little was known about Colter until the early 1900s. That he accompanied Lewis and Clark was familiar to many and may provide a connection to Hayden crewmembers and a hoax using Clark's name.

In 1889, an inscription was found on a tree on the bank of Coulter Creek in northern Teton Basin. The initials "JC" were carved under a large "X." Western writer Philip Ashton Rollins and two guides examined the carving, and optimistic that the carving was evidence of trapper John Colter's presence in the Basin, concluded it was about eighty years old. Shortly after reporting the find, Yellowstone National Park employees cut the tree down and salvaged the portion bearing the 5-½" tall initials. The log was to be placed in the park museum, but as luck would have it, disappeared in transit.[43]

This monument to John Colter stands outside the old Teton Valley Courthouse in Driggs, Idaho. It was erected by the Daughters of the Utah Pioneers in 1938, seven years after the discovery of the Colter Stone, and touts the erroneous "Battle of the Flats." JIM HARDEE PHOTO

Historian Aubrey Haines theorized the lost inscriptions were those of John Merle Coulter, a botanist with the 1872 Hayden Survey and for whom Coulter Creek was named in 1885.[44] The inscription found in 1889 had not been eighty years old, but closer to seventeen years old.

The vicinity of Coulter Creek is dense with lodgepole pine even today. An eighty-year-old carving would have been invisible, obscured by accumulated pitch and the natural growth and scarring in tree bark. According to author Frank Calkins, "blazes cut by CCC boys thirty-five years ago are barely discernible today." An examination of growth rings indicated sizable trees in the vicinity would have been about two inches in diameter at the time trapper John Colter had supposedly been in the valley.[45] This seems to settle the question of John Coulter versus John Colter, and which one carved his name in the trees and stones of Teton Basin.

Most historians agree that John Colter traveled 500 miles from Fort Remon looking for Crow Indians the winter of 1807. The areas of contention, however, are legion and there is no evidence to lay the questions to rest. In the end, any conclusion is based on inconclusive evidence.[46] Colter's exact route will probably never be determined and whether he entered the Teton Basin is likely to always remain a controversy. As it turned out, the boots Lyon traded Beard for the Colter Stone did not fit, and frankly, neither do most aspects of the story.

John Colter left the West for good in 1810, moving back to Missouri where he settled down and married. His property near La Charette, Missouri was at the mouth of Big Boeuf Creek where it enters the Missouri River. A life of farming seems ill-suited for so glorious a frontiersman. Colter died, apparently of jaundice, May 7, 1812, approximately 38 years of age.[47]

6

ANDREW HENRY AND THE ST. LOUIS MISSOURI FUR COMPANY: 1809-1810

During the winter of 1808-1809, Manuel Lisa established the St. Louis Missouri Fur Company. The principal investors included Pierre Chouteau, Auguste Chouteau, Pierre Menard, Andrew Henry, Sylvestre Labbadie, Reuben Lewis and William Clark – some of the most influential men in St. Louis.[1] Lisa took men up the Missouri River who would find their way to Pierre's Hole.

The historical record hints that other trappers and traders were in the Snake River area in the earliest years of the 1800s, before Lisa arrived. These men may have seen the Tetons and explored Pierre's Hole, yet, so shadowy are these tales that the exact whereabouts of these men are unknowable. Names like Jeremy Pinch and "Mr. Courter" peek provocatively from the pages of early journals and letters, testing the mettle of historians trying to make sense of it all.[2]

Al Austin, who came to the Jackson Hole region before 1900, claimed to have found the barrel of a flintlock rifle in a canyon off the Hoback River. The barrel was stamped "London 1776," which does not necessarily mean the rifle was lost prior to 1800, but makes it likely the gun belonged to an early fur trader who poked around in the vicinity of Pierre's Hole.[3]

As discussed earlier, Manuel Lisa of St. Louis was determined to tap the immense fur resources of the West. Leaving a crew busily trading with the Crow up river at Fort Remon, he returned to St. Louis in the summer of 1808. He also had contingents out trapping beaver instead of waiting for Indians to bring their pelts to trade. Though primary fur trade documents do not confirm it, some of these men could have entered Pierre's Hole.

Manuel Lisa made innovations in the fur business. Prior to this time, furs had been obtained mainly from local natives through trade. This method had worked all over the East and in the Canadian market. Build a post and they will come. Indians who rapidly became addicted to manufactured trade goods gladly brought furs for exchange. But on the waters of the Upper Missouri,

Manuel Lisa, founder of the St. Louis Missouri Fur Company, in an oil portrait from 1818. MISSOURI HISTORY MUSEUM, ST. LOUIS

this did not result in expected profits because the Natives were less inclined to spend time trapping. Lisa initiated the practice of Company men going out to trap and bringing in skins, bypassing Indian trade as the primary source of peltry.

Lisa recruited a party of sufficient size to keep hostile tribes at bay while his men trapped the streams of the Rocky Mountains. He acquired a license from then governor Meriwether Lewis, brother of company shareholder, Reuben. Like the vast majority of all American licenses issued during the fur trade years, this permit was for trade with various western tribes – not for trapping.

The 1809 expedition of the St. Louis Missouri Fur Company consisted of 350 men divided into two contingents: one mounted on horseback, the other in a flotilla of keelboats.[4] Up river nearly 1400 miles, close to the junction of the Big Knife River and the Missouri, Lisa built Fort Mandan to serve as a trading center with the Hidatsa, also known as the Gros Ventres of the River. Their primary objective, however, was to reach Fort Remon, roughly 500 miles further west at the mouth of the Big Horn.

In October, partner Andrew Henry selected forty men and started overland to Fort Remon. Another partner, Pierre Menard, took fifty men to pilot boats on up the Missouri to the Yellowstone River, intending to meet Henry at Fort Remon with supplies. The remaining men stayed with Lisa at the new post, Fort Mandan. Fatefully, the Yellowstone froze over, forcing Menard to abandon the watercraft, cache the goods and proceed overland on foot.

Once Henry arrived at Fort Remon, he set his men to trapping. The area closely surrounding the post was likely trapped out by those who had been there a year or more. This forced Henry's trappers to travel many miles in their trapping sorties. In spring 1810, Henry took a group of about thirty men, including Pierre Menard, John Colter, George Drouillard, John Dougherty, and Thomas James over to the Three Forks, where the Gallatin, Jefferson and Madison rivers join to form the Missouri, to continue their hunt. On this journey, Colter showed his companions the site of his battle with the Blackfoot mentioned in the previous chapter.

Henry arrived at Three Forks on April 3, 1810.[5] On a neck of land between the Madison and the Jefferson rivers, about two miles up from the confluence, the men began construction of a new fort. The post was reported to have had a double set of stockade walls sunk three feet into the ground and rising ten feet high, enclosing a rather small area of about 300 square feet. Dougherty recorded that he "left the Fort & decended the Missouri in quest of Beaver near 300 miles when the party lost their canoe & were compelled to return."[6]

Though not documented, if others traveled 300 miles in various directions from Three Forks to set traps, some of them could well have entered the Teton Basin in search of pelts.

The Three Forks enterprise began well enough. James reported his party caught beaver on the first day. The second day found a beaver in every one of their twenty-three traps and James was "cheered with the thoughts of making a speedy fortune."[7] But that rosy glow soon dimmed. Indians were seen in the vicinity and the trappers grew increasingly edgy. James wrote, "when we entered the Fort, the whole garrison was drawn up with fingers upon triggers. They were expecting an attack every moment."[8]

Their headquarters was in the heart of Blackfoot country and deadly encounters accumulated over the next several weeks. Three men went out to trap and were never seen again. Attack after attack, death after death; things got so bad no one would go out of the fort alone for anything, much less to set traps. James Cheek expressed his over-arching sense of dread to fellow trapper Thomas James:

It is the general opinion that you will be killed ... But I am afraid for myself as well as you. I know not the cause, but I have felt fear ever since I came to the Forks, and I never was afraid of anything before ... I may be dead when you return.[9]

Early in May, George Drouillard was killed. James testified,

The Blackfeet manifested so determined a hatred and jealousy of our presence, that we could entertain no hope of successfully prosecuting our business. Discouraged by the prospect before us, most of the Americans prepared to go.[10]

Andrew Henry, disheartened by Blackfoot persistence but determined to find an angle to salvage the mission, decided to cross the Continental Divide into the region of the upper Snake River Plains so highly touted by Weiser and Champlain. In early summer, just a few months after their initial arrival at Three Forks, Henry lowered the fort's flag and pulled out. Menard took men and horses to retrieve the supplies cached on the Yellowstone, arranging to resupply Henry's men who were staying to trap across the divide. Once the crew was restocked, Menard went back to St. Louis and never returned to the mountains.

As many as sixty men may have accompanied Henry into this new beaver country on the Snake River. Only a handful of them can be identified: Dougherty, Michael Immel, Nicholas Glineau,

William Weir, Archibald Pelton, P. McBride, B. Jackson, L. Cather, and that intrepid trio, Edward Robinson, John Hoback, and Jacob Reznor. Neither their exact number nor their route is clearly known.[11]

Many historians think Henry made his way up the Madison River and over modern Raynolds' Pass where he discovered the lake that today bears his name. Along the route, Indians harassed him yet again. This time a group of Crow stole some of the trappers' horses – a double blow since these animals not only packed gear, they were a food source in times of necessity.[12]

Henry may have split his party, sending one group with Menard to obtain needed supplies and then head for the Columbia River drainage, while Henry led the remainder on a more direct route south by way of the Madison River. Two maps that provide differing information support this scenario. First is Clark's enigmatic 1810 manuscript map discussed in relationship to Colter. This map also shows a trail leading southward up the Madison, over the Continental Divide (likely via modern Raynolds' Pass), and onto Henry's Fork of the Snake River. Clark initially mislabeled "Henry's River," striking out the name on one stream to get it correctly situated. This route is borne out in a letter by Clark to Secretary of War William Eustis.[13] It would be, as already remarked by Reuben Lewis, "about 5 or 6 days travel to an illigable plan [eligible plain] for a fort on that River."[14] William Clark would also later report that Henry went "over to the head of a South branch of the Columbia to hunt and trade with the Snakes."[15]

As intriguing as Clark's map is, the second map, dubbed, "The Dougherty Map," is more so. The map's reverse bears a narrative account by an unidentified writer describing the activities of John Dougherty in 1810.[16] This map ranks alongside the previously mentioned Clark manuscript and Drouillard maps as one of the earliest known maps of the region prior to 1817.

According to this map, Dougherty and an unknown number of men crossed over to the Yellowstone from the Gallatin River through a breach labeled "18 miles across." Henry sent this party in order to meet Menard at the cache near Clark's Fork of the Yellowstone River for resupply before Menard's return to St. Louis. Dougherty's group then traveled up the Yellowstone, crossed over to the Stinking Water (Shoshone) River and then on to the Big Horn. This is similar to the course Colter took and it may well have been Colter who suggested the route. It also took them farther south, out of Blackfoot territory. If Colter had already visited Pierre's Hole, surely he had regaled Henry with the wonders of that beaver-laden valley, spurring Henry to head for that area.

Dougherty expected to follow the Rio del Norte, or Green River, cross a ridge and come down onto the Snake, or Lewis River, as it was often known in that day. Historian Mark W. Kelly, biographer of John Dougherty, has hiked throughout the region attempting to work out this route.[17] Kelly postulates the party crossed Shoshone Pass onto the Du Noir River drainage and mistook the upper reaches of the Wind River for the Rio del Norte, unaware that the Wind and Big Horn are the same river.[18] Kelly surmises Dougherty and company backtracked up the Wind to present day Togwotee Pass, then down the Buffalo Fork which brought the brigade into Jackson's Big Hole.

Once in Jackson Hole, the party presumably climbed over the Tetons and into Pierre's Hole where it would have met up with Andrew Henry in a few more days of travel. Although Dougherty's description of his journey does not absolutely confirm this route, the Dougherty party may, nonetheless, have been the first non-indigenous people to enter Teton Valley. The only other candidates would have been Colter, Weiser and Champlain whose presence is also impossible to rule out or confirm.

Undoubtedly, if Dougherty gazed upon the fertile valley of Pierre's Hole, he must have been thrilled by the abundance of beaver sign, the prevalence of big game animals, and the company's good prospects for the coming months. Weiser and Champlain had not exaggerated.

Working northward, Dougherty's group followed the down-stream flow of the Teton River. Their view was dominated by *les Trois Tetons* during these few days. B. W. Driggs was erroneously referring to Henry, but should have been speaking of Dougherty, when he wrote, "He found his way over the Continental Divide ... thence over Teton Pass, spent some time in this valley, and then went on to ... Henry's Fork."[19]

Dougherty's party finally reunited with Andrew Henry about forty-five miles northwest of Pierre's Hole, on the banks of the tributary of the Snake River to which Henry's name would also be attached. After constructing their rude quarters, they prepared for the coming season of fur trapping.

Fort Henry, built in 1810 and vacated the following spring, was the first American post built on the western side of the Continental Divide. The Tetons could be seen to the East. Located on the future site of Eagle's Nest Ford, the fort was on the south side of Henry's Fork of the Snake River, about three miles west of present St. Anthony, Idaho (see color plate 6). Historian Louis Clement's attempt to describe the site places the fort "about 200 yards east of the Salem farm-to-farm road." He offers other hints to find the fort:

> *Where the bottomland of pasture rises to the working farmland ... A hole there from the excavation done by Beal ... If you stand directly in front of the monument facing east and look about 10 degrees to the right you can see the actual site of the fort.*[20]

Wilson Price Hunt recorded his visit to the site in October 1811:

> *We reached the fort of Mr. Andrew Henry. It has several small buildings that he constructed in order to spend the past winter there. All stand along a tributary of the Columbia about 300 to 450 feet wide.*[21]

Other fur trade era visitors to the site include Captain Benjamin Bonneville in 1832 and Father De Smet in 1840. Numerous trapper diaries reveal mountaineers traipsing up and down Henry's Fork but do not mention the ruins of a fort. However, oral testimony was collected in 1925 from three elderly Native Americans at Fort Hall; one of these men remembered a cluster of log houses at the site with their roofs falling in.[22] "Fort" is a generous word to describe a rudimentary collection of makeshift huts. The number of buildings supports the idea that more than a mere handful of men were with Henry.

In 1881, William McMinn homesteaded the land on which the site of Fort Henry is located. While farming, he discovered a gun barrel, an axe, and a piece of homemade chain, as well as several piles of lava rocks arranged in a semi-circle.[23] In April 1925, B. W. Driggs noted the discovery of

The Fort Henry monument stands on the Fort Henry Scenic Byway, along the Red Road, about two miles south of Parker, Idaho, on the left bank of Henry's Fork, south of the bridge and west of the fort site. JIM HARDEE PHOTOS

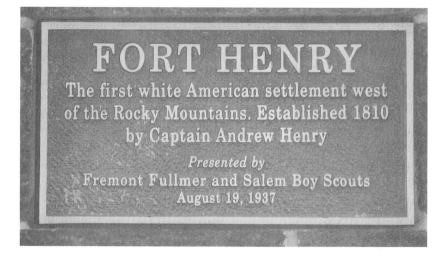

a medallion of bronze, shield-shaped, about the size of the palm of a man's hand ... greatly corroded, and upon it was inscribed sixteen stars arranged in a semicircle. Beneath the stars are two American flags, each with sixteen stars. Crossed cutlasses and crossed pistols are carved on the shield.[24]

Sadly, the location of this particular artifact is currently unknown. Though none of these relics tie directly to Henry, few historians dispute their relationship to his occupation of the area.

Professor Samuel Beal of Ricks College began an archeological dig at the site in 1933. The excavations revealed occasional pockets of ash and slender lines of charcoal marking the position of logs that formed the walls and roof of a ten by twelve foot cabin. Corner positions were also located. The dig uncovered an "upper stratum of clay and sand, next sand and gravel that had pushed in from the sides upon the burning of the walls." At a depth of five feet, the cabin floor emerged, made of harder and finer material than the sand and gravel above. A blue stone about twenty by twelve inches was discovered, inscribed in distinct letters about two inches high, "Fort Henry 1811 by Cap. Hunt."[25] This stone may have been yet another lark perpetrated by a Hayden-party artist.

Inscriptions on the Menan Buttes are probably related to the Henry trapping group. About thirteen miles southwest of Fort Henry, the two conspicuous volcanic cones of Menan Buttes rise six hundred feet above the plain. The area was a prime hunting ground. Names carved on the rocks near an 1810 date include, among several others, those of J. Reznor, J. Day, A. Henry, and W. Weir.[26]

Recently, Donald Faris of Bondurant, Wyoming, reportedly found a blazed tree above the Hoback Canyon, bearing the inscription "IKE WEELER OCT 17 1809." The identity of Weeler or the party to which he may have been attached is unconfirmed. But, based on the date, this alleged presence on the divide between Granite Creek and Shoal Creek may indicate the distance men ranged from Fort Henry while trapping.[27] If men did indeed roam this far from Fort Henry, it indicates the men did not confine themselves to the proximity of the fort for fear of Indian attack as they had at Three Forks.

Once the post was built, it can be assumed Henry's men set about the work for which they had come. In the process of investigating streams likely to produce profitable trapping, the men probably explored the Teton River and found it unpromising. As it exits Pierre's Hole and nears Henry's Fork, the river carves a rather deep canyon – not terrific habitat for setting traps.

Working their way upstream on Henry's Fork, the men would have discovered Fall River, a far superior candidate for beaver trapping. The mouth is but a few miles from Fort Henry and the confluence is broad and inviting. Traveling up Fall River, Henry's employees would find the furry flat-tailed mammals thriving in Squirrel Creek and Conant Creek (see color plate 3 for a typical creek setting showing beaver activity). There is physical evidence of their camp on Conant Creek, about thirty miles from the fort, in Pierre's Hole's northern extremes.

Margaret H. Lindsley, author of *Major Andrew Henry in Idaho*, tells of contention between the Kentucky trio and others at the fort. Lindsley found enough evidence in researching Henry to suggest Hoback, Robinson and Reznor may have pulled away from the main group and set up their own bivouac some distance away. That may explain the existence of the camp.[28] But, given that Henry occupied the Conant Creek site, it was likely an outpost of the main fort.

Inscriptions on several rocks at this location indicate the trappers' presence east of present day Drummond, Idaho, on the Finlandia Ranch (see color plate 7). These inscriptions suggest at least five individuals inhabited the site during September 1810. The engraved rocks were found in the spring of 1917 by Hazen Hawkes while working for the Conant Creek Canal Company.[29]

One stone includes the names of five men, a face, a cross and the year 1810. The names on the rock are A. Henry, J. Hoback, P. McBride, B. Jackson and L. Cather. Because L. Cather's name appears on the side of the stone, one examiner conjectured that, in a starving condition, Cather carved the names as a grave marker, hence the cross, adding his name at the last. Since only one of the Kentuckians' names appears, it is not likely this was the separate camp suggested by Lindsley, although it is possible the men moved back and forth between the fort and this location. Perhaps there were other outpost camps as well.[30]

A few years after the initial discovery, Hawkes was riding through the meadow below the site where the original rock was found and ran across a rock bearing the inscription "Camp Henry" and "Sept 1810." A smaller rock nearby bore the initials "L.C." These rocks are still in situ and have been protected by a shelter erected through a local Boy Scout service project in 1965.

L. Cather may have scratched on these stones, perhaps while on horse guard, since the meadow would have been an exposed place to camp. Historians Louis J. Clements and Harold S. Forbush speculate this site was merely a stopover as the men departed the area, but carving these stones would probably have required more time than an overnight bivouac.[31]

Numerous sources report Henry and his men, though not molested by Indians, found virtually no game in the vicinity of either Fort Henry or Camp Henry. Many animals had likely starved or been driven from the region during the severe winter of 1807-1808, only two years prior. Animal populations would not have recovered by the time Henry arrived.

Major Thomas Biddle, writing to Colonel Henry Atkinson in 1819, made reference to the hardships of Henry and his men, saying, "they suffered much for provisions, and were compelled to live for some months entirely upon their horses. The party by this time had become dispirited, and began to separate."[32]

The winter of 1810-1811 was severe as well. Deep snow and heavy spring rains only added to the party's hunger and hardship. Appropriately enough, Fort Henry was in an area the Shoshone called "Egin," which means "cold."[33]

One St. Louis newspaper recounted that Henry "subsisted principally on roots, and having lost his clothes like another Crusoe dressed himself from head to foot in skins."[34] Had Henry located his post just fifty miles farther downstream in territory frequently utilized by the Bannock and Snake Indians, he would not have suffered so severely. That traditional wintering ground is near the site of historic Fort Hall, near today's Pocatello, Idaho.[35] As it was, the trappers evidently resorted to eating their horses to stay alive. By the end of the winter, they were boiling the hides for soup.

The following year, Wilson Hunt visited the remains of Fort Henry:

The people of this area must suffer terribly from the lack of game ... During our stay in this district the wind blew constantly from the west, often quite violently ... where it causes

Several inscriptions are thought to mark the site of Camp Henry. The large rock in the top photo, held by Hazen Hawkes, is now at the Idaho Falls Museum. The inscribed boulder in the bottom photo is still in place near Drummond, Idaho.
COURTESY OF MUSEUM OF IDAHO

considerable damage, uprooting large trees over a vast area and blowing their branches for great distances.[36]

Despite the wintry conditions before they left, Henry and his men managed to procure some forty packs of beaver. Whether these were gathered through trade with local Shoshone or from actual trapping at either the Three Forks post or on Henry's Fork is unknown. Probably the beaver were garnered via trapping since trade with local Indians would likely have forewarned Henry of his unfavorable wintering site. The harvest of forty packs is a fairly significant accomplishment, considering a typical pack weighs nearly one hundred pounds and had a value of about five dollars per pound – roughly $20,000 for the winter's efforts. It would have taken fifteen to twenty pack animals to get the hides to market, thus Henry either did not eat all of the brigade's pack animals or was able to trade for more in the spring. Significantly, there were no attacks from Blackfoot war parties, which must have been a welcome relief.

Little else has come to light concerning Henry's brigade in Idaho. With the spring of 1811, Henry's Fort was abandoned. Archibald Pelton apparently wandered off on his own, for he was later discovered by the Wilson Hunt party in the vicinity of today's Lewiston, Idaho. Gabriel Franchère, in his narrative of events about Astoria, reported:

> *[Hunt's party] also came upon a young American who was deranged, but who had some lucid moments. The young man told them, during one of his clearer intervals, that he was from Connecticut, and was named Archibald Petton. He said that he had come up the Missouri with Mr. Henry and that all the people at the trader's post had been massacred. He alone had escaped and had wandered for three years among the Indians. Our people took this young man with them.*[37]

Another Astorian, Ross Cox, also reported Pelton among the Snake Indians. Since there is no record of Fort Henry being attacked by any tribe, it is reasonable to conclude Pelton was alluding to the numerous confrontations with Blackfoot while he was with Henry at Three Forks. His suffering must have impressed the Indians around Astoria because Pelton's name became a word in Chinook jargon signifying mental derangement.[38]

Meanwhile, Henry's starving troop divided into three groups and headed in different directions. One party proceeded south toward the Spanish settlements. This group may have heard rumors that others from the St. Louis Missouri Fur Company were trapping in that vicinity.

The second group, consisting of Hoback, Robinson and Reznor, determined to return to their old Kentucky home. These men traversed Pierre's Hole, crossed east into Jackson Hole and over Togwotee Pass, then followed the Wind River. They will be seen again in the next chapter.

The remaining party, presumably led by Henry, reversed the route earlier described by Dougherty, northeast to the Missouri River's forks. The *St. Louis Gazette* reported Henry was still en route to Fort Lisa on August 8 so it appears Henry's company began its homeward march considerably later than the other groups.[39] Whether he continued trapping during the spring season, wanted to allow his remaining livestock more time to recover or had to retrieve hides cached at Three Forks is unclear. Henry had many packs of fur to transport and would need a healthy herd. Additionally, getting loaded horses through the mountains would take longer than would a handful of men traveling relatively lightly.

The *Louisiana Gazette* reported on October 26, 1811:

Arrived on last Monday, Mr. Manuel Lisa from the Mandan village, and the upper part of the Missouri. We are happy to find him accompanied by Messrs. Reuben Lewis and Andrew Henry, members of the company, who have been absent from civilized life for nearly three years. The sufferings of Mr. Henry and his party on the Columbia and in crossing the mountains have been seldom exceeded.[40]

In spite of the loss of men, horses and equipment, Andrew Henry's efforts put the St. Louis Missouri Fur Company on better footing than it perhaps had a right to be. The company charter expired in January of 1812, a few months after Henry's return. The partners reorganized under the simpler name, "Missouri Fur Company," but Henry would not return to the Rockies for over ten years.

7

WILSON PRICE HUNT AND THE
PACIFIC FUR COMPANY: 1811

John Jacob Astor became the first multi-millionaire in America through a profitable trade in pelts that began in the late 1700s, buying from hunters and trappers in the wilderness of upstate New York.[1] A keen entrepreneur who lifted himself almost literally from rags to riches via the fur trade, Astor subsequently dabbled in a variety of businesses – land speculation and opium smuggling, for two.[2] Sensing that a handsome return on investment might be had from a fur trade enterprise on the west coast, he organized the Pacific Fur Company in 1810. The same year, Astor launched two expeditions to the mouth of the Columbia River. One went by sea, leaving from New York, rounding Cape Horn and coasting up the Pacific shoreline. This party arrived in late March 1811 and constructed Fort Astoria in what is now Clatsop County, Oregon.

The other division went overland, across the plains, into the Rockies and beyond, passing through Pierre's Hole on its way. Wilson Price Hunt, a twenty-seven-year-old merchant with little frontier experience, headed this part of Astor's enterprise. Hunt started from St. Louis in October 1810 with a large contingent of men. Late in the year as it was, the group went only as far as the mouth of the Nodaway River in northwest Missouri, and there established winter quarters. Pierre Dorion Jr., who with his father had limited involvement as an interpreter for Lewis and Clark, was one of the guides.[3] Dorion's Iowa Indian wife, Marie, with their two young children in tow, became the first woman to cross the continent from St. Louis to the Pacific.

Reluctant to spend a cold winter on the river and having business yet to complete, Hunt returned to St. Louis to finalize last-minute plans. Come spring 1811, he went back up the Missouri by keel boat. Near La Charette, Missouri, the party stopped to visit John Colter, gleaning tips about the route ahead. Colter declined an invitation to join the expedition "after balancing in his mind the charms of his bride against those of the Rocky Mountains," according to

Wilson Price Hunt, leader of the overland Astorians,
pictured in a nineteenth-century pastel by O. L. Erickson.
MISSOURI HISTORY MUSEUM, ST. LOUIS

Washington Irving, who would publish a romantic account of the Pacific Fur Company's adventures in his book, *Astoria.*[4]

As Hunt pressed upstream, against the flow of the muddy Missouri, Manuel Lisa shoved off from the St. Louis docks on April 2. The Spaniard's Missouri Fur Company boat, loaded with trade goods, was advancing his own enterprise into the Rockies. Lisa was several weeks behind Hunt and his endeavors to catch the Pacific Fur Company triggered one of the most incredible boat races in fur trade history.[5]

On May 26, near the mouth of Rapid River, today's Niobrara, Hunt met three trappers in a near-starved condition. John Hoback, Edward Robinson and Jacob Reznor had recently been plundered by unfriendly Indians and had barely escaped with their lives. As their tale unfolded, Hunt must have been elated to discover that the three Kentuckians knew so many details about travel in the West. He persuaded them to sign on as guides and hunters.

Meanwhile, Lisa pushed his crew at a herculean pace and managed to catch Hunt on June 2 at Cedar Island on the north bank of the Missouri River near modern Jefferson City, Missouri. From that point, both parties ascended the Missouri together to the Arikara villages in what is now central North Dakota. As they ascended the river, Hunt managed to recruit other Henry men returning from the West. These stalwarts had been with Andrew Henry, having endured the hostile attacks at Three Forks and a dreadful Rocky Mountain winter on Henry's Fork of the Snake River.

Edward Rose, Alexander Carson and Benjamin Jones signed on to go to Astoria. Hunt then chose to abandon the river and go west by land when they departed the Arikara town. Most historian believe the Kentuckians' description of their dreadful encounters with Blackfoot may have influenced this decision. On July 18, 1811, eighty-two horses, sixty-two men, and Pierre Dorion's wife and two children formed a caravan that retraced much of the route over which Hoback and his east-bound companions had so recently come.[6]

In the middle of September, they reached today's Union Pass high in the Wind River Mountain Range of western Wyoming. It was probably Hoback who pointed out the Tetons on the western horizon. Hunt wrote in his journal, "One of our hunters who had been on the banks of the Columbia pointed out three immense and snow-covered peaks which, he said, bordered a tributary of the river."[7] Irving, in the poetic style of the day, expanded that brief entry to:

In the course of the day, they came to a height that commanded an almost boundless prospect. Here one of the guides paused, and, after considering the vast landscape attentively, pointed to three mountain peaks glistening with snow, which rose, he said, above a fork of Columbia River. They were hailed by the travellers with that joy with which a beacon on a seashore is hailed by mariners after a long and dangerous voyage.

It is true there was many a weary league to be traversed before they should reach these landmarks, for, allowing for their evident height and the extreme transparency of the atmosphere, they could not be much less than a hundred miles

*distant. Even after reaching them, there would yet remain
hundreds of miles of their journey to be accomplished. All these
matters were forgotten in the joy at seeing the first landmarks
of the Columbia, that river which formed the bourne of the
expedition. These remarkable peaks were known as the Tetons;
as guiding points for many days, to Mr. Hunt, he gave them
the names of the Pilot Knobs.*[8]

This is the earliest published reference to the Tetons. Oddly
enough, the map included in Irving's book did not show the Teton
Range.[9]

The party worked its way down from Union Pass, knowing
that Hoback and his friends had wintered on a tributary of the
Columbia River just on the other side of those Tetons. Descending
to the Green River Valley, they took time to hunt buffalo and dry
enough meat to last until they reached the abandoned Fort Henry
on Henry's Fork. As they neared the majestic spires, the going got
harder: down present Hoback Canyon, crossing and re-crossing the
same stream, sometimes scrambling up the rugged hillside when
the banks closed in on the river. At one point, possibly along the
sandstone cliffs sometimes known as the "Red Ledges," one of the
pack horses rolled, load and all, "into the river from a height of
nearly two hundred feet but was not hurt."[10] Hunt christened this
stream the Hoback River, after his guide.[11]

As the end of September drew near, the Astorians pitched their
tents and camped at present day Hoback Junction, the confluence
of the Hoback and Snake rivers. Hunt was afraid the larger, swifter
current formed by the uniting waterways would not be navigable, so
he dispatched John Reed and two men to explore the Snake River
Canyon. After two days, Reed

*had been obliged to leave his horses which were of no help to
him in climbing the mountains and crags. After an hour's
effort to get through on foot along the river banks he had been
forced to abandon his attempt. To try to get across the peaks
would have been endless labor. The river became very narrow,
its twisting course obstructed by many rapids ... So far as Mr.
Reed could see, the river continued to flow through the heart of
the mountains.*[12]

The Tetons as seen looking west from Union Pass. Wilson Price Hunt would have enjoyed a similar view in September 1811. MARK KELLY PHOTO

Hunt's fears had been realized.

Two visiting Shoshone men professed to know how to reach Fort Henry and Hunt paid them to conduct the party the rest of the way. Hunt wrote that "two of our hunters had the year before come through this area," probably referring to Robinson and Reznor.[13] The fact that all three were not together at that time suggests the trio had split up at Fort Henry the prior year, and had somehow reunited before meeting Hunt on the Missouri. Tellingly, the rock carvings at Camp Henry include only Hoback's name.

Hunt made a tantalizing comment about the Snake River in his journal. He stated matter-of-factly, "Americans call it the Mad River because of its swiftness."[14] Who were these Americans? Had Hunt's Kentucky companions named this river on their trip east in 1810? Or is this another clue, to place alongside the Ike Weeler blazed tree, about the range of Henry's men during their trapping exploits in 1809? In early October, Hunt penned:

The storm ended on the 4th, but all the slopes around us were covered with snow. We forded the Mad River [Snake] with the water up to the bellies of our horses, and camped at the foot of the mountain. On the 5th we climbed it, following an easy and much-traveled trail. Snow whitened the summit and the northern slopes of the heights. The Snakes served as our guides, though two of our hunters had the year before come through this area. (18 miles)[15]

The Pacific Fur Company's overland division had crossed the Tetons, which Hunt referred to as Mad River Mountain, becoming the first non-Indian visitors to Teton Valley verified by the historical record. Partner Ramsay Crooks would later refer to the pass merely as "stupendous ridges."[16] The tracks they followed made an "easy and much-traveled trail," attesting to the Indian population that crossed back and forth between Pierre's Hole and Jackson Hole. Most likely they took the Mosquito Pass trail, as it was more heavily traveled by natives, but the crossing would be known as Hunt's Pass up until 1900.[17]

Eighteen miles and over the Tetons brought the Astorians to the junction of Moose and Mesquite creeks. In those days, all of the main Indian trails over the pass entered Pierre's Hole via the Moose Creek drainage. Hunt's diary reported the Astorians' arrival in Teton Valley:

On the 6th we camped near a little brook that washes the northwest borders of a beautiful plain. The next day we stopped by a river that flows to the northwest, crossing it on the 7th. It joins several other streams and becomes quite large. After merging with another stream of equal size, it runs west. We saw many herds of antelopes. Wild cherries are common, about the size of ordinary red cherries, but they were not yet ripe. About twelve miles northwest of our camp there is a hot spring. I went to it with Mr. Mackenzie and, though it was not boiling, steam constantly spouted from it.[18]

While Hunt occasionally recorded the mileage for the day's travel, on October 6 he did not. Thus, the stream upon which Hunt camped is difficult to identify. The streams in this lower portion of Pierre's

Hole primarily drain the southernmost edges of the valley. By "washes the northwest borders" Hunt may have meant the stream flowed from a southerly direction, carrying its water to the northwest, in which case Trail Creek is Hunt's "little brook." But that is only about six miles which would be a pretty short day of travel.

Alternately, if the translator or transcriber of Hunt's notes had trouble deciphering Hunt's handwriting, it is conceivable this heading should instead be southwest. From this assumption, the party followed Moose Creek west to its junction with Trail Creek. Crossing that stream, they continued west, then turned slightly north, hugging the valley's western edge. Such a route brought Hunt along the south bank of Trail Creek, past present day Victor, Idaho, and down the southern edge of the Palisades Range, nearing the confluence with Little Pine Creek – a day's travel of about fifteen miles which fits better with the company's previous narrations.

Precisely which creek the Pacific Fur Company men camped on is undeterminable. Since Hunt did not mention a river on this day, he must have been far enough south that the Teton River was not yet apparent, though surely its shrub-lined banks down the middle of the valley soon became evident. Little Pine and Trail creeks converge to form the river just downstream from this proposed campsite. Several small tributaries flow from the Big Holes that Hunt crossed in traveling north. They may have progressed as far up the valley as Mahogany (called Bear Creek by Indians) or Horseshoe creeks, given the relatively easy terrain. Yet, the Little Pine Creek alternative seems reasonable based on the journal's wording.

The next day, October 7, Hunt described a river that flowed to the northwest which the group forded before stopping for the night. This is today's Teton River, known in earlier days as Pierre's River or Fork. But at this point, all of the waterways in the valley were unnamed as far as these Americans were concerned. The east bank of the river is joined by "several other steams," as Hunt described. Because Hunt did not write of crossing other streams, it is likely the Astorians kept on the west side of this waterway as they made their way north along the foot of the Big Hole Mountains.

The chronology of the day's entry appears somewhat out of order. It would have made far more sense for Hunt to cross the Teton River once he was out of Pierre's Hole proper at the "stream of equal size." This would have been Bitch Creek, and at this confluence, the united watercourse shifts decidedly westward. The creek's name, bestowed by French Canadian trappers, was originally *biche,* meaning "doe."[19] It probably referred to the many elk found in the area, as Bull Elk Creek is also nearby. The word was corrupted into English which is not surprising since the creek's steep banks make it a son-of-a-gun to cross. Hunt likely negotiated the river at this point, putting him on the north side so he would not have to cross the Teton River again.

Having climbed out of Pierre's Hole onto the right bank of the Teton River, the Astorians would have beheld the Upper Snake River Plains stretching before them toward the setting sun. Here, the Teton River carves a deep canyon, which Hunt avoided by traveling west along its northern rim. Herds of antelope dashed across the open ground. Hunt remarked on seeing lots of cherries, probably choke-cherries; a variant of *Prunus demissa* commonly found growing along the dry banks of creeks in the hills. October is too late in the year for the fruit, which tends to ripen in late summer so he may have identified the plant by its leaves.

Many diaries of early Euro-Americans venturing into the West commented on the number of cherries they found. While on the Snake River in August 1834, John Kirk Townsend, a naturalist, wrote:

> *[August 18] We found ... a considerable quantity of a small fruit called the choke-cherry, a species of prunus, growing on low bushes. When ripe, they are tolerable eating, somewhat astringent, however, producing upon the mouth the same effect, though in a less degree, as the unripe persimmon. They are now generally green, or we should feast luxuriantly upon them, and render more tolerable our miserable provision.*
>
> *[August 26] We bought, of this family, a considerable quantity of dried choke-cherries, these being the only article of commerce which they possessed. This fruit they prepare by pounding it with stones, and drying it in masses in the sun. It is then good tasted, and somewhat nutritive, and it loses, by the process, the whole of the astringency which is so disagreeable in the recent fruit.*[20]

Hunt spoke of finding a hot spring about twelve miles northwest of their camp of October 7. The springs are undoubtedly today's Green Canyon Hot Springs, formerly Pincock Hot Springs, about four miles off Highway 33, up Canyon Creek. However, assuming this chronology is correct, the hot springs are actually twelve miles to the southwest of where Bitch Creek flows into Teton River. This leads to the supposition that a transcriber may have misread northwest for Hunt's southwest.

Today, the hot springs are a recreation destination for many people coming to Pierre's Hole. Advertisements for the resort relay the history of Hunt's visit to the spa. Their story is that Hunt "visited them while spending time at Fort Henry. The rest of the crew built canoes for their ill-fated trip down the Snake River."[21] To be precise, Hunt visited the hot springs on October 7, 1811 – the day before he arrived at Henry's Fort. Nothing in Hunt's diary suggests any of the Astorians slipped off to the hot springs once they reached Henry's Fort. The rest of his men were not building canoes while Hunt soaked in the hot tub, if he bathed there at all.

On October 8, 1811, a windy day with a little snow flying, the Hunt party finally made it to Henry's Fort.[22] Only a few months before, Andrew Henry and his men had vacated the log huts and retreated eastward. Hunt wrote, "It has several small buildings that he constructed in order to spend the past winter here."[23] If Hunt had not decided to cut overland, but had continued up the Missouri River months before, he may well have met Henry's returning party not too far west of the Arikara villages.

Upon reaching Henry's Fort, several in the party were anxious to resume travel by water. Hunt consented and the men soon began constructing fifteen dugout canoes from large cottonwood trees felled along the banks of Henry's Fork. While the canoes were in preparation, hunters ranged about the neighborhood but had little success finding game. They saw days-old buffalo tracks, extremely skittish elk, and antelope "too shy and fleet to be approached."[24] They killed two elk, trapped a few beaver each night and caught "salmon trout of a small size," but the camp subsisted mainly on the dried buffalo meat procured a few weeks prior on the Green River.[25] Hunt had little better luck living off the land than Henry had the winter before.

Eleven days later, the Pacific Fur Company left seventy-seven horses in charge of the two Shoshone men who had traveled with them from Jackson Hole. Hunt trusted them enough to divulge where the saddles were cached, instructing them to keep guard over the livestock until the Americans returned. On October 19, the overland party left the fort behind, pushing off down Henry's Fork and into the Snake River.[26]

Five men, meanwhile, had separated from the Astorian party and stayed in the vicinity to take up trapping, most likely using Henry's Fort as a base. Robinson, Hoback and Reznor, already familiar with the area from the previous seasons, were joined by Martin Cass and Joseph Miller. Miller, a Pacific Fur Company partner, was sufficiently enticed by the potential beaver profits to be made in the region surrounding the fort that he was willing to forgo his affiliation with Astor for the immediate prospect of obtaining valuable pelts.

Washington Irving, in his colorful prose, described the shock felt by Hunt at Miller's resignation as a partner:

Mr. Miller called the partners together and threw up his share in the company, declaring his intentions of joining the party of trappers. This resolution struck every one with astonishment, Mr. Miller being a man of education and of cultivated habits, and little fitted for the rude life of a hunter. Besides, the precarious and slender profits arising from such a life were beneath the prospects of one who held a share in the general enterprise. Mr. Hunt was especially concerned and mortified at his determination, as it was through his advice and influence he had entered into the concern. He endeavored, therefore, to dissuade him from this sudden resolution; representing its rashness, and the hardships and perils to which it would expose him.[27]

These men will reappear in the following chapter with stories of their own.

When William McMinn found the inscriptions while farming his land in 1881, as described in the previous chapter, he also found markings that may have been from Hunt's short occupation of the site. Then again, they may have been from "campfire doodlers" with a later Hayden Survey in 1877.[28] One stone was inscribed, "Fort Henry 1811 by Cap Hunt." Another reads, "Al the cook but nothing to cook." Some researchers have suggested Al the cook was Astorian Alfred Seton. However, Seton was not a member of the overland Astorians, having sailed onboard the *Beaver* to Astoria, arriving in 1812. Yet another rock bears "Gov Camp 1818 H. Wells," but there was no H. Wells known to have been in Hunt's crew, no apparent connection with the government and the date is wrong by six years.

Casting off in cottonwood dugouts, the force of the current hurried the Astoria-bound party westward. In Hunt's words:

> *We were not long in passing the little river that I mentioned on the 7th. Beyond its confluence with the Mad River it becomes large enough to make navigation possible for canoes of all sizes. Its water is light green. Since it had no name, I gave it one: Canoe River.*[29]

Henry's Fork and the Teton River merge near modern Menan, Idaho. The united flow joins the main current of the Snake River shortly after. Hunt dubbed this combined waterway "Canoe River," though today it is the Snake. Two days later, nearly seventy river miles down the Snake from the abandoned Henry's Fort, two canoes swamped in the rapids – an omen of things to come. The men were unhurt but they lost a "good deal of merchandise and many supplies, as well as one of the canoes."[30]

Their portage of a mile and quarter on October 21 was likely around the cascades flowing into today's Idaho Falls, Idaho. Originally called Eagle Rock, citizens voted to rename the town Idaho Falls due to these rapids. A dam was built in the early 1900s to tame these cataracts of the Snake River, creating what is today a picturesque waterfall near the city center.[31]

Mountains rose on their left, paralleling the river. Three snowy summits towered in the distant east. Hunt noted, "We could still see the Pilot Knob that we had seen on September 15."[32] The Tetons are not easily spotted from the vicinity of Idaho Falls for there are only a few places from which a Teton crag peeks over the Big Hole range.

The spirits of the party, once buoyant and elated to be traveling by water again rather than on land, soon flagged. Washington Irving wrote:

> *They knew nothing of the river on which they were floating. It had never been navigated by a white man, nor could they meet*

with an Indian to give them information concerning it. It kept on its course through a vast wilderness of silent and apparently uninhabited mountains, without a savage wigwam upon its banks, or bark upon its waters. The difficulties and perils they had already passed, made them apprehend others before them, that might effectually bar their progress.[33]

Drifting farther west, ever deeper into the Snake River Canyon, high narrow walls restricted the current, creating brutal rapids. Hunt's party met repeated misfortune as it approached the segment of the river east of today's Twin Falls, Idaho. Canoes swamped, several broke up on the rocks and baggage was lost. One man drowned.

Food was increasingly difficult to obtain. Finally, nearly three hundred miles down the Snake River, after a major disaster at a location Hunt named the "Cauldron Linn," the Astorians abandoned the river. Hunt split the party into smaller groups. They cached the majority of their goods and it was, in essence, "every man for himself" over the remaining miles to Astoria, a journey of continued starvation and misery.

Nearly 125 years later, Clifford Starrey discovered several badly rusted objects while fishing in the Snake River during a low water year. He examined the corroded metal and identified the remains of several rifles, axes and beaver traps. These objects were downstream from a rock that met the description of where one of Hunt's canoes had wrecked. Three of these artifacts are on display at the Historical Museum of Boise, Idaho along with the Fort Henry rocks mentioned above (see color plate 8).

Along the trail, Marie Dorion had become pregnant and she gave birth to a boy early on New Year's Eve while the party was crossing the Blue Mountains of Oregon. The party had obtained a few horses and the men insisted she ride. Hunt, apparently awed by the woman's fortitude, scribbled in that day's entry,

[She] rode horseback with her newly born child in her arms. Another child, two years old and wrapped in a blanket, was fastened by her side. One would have thought, from her behavior, that nothing had happened to her.[34]

Sadly, the Dorion baby died about a week later.

The Cauldron Linn on the Snake River. IDAHO STATE HISTORICAL SOCIETY, 72.2.22

On February 15, 1812, Hunt finally arrived at Astoria, now paddling down the Columbia River in six canoes carrying thirty men, a woman and two children. Donald Mackenzie and others from Hunt's company had straggled in about a month before, in the middle of January, after suffering incredible hardships of their own. Satisfied with himself for having blazed a trail across the continent, Hunt wrote:

> *It was a great delight for travelers overcome with weariness to rest comfortably, surrounded by friends, after such a long journey ... We had covered 2,073 miles since leaving the village of the Aricara.*[35]

Yet Hunt would never become a "mountain man." He found his glory not in the wilderness, but as a businessman who happened to have made one long and tremendously adventurous trip west. Back in St. Louis by 1817, he built a grist mill, was appointed postmaster and settled down to the life of a provincial merchant.[36]

Meanwhile, the Pacific Fur Company contingent traveling by ship had arrived at the Columbia River months earlier and had a fort established by the time Hunt dragged in. Those onboard the *Tonquin* had seen challenges of their own. But now trading and trapping were underway, and reports were prepared to update Astor about their accomplishments and defeats. A crew was selected to carry the dispatches east. The adventures of this party include some interesting tales of mishaps in Pierre's Hole.

This engraving shows Fort Astoria as it appeared in 1813.
OREGON HISTORICAL SOCIETY #ORHI 21681

8
ROBERT STUART: 1812

From the initial launch of both delegations of the Pacific Fur Company, two years elapsed before the seafarers and the overland troop reunited at Fort Astoria. During that time John Jacob Astor had heard only snippets of news about his investment in the western trade. Now an account of the venture had to be sent east. Not only did Astor need information, but his men desperately needed supplies. Having lost their ship and its crew in one of the more colorful disasters of the fur trade, the only way to send the information was back overland.[1] The returning Astorians would cross what is today southern Idaho and later in their journey discover a gap in the Rocky Mountains that would enable the pace of westward emigration to explode: South Pass.[2]

Leading the New York-bound team was twenty-six-year-old Robert Stuart. Stuart had come to Astoria by sea, traveling around Cape Horn, and was thus unfamiliar with the overland route. However, all of the men assigned to accompany him knew the terrain. According to Irving:

> It was confided to Robert Stuart, who, though he had never been across the mountains, and a very young man, had given proofs of his competency to the task. Four trusty and well-tried men, who had come overland in Mr. Hunt's expedition, were given as his guides and hunters. These were Ben Jones and John Day, the Kentuckians, and Andri Vallar and Francis Le Clerc, Canadians. Mr. M'Lellan again expressed his determination to take this opportunity of returning to the Atlantic States. In this he was joined by Mr. Crooks, who, notwithstanding all that he had suffered in the dismal journey of the preceding winter, was ready to retrace his steps and brave every danger and hardship, rather than remain at Astoria.[3]

Benjamin Jones had left his Virginia home at the age of sixteen, moved to Kentucky and had been in the mountains since 1807, having arrived as a free trapper in a party led by Ezekiel Williams.[4]

Robert Stuart. MISSOURI HISTORY MUSEUM, ST. LOUIS

Jones would spend many years trapping frontier lands with Alexander Carson, older brother of Kit.[5] When he later retired from his Rocky Mountain adventures, he moved to a tract of land near Wilson Price Hunt on Gravois Creek, about eight miles southwest of St. Louis, Missouri. Jones named one of his sons Wilson Hunt Jones.[6]

John Day relocated from Virginia to Missouri via Kentucky in 1798 where he tried his hand at farming, gave it up for manufacturing gunpowder in 1809, then enlisted in Hunt's overland expedition the following year. Day transferred his allegiance to the North West Company in 1812.[7] Robert McClellan, a Revolutionary War veteran, was one of the earliest Americans to engage in the fur trade. Evidence indicates he ascended the Missouri River in 1802.

McClellan also knew Lewis and Clark, and in September 1806, met them on their return from the West.[8]

Ramsay Crooks had a long history in the fur trade that started in a partnership with Robert McClellan. After his Astorian experience, he became John Jacob Astor's general manager for the American Fur Company and, after Astor sold out, was instrumental in continuing operations of the business until 1842.[9] Regarding the two Canadians, Andrè Vallèe and Francois LeClerc, little is known beyond their participation in the Pacific Fur Company.

Stuart wrote a journal which was later described by Washington Irving as "Travelling Memoranda." Stuart also wrote a revised narrative transcript, and from these two documents a fascinating story unfolds. The portion of the diary involving Pierre's Hole and its surrounding regions is the major focus of this chapter, but the entire journey is well worth reading.[10]

Stuart's party left Fort Astoria on June 29, 1812. Early in the trip, John Day had shown "evident symptoms of mental derangement," so Stuart had hired local Native Americans to escort Day back to Astoria, reducing the party by one man.[11] By mid-August, the party was camped on the Snake River at the mouth of today's Weiser River, about seventy miles northwest of modern Boise, Idaho. An Indian came to the camp late one evening with "grateful tidings of two white men living with his people, about a days march above."[12] Two days later, the Astorians met a band of Shoshone who informed them "that some whites were on the other side of the river."[13] Stuart sent one of the Indians in quest of these men, assuming they were trappers formerly attached to Wilson Price Hunt's overland expedition. Irving related that on August 16,

> some of the party came up, and immediately recognized in the Snake an old friend and ally. He was, in fact, one of the two guides who had conducted Mr. Hunt's party, in the preceding autumn, across Mad River Mountain [Teton Pass] to Fort Henry, and who subsequently departed with Mr. Miller and his fellow trappers, to conduct them to a good trapping ground. The reader may recollect that these two trusty Snakes were engaged by Mr. Hunt to return and take charge of the horses which the party intended to leave at Fort Henry, when they should embark in canoes.

The party now crowded round the Snake, and began to question him with eagerness. His replies were somewhat vague, and but partially understood. He told a long story about the horses, from which it appeared that they had been stolen by various wandering bands, and scattered in different directions. The cache, too, had been plundered, and the saddles and other equipments carried off. His information concerning Mr. Miller and his comrades was not more satisfactory. They had trapped for some time about the upper streams, but had fallen into the hands of a marauding party of Crows, who had robbed them of horses, weapons, and everything.

Further questioning brought forth further intelligence, but all of a disastrous kind. About ten days previously, he had met with three other white men, in very miserable plight, having one horse each, and but one rifle among them. They also had been plundered and maltreated by the Crows, those universal freebooters. The Snake endeavored to pronounce the names of these three men, and as far as his imperfect sounds could be understood, they were supposed to be three of the party of four hunters, namely, Carson, St. Michael, Detaye, and Delaunay, who were detached from Mr. Hunt's party on the 28th of September, to trap beaver on the head waters of the Columbia.[14]

Stuart learned a few tidbits about the fate of Hunt's detachment of trappers, but more importantly, the Shoshone relayed news that "there is a shorter trace to the south than that by which Mr. Hunt traversed the Rocky Mountains."[15] On learning that this Indian was acquainted with the route, Stuart hired him as a guide. The Indian accepted a pistol with gun powder and ammunition, a blue blanket, an axe, a knife, an awl, some blue beads, and a looking-glass as payment for his service.

When the Astorians crawled out of their blankets on the morning of the August 18, the guide was missing – and so were some of the company's horses. Chalking it up as a learning experience, Stuart proceeded on. The next two days were hot and sultry. A couple of the parched men scrambled down the banks of the Snake River for water. Under the overhanging willows of modern Vinson Wash, about three miles northwest of Grandview, Idaho, they were amazed to find John Hoback fishing. Moments later, Edward Robinson, Jacob Reznor and Joseph Miller materialized, primitive fishing poles in hand.

On leaving Henry's Fort the preceding fall, these four mountaineers had traveled two hundred miles south where they trapped on a river they were sure discharged into the Columbia River drainage – likely the Bear River. From there, they steered about two hundred more miles east into what is now south central Wyoming. Here they found about sixty lodges of "Arapayhas" who robbed them of several horses, as well as the greater part of their clothing and equipment.[16]

Barely getting away with their lives, the group wintered about fifty miles further east. In early spring, they were once more accosted by "the same rascals" who stole the remaining horses and most everything else the Americans had. Trading some of their diminutive ammunition supply, they got two of their own horses back.

Martin Cass, the fifth man who had separated from Hunt at Henry's Fort in October 1811, had stolen one of their two recovered horses when he "villainously" left them on the headwaters of the Big Horn River.[17] The second horse had been stolen by the Shoshone a short while later. Historian Edgeley Todd surmises these headwaters may well have been the Popo Agie, which takes its source in the vicinity of South Pass.[18] When they were robbed of their remaining horse "on this side of the Rocky mountains," it is possible they had crossed South Pass to get there.[19] Their description of "all the Southern water courses visited ... abundantly stocked with Beaver, of the largest size and best quality they ever beheld,"[20] was probably the Green River, an area soon destined to draw hordes of trappers to the vicinity of present-day Pinedale, Wyoming.

Having traveled west some 950 hungry, thirsty, fatiguing miles, the quartet was "almost in a state of nature." The desert-like region they had crossed harbored few animals or birds and only by fishing did they survive before meeting Stuart's brigade.[21]

Hoback, Robinson, Reznor and Miller were overjoyed to see Stuart and camp was made then and there. The chance encounter saved the lives of the four men. If Stuart had taken the short cut described by their rapscallion guide or if the dehydrated hikers had stopped for a drink at any other spot on the river, they would not have discovered the famished foursome. Irving, with his marvelous turn of phrase, declared, "the slender stores of the party were ransacked to furnish out a suitable regale."[22]

Days later, Stuart and his ragtag band drew near the caches east of present Twin Falls, Idaho, where Hunt had hidden the overland party's equipment after abandoning the river the previous year. Arriving at the Cauldron Linn, the returning Astorians found six of the underground storage silos opened and their contents plundered. From the numerous wolf tracks, they concluded the canines, attracted by scent of hides buried in the holes, had dug up the skins. The badly torn up ground then attracted Indians who garnered their own prize at the expense of the Americans.

Three of the caches, however, were unmolested and from these, Stuart requisitioned supplies. Intrepid is not a strong enough word to describe the three hunters from Kentucky, for from what minimal provisions were found in the caches, they cobbled together everything they needed to continue trapping beaver. Stuart noted in his journal:

> *I furnished Robinson, Reznor, and Hobach, as far as lay in my power, with everything necessary for a two year's hunt, which they are to make on this river below Henry's Fork, preferring that to returning in their present ragged condition to civilized society – Mr. Millers curiosity and desire of travelling thro' the Indian countries being fully satisfied, he has determined on accompanying us.*[23]

With the addition of Hoback, Robinson, Reznor and Miller, the party continued up the Snake eastward across today's Idaho. Near present day Burley, the three hardy Kentuckians took their leave to get back to trapping beaver. At the Portneuf River, near today's Pocatello, Idaho, Miller, having learned the area during his earlier trapping exploits, guided Stuart's party away from the Snake River, through Marsh Valley, and headed for the southern pass. He hoped to find the trail he had taken before, but it was not long until he conceded nothing was familiar. Rather than a retrograde march, Stuart pushed his party onward.

On September 9, they passed through a gap in the mountains and struck a river in the northern sector of Bear River Valley, probably near today's Soda Springs, Idaho, which Miller pronounced to be the waters he had trapped last fall. In his journal, Stuart called it "Miller's River."[24] Seeing plenty of buffalo sign, the Astorians hoped to find the herd and satisfy their need for fresh meat, but a few antelope and some geese were all they could kill. On the 12th, they "sallied forth with their rods to angle for supper."[25] Stuart was alarmed to find a handful of Crow Indians prowling about the camp when they returned.

A tense encounter centered on one of the few horses in Stuart's possession. Things settled a bit when Stuart offered the Crow twenty charges of powder. He recorded:

Their behavior was insolent in the extreme, and indicated an evident intention to steal, if not to rob – we kept close possession of our Arms, but notwithstanding, our vigilance, they stole a Bag containing the greater part of our kitchen furniture.[26]

Stuart and the men moved east ten more miles before stopping again for the evening. They passed the night quietly, but with one eye open. The next day, three Shoshone told them the Crow were still in the neighborhood. Two more weary, watchful days brought them to Grey's River, east of today's Smoot, Wyoming, but it flowed north – the opposite direction from their goal. Stuart lamented, "on striking this water-course, we easily discovered how far we had failed in attaining the object in view."[27] Translated: they were lost.

Stuart, believing the pass was still to the south, as was a party of Crow that might yet steal everything he had, concluded:

Our best, safest and most certain way would be to follow this river down, and pass the first spur of mountains by the route of the party who came across the continent last year.[28]

Due east of today's Thayne, Wyoming, Stuart reverted to his original plan to connect with the course Hunt followed over the Tetons rather than waste more time searching for the fabled southern pass. On Hunt's trail, they would at least be sure of where they were going even if it made the trip longer. Besides, Stuart reasoned, maybe the two Shoshone left in charge of the horses at Fort Henry were still in that neighborhood and could provide mounts.

Six days elapsed with no sign of the Crow, yet the possible presence of Indians shook the party badly. They reached modern

Alpine, Wyoming and noted two rivers joining the Grey. Confident one was the Snake River, Benjamin Jones was sent to reconnoiter the area and determine a feasible passage. One of these streams was Salt River, the other was indeed the Snake. Jones was unsuccessful in determining a trail through the impenetrable Snake River Canyon, so they continued down the river. This decision would lead the group back to Pierre's Hole, and the route taken would ultimately become a major trail between that basin and the Green River Valley.

The portion of the Snake River flowing through this canyon was avoided during the years prior to 1837. Stuart undoubtedly knew Wilson Price Hunt had tried to find a trail through the high walled corridor from the east. Hunt had learned from local Shoshone and his own men's reconnaissance that the river was unnavigable through the gorge. The surrounding terrain was too steep and difficult for mounted riders. In 1832, Warren Ferris described the "deep cut through the mountains, impassable for pack horses."[29]

There appears to be only one account in primary fur trade documents of mountaineers successfully using this difficult route. In June 1837, Osborne Russell and his party crossed the Tetons from Pierre's Hole into Jackson Hole and, along with another trapper, he

> *travelled down the valley to the south end The next day we travelled in a SW direction over high and rugged spurs of Mountain and encamped on a small stream running into Gray's river which empties into Lewis fork above the mouth of Salt river.*[30]

On September 19, while camped along the Snake River in the area now lying beneath Palisades Reservoir, the cry of "To Arms! There are Indians!" filled the morning air.[31] The band of Crow had followed them, and though the horses were hobbled with "good employment for their jaws," the Indians succeeded in driving them off before the Astorians could protect their meager herd.[32] The rest of that day was spent preparing to journey onward – now afoot. Essential supplies were divided into makeshift packs. The next morning, Captain Stuart wrote in his journal:

> *It was 10 A.M. before we were ready to depart, when collecting every article we could not carry, committed to the flames*

whatever would consume, and the remainder we threw into the river; resolved to prevent the villans benefiting more by us.[33]

By this time, the party had only one beaver trap in its possession. It was set each evening in hopes of obtaining meat. Every beaver caught was "cut up, in order that each might carry his share" of the meat.[34] Fish also partially filled the empty space in their bellies and on September 21, a few miles upstream from the vicinity of today's Irwin, Idaho, Stuart noted with a degree of melancholy:

Forty five Trout were the produce of Mr. Miller's and my fishing rods, but they are poor and very indifferent food; and were it not for the little meat we occasionally fall in with, I really think they would not even support life.[35]

The quality of Stuart's fish was likely due to the late season of the year which was near the end of the annual spawn.

Running deep and swift, the Snake was too risky to ford, so a couple of log rafts were made on which to cross to the other side of the river. Just downstream the Astorians could see the drainage of modern Rainey Creek exiting the Snake River Mountains from the northeast. It probably looked like a good prospect for a pass, though Pine Creek, a few miles north, became the favored route into Pierre's Hole from Swan Valley. Perhaps Stuart contemplated going over the mountain through this defile, but once on the river with their rafts, the current was "safe and steady, which, instead of crossing, induced us to continue on."[36] Had they crossed the mountains at this point they could have entered Pierre's Hole on the same day, saving a little over two weeks' travel.

The Snake River flows relatively smoothly through Swan Valley. Stuart's two rafts floated twenty miles with only a short span of rough water. They encamped on "a beautiful low point," probably near the mouth of Fall Creek.[37] Party hunters loaded the meat of a "Fallow Deer and a Wolverine" onto the rafts.[38] On September 23, they drifted another twenty miles, likely camping near Dry Canyon. For the past several days, Stuart had repeatedly noted seeing a great number of beaver. The next day brought them to "a part of the river where the mountains on the right and the bluffs on the left made us apprehensive of rapids" ahead.[39] In the vicinity of Gormer Canyon, Stuart ordered a two-mile portage around a toe of the Snake River Range that put them back in the water near Bear Gulch.

Farther downstream, the men saw several elk on an island. They wounded one which swam downriver trying to escape. They pursued the elk by raft for over a mile before finally overtaking it. While skinning the animal they discovered an arrow point along with their lead ball which convinced Stuart that Blackfoot Indians had been there not too long ago. Camped on the flats near Black Canyon, the autumn weather gave them a taste of rain, hail and snow throughout the day. They remained in camp an extra night.

Saturday, September 26, saw a late start after a long, wet night of rain. At the end of one mile, they stopped again, almost certainly in Fisher Bottom. On the 27th, the rafts carried them thirty-two miles on a course Stuart described as "from every point of the compass" (see color plate 9).[40] A long day's travel brought them to where the Snake "extricates itself from the mountains and divides into innumerable channels, making Islands without number."[41] Here, about three miles downstream from the present Heise Bridge, Stuart's men rested on the south bank, staying in camp an extra day to make new moccasins in preparation for traveling on foot.

As the Snake continued westward, Stuart saw the foothills of the Big Holes extending north. Sometime over the last few days, Stuart changed his mind again, opting to skip Fort Henry and move on eastward. They would have to pass around and over the distant rise to reach Pierre's Hole. Ramsay Crooks was running a fever, but for now, was able and willing to keep up.

The next morning, the men crossed the river then left the rafts behind. Forcing passage through an extensive bottomland of cottonwood and hawthorn, they hiked north along the western edge of the Big Hole Mountains. Each man toted nearly twenty pounds of meat and though they saw antelope, they were afraid to shoot for fear gunshots would attract the Blackfoot, whom they were convinced were close by.

Cutting the periphery of the foothills, they veered eastward over rough ground, camping on Moody Creek, several miles due south of today's Newdale, Idaho. An established Indian trail led from the south fork of the Snake, crossing Moody Creek immediately above the junction of the creek's two parent forks: Stuart likely took this path. This confluence, near Graham Hollow, may be where they camped.

On September 30, 1812, a couple of miles before reaching their evening's camp, Stuart spied what appeared to be smoke rising into the sky ahead of them. To investigate its source, Stuart headed toward these wispy tendrils. Nineteen miles of hiking found the night's lodging in a deep gully along Canyon Creek; concealed, they felt, from the lurking Blackfoot, having satisfied themselves that the "smoke" they had seen was not from an enemy campfire.

Phillip A. Rollins, who published an edited version of Stuart's travel narrative, suggests the returning Astorians settled for the night near a spot where Hunt had camped on his way west, October 7, 1811. In his diary, Stuart described a landmark from Hunt's earlier trip:

> *A little to one side of our camp, one of the Canadians (in searching for good water) discovered several very astonishing springs of various qualities and temperatures, some of them are cold, others hot: one of the cold we found to be aciduated and impregnated in a small degree with iron; but the principal one in the group is very hot & sulphuric, the water is oily to the touch and foams like soap suds; its margin is covered with a yellow efflorescence of sulphur, which affects the sense of smelling at some distance, and the volume of smoke that issues immediately from this spring may be distinguished at least two miles off.*[42]

Like Hunt, Stuart's party had found today's Green Canyon Hot Springs. The "smoke" Stuart saw was steam rising from the heated pools. The water issuing from these springs reaches temperatures of 115 degrees. The historical record provides no evidence that anyone from the party took time for a soak, but after days of hard traveling, relaxing in the hot water would surely have been welcomed.

Sick for the past three days, Ramsay Crooks was, in Stuart's words, "a good deal indisposed and has a considerable fever."[43] On October 1, the party prepared to cross over the northern rim of Pierre's Hole. Robert McClellan awoke in a surly mood and when the party had climbed to the top of the first hill, he refused to take

Viewed looking east, Canyon Creek flows into this drainage from the lower right. Green Canyon Hot Springs resort sits just left of center, below the dark bluff. The hot spring itself is on the first ledge above the valley floor. Stuart probably camped in the creek-bottom meadow seen to the left, then climbed the hill to cross over the Big Hole Range. Pierre's Hole is beyond the ridge on the eastern horizon. BRUCE BELASON PHOTO

his turn carrying the party's lone trap. Neither would he pack his share of the dried meat. Threatening to leave the group, he declared he could kill enough game to take care of himself.

A dispute about the day's route of travel ensued. Stuart wanted to continue on directly across the Big Hole Range even though the trail was steep and rugged. He argued that route better avoided the Blackfoot. McClellan whined that his feet were too sore and blistered, thus he preferred to continue around the base, alone if necessary, since he knew the lay of the land ahead: he had, after all, crossed the continent with Hunt the prior year.[44]

The cantankerous McClellan was overruled and Stuart started his men across the Big Holes. McClellan rashly abandoned the party

108

and stalked off on his own. By mid-afternoon, the main party had worked its way up and over the ridge, already finding snow deeper than anticipated. It is likely Stuart followed the ridge line between Warm and Wright creeks to where it tops out on Relay Ridge, stayed on the Packsaddle Creek drainage and followed it down into Teton Valley.

From the crest, they could see McClellan ahead of them. He had skirted the edge of the hills, crossed a bench of land and dropped into Pierre's Hole. The lone man stood out on the plain below, clearly visible to any Indians who might be in the vicinity. Whether McClellan saw his companions or not, he showed no disposition to wait for them. His knowledge of the lay of the land apparently found the easier and shorter route because he was miles ahead of Stuart, and would remain so for nearly two weeks when he rejoined the party.

Having descended to the floor of Teton Valley, Stuart's group reached the Teton River six miles from the base of the mountains. The watercourse was fifty yards wide, flowing knee deep, lined with willow and exhibiting an abundance of beaver sign. They likely camped where Horseshoe Creek flows into the Teton River less than a mile south of its juncture with Packsaddle Creek and about five miles southwest of today's Tetonia, Idaho.[45] Stuart's "Travelling Memoranda" reported:

The Plain, from the mountain we traversed today to that of the Pilot Knobs, is about 19 miles in width, and the River running through it falls into Henrys River, half way between his Fork and the mouth of Mad River – the whole of this days march was 18 miles E.S.E.[46]

Ramsay Crooks' condition had worsened. His "indisposition encreased so much this afternoon," Stuart wrote, "that I insisted on his taking a dose of Castor oil, which fortunately had the desired effect."[47] But the man was too sick to continue. The party was forced to stop to give him time to recover.

Several of the men argued strenuously for leaving Crooks and going on without him. It was already the first week in October and they had fought unexpected snow crossing the Big Holes. More delays increased the chance of finding heavier snow pack in the higher passes. Currently out of food, with Indians about, it was too dangerous to hunt. They almost succeeded in persuading Stuart, but in the end, "the thoughts of leaving a fellow creature in such a forlorn situation were too repugnant to my feelings to require long deliberation."[48] Stuart ordered the company to stay put until Crooks was well enough to travel.

On Friday morning, October 2, Benjamin Jones was searching for a prime spot in which to set the party's beaver trap when he was attacked by a grizzly bear. In self defense, he broke Stuart's prohibition on gunfire, but merely wounded the bruin, which escaped. Nevertheless, the silence had been breached, so Stuart sent Jones back out to hunt. If the Indians had not been attracted by the earlier gunshot, they must have cleared the valley.

Jones returned about two hours later with the joyful news of having killed five elk. The party packed up and moved six miles up the creek to recover the elk carcasses where Jones had left them at the base of the mountains.[49] The camp thus relocated into Horseshoe Canyon. Crooks, unable to walk by himself, had to be supported the entire way.

The supply of castor oil soon exhausted, Stuart had no more medicine to treat Crooks who was still too weak to proceed. With the weather "principally cold" the past few days, the group resorted to a Native American remedy – the sweat bath. Constructing a dome-like shelter, they covered it with blankets, tarps and hides, then built a fire inside. Water was poured on heated stones, creating thick clouds of steam. The naked patient was put into the primitive sauna to benefit from the therapeutic effects of the dense, hot vapors. But the process cost them another day of travel.

The results were encouraging, however, and on Monday, by carrying Crooks' belongings for him, the party advanced south through the valley another eight miles, a little beyond Mahogany Creek. Here they found plenty of firewood and the ground rising a bit, becoming less swampy than what they had slogged through most of the day. Along the way, they killed a grizzly bear with three and a half inches of fat on its rump which was "an agreeable addition" to their supply of meat.[50]

Stuart wrote, "several Branches issue from the Pilot Knob Mountain on the East, which, on reaching low grounds, are dammed up by Beaver and occasion the Swamps through which we passed to day."[51] Numerous creeks join the Teton River on the east side of the valley, issuing from the Teton Range rather than the Tetons themselves. The most notable of these streams are today named Leigh, Teton, Darby, and Fox creeks, and are all on the opposite side of the river from Stuart's line of march. Even today, marshy lowlands along the Teton River extend from both sides for much of its course throughout the valley.

On October 6, the Astorians set out early, veering away from the swamps and keeping closer to the foothills. They traversed the plain thirteen miles in a southerly direction before crossing Little Pine Creek. This route kept the boggiest wetlands, in the southwest corner of Pierre's Hole, on their right. The Teton River transitions to Trail Creek, which the Astorians had also shadowed the year before. During this day's march, they passed the site that would become the town of Victor, Idaho. At the junction of Trail and Moose creeks, the extreme southern end of Pierre's Hole, Stuart halted after a long day of hiking and "encamped where it divides nearly into equal branches."[52] Crooks continued to mend and carried his rifle and pistol for most of the day.

Stuart clearly stated he picked the right hand fork, Moose Creek, for the next day's travels.[53] Significantly, the main Indian trail out of Teton Valley ascended Moose Creek so they logically would have kept to this proven path. It was a reverse of the same route Hunt used the year prior; several of Stuart's party were familiar with it. Thus, following up the well-trodden Moose Creek trail, the Astorians made their way thirteen miles to

> the summit of the Pilot Knob mountains, on which we found about nine inches snow – 9 miles same course brought us to mad river, and in 2 more reached the opposite bank, having crossed five channels of from 30 to 60 yds. wide each and from 2 to 3 ½ feet water, a very rapid current, and in every respect of the same character as the part we descended on the rafts.[54]

Now out of Teton Valley, their trek led them down the Snake River, up one of its tributaries, Horse Creek, and eventually to the Hoback Canyon. Stuart reached this point on Friday, October 9.[55]

If, in September, Stuart's scout had been successful in locating a route through the Snake River Canyon from today's Alpine Junction, the group would have reached this same destination, the junction of the Hoback and Snake rivers, eighteen days prior. However, the route Stuart chose instead, through Pierre's Hole, would become a major crossroads for travelers to and from the Green River area until a trail was eventually established through Snake River Canyon in the late 1830s.

Traveling about twelve miles up the north side of the Hoback River brought them to Granite Creek. Here the walls of Hoback Canyon are remarkably steep with a boiling, boulder-strewn river for a floor. The returning Astorians were forced to work their way around present day Battle Mountain and Game Hill. Stuart calls this prominence "Henry's Hill," which may be another reference to the range of Andrew Henry in prior years.[56]

The rest of Stuart's enterprising journey is fully chronicled in his *Narratives*, but will be summarized here. Two days after Henry's Hill, with food hard to come by, the party discovered a recent campfire and supposed it to be "where Mr. McClellan had encamped and supped upon the carcase of a poor wolf the night before."[57] Stopping at the same spot, Stuart's men bedded down with nothing to eat.

The party's spirit was "greatly damped" the next morning upon finding only the forepaw of a large beaver in their solitary trap.[58] Entering the Green River Valley on October 12, 1812, they saw smoke ahead so LeClerc was sent to reconnoiter. It was McClellan, whose unattended fire had set the surroundings ablaze while he was away fishing. He told LeClerc he wanted to rejoin the group, partly in hopes they would have food. Stuart's group, though in the same predicament as McClellan with food stores depleted, welcomed their colleague back into the fold when they reached his camp. Stuart reported:

> *on our getting to him, he was lying on a parcel of straw, emaciated and worn to a perfect skeleton, hardly able to raise his head or speak from extreme debility, but our presence seemed to revive him considerably – and by a good deal of persuasion, we prevailed on him to accompany us.*[59]

As the Astorians prepared to retire that night, one of the Canadians approached Stuart, rifle in hand. Admitting there was little prospect of killing game, LeClerc suggested lots be cast that "one should die to save the rest."[60] Stuart shuddered at the thought of cannibalism but LeClerc would not be dissuaded. Grabbing up his own gun, Stuart cocked and pointed it at the Canadian. This act so terrified LeClerc that he fell to his knees asking the entire party's pardon.

After five days with no food, they managed to kill "an old run down Buffalo Bull."[61] The men ate part of it raw in their haste to fill their stomachs. The next afternoon, they ran into a Shoshone band with whom they traded for the only horse the Indians had, worn down as it was. Stuart finally found, and crossed, South Pass on October 22 but it is doubtful the party recognized the significance of its achievement.[62] While an epic moment in Western American history, it was just another day of drudgery for Stuart and his men.

The rest of the journey east continued to bring one adventure after another. The Astorians reached St. Louis on April 30, 1813. Regarding that auspicious occasion, Stuart said:

> *This day after descending 35 miles, a little before sunset we reached the Town of St. Louis all in the most perfect health after a voyage of ten months from Astoria, during which time we underwent many dangers, hardships, & fatigues, in short, I may say, all the privations human nature is capable of.*[63]

Anxious to turn over his dispatches to Astor, Stuart traveled on to New York, arriving there June 23.[64] Astor was expecting him since newspaper stories had already spread the word about the incredible journey of the returning Astorians.

Stuart's accomplishments, including the discovery of South Pass, were largely forgotten upon his return. According to writer Layton McCartney, Astor was reluctant to make Stuart's narratives available to the public. The wealthy entrepreneur viewed the journals as proprietary information; they contained extensive intelligence regarding the fur trade business. However, the October after Stuart's arrival in St. Louis, the *Missouri Gazette* ran the following item:

> *By information received from these gentlemen, it appears that*
> *a journey across the continent of North America, might be*
> *performed with a wagon, there being no obstruction in the*
> *whole route that any person would dare to call a mountain.*

While Astor may have tried to keep Stuart's information close to his vest, along with other papers regarding the Astoria Project, word of the new pass had leaked in a few short months. In the mid-1830s, Astor gave the diaries to Washington Irving to use in writing *Astoria.*[65]

Months after Stuart's return to New York, in the autumn of 1813, Hoback, Robinson and Reznor headed to the Boise River on another trapping venture, this time led by their old Astorian compatriot, John Reed. They were accompanied by Pierre and Marie Dorion and several others. That winter would see the three Kentuckians and the rest of their cohorts massacred by Bannocks, leaving only Marie and her children to struggle back to Astoria in one of the epic survival tales of the fur trade.[66]

A final addendum to the Astorians in Idaho regards an obscure inscription on the rocks along the Snake River, southeast of the Heise Bridge. Parts of the carving are unreadable but it appears to be "J [H?] 181[2?]." The unknown letter could be an H or K. As for the last number in the date, there is clearly a horizontal scratch at its top. It could be a 2 or 7 but the spacing also allows for an incomplete zero. It is mentioned here because it could indicate that John Hoback traveled along the Snake in this vicinity.

This inscription, "J [H?] 181[2?]" is carved on a rock along the Snake River near Heise, Idaho. BRUCE BELASON PHOTO

9
THE SNAKE COUNTRY EXPEDITIONS: 1816-1831

Nolie Mumey got it right in his history of the Pierre's Hole area: "Very little has been recorded about the activities in the region around the Tetons from 1812 to 1822."[1] Undoubtedly, the country was trapped consistently throughout this period as NWC brigades from Canada operated along the Snake and Salmon rivers. Though Pierre's Hole may have been overrun by beaver hunters as they exploited this richly furred section along the base of the Tetons, the record is rather silent regarding details. From 1816 on, there is a little more in the historical record to go on.

From 1812 to 1822, the American fur trade was virtually dormant in the Rocky Mountains for several reasons. First and foremost was the War of 1812. Many men who might have ventured west to trap were diverted to fighting battles waged in the eastern United States. In addition, capital that would have been used to finance fur companies' trapping expeditions was instead channeled into the war effort. Perhaps worst of all, Fort Astoria was lost to American fur trade interests and became British property, which in many ways signaled a loss of American control over the Pacific Northwest. With a British takeover probable and rumors of a British warship sailing toward the mouth of the Columbia, Fort Astoria was sold at a better-than-bargain price to the NWC, without Astor's consent, and the name changed to Fort George. Many of Astor's employees, particularly the Canadians, signed up with the new owners. British trappers then moved freely into this quarter with virtually no competition.

Second, large portions of the Missouri River regions of the modern Dakotas and eastern Montana had been trapped so heavily in the years from Lewis and Clark's return in 1806 up until the War of 1812, that beaver populations neared depletion. The only trapping areas still potentially profitable were farther up river, in the lands of the Blackfoot nation – generally unfriendly to American trappers.

Finally, an economic depression followed the war and greatly reduced the discretionary income of many Americans who might otherwise have purchased beaver felt hats. This caused the demand for pelts to temporarily plummet.

The Treaty of Ghent officially ended the war in December 1814. In the first years following the war, the NWC did not actively trap beaver in the Snake River country because of the greater availability of beaver in more northern regions. Few attempts had been made to penetrate what is now southern Idaho since John Reed's Astorian party had been killed by Indians in the early days of 1814.

In 1816, however, the NWC decided to resupply Fort George and step up beaver harvests in the West to better compete with the HBC. The man appointed to take charge of the NWC's Columbia Department and its interior trade, and who helped introduce another twist in the fur trade's practice, was Donald Mackenzie. He had been a partner in Astor's Pacific Fur Company, had traveled with Hunt's overland party, and had first-hand knowledge of the country.[2]

Mackenzie put into motion an annual Snake River trapping expedition in which skilled trappers in large brigades replaced trading posts as the active method for obtaining peltry. Barton Barbour, Jedediah Smith's biographer, points out several innovations introduced by Mackenzie's NWC regiments:

Mackenzie's system reduced the necessity to build, stock, and maintain expensive trading posts, and it used horses instead of boats to carry peltry from the field to transshipment depots. Furthermore, even as it maximized trappers' productivity, it also tended to increase their dependence upon the company (and its goods), since they might remain in the field for years at a stretch. Most importantly, Mackenzie's North West Company brigades began returning profits from a region that formerly produced lackluster fur harvests.[3]

Respectable annual harvests kept the enterprise going. These brigades sought hides in many regions the United States then claimed as part of the Louisiana Purchase, and employed quite a few displaced Iroquois, such as Pierre Tevanitagon.

Mackenzie was a poor record keeper. Alexander Ross, second in command on some of Mackenzie's early treks into the Snake River region, wrote that his superior

Donald Mackenzie instituted the Snake Country Expeditions. CHAUTAUQUA COUNTY HISTORICAL SOCIETY, WESTFIELD, NEW YORK.

detested spending five minutes scribbling in a journal. His traveling notes were often kept on a beaver skin written hiero- glyphically with a pencil or a piece of coal; and he would com- plain of the drudgery of keeping accounts.[4]

For this reason, Mackenzie's whereabouts and activities during the winter of 1816-1817 are unknown. Fortunately, Ross was a prolific writer and much of what is known regarding Mackenzie comes from him.

The 1817 brigade spent most of its time in the country south of Snake River, so its field men probably did not come into Pierre's Hole that year. But the following year, 1818, Mackenzie appears to have undertaken a grand expedition that included Teton Valley. This excursion, departing from Fort Nez Perces (also known as Fort Walla Walla) in September, consisted of fifty-five men of multifarious ethnicities and 195 horses. Along with a considerable stock of supplies, they carried 300 beaver traps.[5] Ross, in charge at the fort, left an elaborate account of the Snake River territory described to him by Mackenzie upon his return:

The Rocky Mountains skirting this country on the east, dwindle from stupendous heights into sloping ridges, which divide the country into a thousand luxurious vales, watered by streams which abound with fish. The most remarkable heights in any part of the great backbone of America are three elevated insular mountains, or peaks, which are seen at the distance of one hundred and fifty miles: the hunters very aptly designate them the Pilot Knobs.[6]

Ross compiled his history several years after the fact, and appended to the above statement, "they are now generally known as the Three Paps, or 'Tetons;' and the source of the Great Snake River is in their neighborhood."[7] It was apparently this trip that resulted in the naming of "Pierre's Hole" and "Grand Tetons," probably coined by the French-Canadian trappers or Iroquois who accompanied Mackenzie.

The Snake Country Expedition did not return to Pierre's Hole until several years later. The 1819 Snake Country Expedition appears to have gone to Bear Lake during its five months on the trail. Mackenzie therefore led the first group of non-Indians to penetrate this eastern portion of the Great Basin.[8]

Despite the brevity of the tour, some historians credit Mackenzie with reaching the confines of Yellowstone National Park during the 1819 expedition.[9] In 1880, Colonel Philetus W. Norris, then superintendent of the park, discovered a barely discernable inscription carved in a pine tree above the Upper Falls of the Yellowstone River.[10] It read:

J.O.R.
Aug. 29, 1819

While this is the earliest record, outside that of John Colter, indicating the presence of white men within the limits of the park, identifying the engraver as a member of Mackenzie's party is erroneous since the brigade was not in the Yellowstone area.

During Mackenzie's 1819 expedition, a key innovation was having a caravan of goods escorted to the Boise River region – a prototype of the rendezvous. William Kittson left Fort Nez Perces in late spring, rendezvoused with the Snake Brigade, and delivered needed supplies. Mackenzie "contrived to assemble and bring together the greater part of his [men]" which included the Iroquois Pierre Tevanitagon. Kittson then loaded up the furs collected thus far and was back at the fort by July 7, 1819.[11]

In 1821, the Northwest Company merged with the Hudson's Bay Company. From that year on, the Snake Country Expeditions outfitted as regiments of the HBC, the name by which the new conglomerate was identified. Little is known, however, of the details relating to these early expeditions.

The Iroquois chief, Pierre Tevanitagon, was with Mackenzie on several of these forays; on at least one of these journeys Pierre was introduced to Teton Valley. B. W. Driggs stated the year as 1818 and that may well be, given that Ross described the Tetons in the journal from that trek as noted above.[12] The record is admittedly skimpy, however.

1822 saw the brigade led by Michel Bourdon, who had been with Mackenzie in 1818-1819. Bourdon's party was outfitted as freemen – contract trappers who could settle their accounts at the end of the season. Finan McDonald was in charge of a small contingent of engagés and Pierre Tevanitagon was a member of that year's expedition. Bourdon took his group as far as Cache Valley, Utah, trapping the waters of Bear River, and appears to have spent time in Pierre's Hole though the actual dates are not clear.[13]

When fourteen of his men deserted, the short-handed Bourdon was forced to cache 700 of the approximately 2,000 pelts they had collected. In September, he withdrew to the HBC post at Spokane House, reprovisioned, then returned a few weeks later over the same route to retrieve the buried skins. This may have included revisiting Pierre's Hole. A battle with the Blackfoot occurred on Henry's Fork, so they at least saw the Tetons if the skies were clear. Bourdon and five other trappers lost their lives in this clash.

Finan McDonald was captain of the HBC Snake Country Expedition in 1823.[14] He pushed his trappers over the Salmon River Mountains, then south through Teton Valley, the Pilot Knobs leading the way. He trapped as far down as the Bear River and may have crossed over to the Green River. On his return, he headed back to the Snake River via Jackson Hole, over the Tetons into Pierre's Hole, then to Henry's Fork and home. Outside of a run-in with the Blackfoot, this turned out to be a successful trip. He returned with 4,459 beaver skins packed on the horses. Regarding the Indian trouble, McDonald lamented, "I got safe home from the Snake Cuntre ... and when that Cuntre shall see me agane the Beaver will have a Gould Skin."[15]

Alexander Ross took the expedition out as leader in 1823-1824. Leaving Flathead House, near modern Thompson Falls, Montana in November, it was not long before the Iroquois acted up, Pierre Tevanitagon in the lead. As described earlier, Pierre often provided his share of grief to the brigade leadership. Camped on Finley Creek, due south of Montana's Flathead Lake, he asked Ross to show him the accounts of his brethren, a "reasonable demand, although somewhat out of place," from Ross' perspective.[16] They had all seen their accounts prior to leaving the post, thus Ross knew this was leading up to something. According to Ross, after reviewing the books Tevanitagon stated, "Our debts are heavy, and we are never able to reduce them in a large party, allow us to go off by ourselves and we shall do much better."[17]

Ross persuaded the Iroquois to stay with the main party, which was effective for a few days. However, soon the Iroquois lagged behind. One evening, they arrived late to camp, and set up some distance from everyone else. Ross sent for Pierre and learned from him that John Grey was "a plotting busybody," stirring up his brethren.[18] Nevertheless, nothing material transpired and life proceeded as normal for a few more days.

Ross soon noticed an Iroquois named Jacob had deserted. Some days later, after a visit from eight Piegans of the Blackfoot Confederacy, two more Iroquois, Laurent and Lizard, turned back. Ross took four men to go after these two fugitives and found them sixteen miles to the rear. Ross threatened to tie Lizard to a horse's tail and drag him back before the unwilling trapper consented to return quietly.

By now it was mid-March 1824 and Ross was forcing his way through the Bitterroot Valley. They were riding for today's Gibbon

Pass in the Bitterroot Range, headed for the Big Hole Valley, hoping to be there in time to begin the spring trapping season. The snow was seven feet deep. Ross held a council to decide how to get over the mountain and it was Old Pierre who suggested using horses to trample a road. After discussion, Ross wrote:

> *Old Pierre again spoke in favor of trying the road, some others spoke to the same effect! On this occasion, I had every reason to be satisfied with the conduct of old Pierre the Iroquois while on the other hand John Grey and his confederates opposed those who were for making the road.*[19]

Grey seemed opposed to everything except turning back, but at last everyone agreed to try opening the road. Unexpectedly, Pierre began to waver after a foot of new snow fell during the night. Finally, forty-five men with eighty horses began the tedious process of breaking trail. A man on snowshoes took the first horse by the bridle and led it forward while a second man applied the whip, urging the animal ahead. After several plunges, it got so tired, it lay there, head and shoulders barely above the snow's surface, while another horse was maneuvered into place and the whole scene repeated. The second horse would make it six or seven yards in front of the first before it played out. Then a third did the same, and so on.

The difficulty of getting the horses dug out of the snow was greater than that of goading them forward, but Ross reported, "we were partly recompensed by the novelty of the scene and the mirth and glee the operation diffused among the people ... but the men and horses soon got tired of it."[20] Nine hours later, they had managed less than 600 yards of road.

On the second day of such effort, only twenty-eight men and fifty horses showed up for road duty. They made less than a quarter of a mile of progress. They started trail work on March 20 and finally, on April 14, made it over the pass. After staggering exertion, they said farewell to the "Valley of Troubles," as Ross named it.[21] It would come to be known as Ross's Hole, in modern Ravali County, Montana.

While on Little Lost River, Ross noted, "We had reached a point where it became necessary for us to decide on the course we intended to pursue the rest of the season."[22] Calling the men together, he left

Alexander Ross, Snake Brigade Leader.
ARCHIVES OF MANITOBA, ALEXANDER ROSS 1 (N20030)

the choice to them. After some debate, it was determined to steer east. Once the party was employed in the tasks of the trade, Ross set off with ten men to examine the country to the southeast and was gone for four days. He recorded that "at the extent of our journey we ascended high mountains, had a good view of the country, and saw the three Pilot Knobs quite plain, in the direction of east."[23] Several days later, Ross went to examine

> *the Trois Tetons, so named from their appearance, these three little hills standing in a group are very conspicuous in the middle of an open plain, having hot springs at their base but no cold water nearer than the south end of Goddin's River.*[24]

Here, then, is one of those confusing references to the modern Twin Buttes and Big Southern Butte of the Snake River Plains, and not the pinnacles of the Grand Tetons seen from Pierre's Hole. It is easy to see how references to various landmarks confound historians trying to sort out the early days of the fur trade.

All this time, the Iroquois had been plotting to abandon the main party and hunt by themselves. Since the Valley of Troubles, John Grey had been creating an undercurrent against Ross's command. "At last Old Pierre was drawn into the cabal," and approached Ross about the Iroquois going off on their own. The two men chewed it over, but Pierre did not change his mind. Ross wrote, "I fitted them out and we parted friends, but to my surprise, Grey and Martin gave up the idea, saying they would still prefer remaining with the main party."[25] Ross and Tevanitagon agreed to meet on the first of October at the Trois Tetons (the Buttes, not the pinnacles) near Godin's River. Trappers originally named the Big Lost River after Thyery Godin who had explored it while working with Mackenzie's Snake Country Brigade.

Both parties went their separate ways in pursuit of beaver. Old Pierre made first for Henry's Fork, on into Pierre's Hole, and probably exited the basin via Pine Creek Pass. He then trapped down the south bank of the Snake River as far as the Blackfoot and Portneuf rivers. Come time to rendezvous at the Buttes, the Iroquois brigade arrived "trapless and beaverless, naked and destitute of nearly everything!" Ross exclaimed.[26]

Note here again, Ross used "Trois Tetons." This reference has caused some writers, including Jedediah Smith biographer Maurice Sullivan, to assume the reunion happened in Pierre's Hole. Sullivan wrote of the unlucky Iroquois' chance salvation by the American trappers, "Captain Smith now ... agreed to guide them to the place known in Western history as Pierre's Hole, in the northeastern part of modern Idaho."[27] This is another example of mixing up the Buttes, known earlier as the Trois Tetons, and the modern Tetons, known earlier as the Pilot Knobs. The meeting between Ross and Smith occurred, for certain, at the Buttes.

Old Pierre staunchly defended his compatriots' position, though "in debt to the American trappers for having conveyed them to the Trois Tetons." According to Ross, Tevanitagon claimed:

> *We trapped with good success for nearly two months. At last some of the Snakes found us out. Cantayehari [an Iroquois*

trapper] took one of their women for a wife, for whom he gave one of his horses. The Indians wished for another horse, but were refused. The wife deserted and we changed to another place to avoid the Indians. There a war party fell on us and robbed us of everything. We had 900 beaver, 54 steel traps, and 27 horses, all of which together with five of our guns and nearly all of our clothing the Indians carried off! Naked and destitute as we then were we promised [the Americans] forty dollars to escort us back to Goddin's River, where we arrived the morning before the men you sent to meet us.[28]

The HBC brigade leader then questioned the Americans and their superior, Jedediah Smith. Ross claimed they "appeared to be shrewd men."[29] Smith acknowledged having received 105 beaver skins, worth far more than forty dollars, to provide an armed escort for the Iroquois to the meeting site at the Buttes. Ross continued:

No two of them, however, told the same story the same way. Nor did the Americans agree in their version of it. So that it appeared to me to be a piece of trickery from beginning to end.[30]

Ross later heard the Americans had, in two different caches, 900 beaver, which would be a tremendous catch for a three month hunt with only seven men – and coincidentally the same number of pelts Tevanitagon had reported stolen by Shoshone raiders. It did not take Ross long to put two and two together, especially when he began to hear rumblings from other brigade members that Pierre's story might not be true. The rumor was that the Iroquois had been seduced by the Americans, who had promised them five dollars per hide. Thus, the Iroquois left their furs cached with those of the Americans and had come back, not with the intention of remaining with the British brigade, but of convincing other HBC Iroquois comrades to desert as well.[31]

The arrival of these seven Americans under Jedediah Smith signaled that the British reign over this region was drawing to a close. Smith embodied a threat that had been very much on the minds of the HBC for several years. Competition was increasing, as Ross so clearly illustrated in his journal:

The quarter is swarming with trappers who next season are to penetrate the Snake country with a Mr. Henry at their head, the same gentleman who fifteen years ago wintered on the Snake River.[32]

Jedediah Smith accompanied the Snake Country Expedition back to its base at Flathead House, arriving in late November, 1824. Ross concluded his report to HBC officials, noting:

We may say that all things considered our returns were the most profitable ever brought from the Snake country in one year, amounting to 5000 beaver, exclusive of other peltries ... Which brings our Snake Adventure to a close.[33]

In fact, the Snake Country Expeditions would continue as a part of the HBC strategy well into the 1840s under different brigade leaders. Peter Skene Ogden led the expeditions for several years in a row from 1824 through 1829. Like so many other Hudson's Bay Company brigades, most of these were mostly composed of French Canadians and "natives" – the company term for half-bloods as well as Indians in their employ. In most cases, wives and children increased the size of the party.[34]

HBC Governor George Simpson ordered Ogden to start with a winter hunt, thoroughly explore the country, and do his absolute best to trap it out. Simpson hoped that making a "fur desert" out of the Snake River region would act as a buffer to the encroaching American trappers, keeping them on their side of the Continental Divide.[35] The definition of Snake Country was eventually enlarged to include the drainages of the Humboldt River in what is now Nevada as well. Subsequent Snake Country Expeditions would fulfill Simpson's goal, unwittingly assisted by American trappers in their own quest for profits.

The international incident described earlier, in which Ogden attempted to prevent the American Johnson Gardner from luring away his men, had occurred on Ogden's first Snake River Expedition, 1824-1825. Fearing yet more desertions, Ogden did not dawdle on the American-infested Weber River in the northwestern sector of modern Utah, but proceeded north on May 26, 1825.[36] Three days later, three more HBC men left to join the American opposition. These trappers were in such a hurry they sacrificed everything they had to catch up to them, leaving their women, children, horses, traps and furs behind.

In a week's time, Ogden's dwindling crew was camped on a branch of the Portneuf, the Three Buttes in view, several miles to the west. After crossing the Snake near the confluence of the Blackfoot River, they took a westerly course, cruising for the "lower Bute."[37] That evening two Flathead men came into camp, reporting they had been searching for the HBC brigade. It seemed their chief, waiting in the vicinity of Henry's Fork, had mail for Ogden. The letter was delivered a couple of days later. It was a memo from Governor Simpson ordering him to return to Fort George.

On June 10, 1825 as he continued north, Ogden scribbled in his journal, "We this day had a Sight of the Trois Tettons bearing due East, they appear not very far distant, but as they are very high the distance must be great."[38] June 14 found them spending the night on Henry's Fork where they unexpectedly found the area entirely destitute of beaver. The next day, Ogden and his men found the main Flathead camp, "consisting of 30 lodges" strung along the waterfront.[39] The stream they were on, Ogden wrote, "takes [its] rise in the Vicinity of the Trois Tettons which were visible this day & appear very high."[40]

The preceding two quotes are the only indications that Ogden was even remotely close to Pierre's Hole on the 1824-1825 expedition. Following Simpson's instructions, Ogden turned west and was back at Fort Nez Perce, near present Wallula, Washington, in early November, 1825. The next season's Snake Country Expedition did not approach Pierre's Hole at all.

The 1827-1828 trip, much like Ogden's first command in the region, caught just a glimpse of the Tetons. Stopping for the day at sunset, directly east of present Howe, Idaho, on November 16, 1827, Ogden wrote:

When we reached the great barren Snake Plain and in full view of both the Pilot Knobs as also the three knobs nearly in the centre of the plain, the former joining the sources of the Snake River and dividing ridge of the Columbia waters and Missouri also the waters of the Spanish River; the latter is no doubt a guide to travellers as they are most conveniently placed

*Peter Skene Ogden led several HBC Snake
Country Expeditions.* COURTESY OF OREGON STATE LIBRARY

*and are to be seen at a great distance and water to be found
near each, and the only places there is any between this and the
Snake River.*[41]

The party wintered in the general vicinity of today's Pocatello,
Idaho, and was periodically snowbound. American trappers under
Samuel Tullock, an employee of the Smith, Jackson and Sublette
Fur Company at the time, had their winter quarters close enough to
the HBC brigade to visit occasionally throughout the season. It was
one of the worst winters many of these trappers had endured.

Ogden felt competitive pressure from Tullock's proximity and,
noting the Americans did not have snowshoes, forbade his men from
constructing such equipment for the SJS crew. Ogden was afraid

HBC Snake Country Expedition leader, John Work.
IMAGE HP075560 COURTESY OF THE ROYAL BC MUSEUM, BC ARCHIVES

that with snowshoes, Tullock could make his way to the American supply depot and return with trade goods, including alcohol, and wind up with every beaver hide in camp. The Americans offered up to twenty-five dollars for a pair of snowshoes, but whatever influence Ogden exerted seemed to work as no pelts were sold and no snowshoes were made for the Americans.[42]

When spring finally arrived, Ogden began trapping in earnest, moving up the Snake River about thirteen miles north of modern day Idaho Falls, Idaho before reversing direction on May 18, 1828.[43] It does not seem feasible that any of Ogden's trappers roamed as far eastward as Pierre's Hole during this time.

Future expeditions, including Ogden's of 1829, went nowhere near Pierre's Hole. But Ogden had taken to heart Simpson's demand of creating a fur desert. In the six years of Ogden's command, his brigades took about 18,000 beaver – over half of the 35,000 pelts collected in the nineteen years the Snake Country Expeditions were under HBC leadership.[44]

The next year's brigade fell under the leadership of John Work, who led future efforts of the Snake Country Expeditions as well, though none as far as Teton Valley. With beaver getting scarce, these expeditions started looking for new trapping grounds. Work's 1830-1831 brigade went up Snake River as far north as today's Pocatello, Idaho, before changing course, never mentioning the Tetons in his journal. This year's itinerary followed much of the same territory Ogden trapped in 1827-1828. Where Ogden had harvested 3,093 hides, Work's men brought in only 866.[45] Though some modern writers place Work in Pierre's Hole, his presence is not supported by existing primary records.

Thanks to the persistent efforts of the Snake Country Expeditions, the HBC did indeed create a fur desert in the regions west of Pierre's Hole. Work's expedition discovered the region was not entirely trapped out of beaver, but certainly did not yield enough pelts to pay the expenses of such operations. Succeeding years sent brigades to the waters of the Salmon River and even south into California. American trappers also began searching for more productive trapping ground elsewhere. The HBC Snake Country brigades had accomplished their intended mission.

It is hard to say definitively how much environmental change or adjustment can be attributed to the HBC's fur desert policy. The presence of beaver in an ecosystem affects the water table, vegetation patterns, erosion rates, sedimentation, and wildlife populations. It is likely the removal of the beaver had subtle but far-reaching consequences on the land.[46]

10
THE HENRY-ASHLEY AND ASHLEY-SMITH COMPANIES: 1822-1826

The conclusion of the War of 1812 saw a resurgence of trapping that brought more mountaineers to Pierre's Hole. Two men who took advantage of this resurgence, and who were instrumental in advancing the fur trade at this time, were Andrew Henry and William H. Ashley. Henry's mountain experience with the St. Louis Missouri Fur Company has been detailed in previous chapters, but in 1822, he found a new partner. Ashley had been elected Lieutenant Governor of the State of Missouri in 1820 though his political ambitions ran much higher. He saw fur trade profits as a means of financing runs for future government offices.[1]

The Henry-Ashley Fur Company is credited with expanding the American fur trade in the Rocky Mountains through the use of free trappers, and eliminating the necessity of trading for pelts from the Indians. Although laws had mandated the Indian trade, Andrew Henry knew from experience that Indians were not dependable fur hunters and that more money could be made by employing company trappers.[2] This plan had already worked well for Manuel Lisa and for the Northwest Fur Company/Hudson's Bay Company Snake Country Expeditions.

By hiring free trappers, Henry eliminated the necessity of constructing and maintaining forts. He also increased the mobility of his trapping operations. Henry and Ashley may have initially planned a series of forts to supply their men, such as the one they built at the mouth of the Yellowstone in the fall of 1822, but gradually transitioned to an annual rendezvous system at a predetermined time. The first official rendezvous occurred in 1825 on Henry's Fork of the Green River, in today's extreme southwestern Wyoming. The tradition served until 1840 and the end of the Rocky Mountain fur trade.

By holding annual rendezvous in the mountains the men could stay near the trapping grounds for literally years at a time. Needed supplies and equipment were brought to rendezvous via pack trains and later on, wagons, from St. Louis and other commercial centers in Missouri. At this summer meeting, in exchange for the furs they had secured during their fall and spring hunts, trappers replenished the needed paraphernalia of their trade. This more efficient method, in theory, provided more income for the trapper as well as for the company.

The rendezvous concept as it was pursued in the American Rockies has generally been attributed to Henry and Ashley although its introduction may have begun as a happy accident. A battle with the Arikara in 1823 effectively closed the Missouri River to trappers headed up river, denying the Ashley boat access to its post. This forced an overland expedition to established trapping grounds. As it turned out, the short-term solution evolved into a successful pattern, in part because Henry's prior experience in the mountains gave him particular insight into what did and did not work in the field. Traveling by land, finding new beaver territory and spreading its trappers over an increasingly wider terrain, the fur company expanded its strategy to include a mobile supply depot: the rendezvous.

Whether Ashley and Henry were aware of it remains unknown, but their rendezvous model was similar to aboriginal trading fairs that had been held in adjacent areas long before the arrival of the "mountain man." The rendezvous may simply have been an adaptation of that tradition. Other precedents which the Americans would surely have heard of include the annual Northwest Company rendezvous at Grand Portage, and later at Fort William on Thunder Bay, as well as comparable events sponsored by the HBC.[3] Take, for instance, this description by independent trader Peter Pond of a rendezvous at Mackinac in the 1770s:

> *While Others are amuseing themselves in Good Cumpany at Billards Drinking fresh Punch Wine & Eney thing thay Please to Call for While the Mo[re] valgear Ware fiteing Each other feasting was Much atended to Dansing at Nite with Respcttabel Parsons.*[4]

Moreover, as recently as 1819, Donald Mackenzie had instituted annual supply delivery to Snake Country Brigade trappers in the field. So the rendezvous concept was not new to the trapping business, but the Henry-Ashley Company and the mountain men would make it legendary.[5]

Regarding the Henry-Ashley transition to a rendezvous system in the years 1824-1825, historian Don Berry draws the following conclusions:

> *It is certain that Ashley had not yet realized how important the idea of rendezvous was; it is equally certain that by the end of the first one he had been struck by the inescapable logic of it ... The logic of permanent residence in the mountains must have occurred to many men during this rendezvous; it certainly occurred to Ashley himself, and probably through his conversations with the knowledgeable old Iroquois Pierre Tevanitagon. In talking with Pierre, a whole new picture of mountain operations must have been shaped in Ashley's mind.*[6]

To grant Pierre credit for creating the rendezvous is obviously a precarious notion. Nevertheless, he could have observed an NWC rendezvous when he was posted at Fort William early in his fur trade career; he was with Mackenzie in 1819 at the Snake River Brigade rendezvous on the Boise River; he was with Ashley in 1825 at the "first" rendezvous; and he jumped at the opportunity for profit by ordering an outfit of his own through Ashley at that rendezvous. It will never be known how much he may have influenced Ashley's awareness of the rendezvous' potential.

The term "mountain man" has become synonymous with those Rocky Mountain trappers who lived a carefree and raucous lifestyle, hearty souls who braved icy streams in search of beaver. However, historical use of the phrase is scarce prior to the waning days of the beaver trade. It can be found as early as 1834 in John Townsend's *Narrative of a Journey Across the Rocky Mountains*, but in primary source documents from the period, such as journals and diaries, "mountaineer" appears to be a far more widely accepted term for these men who trapped valuable pelts in the Rockies.[7]

Mountaineers who signed on with Henry and Ashley, and who would proudly call themselves "Ashley men," soon found their way to Pierre's Hole. Two of the annual rendezvous would eventually be held in Teton Valley, introducing even more trappers to the beauty and grandeur of *les Trois Tetons*.

In 1822, Henry and Ashley ran the now-famous advertisements in St. Louis newspapers seeking to hire men for their expedition. With the advertiser shown as William Ashley, it is easy to see why many people refer to the company as being Ashley's or, just as commonly, Ashley and Henry. Frequently, the business is identified as the Rocky Mountain Fur Company, but in truth, the firm was called "Henry and Ashley." This is borne out in a government document submitted by the two principles for reimbursement in January 1824.[8] The partnership known as the Rocky Mountain Fur Company, made up of five other men, did not come into legal existence until the summer of 1830.

Henry took the first group of "enterprising young men" up the Missouri River by keel boat in April 1822. A second boat sank, losing the entire $10,000 worth of equipment. A third boat dropped men and supplies at the mouth of the Yellowstone River. Henry's mountaineers wintered on the Upper Missouri in a small picketed enclosure they wasted no time in erecting. Two trapping parties, one under Henry and one under John Weber, got to work gathering fur. One group trapped up the Missouri to the mouth of the Musselshell

TO
Enterprising Young Men.

THE subscriber wishes to engage ONE HUNDRED MEN, to ascend the river Missouri to its source, there to be employed for one, two or three years.—For particulars, enquire of Major Andrew Henry, near the Lead Mines, in the County of Washington, (who will ascend with, and command the party) or to the subscriber at St. Louis.

Wm. H. Ashley.

February 13   ——98 tf

This ad ran in the Missouri Republican *newspaper to recruit men for the Henry and Ashley Fur Company trapping expedition in 1822.*

MISSOURI HISTORY MUSEUM, ST. LOUIS

River; the other brigade ascended the Yellowstone to the Powder. The Blackfoot were not happy that American hunters were on their lands again. Making their dissatisfaction known, four men were killed and several horses were stolen. American trappers would not trap that region again for six years.

In spring 1823, Ashley left St. Louis with two more heavily-laden keelboats to strengthen the crews working the Upper Missouri. On the way upriver, Ashley was attacked by the Arikara. Fifteen men died and large amounts of cargo were lost. The ensuing "war" drew Henry's men and the United States military to the battlefield. At its conclusion, the Henry-Ashley Company took overland trails westward, forgoing the river route.[9]

Splitting his trappers into two groups again, Henry took one party of men back to the Yellowstone post, relocated to the mouth of the Big Horn River, and constructed another fort. A second brigade of eleven men, led by twenty-four-year-old Jedediah Smith, went into Crow territory in what is now northwestern Wyoming and wintered with them.[10]

The Crow told Smith of country just over the Wind River Mountains that abounded with beaver so plentiful they could be clubbed without the need for traps.[11] Anxious, Smith's party tried to cross Union Pass in February 1824 but was unable to force a passage so early in the year. It is not known how far they got, but it is doubtful they were high enough to see the Tetons.

Later in the spring Smith traveled south. On the Sweetwater River the trappers cached powder, lead and other supplies, then crossed South Pass and entered the Green River Valley.[12] As the Crow had described, they found an immense number of beaver. Smith divided his undersized brigade into even smaller teams to trap, agreeing to regroup on the Sweetwater by the first of June.

The opening weeks of June 1824 saw the first quasi-rendezvous of Henry-Ashley men as Smith's men gathered to resupply and arrange to get their furs to market. Thomas Fitzpatrick led a small crew that floated the furs down the Sweetwater and on to St. Louis. One trapper, James Clyman, did not show up at the appointed time and a year would pass before Smith learned he was still alive.[13]

After bidding farewell to the St. Louis-bound crew, the remaining Americans headed west, back over South Pass. From the Green

River, Smith is presumed to have traveled northwest into the Bondurant basin and the Hoback River, down the Hoback to Jackson Hole, then across the southern end of the Teton Range and into the heart of British trapping grounds. Thus, sometime in the summer of 1824, Jedediah Smith and his party entered Pierre's Hole and trapped their way along Pierre's Fork.

According to Washington Hood, a captain in the U. S. Army Corps of Topographical Engineers, Smith went north through Jackson Hole then entered Teton Valley by Conant Pass. Hood's 1839 manuscript map speculates Smith would:

> *Follow down Jackson's fork [Hoback River] to its mouth and decline to the northward along Lewis' fork [Snake River], passing through Jackson's Big Hole to about twelve miles beyond the Yellowstone pass [Two Ocean Pass], crossing on the route a nameless beaver stream. Here the route passes due west over another prong of the ridge [Conant Pass], a fraction worse than the former, followed until it attained the headwaters of Pierre's Hole, crossing the Big Teton, the battleground of the Blacksmith's Fork; ford Pierre's fork eastward of the butte at its mouth and Lewis fork also, thence pass to the mouth of Lewis fork.*[14]

In examining Hood's proposal, historian Merrill Mattes offered the understatement that, "because of unfamiliar nomenclature, this description is a bit confusing."[15] Hood's map is nonetheless interesting precisely because of its nomenclature, specifically for some of the creek names. Today's Teton Creek appears as Big Teton Fork, what is likely Leigh Creek is marked as Battle Ground Fork and Bitch Creek is charted as Blacksmith's Fork. Hood's reference in the narrative to "the battleground of the Blacksmith's Fork" is certainly intriguing as no other historical reference to such an event has been found.[16]

If Smith crossed Conant Pass, he probably followed a well-used Indian trail known to lead from Jackson Hole to the northern expanses of Teton Basin. That trail descended through Jackass Meadows and down the ridge north of Conant Creek. With Smith on this track, he obviously saw the Tetons, but may not have come very far into Pierre's Hole.

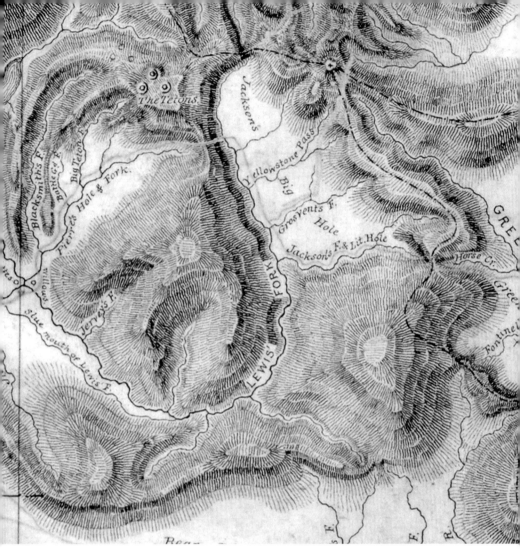

A detail of Captain Washington Hood's 1839 manuscript map shows Pierre's Hole in the upper left. COURTESY NATIONAL ARCHIVES, RG-77: CWMF TREASURE ITEM US 110B

Either way, Smith's party came out on the Snake River Plains in mid-September 1824 where it fell in with the impoverished band of Iroquois led by Pierre Tevanitagon, as told in a previous chapter, and escorted the Iroquois back to the Snake Country Expedition of Alexander Ross. Smith tagged along with Ross all the way to the HBC Flathead Post near modern Thompson's Falls, Montana, much to the chagrin of not only Ross, but other leaders at the fort as well. At the expense of the British, whose operations he sized up along the way, Smith was now familiar with choice beaver country west of the Tetons.

Peter Skene Ogden, assigned to take command of Ross's men, reached the Flathead Post just a few hours before Smith, Ross and the Snake Country Expedition arrived on November 26. Ogden brought with him plenty of equipment to restock the crew, enough to stay in the field throughout the coming year. When Smith's party and the annual brigade departed together three weeks later, the British brigade comprised ten engagés and fifty-three "Fremen and lads," and – bigger shock to the Americans who worked in a men-only environment – thirty women and thirty-five children.[17]

According to historian Harrison Dale, this expedition of Smith's made him

> *the first American since Lewis and Clark, of whom there is definite information, to cross the continental divide within the area lying north and west of the Three Forks of the Missouri. He was the first since Andrew Henry, in 1810, to explore the Columbia drainage area south and west of the Three Forks, the country, that is to say, of Pierre's Hole and upper Snake river.*[18]

Traveling together for the first few months, Ogden's and Smith's parties began leap-frogging their way to the Blackfoot River, the Tetons rising on their eastern flank for part of the trip. Meanwhile, back in St. Louis, Ashley was making plans to bring a caravan of fifty pack horses and a wagon loaded with supplies to the Rockies.[19] He left Fort Atkinson, just north of modern Omaha, Nebraska, on November 3, 1824 and arrived on the Green River, which Ashley called the "Shetkadee," on April 19, 1825.[20] The wagon was evidently abandoned along the way due to deep snow. Ashley dispersed teams to trap the surrounding areas and made three different caches of supplies as he, too, set out to explore. He had already instructed his team leaders regarding "The place of rendavoze for all our parties on or before the 10th July next."[21]

The first of what would become annual rendezvous was held on July 1, 1825. It was located twenty miles up Henry's Fork of the Green River on the bench between Burnt Fork and Birch Creek, along a stream Ashley named "Randavouze Creek."[22] Unlike the trade fairs to come, this one lasted only one day, though many of the mountaineers had arrived at the site several days ahead of the boss. One other notable difference was that Ashley's detailed list of supplies included no mention of alcohol, something he amended in future years.

During this first rendezvous, Smith or some of the men who accompanied him may have regaled fellow trappers with glowing accounts of the Tetons. As historian Mattes relates, "Whatever the inspiration, Fitzpatrick, along with Jim Bridger, was reported to have headed there to resume trapping operations" once the 1825 rendezvous broke up and the previous year's fur harvest was on its way east.[23]

Though smaller parties had trapped the regions around Jackson Hole, Fitzpatrick and Bridger's thirty man brigade was likely the first large scale assault on the beaver populations in all the tributaries on either side of the Tetons.[24] Neither man kept a journal, so there is no primary documentation for this trip.[25]

At the close of the 1825 rendezvous, Ashley gathered up 9,700 pounds of beaver valued at $48,000, then turned toward the rising sun.[26] Smith accompanied him back to civilization. Along the way, Ashley engaged his young protégé in important discussions about the future of the company. Andrew Henry was retiring from the mountain trade and Ashley was in need of a new partner. Ashley also had his eye set on becoming Missouri's governor, so he could not afford to be absent for long periods. He was desperate for a field captain with energy, integrity and business acumen similar to Henry's. Jedediah Smith appeared to fit the bill.[27]

Ashley arrived back in St. Louis on October 4, with Smith having agreed, somewhere between the rendezvous and the Missouri, to pitch in with Ashley and make a go of it. About four weeks later, the new firm of Ashley and Smith was ready to return to the mountains under Smith's leadership, fully equipped "for prosecuting our business Wt of the Rocky Mount," Smith would later write.[28] Robert Campbell, on his maiden voyage to the mountains, was with Smith along with about sixty others, carrying supplies back to the trappers.

According to cartographer David H. Burr's 1839 map, Smith plodded west on what would become the Oregon Trail and when he reached the Green River Valley, took what was becoming the typical route down the Hoback River into Jackson Hole. From there, Smith crossed the Tetons and descended into Pierre's Hole.

Having trapped there the previous year, he did not linger in the fall of 1825 but traversed the valley steering north, crossing over to Henry's Fork.

The map hints at a route ascending the Snake River all the way to the Salt River. Once on the Salt, Smith followed it south, upstream to its head, then went down Smith's Fork to the mouth of Bear River, where he spent the rest of the winter.[29] But the Burr map is often contradictory and difficult to make out, so there are doubts about this route. For a Salt River destination, it seems more logical to exit Pierre's Hole west, over Pine Creek Pass, and turn south, than to traverse cross country to Henry's Fork and down to the confluence of the Snake River. Either route in the dead of winter is a remarkable feat.

Smith broke camp as the spring thaw of 1826 arrived and pushed his pack-laden caravan down Bear River to the Great Salt Lake, the Boise River and beyond. No more beaver were to be had, however.[30] The HBC Snake Country brigades had done their job of creating a fur-free buffer. Smith's party would have a long hard trail to the next rendezvous, in today's Cache Valley.

Dale Morgan penned the biography of Jedediah Smith in 1953. In 1964, Morgan assembled a mass of primary documents and published *The West of William H. Ashley*.[31] Among the original narratives Morgan included in this substantial tome were the dictated reminiscences of Robert Campbell, who left St. Louis with Smith in late 1825. This information had been unavailable when Morgan wrote the Smith biography.[32] Campbell provided a quite different version of the 1825-1826 adventure:

> *An expedition was in the fall of 1825 – fitted out, under the firm of Ashley & Smith ... Jedediah Smith was Ashley's partner ... We left St. Louis on the first of November. It was wrong to start at that season, because we had the winter to encounter ... We wintered all along the Republican Fork, and suffered very much for want of provisions. One-third of our mules died that winter, and we sent back for more mules to St. Louis ... We suffered great privation until joined by General Ashley from St. Louis. He overtook us at Grand Island on the Platte about the first of April with supplies. He then sent off Smith and Harris to the Trappers in the*

*Mountains to arrange in advance for a rendezvous, which
was about twenty miles north of Salt Lake in Utah, called
Cache or Willow Valley.*[33]

It was a miserable beginning to Campbell's fur trade career.
Mountaineer Jim Beckwourth included a related version of these
events in his own memoirs. Beckwourth confirmed the encampment
on Kansas River, of which the Republican Fork is a branch. "Here
it was found the company was in need of horses," so he and Moses
Harris took a message back to Ashley.[34] On the Platte River, headed
back to the mountains, Beckwourth said they found

*the men, twenty-six in number, reduced to short rations, in
weakly condition, and in a discouraged state of mind. They had
been expecting the arrival of a large company with abundant
supplies, and when we rejoined them without any provisions,
they were greatly disappointed. General Ashley exerted himself
to infuse fresh courage into their disconsolate breasts, well
knowing himself, however, that unless we could find game, the
chances were hard against us.*[35]

Smith's crew had been snowed in on the Republican River in
early January 1826, near where Fort Riley would later be built in
northeast Kansas.

Several period newspapers published accounts of Ashley setting
out from St. Louis on or about March 8, 1826 with a second supply
train, headed for the Cache Valley rendezvous.[36] On receiving their
orders from Ashley at the Grand Island resupply in early April,
Smith and Harris may have sped through Teton Valley, pursuing
their mission of rounding up mountaineers wherever they could be
found, to spread the word of the upcoming rendezvous.[37]

Cache Valley played a minor role in the later history of Pierre's
Hole. Jim Beckwourth related a story about why Willow Valley's
name was changed:

*Soon after we arrived we commenced digging caches to secure
seventy-five packs of beaver-skins in the possession of our party.
While digging a cache in the bank, the earth caved in, killing
two of our party, who were Canadians.*[38]

Warren Ferris provided a similar story in his journal, describing an event in 1827:

> *[Cache Valley] received its name from a melancholy incident that occurred in it a few years ago. The circumstances are briefly these: A man in the employ of Smith, Sublette and Jackson, was engaged with a detached party, in constructing one of those subterranean vaults for the reception of furs ... The cache was nearly completed, when a large quantity of earth fell in upon the poor fellow, and completely buried him alive. His companions believed him to have been instantly killed, knew him to be well buried, and the cache destroyed, and therefore left him 'Unknelled, uncoffined, ne'er to rise, Till Gabriel's trumpet shakes the skies,' and accomplished their object elsewhere.*[39]

Ferris often quoted poets of the day such as the shaky Byron interpretation above. Still, he is more believable in many cases than Beckwourth. The connection to Pierre's Hole is that, according to B. W. Driggs, in the late 1880s, Mormon settlers from Cache Valley relocated to Pierre's Hole, naming their new community "Cache."[40] Though the hamlet no longer exists today, an area in Teton Valley between Driggs and Tetonia is often identified as Cache.

11

THE SMITH, JACKSON AND SUBLETTE
FUR COMPANY AND THE 1829 RENDEZVOUS

At the Cache Valley rendezvous, yet another change in the leadership of the Rocky Mountain trappers transpired. His fortune secure, William Ashley sold out his interest in the Ashley-Smith firm to a new partnership comprised of Jedediah Smith, David Jackson and William Sublette. The company was known as Smith, Jackson and Sublette, frequently shortened to SJS. Sublette had been with Smith during most of his travels thus far, so it is likely they knew each other fairly well. Less is known about Jackson, but he obviously had a strong enough relationship to connect with Smith and Sublette, at least on a business level. The SJS Fur Company would host the first rendezvous to be held in Pierre's Hole.

In August 1826, after rendezvous broke up, Smith left Cache Valley, rode southwest, and wound up in California. Ostensibly, the trip was to search for unspoiled trapping grounds but it may also have been, to some degree, an effort to satisfy Smith's need to explore. Information regarding the fall 1826 operations of Sublette and Jackson is scant. Robert Campbell was among the party and wrote in his narrative, "When Smith left for Colorado, Jackson and Sublette with myself ascended the Snake river and tributaries near the Three Tetons and hunted along to the forks of the Missouri."[1] Jim Bridger was likely with this brigade as well.

That brief snippet, combined with another hint from Daniel Potts, provide further clues that a trapping party ventured near the vicinity of Pierre's Hole that fall. Potts, a young man from Pennsylvania, had hoped to accompany Smith westward but was not selected. It appears he went with Sublette and Jackson. Potts wrote his brother:

I took my departure for the Black-foot Country much against my will as I could not make a party for any other rout. We took a northerly direction about fifty miles where we cross the Snake river or South fork of Columbia at the forks of Henrys & Lewis's forks at this place we was dayly harrased by the Black-feet from thence up Henrys or North fork which bears North of

*East thirty miles and crossed a large rugged Mountain which
sepparates the two forks from thence East up the other fork to
its source which heads on the top of the great chain of Rocky
Mountains which sepparates the waters of the Atlantic from
that of the Pacific.*[2]

When Potts had begun this series of letters to his brother
two years prior, he asked the reader to excuse him from "bad
spelling and writing" and it is easy to see why.[3] The "large rugged
Mountain" was probably the Teton Range. The "two forks" Potts
referred to were both the Snake River – on the west side of the
Tetons, he called it the "South fork of Columbia" and on the east
side of the divide, he named it "Lewis's fork."

One final scrap of evidence comes from the reminiscences of
Jim Beckwourth, who says he joined the main party on "Lewis's
Fork of the Columbia."[4] Following an encounter with Blackfoot
Indians, "all moved on together for the head of Green River."[5] If
Beckwourth started from the west side of the Big Hole Mountains,
such a trip from the Snake River to the Green River would also
include Pierre's Hole.[6]

It appears the party, led by SJS partners Sublette and Jackson,
followed Henry's Fork, cutting east to the foot of the Tetons, the
"rugged mountains" referred to by Potts. Whether they crossed
via Conant Pass or Teton Pass is conjectural. A 2006 Museum of
the Mountain Man presentation publication by Dr. Fred Gowans,
one of the foremost authorities on the Rocky Mountain fur trade,
indicates Teton Pass.[7] If this was indeed the SJS itinerary, the
brigade traversed the length of Pierre's Hole.

Smith biographer Dale Morgan, however, says Sublette "circled
around the Tetons into upper Jackson Hole," which better favors
Conant Pass at the northern extremity of the Teton Range.[8]
Historian Merrill Mattes also leans toward Conant Pass.[9] In this
direction of travel, they likely did not go into the basin proper, but
cut its uppermost northern quarter. Once on the east side, Potts
wrote the earliest description known of the geyser region that is
now Yellowstone National Park. During this trek, they passed
Yellowstone Lake, which for a time was called "Soublett Lake," after
the brigade leader.[10]

Jim Beckwourth often confused the chronology of events in his life story; in this case, he squeezed the events of three years into one and scrambled them as well. His account of this brigade's action could be interpreted as occurring in 1827 instead of 1826.[11] That appears to be a dilemma for historian Don Berry who described Sublette trapping "both flanks of the Tetons and the Pierre's Hole area," in the spring of 1828.[12] Otherwise, Sublette's maneuvers are not documented.

Pierre's Hole was rapidly gaining a reputation among the international trapping community, particularly as a gateway from the Green River to the upper reaches of the Snake River Plain. No trail yet forced a way west through the steep gorge of the Snake beyond its junction with the Hoback. Trappers typically avoided the Snake River canyon altogether. Westward travelers departed the Snake near its confluence with the Hoback, headed northwest over the Tetons, and dropped into the southernmost end of Teton Valley.[13] By exiting the valley at Pine Creek Pass, they picked up the Snake River again, marched upstream, and arrived at its confluence with the Salt and Grey's rivers, where the Snake exits the ravine. Alpine Junction, Wyoming occupies this site today. A second option was to traverse Teton Valley to the northwest, then head due west and hit Henry's Fork, following it downstream to its junction with the Snake.

Significant beaver populations also made the locale legendary. In March 1827, John McLoughlin, in charge at HBC Fort Vancouver, advocated sending a party of fifty men into Oregon country from the Red River Settlement near present Winnipeg, Manitoba to compete with the expanding American fur companies, which were not only acquiring valuable hides but recruiting HBC deserters. He wrote his boss, Governor George Simpson:

> *If such a party was sent they should go direct to Trois Tettons and hunt up that place, turn North and hunt all the head branches of the Missouries in the vicinity of where Mr Ogden was in the Summer 1825, in three years they would do this which would destroy the Inducements the American trappers from the other side have to push to the Head waters of the Columbia and by hunting the Head branches of the Missouries where I state, diminish the inducements the Americans have to equip hunting*

145

parties from this of the Mountains and to interfere with our Saskatchewan trade sooner than they otherwise would.[14]

McLoughlin was reiterating a letter written six months earlier in which he advocated sending eighty men to the Henry's Fork-Tetons region for a three-year trapping stint.[15] It is odd that McLoughlin would suggest so illegal a maneuver in this latter dispatch since the Three Forks area, clearly on the east side of the Continental Divide, was American territory and not open to British commercial enterprises. Such an expedition never materialized.

Jedediah Smith appeared at the 1827 rendezvous at Bear Lake having made the first crossing of Nevada's Great Basin from west to east. He made a brief report to his partners about his expedition into California, arranged to meet them in two years in the upper Snake River country, and with only a ten-day respite, hit the trail back to California.[16] His cohorts would not see the senior partner of SJS until the 1829 rendezvous at Pierre's Hole.

For almost two years, from the winter of 1826-1827 through the summer of 1829, the record is virtually silent regarding any trapping parties, HBC or otherwise, coming close to Pierre's Hole. Sublette seems to have worked his way through Teton Pass down the Teton River, and on to Henry's Fork, with Campbell's brigade somewhere nearby.[17] Pierre's Hole was a familiar location to so many fur brigades that the region surely saw streams of trappers on a continual basis. It may be more accurate to state that during this period no literate mountaineers equipped with paper and ink journeyed into Teton Valley.

Sublette took the furs from the 1828 rendezvous at Sweet Lake (called Bear Lake today) to St. Louis and spent the winter there. In March 1829 Sublette wrestled a heavily-laden caravan of horses and mules back to the Rockies. Four new recruits on this trip left records of their travels. Robert Newell, twenty-two years old, and Joe Meek, just over nineteen, would stay in the Rocky Mountains until the final rendezvous in 1840. Both men ultimately took up residence in Oregon Country. Meek would relay his chronicle through his biographer, Mrs. Frances Victor. Newell's memorandum, far more brief than desired, was begun in 1836 and continued periodically until he left the Rockies. George Ebberts dictated his account to

Hubert H. Bancroft in 1878 and William Craig's recollections were recorded in a Lewiston, Idaho newspaper story of 1918.

Two rendezvous took place in the summer of 1829. The first was in mid-July on Wind River near the mouth of the Popo Agie River by modern Lander, Wyoming. The second was in Teton Valley, in August. The latter one in Pierre's Hole is considered by most historians to have been the "official" rendezvous for the season, though few details are available. Campbell and his men were at the July resupply. Following that rendezvous, Campbell took the furs to St. Louis, then went on to Scotland, his homeland, to deal with family matters. Sublette led his supply train up the Wind and over Togwotee Pass, aiming for the Snake River. He knew the returning Smith, of whom nothing had been heard for two years, should be in the vicinity and sent scouts ahead to locate him.

As it turns out, Smith's party had had a deadly encounter with Indians in July 1828 on the Umpqua River in Oregon, where all but he and three of his men had been killed. The four survivors found their way to Fort Vancouver and spent the winter of 1828-1829 under the hospitality of the Hudson's Bay Company.[18] Only Smith and one other man, Arthur Black, departed from the HBC fort in the spring to meet the SJS partners on the Snake River. Smith was in Pierre's Hole when Sublette's scouts found him.

The reunion of Smith, Jackson and Sublette has been told in a variety of ways by different historians. The following three passages illustrate why there are discrepancies in the records. Meek himself related that:

> *Sublette led his company up the valley of the Wind River, across the mountains, and on to the very head-waters of the Lewis or Snake River. Here he fell in with Jackson, in the valley of Lewis Lake, called Jackson's Hole, and remained on the borders of this lake for some time, waiting for Smith, whose non-appearance began to create a good deal of uneasiness. At length runners were dispatched in all directions looking for the lost Booshway.*

> *The detachment to which Meek was assigned had the pleasure and honor of discovering the hiding place of the missing partner, which was in Pierre's Hole, a mountain valley about thirty miles long and of half that width, which subsequently was*

much frequented by the camps of the various fur companies. He was found trapping and exploring.[19]

Newell summed up his recollection succinctly:

on piers fork we fell in with Messrs Smith & Jackson partners of Mr Subletts august 20 held Randezvous and seperated for Beever hunting when all together about 175 men.[20]

And George Ebberts wrote:

We were lying in Jackson's Hole when the express came back to us at the Three Tetons. We were lying there & Fitzpatrick, he came back to us ... then we moved to the – to Smith's ... We met him near what is called Pier's Hole in the Teton Mountains ... We were in a company consisting of 52 men and two Indians, 54 altogether. The Rendezvous was in Pier's Hole ... we came over by the Three Tetons.[21]

A letter probably written by Smith to William Clark in December 1829, and signed "Smith, Jackson & Sublette," should clarify the inconsistencies. The letter says that after joining Jackson, "[Smith] proceeded and joined Mr W. L. Sublette, on the 5th August 1829, at the Tetons on Henry's Fork S. branch Columbia."[22] What matters here is their collective presence in Pierre's Hole and, for the first time in two years, all three partners were together.

Although Newell appears to be claiming there were 175 men present (some historians who have examined his handwriting make the number to be 45 or maybe 55), at its peak, SJS likely employed only about 120 men.[23] Thus, if Newell's "175" is correct, a number of men in attendance were not attached to SJS, but were free trappers. Meek offered a good sketch of these freelancers as compared to others in the trapping fraternity:

The difference between a hired and a free trapper was greatly in favor of the latter. The hired trapper was regularly indentured, and bound not only to hunt and trap for his employers, but also to perform any duty required of him in camp. The Booshway, or the trader, or the partisan, (leader of the detachment) had him under his command, to make him take charge of, load and unload the horses, stand guard, cook, hunt fuel, or, in short, do any and every duty. In return for this toilsome service he received an outfit of traps, arms and ammunition, horses, and whatever his service required. Besides his outfit, he received no more than three or four hundred dollars a year as wages.

There was also a class of free trappers, who were furnished with their outfit by the company they trapped for, and who were obliged to agree to a certain stipulated price for their furs before the hunt commenced. But the genuine free trapper regarded himself as greatly the superior of either of the foregoing classes. He had his own horses and accoutrements, arms and ammunition. He took what route he thought fit, hunted and trapped when and where he chose; traded with the Indians; sold his furs to whoever offered highest for them; dressed flauntingly, and generally had an Indian wife and half-breed children. They prided themselves on their hardihood and courage; even on their recklessness and profligacy. Each claimed to own the best horse; to have had the wildest adventures; to have made the most narrow escapes; to have killed the greatest number of bears and Indians; to be the greatest favorite with the Indian belles, the greatest consumer of alcohol, and to have the most money to spend, i.e. the largest credit on the books of the company. If his hearers did not believe him, he was ready to run a race with him, to beat him at "old sledge," or to fight, if fighting was preferred, – ready to prove what he affirmed in any manner the company pleased.[24]

Of his first experience at the trappers' annual assembly, Meek reported:

The Summer rendezvous was always chosen in some valley where there was grass for the animals, and game for the camp. The plains along the Popo Agie, besides furnishing these necessary bounties, were bordered by picturesque mountain ranges, whose naked bluffs of red sandstone glowed in the morning and evening sun with a mellowness of coloring charming to the eye of the Virginia recruit. The waving grass of the plain, variegated with wild flowers; the clear summer heavens flecked with white clouds that threw soft shadows in passing; the grazing animals *scattered about the meadows; the lodges of the Booshways, around which clustered the camp in motley garb and brilliant coloring; gay laughter, and the murmur of soft Indian voices, all made up a most spirited and enchanting picture, in which the eye of an artist could not fail to delight.*

But as the goods were opened the scene grew livelier. All were eager to purchase, most of the trappers to the full amount of their year's wages; and some of them, generally free trappers, went in debt to the company to a very considerable amount, after spending the value of a year's labor, privation, and danger, at the rate of several hundred dollars in a single day.[25]

As for the 1829 rendezvous in Pierre's Hole specifically:

Meek found time to admire the magnificent scenery of the valley, which is bounded on two sides by broken and picturesque ranges, and overlooked by that magnificent group of mountains, called the Three Tetons, towering to a height of fourteen thousand feet. This emerald cup set in its rim of amethystine mountains, was so pleasant a sight to the mountain-men that camp was moved to it without delay, where it remained until some time in September, recruiting its animals and preparing for the fall hunt.

Here again the trappers indulged in their noisy sports and rejoicing, ostensibly on account of the return of the long-absent Booshway. There was little said of the men who had perished in that unfortunate expedition. "Poor fellow! out of luck;" was the usual burial rite which the memory of a dead comrade received. So much and no more. They could indulge in noisy rejoicings over a lost comrade restored; but the dead one was not mentioned. Nor was this apparently heartless and heedless manner so irrational or unfeeling as it seemed. Everybody understood one thing in the mountains – that he must keep his life by his own courage and valor, or at the least by his own prudence. Unseen dangers always lay in wait for him. The arrow or tomahawk of the Indian, the blow of the grizzly bear, the mis-step on the dizzy or slippery height, the rush of boiling and foaming floods, freezing cold, famine – these were the most common forms of peril, yet did not embrace even then all the forms in which Death sought his victims in the wilderness.[26]

Several mountaineers left similar glowing accounts of the beauty of Teton Valley. Benjamin Bonneville, for example, would later say:

The valley called Pierre's Hole is about thirty miles in length and fifteen in width, bounded to the west and south by low and broken ridges, and overlooked to the east by three lofty mountains, called the three Tetons, which domineer as landmarks over a vast extent of country.

A fine stream, fed by rivulets and mountain springs, pours through the valley toward the north, dividing it into nearly equal parts. The meadows on its borders are broad and extensive, covered with willow and cotton-wood trees, so closely interlocked and matted together as to be nearly impassable.[27]

Jim Bridger was totally smitten. According to General William F. Raynolds, whom he guided during the latter's land surveys of the area nearly thirty years later, Bridger called the Teton Basin, "the finest valley in the mountains!"[28]

It is unfortunate that within the sparse primary sources, no hints indicate the specific site of the rendezvous. Historians are left to guess where the SJS men set up their camps for trading. A number of artifacts have been found along Darby Creek on the west side of today's Highway 33 about three miles south of Driggs, Idaho, including such trade goods as knives, bells, tomahawks, and a large assortment of trade beads. This location is a good consideration for the rendezvous grounds.

There is reason to believe that during meetings between the partners, Smith convinced Sublette and Jackson they should divvy up the mountains with the HBC, the Americans sticking to their side of the Continental Divide. Meek, again, was the primary source:

In the conference which took place between Smith and Sublette, the former insisted that on account of the kind services of the Hudson's Bay Company toward himself and the three other survivors of his party, they should withdraw their trappers and

151

*traders from the western side of the mountains for the present, so
as not to have them come in conflict with those of that company.
To this proposition Sublette reluctantly consented, and orders
were issued for moving once more to the east, before going into
winter camp, which was appointed for the Wind River Valley.*[29]

In spite of this, American trappers continued to rid the
mountains of the beaver population. Whatever marginal attempt
they may have made to honor Smith's request was short lived. Even
if SJS had agreed with Smith, the partners had little if any control
over free trappers.

This Pierre's Hole rendezvous broke up in late September 1829.
How many additional beaver skins may have been acquired at this
second assembly was not recorded. Robert Campbell returned to St.
Louis with forty-five packs of beaver from the July meeting on the
Popo Agie. Beaver was then selling for $5.25 per pound and he had
4,076 pounds loaded on the mules. Those hides, a few otter skins
and fourteen pounds of castoreum brought the company $22,476.[30]
Meanwhile, three SJS brigades set out for the fall hunt. One
contingent included newcomer Joe Meek, who

*was sent out with a party to take his first hunt for beaver as a
hired trapper. The detachment to which he belonged traveled
down Pierre's fork, the stream which watered the valley of
Pierre's Hole, to its junction with Lewis' and Henry's forks
where they unite to form the great Snake River. While trapping
in this locality the party became aware of the vicinity of a
roving band of Blackfeet, and in consequence, redoubled their
usual precautions while on the march.*[31]

David Jackson may have stayed around the Pierre's Hole
neighborhood, trapping its streams, then crossed directly over Teton
Pass, traveling to the Wind River region.[32] Alternatively, Jackson
may have trapped the Snake country during the spring 1830
hunt.[33] Smith and Sublette, meanwhile, led their men down Pierre's
River, today's Teton River, west to the Snake and up Henry's Fork
into Blackfoot territory. Following numerous skirmishes, all three
partners eventually found their way to the Wind River in time for
the 1830 rendezvous.

Further evidence of trappers in Pierre's Hole in the second half of 1829 is lacking. The forty man brigade led by Milton Sublette, Henry Fraeb and Jean-Baptiste Gervais might have returned to Pierre's Hole in late fall. This group left the Popo Agie and trapped through the Big Horn Basin. After a possible visit to Teton Valley, they relocated to winter quarters on Wind River.[34]

Several accounts of events in Pierre's Hole are inaccurate or have no supporting evidence. B. W. Driggs described a battle in the fall of 1829 "in this vicinity," in which Thomas Fitzpatrick played a prominent role in keeping the company horses from being stolen.[35] According to B. W. Driggs, Blackfoot warriors attacked the camp early one morning – too early in fact, as the herd had not yet been turned out to graze. As Indians charged, guns blazing, trying to stampede the horses, Fitzpatrick mounted and rode around and around the camp to keep the livestock in check. Two horses were shot out from under him, but the stock was saved. After six hours of fighting, the Blackfoot war party left the area, at which time, "the trappers then moved off in a northwesterly direction through the pine forests in the north end of Pierre's Hole."[36]

Joe Meek related this battle pretty much as described, but with two important differences. First, Meek's account places the event in the fall of 1830 rather than 1829. Second, the site was nowhere near Pierre's Hole but was on Henry's Fork of the Snake. Meek reported that after the skirmish, the camp moved in a northeasterly direction, "through the pine forests between Pierre's Hole and the head-waters of the Missouri."[37] Meek's version therefore puts the trappers enroute to the Three Forks in search of beaver.

12

The Rocky Mountain Fur Company: 1830-1832

Primary evidence of trappers in Pierre's Hole between the rendezvous of 1829 and 1832, both held in Teton Valley, is sparse.[1] A Euro-American party toured Pierre's Hole sometime in early to mid-1830. Paul Wilhelm, Duke of Württemberg, in southwest Germany, visited the valley during his second adventure into the American West. Wilhelm was by avocation a scientist specializing in botany and zoology, thus his outings focused on scientific research and exploration. On his initial trip to this country in 1823, he had met eighteen-year-old Jean-Baptiste Charbonneau, son of Toussaint and Sacagawea of the Lewis and Clark Expedition. The young Charbonneau had then traveled to Europe with the Duke, remaining there for several years.

In April, 1829, the two friends departed Europe for a tour of several islands in the West Indies.[2] After several months on various Caribbean islands, they arrived in New Orleans in late November. Obtaining necessary permits from Superintendant of Indian Affairs William Clark to go at least as far as the Columbia, the Duke set off from St. Louis for the Rocky Mountains on December 23, 1829.[3] He was accompanied by a clerk, two servants, and two hired men of the American Fur Company, one of whom was likely Jean-Baptiste Charbonneau.[4]

Records at Fort Union, on the Missouri River near today's Montana-North Dakota border, indicate the Duke's party had arrived there by mid-May, 1830.[5] Wilhelm arrived in the Rockies on July 18, just two days after William Sublette's supply caravan made it to the Wind River rendezvous site, causing some to suggest the Duke and Charbonneau attended this gathering.[6] If true, the two men parted ways shortly thereafter because Warren Ferris places Charbonneau solidly in an AFC brigade under Joseph Robidoux by late August.[7]

Wilhelm wrote about the Tetons, the Wind River Range and the buttes of the Snake River plain:

Far back from the front range ... rise the Wind River Mountains. In the extreme northwest are the lofty peaks of the three Titans, called the Triple Snow Peaks. These are covered with perpetual ice and snow, perhaps the loftiest mountains in all the scenery of the North-American Alps. Between, and farther south, are the Three Knobs ... All these I had visited in 1830-1831.[8]

Regarding Wilhelm's trip to Pierre's Hole, Margaret Sanborn speculated:

Since it is known that Paul went to the Missouri's Three Forks, it is logical that he accompanied one of the trapping parties there after rendezvous. The fact that in later writings he describes his delight at meeting again that 'lovable old huntsman' Tom Fitzpatrick, makes it almost certain that he joined Fitzpatrick, Bridger and Milton Sublette, who are known to have taken their men to the Three Forks that fall. Their trail ran north through the Bighorn Basin to the Yellowstone River (where Paul tells of finding coal deposits), and then turned west to the Missouri's headwaters. From there they followed the Jefferson, crossed the Divide, and worked south through Pierre's Hole where Paul would have seen the Tetons for either the first or second time.[9]

Chroniclers Joe Meek, Robert Newell and George Ebberts were all with Fitzpatrick, Bridger and Milton Sublette on the 1830 trip but make no mention of the Duke. It seems clear Wilhelm saw the Tetons on this trip, though the likelihood he was with this RMFC brigade is slim. This almost certainly indicates two separate parties traversed Pierre's Hole during 1830.

Duke Paul Wilhelm had returned to the East by October 1830.[10] He was the first scientifically trained visitor to the Tetons so it is unfortunate that his journals, notes and drawings are unavailable. Significant observations of flora and fauna such as appear in the Duke's existing diaries would likely have provided an invaluable resource for reconstructing the natural history of Pierre's Hole.[11]

The 1830 rendezvous on Wind River was historic for several reasons. First, Sublette brought supplies via wagons, rather than pack train, for the first time. Then, on August 4, 1830, Smith, Jackson and

Sublette sold out their interest in the fur company to James Bridger, Thomas Fitzpatrick, Milton Sublette, Henry Fraeb and Jean-Baptiste Gervais. The legendary "Rocky Mountain Fur Company" (RMFC) was now an official entity for the first time.[12]

This year also saw the emergence of the American Fur Company as a competitor in the field. Led primarily by Andrew Drips and Luciene Fontenelle, this new challenger had been resurrected from Astor's earlier efforts in the Rocky Mountain fur trade. Competition from AFC would impact which company garnered the most beaver over the next several years. Warren Ferris, a member of the AFC brigade, kept a detailed journal that provides rich details of the workings of the company. Joe Meek summed up the 1830-1831 fall and spring hunts:

> *Fitzpatrick, Bridger and Sublette completed their spring and summer campaign without any material loss in men or animals, and with considerable gain in beaver skins. Having once more visited the Yellowstone, they turned to the south again, crossing the mountains into Pierre's Hole, on to Snake river; thence to Salt river; thence to Bear river; and thence to Green river to rendezvous.*[13]

This rather vague itinerary indicates the party visited what is now Yellowstone National Park and then followed the Snake River through Jackson Hole. In that they "turned to the south" from Yellowstone, it seems they crossed Conant Pass to reach Pierre's Hole. Some sources suggest they sojourned in the valley for a while before continuing on to Henry's Fork. Others propose a trip across Pine Creek Pass, headed for Salt River and the Bear.

Apart from Meek's account, little mention is made of Teton Valley in the meager extant records for 1831. In October, two unidentified men from the American Fur Company, along with three or four Indians, probably passed through Pierre's Hole on their way from the Salmon River to meet Andrew Drips, who was expected from Council Bluffs with a supply train.[14]

There is some confusion as to the site of the 1831 rendezvous. It may have been held in Cache Valley, or it may have been on the Green River. More evidence points to Cache Valley, but it is not conclusive.[15] The rendezvous was supplied via Santa Fe, New

Mexico because Fitzpatrick did not depart for St. Louis in time to make arrangements for merchandise. Having made a late start for Missouri, he had met Smith, Jackson, and Sublette with a caravan of merchants bound for Santa Fe. Fitzpatrick was persuaded to join them in order to put together an outfit at their destination. It was on this trip along the Santa Fe Trail that Jedediah Smith was killed.

For the return journey, Fitzpatrick hired a few men, including young Kit Carson, to help with the pack mules carrying supplies to the rendezvous. Fitzpatrick, behind schedule, did not get back to the mountains until sometime in September. Many trappers had already left, taking their beaver skins with them, determined to make the fall hunt with what little supplies remained from the previous year. The lucky ones still waiting were rewarded: Fitzpatrick had brought liquor, probably good old *aguardiente de Taos*.

In the mountains, Fitzpatrick turned over the trade goods to Henry Fraeb and immediately headed back to St. Louis to secure the coming year's supplies. Fraeb rambled through the Rockies with the pack train, trying to locate and reprovision the isolated RMFC trapping brigades. Only a few furs made it to the eastern market.

Joe Meek's abbreviated 1831 narrative may have been due to his possible absence from the brigade during part of the time. Meek and Milton Sublette had separated from the main party at least by the early spring of 1832, if not sooner. Sublette had been stabbed and severely wounded in a brawl with a Bannock chief.[16] Meek stayed behind to bury his friend, if necessary, but six weeks later, Milton was satisfactorily healed. He and Joe Meek rode off to find their brigade, but met a Shoshone party on the Green River. Here they encountered Umentucken Tukutsey Undewatsey – the Mountain Lamb – the most beautiful Native American woman either man had ever laid eyes on. Milton Sublette would soon marry her, then two years later, after he had left the Rockies for good, Meek would take her to wife. But for the immediate future, the two trappers pursued a course to Pierre's Hole, hoping to get there by summer.

The spring of 1832 saw an AFC crew of forty-eight escalating fur trade competition in the mountains. According to Newell, Fraeb's brigade hunted "from Psalmon River to henrys fork to Lewises fork up Salt River Round to Piers hole."[17] On top of that, the AFC fielded fifty additional men out of Fort Union. That many trappers in the Rocky Mountains pointed to a busy summer's rendezvous, again slated for Pierre's Hole.

Meanwhile, Robert Campbell had returned from Ireland and William Sublette had approached him about becoming business partners. Unfortunately, Campbell's savings were nearly exhausted so he needed to raise the capital for his share in such an arrangement. To do this, Campbell hired on with Sublette as his lieutenant but also purchased his own small outfit of trade goods to take to rendezvous. The sale of this merchandise would provide the stake he needed to officially join Sublette in business.

The caravan pulled out of St. Louis on April 25, 1832. Campbell's five employees led ten horses loaded with $363.75 worth of stock. He had also purchased a new P. Carmer rifle and a brace of Hawken flintlock pistols.[18] Sublette had fifty men in service to manage the pack string.[19] By the time they left Independence, Missouri two weeks later, they had been joined by Thomas Fitzpatrick and Bostonian Nathaniel Wyeth, along with his twenty-five followers. All together, a force of eight-six men and 300 head of livestock headed west to the most competitive and potentially profitable rendezvous of them all.[20]

13

RENDEZVOUS 1832

The pinnacle of all fur trade extravaganzas may have been the grand rendezvous of 1832, the second and last to be conducted in Pierre's Hole. Mountaineers began converging on the valley in June, anxious to celebrate the high point of the annual Rocky Mountain fur trade cycle. More people attended this particular event than any of the prior summer gatherings, and more than any rendezvous to come. The weather was cold and wet: a typical mountain summer. Snow and hail plagued the trappers well into the month of July. Despite the conditions, it was likely the most important rendezvous ever held.

In the first week of July, William Sublette wrangled a pack train of seventy-eight men and 150 horses over Teton Pass. For animal and human, footing was precarious. The animals' hooves were already worn thin from sharp stones, others were lame. Several horses slipped, a few rolled down the slope. At the summit, Sublette made camp and waited for sick and inexperienced men to catch up. A snow storm struck that night. They had to dig out of the snow before continuing their descent to Teton Valley and the waiting trappers.

More first-person accounts of this rendezvous and associated events exist than for any other – as many as fourteen men wrote journals or letters or otherwise recorded their summer experience. Following are excerpts by trappers and traders who were actually there.[1]

Nathaniel J. Wyeth was a Boston ice merchant with dreams of founding a new company in the Oregon Territory on the Columbia River. His expedition included his brother, Dr. Jacob Wyeth, and a young cousin, John. Before departing Independence, Missouri, Wyeth's Pacific Trading Company linked up with Sublette on his way west. The greenhorn Nathaniel told of his approach to Pierre's Hole from the Jackson Hole side of the mountains:

> We marched early and at 2 ock stoped on Lewis river and
> within 20 miles of the Trois Tetons three very conspicuous
> snow covered mountains visible in all this region this river here

159

runs nearly S. and is divided over a bottom about 2 miles and into 8 streams very rapid and difficult these we forded which consumed the time until night and encamped after making 18 miles on the W. bank with no grass. in the morning of the 7th [July] we proceed up a small brook coming from a gap of the mountains due south of the Trois Tetons and passed the range of mountains of this range without much difficulty it is a good pass for such a range and fresh animals would have no difficulty in passing through it On the highest point we had snow accompanied with heavy thunder and being out of meat fed upon the inner bark of the Balsam trees a tree similar if not the same with the Eastern Balsam At Night we encamped at the foot of the pass on the western side and at the commencement of a large valley with several streams running through it into Lewis River surrounded with high and snow clad mountains The weather is here warm in the day time but frost every night the grass is good the land ordinary.[2]

Young John Wyeth wrote about the same leg of the journey:

On the 4th of July, 1832, we arrived at Lewis's fork, one of the largest rivers in these rocky mountains. It took us all day to cross it. It is half a mile wide, deep, and rapid. The way we managed was this: one man unloaded his horse, and swam across with him, leading two loaded ones, and unloading the two, brought them back, for two more, and as Sublet's company and our own made over a hundred and fifty, we were all day in passing the river. In returning, my mule, by treading on a round stone, stumbled and threw me off, and the current was so strong, that a bush which I caught hold of only saved me from drowning. This being Independence-Day, we drank the health of our friends in Massachusetts, in good clear water, as that was the only liquor we had to drink in remembrance of our homes and dear connexions. If I may judge by my own feelings and by the looks of my companions, there was more of melancholy than joy amongst us. We were almost four thousand miles from Boston, and in saying Boston we mean at the same time our native spot Cambridge, as they are separated by a wooden bridge only. From the north fork of Lewis's river we passed on to an eminence called Teton mountain, where we spent the night.

The next day was pleasant, and serene. Captain Sublet came in the evening to inquire how many of our company were sick, as they must ride, it being impossible for them to go on foot any farther. His kindness and attention I never can forget. Dr. Jacob Wyeth, the Captain's brother, George More, and Stephen Burdit, were too weak to walk. To accommodate them with horses, Captain Wyeth was obliged to dig a hole in the earth, and therein bury the goods which had been hitherto carried on horseback. In the language of the Trappers this hiding of goods was called cacher or hidden treasure, being the French term for 'to hide.' When they dig these hiding-holes they carefully carry the earth on a buffalo-skin to a distance, so as to leave no marks or traces of the ground being dug up or disturbed: and this was done to secure the cache from being stolen by the Indians or the white men. The goods so hidden are wrapt up in buffalo-skins to keep them dry, before the earth is put over them. Nor is this all; they make a fire over the spot, and all this to prevent the Indians from suspecting that treasure is cache, or hidden there, while the owner of it takes care to mark the bearing of the spot on some tree, or rock, or some other object that may lead him to recognise the place again. But I have my doubts whether they who hid the goods will ever return that way to dig up their hidden treasure. We did not meddle with it on our return with Captain Sublet.

On the 5th of July we started afresh rather low spirited. We looked with sadness on the way before us. The mountain was here pretty thickly timbered down its slopes, and wherever the ground is level. The pines and hemlock trees were generally about eighteen inches through. It had snowed, and we were now at a height where the snow commonly lies all the year round. Which ever way we looked, the region presented a dreary aspect. No one could wonder that even some of us who were in health, were, at times, somewhat homesick. If this was the case with us, what must have been the feelings of our three sick fellow travellers. We passed through a snow bank three feet deep. We well ones passed on with Captain Sublet to the top of the mountain, and there waited until our sick men came up with us. George More fell from his horse through weakness. He might have maintained his seat on level ground, but ascending and descending required more exertion than he could call forth; and this was the case also with Dr. Wyeth. Burdit made out a little better.

When we encamped at night, we endured a snow storm. Sublet's company encamped about two miles from us; for at best we could hardly keep up with his veteran company. They were old and experienced trappers, and we, compared with them, young and inexperienced soldiers, little imagining that we should ever have to encounter such hardships, in realizing our dreams of making a fortune. Ignorance of the future is not always to be considered among the calamities of man.

Captain Sublet's grand rendezvous, or Head Quarters, was about twelve miles from our encampment. He had there about two hundred trappers, or beaver-hunters; or more properly speaking, skinners of entrapped animals; or peltry-hunters, for they chased but few of the captured beasts. To these were added about five hundred Indians, of the rank of warriors, all engaged in the same pursuit and traffic of the fur-trade. They were principally the Flat-heads ...

The spot where we now were, is a valley, between two mountains, about ten miles wide, so lofty that their tops are covered with snow, while it was warm and pleasant where we pitched our tent. This agreeable valley is called by the trappers Pierre's-Hole, as if it were a dismal residence; and was the most western point that I visited, being about, we conjectured, four hundred miles short of the mouth of the Oregon river, whence the territory derives its name.[3]

Nathaniel Wyeth further revealed:

On the 8th we proceed into the plain and after a march of 10 miles arrived at the rendezvous of the hunters of this region here we found about 120 Lodges of the Nez Perces and about 80 of the Flatheads a company of trappers of about 90 under Mr. Dripps of the firm of Dripps & Fontenelle connected with the American Fur Co. Many independent Hunters and about 100 men of the Rocky Mountain Fur Co under Mess Milton Sublette and Mr. Frapp.[4]

John Ball, also a member of the Wyeth's Pacific Trading Company, wrote:

four days of hard working our way through ragged ravines and over steep ridges brought us out on to a fine grassy plain among the mountains, called Pierre's Hole and to the grand encampment, where they had for some time been awaiting our arrival.[5]

Although John Wyeth did not get all of his facts entirely straight, he was clearly impressed with Sublette and the rendezvous concept:

Captain Sublet has, for several years, had about two hundred of these trappers in his pay, in and around the Rocky Mountains, and this troop was a party of them. His place of rendezvous for them is at Pierre's Hole, by which name they call one of those deep and verdant valleys which are to be found in the Rocky Mountains from the eastern boundary of them to their extreme edge in the west, where the Oregon or Columbia river commences under the name of Clark's river, some branches of which inosculate with the mighty Missouri on the east. It is to Pierre's valley or Hole, that his trappers resort to meet their employer every summer. It is here they bring their peltry and receive their pay; and this traffic has been kept up between them a number of years with good faith on both sides, and to mutual satisfaction and encouragement. When Sublet leaves St. Louis, he brings up tobacco, coffee, rice, powder, shot, paint, beads, handkerchiefs and all those articles of finery that please both Indian women and men; and having established that sort of traffic with his friends, the Indians on and in the vicinity of the Rocky Mountains, what chance was there that any small band from Boston, or even Cambridge, could supplant him in the friendship and confidence of his old acquaintance, the Shoshonees, the Black-feet, or any other tribe?[6]

John Wyeth continued:

Captain Sublet encamped his forces; and then pointed out to Captain Wyeth the ground which he thought would be most proper for us; and altogether we looked like a little army. Not but what we felt small compared with our great and powerful allies.

We were overjoyed to think that we had got to a resting place, where we could repose our weary limbs, and recruit the lost strength of our sick. While Sublet was finishing his business with his Indian trappers, they delivering their peltry, and he remunerating them in his way with cloth, powder, ball, beads, knives, handkerchiefs, and all that gawdy trumpery which Indians admire, together with coffee, rice, and corn, also leather, and other articles, – we, being idle, had time to think, to reflect.[7]

The AFC brigade, including Warren Ferris, also showed up in Pierre's Hole. Ferris described the days leading up to rendezvous:

We continued slowly up Henrie's fork, and halted two or three days on the East fork, to dry meat, knowing that we should remain one or two days at rendezvous, and that buffalo would soon be driven far from us. We ... continued thirty miles South Eastward over prairie hills, decked with groves of Aspen trees, to the Northern extremity of Pierre's Hole. This pleasant retreat is twenty miles long, and two wide, extending from Southeast to Northwest; and is surrounded by lofty mountains, save on the west side, where prairie hills appear. It is watered by numbers of small streams, which unite and form Pierre's fork, a fine stream thirty or forty paces in width, which cuts its way out of the valley, in a deep canal of bluff rocks. On the east side of the valley, three majestic peaks of naked rock, rise far above the rest, and are well known to mountain rovers by the name of 'The Trois Tetons.' The mountains are very abrupt, as far as the pines extend, and the huge pyramids above are absolutely inaccessible. This valley is noted for the large extent of excellent pasturage, along the borders of its waters; and has been selected as a pleasant place for a general rendezvous, by the R.M.F.C., Vanderburgh and ourselves: it receives its name from an Iroquois chieftain, who first discovered it; and was killed in 1827, on the source of the Jefferson River. On reaching this valley, we found the Rocky Mountain Fur Co. already here, awaiting the arrival of Mr. Fitzpatrick, with supplies from Saint Louis. Mr. Vanderburgh expected a Mr. Provenu, with an equipment from fort Union, at the mouth of the Yellow Stone; and we as anxiously looked forward for Mr. Fontenelle, who was expected from the Council Bluffs.

Some days after we entered Pierre's Hole, a party of trappers returned, having made their hunt to the Southward. They saw Captain Ghant, at the head of fifty or sixty men, on Green river; he had procured horses from the Spaniards of New Mexico, and had made his hunt on the sources of the Arkansas, and tributaries of Green river, without molestation by the Indians. Two men were despatched by the R.M.F. Co. about this time, to meet the Saint Louis companies, and six of our men followed a few days afterwards for the same object.

On the 29th of June, the two men despatched by the R.M.F. Co. returned in a miserable plight; they had proceeded as far as Laramie's fork, at the foot of the Black hills, and were robbed by a party of Crow Indians, of their horses; after which they retraced their steps to camp, and suffered extremely for want of provisions, or from cold, rain, and fatigue. Throughout the month of June, scarcely a day passed without either rain, hail, or snow, and during the last three days of the month, a snow storm continued without intermission, the whole time, night and day; but disappeared from the earth a few hours after the sun reappeared.

On the third of July, one of our men who was sent in quest of the St. Louis companies returned, and reported that William Sublett, at the head of one hundred men, was now on his way here. *This numerous company was composed of fifty hired men; a party of twenty-two men, detached from Ghant's company; a party of thirteen men from the Rio del Norte, and a Mr. Wythe with ten or twelve followers, who was on some secret expedition to the mouth of the Oregon, or Columbia River. We learned that Mr. Fitzpatrick left the company at the Red Hills, with two horses, and set out to reach us, in advance of Sublett; but had not since been heard of. Two or three nights before our express reached them, their camp was fired upon by a party of unknown Indians, but no one injured. Several horses were stolen, however; from Sublett, our express could learn nothing of Fontenelle; and determined to proceed on until they should meet him, but the day after their departure from Sublett's Camp, they were charged upon by a party of mounted Indians, who compelled them to return.*

On the 8th Sublett arrived, and halted in the middle of the hole, with the R.M.F. Co., for whom he brought one hundred mules, laden with merchandise. The same evening Mr. Thos. Fitzpatrick, to our great joy, came into camp, though in a most pitiable condition. It appears that this traveller, on his way to Pierre's Hole, came suddenly upon a large Village of Indians, who mounted their horses and immediately gave chase; however, he had fortunately taken the precaution to furnish himself with two horses, previous to his departure from camp, one of which had the reputation of being fleet. This last he led by the halter, ever saddled, and bridled, as a resource in case he should be compelled to seek safety by flight. So soon as he found himself discovered and pursued, he sprang upon his favorite horse, and fled, directing his course towards the mountains, which were about three miles distant. When he reached the mountains, the Indians were so far behind, that he hoped to elude them by concealment, and immediately placed his horse in a thicket, and sought a crevice in the rocks, where he concealed himself. In a few moments the blood hounds came up, and soon discovered his horse; from his place of concealment he saw them searching every nook and crevice for him, and the search was not discontinued, until the next step would have placed him before the eyes of a blood thirsty set of wretches, whose clemency in the first instance, is yet to be recorded. Fortunately for him, the search was abandoned, and the Indians returned to camp, at the same time he chose a point, whence he could discover any passing object, in the plain beneath him; and determined to remain, until the company should pass, and join them at that time. At the expiration of three days, he discovered six men, passing in the valley, and immediately descended the mountain to join them, but ere he could effect this, a party of Indians appeared from another quarter, and gave chase to the six men, who wheeled and fled; in the meantime, he fled back to his place of refuge. At length he became confident, that the company had passed him without his knowledge, and set out for Pierre's Hole in the night; his moccasins became worn out, and he was forced to make others of his hat, he likewise lost his powder in swimming a river, and suffered from the combined effects of hunger, cold, and fatigue, until he was reduced to a mere skeleton, and could scarcely be recognized when he finally reached camp. He informs us, that the Indians were doubtless a band of Grosvents of the prairie, who passed from the Missouri to the head of the Arkansas three years ago, and were now on their return to their own country. They are the same Indians who encamped with Smith, Sublett and Jackson, on the Arkansas last summer, and there buried their hatchets and animosity together. But it appears from their proceedings this far, that they have raised both since.[8]

Fitzpatrick's experience, described in several trappers' journals, goes down in the annals of fur trade lore as one of the most harrowing escapades one man might ever have to face, rivaling the adventures of John Colter or Hugh Glass.[9] According to the story, Fitzpatrick's hair turned white from the stress and fear accompanying his traumatic exploit. Glad to be alive, he made his way to Pierre's Hole, where the trappers celebrated his arrival as well as that of Sublette and the supplies – including the liquor.

Teton Valley saw a greater variety of fur companies at this affair than at any other rendezvous. The enterprises included the well known Rocky Mountain and American Fur Companies, but several independent concerns had also sprung up. These included some now unemployed men of the Gantt and Blackwell outfit, other free trappers and the newborn Wyeth outfit.[10] A small pack outfit under partners Robert Bean and Alexander Sinclair arrived on July 3. Their company had split in May, disagreeing on where to trap. While this group had chosen to work the Platte River and then travel on to Pierre's Hole, the destination of the other faction is unknown.[11] Several Indian tribes attended, predominantly Flathead and Nez Perce. The occasional band of Iroquois, Shawnee and Delaware were generally counted amongst the trappers due to enduring collaboration with Euro-Americans.[12]

The 1832 rendezvous had been coordinated primarily by RMFC to outfit its men. AFC had not been expressly invited, but word traveled fast in the mountains. For example, George Nidever, a member of the Bean-Sinclair party, told of meeting other men on the Platte River some time after May of 1832:

> At this place we met a trader by the name of O'Felon, an Irishman, who with a half doz. mules had brought liquor and a few articles such as blankets, &c., to trade with the trappers. He was accompanied by a trapper by the name of Harris, and had 6 or 7 Mexicans to attend to his mules and packs. He was bound for Pierre's Hole, a deep valley situated between the Lewis and Henry's Forks, and the appointed rendezvous of the trappers and traders for that year. This would take place in July, so I determined to accompany O'Felon.[13]

William O. Fallon's small outfit was apparently intended to supplement the American Fur Company's needed supplies, thus AFC had already gotten wind of the rendezvous arrangements and planned to crash the party.[14] Joe Meek, employed by RMFC, complained that AFC partisans

> tampered with the trappers, and ferreted out the secret of the next rendezvous; they followed on their trail, making them pilots to the trapping grounds; they sold goods to the Indians, and what was worse, to the hired trappers. In this way grew up that fierce conflict of interests, which made it "as much as his life was worth" for a trapper to suffer himself to be inveigled into the service of a rival company, which about this time or a little later, was at its highest.[15]

168

RMFC and AFC had an intense rivalry going and Ferris indicated the two factions camped about a mile apart during the rendezvous. Each outfit awaited its own supply train, and whoever got to Pierre's Hole first would also get the independent trade of Indians and free trappers. Historians estimate that about 1,000 people and 2,000 to 3,000 head of livestock camped in Teton Basin for this get-together. John Ball recorded:

> *Grand Rendezvous – Here we found not only Sublette's traders and trappers, but a party of the American Fur Company, and bands of Nez Perce and Flat Head Indians, who had by appointment met the traders here with their furs and five or six hundred horses. Many of them they sold us to take the place of our lean ones. They would allow something for the lean ones for with them, in their slow way of journeying they would recruit. But the full price of a pony was but a blanket and a cheap knife. So we supplied ourselves with all we needed. These mountain horses are of the Arabian stock, brought to Mexico by the early Spanish settlers - light of limb and fleet. It was a grand sight to look on their immense herd out on the prairie of all colors from white to black and many spotted ones. For during the day they would send them out on to the open prairie to feed with the mounted guard with them, to run them into camp, if the Blackfeet, in whose country we were, should make a dash down the mountain side to steal them. At night they would bring them into camp where they would quietly remain among their owners' tents till morning.*

> *Pierre's Hole – Here in Pierre's Hole was for us a grand time of rest and recruit. The Indians had an abundance of good, dried buffalo meat which we bought of them and on which we feasted, took a bite of the fat part with the lean, eating it like bread and cheese, uncooked or slightly roasted on the coals as we chose. And I never witnessed such recuperation of men as during the two weeks we lay at our ease in this camp, feeding on the dried buffalo meat, and our drink the pure cool mountain creek, a branch of the Lewis river, on which we were encamped. And among us, a varied congregation of some two hundred white men and perhaps nearly as many Indians, there was quite a*

social time, and a great exchange of talk and interesting indeed, from the wide and varied experiences of the narrators. There were cultured men from city and country down to white men lower than the Indian himself. Men of high-toned morals, down to such as had left their country for its good, or perhaps rather personal safety.

Some made the season's trip from the miasmic air of the Mississippi and its city follies to recuperate their bodily and mental derangement. And it proved a grand specific. This mountain-pure air and ever-shining sun is a grand, helpful thing for both soul and body, especially when feeding on only meat and water.[16]

Joe Meek further conveyed the mood of the rendezvous:

All the parties were now safely in. The lonely mountain valley was populous with the different camps. The Rocky Mountain and American companies had their separate camps; Wyeth had his; a company of free trappers, fifteen in number, led by a man named Sinclair, from Arkansas, had the fourth; the Nez Perces and Flatheads, the allies of the Rocky Mountain company, and the friends of the whites, had their lodges along all the streams; so that altogether there could not have been less than one thousand souls, and two or three thousand horses and mules gathered in this place.

"When the pie was opened then the birds began to sing." When Captain Sublette's goods were opened and distributed among the trappers and Indians, then began the usual gay carousel; and the "fast young men" of the mountains outvied each other in all manner of mad pranks. In the beginning of their spree many feats of horsemanship and personal strength were exhibited, which were regarded with admiring wonder by the sober and inexperienced New Englanders under Mr. Wyeth's command. And as nothing stimulated the vanity of the mountain-men like an audience of this sort, the feats they performed were apt to astonish themselves. In exhibitions of the kind, the free trappers took the lead, and usually carried off the palm, like the privileged class that they were.

But the horse-racing, fine riding, wrestling, and all the manlier sports, soon degenerated into the baser exhibitions of a "crazy drunk" condition. The vessel in which the trapper received and carried about his supply of alcohol was one of the small camp kettles. "Passing round" this clumsy goblet very freely, it was not long before a goodly number were in the condition just named, and ready for any mad freak whatever. It is reported by several of the mountain-men that on the occasion of one of these "frolics," one of their number seized a kettle of alcohol, and poured it over the head of a tall, lank, redheaded fellow, repeating as he did so the baptismal ceremony. No sooner had he concluded, than another man with a lighted stick, touched him with the blaze, when in an instant he was enveloped in flames. Luckily some of the company had sense enough left to perceive his danger, and began beating him with pack-saddles to put out the blaze. But between the burning and the beating, the unhappy wretch nearly lost his life, and never recovered from the effects of his baptism by fire.

Beaver being plenty in camp, business was correspondingly lively, there being a great demand for goods. When this demand was supplied, as it was in the course of about three weeks, the different brigades were set in motion.[17]

In a letter home, John Ball relayed to his parents:

We are in a valley 6 or 8 miles wide with mountains covered with snow on both sides, still the weather very fine & good feed for our horses. Sometimes a frost at night. Here they come from the states to trade with the Indians & those that hunt beaver, no other fur is worth carrying so far, bring traps arms & ahminition, beads & other trinkets, and all sorts of groceries, flower rice &c. flower and rice $1.50 pr. Pound, sugar coffee ea. $2. all in proportion. A few yards of scarlet cloth, string of beads & paper of vermilion, awl & fishhook will buy a horse. The indians have many. It is known before hand where the traders are to come & the indians & hunters assemble. there are in this place within five miles Seven or 8 thousand horses &

mules, & one or two thousand whites & indians. But in a few weeks they will scatter to the four winds of heaven, buffalow & other wild animals resume their pasture.[18]

George Nidever, who noted the reunion of the splintered Bean and Sinclair outfit, described the rendezvous this way:

We arrived at Pierre's Hole just before 4th of July. On our way we had crossed several mountains, and the last one just before reaching Pierre's Hole. Morning found us wading through the snow on its tip and by evening we were in the midst of green grass and summer weather at its foot. At Pierre's Hole we found already arrived some 50 or more hunters and trappers. A few days later, a company of 150 trappers under Wm. Sublette arrived from St. Louis bringing supplies. The second in command, Fitzpatrick, they had lost while crossing the Green River. Having gone in advance to reconnoiter, he was cut off by the Indians and so hard pressed that he was obliged to abandon his horse and take to the rocks. His companions supposed him killed.

A week or so after the arrival of the company, a trapper by name of Poe and I went out for a short hunt, and met Fitzpatrick crossing the Lewis Fork. He was mounted, having by the merest chance caught a horse saddled and bridled, that had escaped from one of the men at Pierre's Hole and wandered to where he was found by Fitzpatrick. Fitzpatrick was shoeless, hatless, and almost naked. In crossing a river his powder horn was lost, and this rendered useless his gun and pistols, which he threw away. For ten days or thereabouts he had wandered about, having in that time eaten of no food excepting a very small piece of dried meat. We piloted him back to camp.

Other hunters, singly and by small companies, continued to arrive at the rendezvous until they numbered in all about 500. This was the favorite rendezvous for trappers West of the Rocky Mts. and had been the center of a rich beaver country. At this time, however, it was well nigh trapped out. The companies then at the rendezvous were, as near as I can remember,

William Sublette's, of 150 men – they had come out expressly for trading purposes and returned with about 100 men to St. Louis when the rendezvous broke up; Milton Sublette's, a brother of Wm., composed of about 30 men; Frapp's company, also about 30 men; Wyatt's company of emigrants of about 12 to 16, who were going to the mouth of the Columbia to explore [the] country; Perkin's company of about 3 to 5 men.

Our own company had also got together again, making some 14 or 15 more. When we separated on the Green River, the majority of them finally agreed to make a hunt on the Platte River, but having found the country filled with Indians and lost one of their men by them, they turned back. The rest of the trappers at the rendezvous were a class that hunted singly in parts of the Mts. free from the Indians, or in unorganized bands and with no recognized leader; many of these men never leaving the mountains. At the yearly rendezvous they would exchange their pelts for what few supplies they required and then return to the mountains.[19]

While at rendezvous, Nathaniel Wyeth experienced difficulties that had been brewing among his men for some time. His cousin John, one of the disgruntled, divulged some details of their unhappiness (all emphases in original):

We had been dissatisfied for some time, but we had not leisure to communicate it and systematize our grievances. I, with others, had spoken with Captain Sublet, and him we found conversable and communicative. Myself and some others requested Captain Wyeth to call a meeting of his followers, to ask information, and to know what we were now to expect, seeing we had passed over as we supposed the greatest difficulties, and were now nearly four thousand miles from the <u>Atlantic</u>, and within four hundred miles of the <u>Pacific Ocean</u>, the end and aim of our laborious expedition, the field where we expected to reap our promised harvest. We wished to have what we had been used to at home, – a town meeting, – or a parish meeting, where every freeman has an equal right to speak his sentiments, and to vote thereon. But Captain Wyeth *was by no means inclined to this democratical procedure. The most he seemed inclined to, was a <u>caucus</u> with a select few; of whom neither his own brother, though older than himself, nor myself, was to be of the number. After considerable altercation, he concluded to call a meeting of the whole, on business interesting and applicable to all. We accordingly met, Captain Wyeth in the chair, or on the stump, I forget which. Instead of every man speaking his own mind, or asking such questions as related to matters that lay heaviest on his mind, the Captain commenced the business by ordering the roll to be called; and as the names were called, the clerk asked the person if he would go on. The first name was Nathaniel J. Wyeth, whom we had dubbed <u>Captain</u>, who answered – "I shall go on." – The next was William Nud, who, before he answered, wished to know what the Captain's plan and intentions were, whether to try to commence a small colony, or to trap and trade for beaver? To which Captain Wyeth replied, that <u>that</u> was none of our business. Then Mr. Nud said, "I shall not go on;" and as the names of the rest were called, there appeared <u>seven</u> persons out of the <u>twenty one</u>, who were determined to return home. Of the number so determined was, besides myself, Dr. Jacob Wyeth, the Captain's brother, whose strength had never been equal to such a journey. His constitution forbade it. He was brought up at College. Here were discontents on both sides; criminations and recriminations. A commander of a band of associated adventurers has a very hard task. The commanded, whether in a school, or in a regiment, or company, naturally combine in feeling against their leader; and this is so natural that armies are obliged to make very strict rules, and to pursue rigid discipline. It is so also on ship-board. Our merchant ships cannot sail in safety without exacting prompt obedience; and disobedience in the common seamen is mutiny, and mutiny is a high crime, and approximates to piracy. It is pretty much so in these long and distant exploring expeditions. The Captain cannot always with safety satisfy all the questions put to him by those under his command; and it would lead to great inconvenience to entrust any, even a brother, with any information concealed from the rest. There must be secrecy, and* there must be confidence. We had travelled through a dreary wilderness, an infinitely worse country than Palestine; yet Moses himself could not have kept together the Israelites without the aid of miracles; and the history we have given of our boat-like arks, and the wreck of our raft, and the loss of our heaviest articles may lead most readers to suspect that our Leader to his Land of Promise was not an inspired man. In saying this, we censure no one, we only lament our common frailty. Reflect a moment, considerate reader! on our humble means, for an expedition of FOUR THOUSAND <u>miles</u>, compared with the ample means, rich and complete out-fit, letters of credit, and every thing deemed needful, given to <u>Captains Lewis</u> and <u>Clarke</u>, under the orders of the government of the United States; and yet they several times came very near starving for the want of food and of <u>fuel</u>, even in the <u>Oregon</u> territory! In all books of voyages and travels, who ever heard of the utmost distress for want of wood, leaves, roots, coal, or turf to cook with? Yet all through the dreary wilderness of Missouri, we were obliged to use the dung of buffaloes, or eat raw flesh. The reader will scarcely believe that this was the case even at mouth of the Oregon river. Clarke and Lewis had to buy wood of the Indians, who had hardly enough for themselves. To be deprived of solid food soon ends in death; but we were often deprived of the two elements out of four, <u>fire</u> and <u>water</u>, and when on the Rocky mountains, of a <u>third</u>, I mean <u>earth;</u> for everything beneath our feet and around us was stone. We had, be sure, <u>air</u> enough, and too much too, sometimes enough almost to blow our hair off.

But to return to our dismal list of grievances. Almost everyone of the company wished to go no farther; but they found themselves too feeble and exhausted to think of encountering the risk of a march on foot of three thousand five hundred miles through such a country as we came. We asked Captain Wyeth to let us have our muskets and a sufficiency of ammunition, which request he refused. Afterwards, he collected all the guns, and after selecting such as he and his companions preferred, he gave us the refuse; many of which were unfit for use. There were *two tents belonging to the company, of which he gave us one; which we pitched about a quarter of a mile from his. George More expressed his determination of returning home, and asked for a horse, which after considerable difficulty he obtained. This was July 10th. The Captain likewise supplied his brother with a horse and a hundred dollars.*

On the 12th of July, Captain Wyeth, after moving his tent half a mile farther from ours, put himself under the command of Mr. Milton Sublet, brother of Captain William Sublet so often mentioned. This Captain Milton Sublet had about twenty men under his command, all trappers; so that hereafter as far as I know, it was Wyeth, Sublet and Co.; so that the reader will understand, that Dr. Jacob Wyeth, Palmer, Law, Batch, and myself concluded to retrace our steps to St. Louis in company with Captain William Sublet, while Captain Nathaniel J. Wyeth remained with Milton Sublet, and his twenty men. I have been unreasonably blamed for leaving my kinsman beyond the Rocky Mountains with only eleven of his company, and that too when we were within about four hundred miles of the mouth of the Columbia, <u>alias</u> Oregon river, where it pours into the <u>boisterous</u> Pacific Ocean, for such Lewis and Clarke found it to their cost.[20]

To which Nathaniel Wyeth countered in his journal:

I remained at this encampment until the 17th during which time all my men but 11 left me to these I gave such articles as I could spare from the necesities of my own Party and let them go. While here I obtained 18 Horses in exchange for those which were worn out and for a few toys such as Beads Bells red and Blue cloth, Powder and Balls fish hooks vermillion old Blanketts We also supplied ourselves with Buffaloe robes we have now a good outfit and here we found plenty of meat which can be had of the Indians for a trifle.[21]

As noted above, Wyeth's party had experienced trouble from early on in the expedition. Granted, Nathaniel was a rather autocratic leader who rankled members of the party. His cousin John was an inexperienced eighteen-year-old clearly not used to being away from his home city. Several of the least satisfied men decided to return east with William Sublette, leaving Nathaniel and eleven others to continue on to the Pacific. Wyeth's brother Jacob and cousin John were two of those who apparently had had enough of wilderness life and went home.

Trapper Zenas Leonard had come to the mountains as a member of the Gantt and Blackwell Company. That enterprise had been reported as insolvent before rendezvous, leaving the men to believe they had no official employer, so several came on to rendezvous in hopes of selling what fur they possessed. Leonard offers this description of the location and the wonder of the scene:

> *There was at this rendezvous at this time, about four hundred white people, who lived in constant intercourse with the flatheads and "Nez Perces," or Pierced Nose tribes, which latter consists of one thousand warriors ... This valley is situated on the river of the same name, and is from seventy to eighty miles in length, with a high mountain on the east and west – each so high that it is impossible to pass over them, and is from eight to ten miles wide. The river runs immediately through the centre, with a beautiful grove of timber along either bank; from this timber to the mountain, a distance of four or five miles, there is nothing but a smooth plain. This meadow or prairie is so perfectly level that a person may look up or down as far as the eye will reach without meeting any thing to obstruct the sight, until the earth and sky appear to meet.*[22]

Rocky Mountain Fur Company trapper Robert Newell, in his concise manner, said:

> *Met all hunters of these parts Vanderberg Drips & Co with about 175 men   William Sublette arived with Supplies for our Camp   Mr fitzpatrick who was with Sublette left to come to us but was chased by the indians and Detained and Just escaped death [to] come to us   this is to be Remembered to be the largest party of whites ever Seen together north west or west of the yellow stones mouth or even thare except our American troops (aug 1832) up to the above date   I think our number to exceed 350 but not much but in all whites and indians all sorts*

> *and kinds of men about 600, (a [s]crimmage with the Black-*
> *feet-) Into Rondezvous got our Supplies and Scatterd in the*
> *following courses to our profession Wm Sublette to the States*
> *with the Returns*[23]

Newell's "scrimmage with the Black-feet" is understated. What has become known as the Battle of Pierre's Hole is perhaps the most famous episode of the Rocky Mountain fur trade. The details of that encounter are covered in the next chapter.

A diverse group indeed gathered that summer in Teton Valley.[24] Competition for fur in the Rockies reached its highest pitch as trappers converged for the eighth annual rendezvous. Rocky Mountain Fur Company fielded about one hundred men while American Fur Company showed up with around ninety mountaineers. The Gantt and Blackwell Company, though bankrupt, was still represented by about twenty-two now independent trappers. The Bean and Sinclair outfit was manned by about fifteen. Wyeth led about a dozen greenhorns. William Sublette's supply train was staffed by around eighty-five men. This makes a total of about 325 non-native people in the Basin. With 120 lodges of Nez Perce and about eighty lodges of Flathead anxious to trade for the Americans' goods, the Indian presence far outnumbered the whites – probably close to 1,500 native men, women and children.

Camps were spread over many miles within the valley. The exact locations are not known and little detail is provided in the first-hand accounts, though according to John Ball, camps stretched out in about a five mile radius. RMFC was host for the event and its camp was close to the center of the valley. Ferris indicates RMFC "encamped about a mile from us." Once Sublette arrived with the trade goods, his merchandise certainly became the center of attention.

Some writers have placed the site of Sublette's camp on Teton Creek, which was called Beaver Creek by the trappers, just south of the modern town of Driggs, Idaho. However, from the few specifics available, it was likely a little farther east up Teton Creek, closer to the base of the mountain. In all probability, RMFC camps filled the glade between Teton and Spring creeks, spilling across the grassy regions on both sides of these streams. This conclusion is based on the numerous eyewitness reports that brigades leaving rendezvous went "southwest" before climbing over a pass out of the valley. Camping farther up Teton Creek makes the compass bear more southwest at the time of departure. Nathaniel Wyeth put the base camp ten miles from the bottom of the pass, indicating his company may have been a bit farther up the creek. Since RMFC was already in the valley when AFC arrived from the north, Ferris and his companions probably stopped on the north side of Teton Creek, roughly a mile from RMFC.

Many authors have speculated on the positions of the Indian camps, but the only reference to them in primary sources stated that the tribes had "lodges along all the streams."[25] B. W. Driggs reported, "Leigh Creek was called Indian Creek by the trappers, it being the favorite Indian camping place and rendezvous for hunting trips," though he stops short of saying this is where anyone camped during the 1832 event.[26]

In his *History of Teton Valley*, B. W. Driggs says the camp, according to early settler lore, was

> *at the spring that gushes out of the ground into a flowing stream where the slaughter yards are now situated. It was a little southwest of Driggs, where a log house was constructed for storing goods and alcohol, and at that time was like a tented city.*[27]

Oral history records the ruins of a rude cabin, identified by Indians as the rendezvous liquor storehouse, still standing at the big spring just southwest of Driggs, Idaho when the first settlers arrived.[28] Although primary documentation does not include a structure of any kind at either of the two rendezvous held in Pierre's Hole, log constructions at the 1828 and 1838 rendezvous were recorded so the idea of some kind of structure is not out of the question.[29] However, it might easily have been a storage cabin from later inhabitants like the cattle rustlers or horse thieves that frequented the valley in the years between 1840, the end of the fur trade, and the late 1880s, when the settlers arrived.

As for a "tent city," most journals indicate tents were not often used by mountain men. Wyeth, for example, says their party had only two tents. John Ball, tenderfoot that he was, indicated in a letter to his parents from Pierre's Hole that

> *We have a tent that we sometimes pitch, but oftener than otherwise my bed has been a buffalow skin on the ground & small pack under my head, my oald cloak with the cape thrown over my head around me & a blanket over my feet & the havens above, & never have I slept better.*[30]

It is likely Indian and mountain man camps extended from Fox Creek, well below the south end of Driggs, Idaho, north along the east side of the Teton River, perhaps as far as Tetonia, Idaho. Local treasure hunters have found numerous artifacts on both sides of Teton Creek east of the bridge on Idaho State Highway 33, south of Driggs, Idaho.

These relics include tomahawk and axe heads, various bells, lead balls, a few gun parts, awls, fire steels, clay pipes and a selection of knife blades (see photos on next two pages and color plate 11). An exceptional example of a trade silver Jesuit cross was also uncovered.

A remarkable assortment of glass trade beads, including small "Hudson's Bay white hearts," large "Cornaline d'Aleppo," "Padres" and a variety of chevrons in a myriad of sizes have also been dug up, along with pony and pound beads and other Venetian beads. "Russian" faceted beads in several colors, sand cast beads, bone hair pipes and several abalone buttons have also been picked up. Two strands were found still strung on sinew, and a leather-wrapped bundle of various colored beads was unearthed, though the buckskin was crusty and crumbling (see color plates 12 and 13).

With the number of horses present, keeping the various herds separated and supplied with ample feed for the duration of the rendezvous must have been a challenge. But it is easy to visualize camps along both side of Fox, Darby, Spring, Leigh and Teton creeks where there would have been water, fuel and grass in the flats between streams. It is doubtful there were any camps on the west side of the Teton River as it would have meant repeated crossings to get in on the action of rendezvous.

As noted in the journal accounts, the AFC men were anxiously awaiting a shipment of merchandise from their own company. These

The photos on this page and the next, as well as color plates 11-13, demonstrate some of the artifacts collected by Jim and Debbie Wood of Rigby, Idaho along Teton Creek in Pierre's Hole. The top photo includes a variety of bells, knife blades, bone buttons, lead shot, and a fire steel. At left is a Jesuit cross fashioned of trade silver. The items are believed to be remnants of rendezvous trade goods. JIM HARDEE PHOTOS

181

Possible rendezvous artifacts collected along Teton Creek in Pierre's Hole include belt buckles, a beaver trap pan, gun parts, metal arrow heads, and knife blades. JIM HARDEE PHOTOS

goods had come up the Missouri River by steamboat as far as Fort Union. Lucien Fontenelle was to bring the goods to Pierre's Hole but unfortunately the steamboat "Yellowstone" was late arriving at the fort. The boat finally made it to Fort Union on May 31, and by June 6, Fontenelle was packed and ready to head west with "40 and odd men ... with 110 or 15 Horses," according to fort records.[31] But the delay cost him dearly as he never made it to Pierre's Hole. He missed the rendezvous altogether.[32]

Yet all the mountaineers, including those in the American Fur Company, purchased equipment and supplies for the coming trapping season. Independent trader Robert Campbell kept busy, and many of his sales receipts still exist to provide a few examples of the items traded and the variety of transactions (see next two pages).

182

John Gray

July 17th To .... I powder Horn.. 5.00

6 Bunches small Beads 150........................ 5.00

I " white Beads.. 3.00

" Green Beads.. 3.00............ 22.00

"   By 51/2 Beaver Furr..4$............. 22.00

To 2 Cakes Shaving Soap............................ 1.00

Robert Newell

July 17 To .... I Powder Horn.................................... 5.00 ....5.00

Cr

By amt Charged to N Provo 5.00

1832 Madam Pierre[33]

July 17 To .... [?] " Beads...1.50

" 5 Bunches Garnishing Beads.................. 8.00

" Blanket Saddle.. 5.00............$14.50

Thomma Pierre

7 cups sugar}

5 " coffee}

2 cakes Soap}..25.00

½ Beads...2.50

                                                                                           $42.00

By Amount assumed by Dripps................................ 42.00

1832 Narcissa Provo[34]

July 17 To .... I powder Horn... 5.00

" I fine Comb.. 1.00

" 4 Bunches Blue Beads 4$...................... 16.00

" 2 " fine Garnishing 150............................ 3.00

" 2 " white & Blue 1$ .... 2.00............ 27.00

" I Blk Silk Hdkf 3.00

                                                                                           $30.00

By Mr Sublette..3.00

                                                                                           $27.00

To Amt assumed for Doctor 5.00

                                                                                           $32.00

By assumpsit Rocky Mountain 30.00

Profit & Loss... $2.00

1832 Fontenelle & Dripps

July 21 To amt of 8 cups Sugar & 6 cups coffee }

" to Grand Eneas per verbal order } 28.00

" " Baptist Nor[?]uest 6 cups sugar 6 cups coffee 24.00

" " Thomma Pierre 70.00

" " Horse Shoes to Palo on Seedskerdie 5.00

127.00

" " to amt Baptiste Iroquois account 40.00

" " Thomma & Madam Pierre 42.00

27 " amt for John Gray (Bridle) 15.00

Thomas Fitzpatrick

To Paley Philosophy 2.25

" 4 Books 1$ 4.00

" 2 Hdkfs 2$ 4.00

" 1 port Folio paper cutter &c 4.00

Dr.	The Rockey Mountain Furr Co		

1832

July 12 To .... 1 Blue Blanket to Fraeb $18.00

" " " .... 1 pr Socks " Do ....2.00 ....20.00

" " " .... 1 powder Horn to Antoine Goodin 5.00

" 17 " .... Beads per verbal order Do Do .... 10.00 .... 15.00

2 coarse & 2 fine combs Do 1$ 4.00

2 Bunches Garnishing Beads (Milton) 3.00

1 Blk Silk Hdkf (Fraeb) .... 3.00 ....

1 fine & 1 coarse comb (to Mytingor) ..... 2.00 ....8.00

47.00

" " " .... 1 Gun Lock to Hockaday 15.00

" 21 " .... Beads to Phillipson 4.00

" 22 " .... " " Hockaday 4.00

" 23 " .... 1 fine & 1 coarse comb (to Robinson) 2.00

66.00

To amt of Provo's account   30.00

$96.00[35]

The 1832 Rendezvous in Pierre's Hole saw substantial maneuvering among the fur trade companies. With the competition heating, RMFC made an attempt to divide the trapping grounds between itself and the AFC. However, AFC had been rapidly learning the ropes of the beaver trade by dogging the trail of RMFC trappers – a tactic not appreciated by the RMFC. AFC declined the offer to split up the territory.

Meanwhile, William Sublette, acting as an independent agent, struck a canny business arrangement with the RMFC partners. On July 25, 1832, Sublette sat down with the company primaries and signed a contract making him their main supplier. It begins:

> *Articles and Agreement made and entered into on the Teton Fork of the Columbia River and under the Three Teton mountains this Twenty fifth day of July in the Year One Thousand Eight Hundred and Thirty Two, by and between William L. Sublette of the first part and Thomas Fitzpatrick Milton G. Sublette John Baptiste Jarvie James Bridger and Henry Fraeb trading under the name and Style of the Rockey Mountain Furr Co. of the Second part.*[36]

The formal agreement lined out the unpaid balance on the invoice for merchandise delivered to Pierre's Hole, the cost of transporting the RMFC furs back to St. Louis, the remaining principle and interest on various notes payable, the quantity of beaver and other furs Sublette was to transport, etc. This contract was totally in favor of the party of the first part, putting William Sublette in position to virtually control the fur company. He had been the main supplier for this year's rendezvous and was guaranteed next year's business as well.[37]

Interestingly, Sublette renewed his fur trade license in St. Louis prior to his departure for the Rockies. By law, he was allowed to take whiskey for his boatmen to the tune of 450 gallons, but had to post a bond not to sell whiskey to the Indians. However, Sublette took his caravan of horses and mules along an overland route to the Pierre's Hole rendezvous, and thus did not require the use of boatmen. The whiskey was obviously for illegal trade.[38]

Sublette set out for St. Louis from Teton Valley on July 30 with 169 packs of fur. He traveled back over Teton Pass and ascended the

Gros Ventre River to Union Pass. Descending Wind River, in due course he hit the Sweetwater which he followed down to the Platte, eventually arriving in St. Louis on October 3.[39] There he received $4.25 per pound on the beaver skins. RMFC's 13,719 pounds of beaver brought in $58,305.75. The company's debts, delineated in the agreement made "under the Three Teton mountains" and mostly owed to Sublette, totaled $46,751.13. The nearly $12,000 of gross profit was eaten up rapidly – $7,000 alone would go to transportation costs. Charges for cleaning and packaging, insurance, dealer commissions and interest would leave RMFC still in debt to Sublette to the tune of $5,400. Such a weighty balance due was exactly the sort of control Sublette wanted over the company.[40]

Rendezvous 1832 was probably the most important rendezvous ever held. It had the highest attendance of both trappers and Indians. The intermingling of so many important fur trade personalities impacted the future of the industry by shaping several key transactions as competition grew between the various commercial concerns. Fitzpatrick's remarkable adventure also added to the event's legendary nature. One has to wonder whether the men who recorded their observations might have been aware of the momentousness of this gathering.

14
THE BATTLE OF PIERRE'S HOLE

The most significant event at the 1832 rendezvous was undoubtedly the battle that occurred on July 18 between trappers and Indians as the various camps were breaking up to begin the fall hunt. A remarkable number of primary sources tell the story, perhaps more than for any other single incident in fur trade history. Eleven trapper journals, several letters and one oral interview provide first-hand information about this encounter. But, as with many eye witness reports, there are great discrepancies among the assorted versions. Several historians have attempted to distill these accounts into a coherent chain of events, but there is so much disagreement in the details that an irrefutable analysis is virtually impossible.[1]

A few trappers reported that the Indian antagonists were Blackfoot. However, it is clear from other mountaineers that the adversary was actually the Gros Ventres of the Prairie. Sometimes called Atsina, they were considered a band of the Blackfeet Confederacy, along with the Bloods, Piegans, Blackfoot and Sarsi. Since the Gros Ventre language is difficult, they often spoke to strangers in the Blackfoot tongue, which might have obscured their identity in Pierre's Hole. The Gros Ventres referred to themselves as A'ani or "White Clay People" and did not use the Atsina designation.[2]

The French translation of *Gros Ventre* is Big Belly, a mis-interpretation of tribal hand signs for the numerous waterfalls in their lands. Some Canadian tribes called them the Falls or Rapids people due to these same cascades on the Saskatchewan River.[3] The A'ani, or Gros Ventres of the Prairie, should not be confused with the Gros Ventres of the River, better known as the Hidatsa. These people lived along the Missouri River.

At the time of the Pierre's Hole clash, this band of Gros Ventres was returning from a lengthy sojourn, perhaps as long as six years, with Arapahoe relatives in what is now southern Colorado. They appear to have gone to visit their cousins in the late 1820s.[4] Gros Ventre tradition attributes this migration to Old Bald Eagle, a chief whose wife had run off with a young brave. Old Bald Eagle was so filled with longing he convinced the entire tribe to follow the runaways to the Arapahos, where they had taken asylum. This trip was referred to as "the return to their people," because the Gros Ventres stayed there for several years. Several bands, including those led by Bear Tooth, Elk Tongue and Iron Robe, went south to visit their cousins at about the same time.[5]

The band was certainly along the Arkansas River in 1831 when it attacked Santa Fe-bound caravans. Josiah Gregg reported such an encounter and also related that William Sublette

narrowly escaped a total destruction. They had fallen in with that immense horde of Blackfeet and Gros Ventres, with whom we afterward met, and, as the traders were literally but a handful among their thousands, they fancied themselves for awhile in imminent peril of being virtually "eaten up."[6]

Gregg credited the wagon train's lack of serious molestation to Sublette's considerable experience with "treacherous savages."

According to tribal history, 1832 was a rough year for the tribe. Shortly after the Pierre's Hole battle, the Gros Ventres had a disastrous run-in with the Crow. The year's ominous events had begun during their extended visit with the Arapahoe. The Gros Ventres had traded extensively with Mexicans. One Gros Ventre chief wanted all the goods and killed an Araphoe leader in the ensuing quarrel. A clash erupted, but was soon quelled and the Gros Ventres headed north to their homelands shortly thereafter.[7] Some of their close Arapahoe relatives accompanied them.

Normally, the route would have taken the band in a more easterly direction, through the Big Horn River area, but a clash with the Crow pushed the Gros Ventres to the west, into the Green River drainage. They crossed the path of Sublette's supply caravan in early July. Sublette described a skirmish with three hundred Indians that lasted almost an hour. Before the warriors withdrew, they had five of Sublette's horses in tow and had left several animals dead.[8] This same band of Gros Ventres harassed Thomas Fitzpatrick as described in several of the previous rendezvous accounts.

The homeward-bound Gros Ventres, led by their chief, Biahoh, met the trappers head-on in Pierre's Hole on the morning of July 18, 1832. An unfortunate incident led to a brief exchange of gunfire with a trapping brigade heading southwest out of the valley. The White Clay band fell back into a grove of cottonwoods along a creek and built fortifications from downed logs. Reinforcements from the main trapper camp arrived and laid siege to the Indian stronghold. A long afternoon of battle brought fatalities to both sides. Death tolls range in various accounts from three to twelve on the trappers' side and nine to fifty Gros Ventres killed. During the night, the Gros Ventres slipped away.

Following are accounts of the battle and related events presented in alphabetical order according to the writer's surname.

John Ball

John Ball was a member of Nathaniel Wyeth's expedition to the Rockies and was at the battle though he did not take part. He went on to Oregon and became the first teacher in Oregon Country. Ball wrote an autobiography in 1874, his 80th year, working from scant diaries kept at various periods of his life and from old letters sent home, as well as from memory. The manuscript was compiled by his three daughters and was published in 1925. The following are excerpts from Ball's autobiography, diary and letters.

Diary – July 16 [1832] – We twelve moved our camp up the creek towards Vanderburgh, eight miles, with Mr. Frap and Milton Sublette, a brother of Capt. William Sublette, and with twenty-two of their trappers and sixteen independent trappers, including some half-breeds and Indians, hoping to come out somewhere all right. Mr. Frap took the lead. We had a quiet night.

On the following morning, just as we packed, ready for march, we saw a band of Indians in the direction we were to go. Mr. Frap sent an Indian and a half-breed named Antoine to meet them. As they approached, they discovered the Indians were Blackfeet. The chief left the party and came out in a friendly way to meet Antoine and his Indian companion. But Antoine's father had been killed by the Blackfeet; he was going to have his revenge then and there. So he said to the Indian, "I'll appear friendly when we meet, but you watch your chance and shoot him." This he did. Antoine caught his robe or blanket of blue or red, turned and fled to camp. The Blackfeet fired after him, and as he rode into camp he said, "They were Blackfeet. We killed their chief. Here is his robe." We, to our dismay, expected a battle, which we did not like. An express was sent back to Captain Sublette's camp to tell the state of affairs and ask assistance.

The white and Indians returned in great number, Captain Sublette going against the Blackfeet on his own account. The Blackfeet by this time had built a breastwork by the creek, taking their women and horses inside with them.

We had hastily thrown up a breastwork of our saddle. There was a hard fight until sunset. The Indians always lay down on their backs while loading their guns, and sometime fire lying down. The Indians considered the leaden bullet a sort of thunder and lightening death, and the whites did not think the parbed arrows any better. At sundown we retired and encamped. A Mr. Sinclair died of his wounds that night. During the battle I was left in charge of the horses and camp and took care of the wounded.

The next night we returned to the rendezvous, and in the horse pen buried Mr. Sinclair. Mr. Wm. Sublette was wounded. There were eight whites and as many friendly Indians killed, and some others wounded. After breakfast we visited the enemy's camp and found some twenty-five dead horses and two dead women. There were ten scalps taken by our Indians from the blackfeet. We concluded that the reason they had left their dead was because there was not enough of them left to carry them off.

This affair detained us three days. We buried all the dead in the horse pen, as the ground was so well trodden they couldn't be found. They would, we knew, be sought for their scalps.

The wounded were carried on stretchers to Sublette's camp. A bier was made by suspending trees covered with blankets between two horses, one in front of the other.

July 24 — We quit camp, going south by the battleground of the eighteenth; got but ten miles along. The next day was showery, but we traveled to the south. Vegetation was forward, especially flax and currants of an orange color.

July 26 — We crossed the Lewis River in the bull boat, where Fort Hall now is.[9]

Excerpts from a January 1, 1833 letter written at Fort Vancouver to Dr. T. C. Brinsmade *— We stoped at the place where I last wrote you, in the mountains, till the 24th of July, during which time a skirmish took place between the whites and friendly Indians and a party of the Black feet Indians. It lasted the most part of a day, the Black feet having fortified themselves in some timber nigh a creek. We were about a mile distant during the action, being prohibited from our immediate Captain from joining, so I took no other part, than to assist in taking care of the wounded and guarding our own camp. The result was that the whites & their friends retreated at approach of night with 7 killed or mortally wounded and as many Indians, the enemy, they supposed demolished, there probably not being more than fifty of them, tho' but ten scalps were taken and 32 horses killed. the whole appeared to me a needless and rash affray, for the Blackfeet wished to avoid the engagement. Twelve of our party (the rest chusing to return or to trap in the mountains,) started on our journey in company with 40 trapers, first 40 or 50 miles S. across the Lewis river.*[10]

Autobiography *— Many of Mr. Wyeth's men had long before they got here become disheartened and disgusted, but they could not stop or return alone. But now they decided to return with Mr. Sublette's party. And all decided to go no farther, except twelve. For myself I never turned my face back for a moment and resolved to go on, if it was in the company of the Nez Pierces whose country was down near the mouth of the Lewis river. But a Mr. Frapp and Milton Sublette with a trapping party of Sublette's men were to go off trapping somewhere west-ward, so we resolved to go on, joined their party of some forty* *whites, half-breeds and Indians, and so keep on, thinking some way to bring out rightly.*

Mr. Sublette had come out with arms, ammunition, traps, etc., for his business and new men to take the places of those whose term of service had expired, so there was much fixing up to sort out the parties for the different purposes. And our party of trappers under Mr. Frapp one afternoon left the main camp and went out some seven or eight miles and encamped on a prairie near some timber on a little creek, as usually there is timber on the streams and mountainsides.

We had a quiet night but in the morning, as we were about to commence our day's march, Indians were seen in line of march on horseback off across the prairie, say some two miles. And the trappers at once decided they must see who they were. So Frapp told Antoine, the half-breed, to take a good horse and have an Indian of the party go with him and go out and see who they were. As Antoine approached them he saw they were Blackfeet, and their chief left his party and came out in a friendly way to meet him. But his father having been killed by the Blackfeet, he was going to have his revenge. So he said to his companion, "I will appear to be friendly when we meet, but you watch your chance and shoot him." His plan was carried out. He was shot down. Antoine caught his robe, a square of blue and scarlet cloth, and turned and the Blackfeet fired after him, when they saw his treachery. He escaped and came into our camp, said they were Blackfeet, and that he had killed their chief and there was his robe in evidence.

"All right" they said, "they would play friendly now but at night attack our camp." But we twelve could not appreciate the reasoning. But here we were in the company that thus decided. But as we watched to see what they would next do they seemed at first to break up and scatter, but soon we saw that a large band, the warriors, seemed coming directly towards us to make fight. So we immediately tied our horses to bushes near and put up our saddles as a kind of breastwork but before they reached us, they

turned off into some timber on a stream, built a kind of fort of logs, bushes, their saddles and blankets, as a shade if we attacked them, and took their horses into the fort with them.

Fight with the Blackfeet – *The moment that Antoine gave the information that they were Blackfeet, an express flew off back to the old camp to tell we had met the enemy, and in the time, it seemed to me, that race horses could have hardly gone over the ground, some of Sublette's men and the friendly Indians came rushing into our camp inquiring where were the Blackfeet. And on soon finding where they had fortified themselves, each white or Indian, as he felt that his gun was right, and all things ready for his part, would start off. And so they went helter skelter, each on his own hook to fight the common enemy. For the friendly Indians had their own wrongs to avenge. As they thus almost singly approached their brush and saddle fort, they could only see the defences whereas, they, the Blackfeet, could see everyone who approached them. They soon shot down some of the trappers and Flatheads, for the timber was not large enough to shelter a man. And soon wounded men were brought back to our camp.*

We twelve Yankees felt that we had no men to spare to be killed or wounded, that we were not called upon to go out of the way to find danger, but had they attacked our camp, we should have taken our full part, to save ourselves and horses. But we readily assisted in taking care of the wounded and in other ways aid, as far as we felt belonged to us. They kept up a firing at them at, a safer distance, but did not rout them. Six trappers and as many friendly Indians were killed or mortally wounded. And as night approached it was determined to retreat. And the whites took a wounded man on a horse, others riding each side to hold him up. The Indians fixed long fills to a horse letting the ends draw on the smooth ground and fixed onto them a kind of hurdle, onto which they laid the wounded and drew them off easily over the smooth prairie. A better way than ours.

When night came on we encamped in the best manner of defence we could, and the next day expecting surely an attack from them, built a high fence and strong pen for our horses in such case, and a guard on the open prairie to run them in if attacked, and then awaited the result. Their fort was finally visited and a number of dead horses found. But of course they had secreted any men they lost from scalping. We did not go back so far as the old camp.

Buried the Dead – *The man who died in our camp we buried in the horse pen where the ground was so trodden that the enemy could not find the body to scalp it. Another badly wounded was sent to Sublette's camp on a bier suspended between two horses, one ahead of the other. And when we found that the enemy was not near, after a few days, we took up our line of march as originally intended. And after two or three days reached the main Lewis river.*[11]

Benjamin Bonneville

Benjamin Bonneville, a U.S. Army captain on leave from the military, tried his hand in the fur trade. He may have been on a military reconnaissance mission in the Rocky Mountains during this outing, though solid proof is lacking. Washington Irving used a manuscript written by Bonneville to compose *The Adventures of Captain Bonneville,* published in 1837, from which the following account is excerpted. Bonneville was camped on Green River during the rendezvous and the battle in Pierre's Hole. The information credited to him is hearsay, but two of his informants were Robert Campbell and William Sublette, who ran into Bonneville on their way back to St. Louis from the 1832 rendezvous. The account has been dramatized by Irving, thus, there are numerous details that are suspect, particularly when compared to what Campbell and Sublette report.[12]

On the 17th of July, a small brigade of fourteen trappers, led by Milton Sublette, brother of the captain, set out with the intention of proceeding to the southwest. They were accompanied by Sinclair and his fifteen free trappers; Wyeth, also, and his New England band of beaver hunters and salmon fishers, now dwindled down to eleven, took this opportunity to prosecute their cruise in the wilderness, accompanied with such experienced pilots. On the first day, they proceeded about eight miles to the southeast, and encamped for the night, still in the valley of Pierre's Hole. On the following morning, just as they were raising their camp, they observed a long line of people pouring down a defile of the mountains. They at first supposed them to be Fontenelle and his party, whose arrival had been daily expected. Wyeth, however, reconnoitered them with a spy-glass, and soon perceived they were Indians. They were divided into two parties, forming, in the whole, about one hundred and fifty persons, men, women, and children. Some were on horseback, fantastically painted and arrayed, with scarlet blankets fluttering in the wind. The greater part, however, were on foot. They had perceived the trappers before they were themselves discovered, and came down yelling and whooping into the plain. On nearer approach, they were ascertained to be Blackfeet.

One of the trappers of Sublette's brigade, a half-breed named Antoine Godin, now mounted his horse, and rode forth as if to hold a conference. He was the son of an Iroquois hunter, who had been cruelly murdered by the Blackfeet at a small stream below the mountains, which still bears his name. In company with Antoine rode forth a Flathead Indian, whose once powerful tribe had been completely broken down in their wars with the Blackfeet. Both of them, therefore, cherished the most vengeful hostility against these marauders of the mountains. The Blackfeet came to a halt. One of the chiefs advanced singly and unarmed, bearing the pipe of peace. This overture was certainly pacific; but Antoine and the Flathead were predisposed to hostility, and pretended to consider it a treacherous movement.

"Is your piece charged?" said Antoine to his red companion.

"It is."

"Then cock it, and follow me."

They met the Blackfoot chief half way, who extended his hand in friendship. Antoine grasped it.

195

"Fire!" cried he.

The Flathead levelled his piece, and brought the Blackfoot to the ground. Antoine snatched off his scarlet blanket, which was richly ornamented, and galloped off with it as a trophy to the camp, the bullets of the enemy whistling after him. The Indians immediately threw themselves into the edge of a swamp, among willows and cotton-wood trees, interwoven with vines. Here they began to fortify themselves; the women digging a trench, and throwing up a breastwork of logs and branches, deep hid in the bosom of the wood, while the warriors skirmished at the edge to keep the trappers at bay.

The latter took their station in a ravine in front, whence they kept up a scattering fire. As to Wyeth, and his little band of "downeasters," they were perfectly astounded by this second specimen of life in the wilderness; the men, being especially unused to bush-fighting and the use of the rifle, were at a loss how to proceed. Wyeth, however, acted as a skilful commander. He got all his horses into camp and secured them; then, making a breastwork of his packs of goods, he charged his men to remain in garrison, and not to stir out of their fort. For himself, he mingled with the other leaders, determined to take his share in the conflict.

In the meantime, an express had been sent off to the rendezvous for reinforcements. Captain Sublette, and his associate, Campbell, were at their camp when the express came galloping across the plain, waving his cap, and giving the alarm; "Blackfeet! Blackfeet! a fight in the upper part of the valley! – to arms! to arms!"

The alarm was passed from camp to camp. It was a common cause. Every one turned out with horse and rifle. The Nez Percés and Flatheads joined. As fast as horseman could arm and mount he galloped off; the valley was soon alive with white men and red men scouring at full speed.

Sublette ordered his men to keep to the camp, being recruits from St. Louis, and unused to Indian warfare. He and his friend Campbell prepared for action. Throwing off their coats, rolling up their sleeves, and arming themselves with pistols and rifles, they mounted their horses and dashed forward among the first. As they rode along, they made their wills in soldier-like style; each stating how his effects should be disposed of in case of his death, and appointing the other his executor.

The Blackfeet warriors had supposed the brigade of Milton Sublette all the foes they had to deal with, and were astonished to behold the whole valley suddenly swarming with horsemen, galloping to the field of action. They withdrew into their fort, which was completely hid from sight in the dark and tangled wood. Most of their women and children had retreated to the mountains. The trappers now sallied forth and approached the swamp, firing into the thickets at random; the Blackfeet had a better sight at their adversaries, who were in the open field, and a half-breed was wounded in the shoulder.

When Captain Sublette arrived, he urged to penetrate the swamp and storm the fort, but all hung back in awe of the dismal horrors of the place, and the danger of attacking such desperadoes in their savage den. The very Indian allies, though accustomed to bush-fighting, regarded it as almost impenetrable, and full of frightful danger. Sublette was not to be turned from his purpose, but offered to lead the way into the swamp. Campbell stepped forward to accompany him. Before entering the perilous wood, Sublette took his brothers aside, and told them that in case he fell, Campbell, who knew his will, was to be his executor. This done, he grasped his rifle and pushed into the thickets, followed by Campbell. Sinclair, the partisan from Arkansas, was at the edge of the wood with his brother and a few of his men. Excited by the gallant example of the two friends, he pressed forward to share their dangers.

The swamp was produced by the labors of the beaver, which, by damming up a stream, had inundated a portion of the valley.

The place was all overgrown with woods and thickets, so closely matted and entangled that it was impossible to see ten paces ahead, and the three associates in peril had to crawl along, one after another, making their way by putting the branches and vines aside; but doing it with caution, lest they should attract the eye of some lurking marksman. They took the lead by turns, each advancing about twenty yards at a time, and now and then hallooing to their men to follow. Some of the latter gradually entered the swamp, and followed a little distance in their rear.

They had now reached a more open part of the wood, and had glimpses of the rude fortress from between the trees. It was a mere breastwork, as we have said, of logs and branches, with blankets, buffalo robes, and the leathern covers of lodges, extended round the top as a screen. The movements of the leaders, as they groped their way, had been descried by the sharp-sighted enemy. As Sinclair, who was in the advance, was putting some branches aside, he was shot through the body. He fell on the spot. "Take me to my brother," said he to Campbell. The latter gave him in charge to some of the men, who conveyed him out of the swamp.

Sublette now took the advance. As he was reconnoitring the fort, he perceived an Indian peeping through an aperture. In an instant his rifle was levelled and discharged, and the ball struck the savage in the eye. While he was reloading, he called to Campbell, and pointed out to him the hole; "Watch that place," said he, "and you will soon have a fair chance for a shot." Scarce had he uttered the words, when a ball struck him in the shoulder, and almost wheeled him around. His first thought was to take hold of his arm with his other hand, and move it up and down. He ascertained, to his satisfaction, that the bone was not broken. The next moment he was so faint that he could not stand. Campbell took him in his arms and carried him out of the thicket. The same shot that struck Sublette wounded another man in the head.

A brisk fire was now opened by the mountaineers from the wood, answered occasionally from the fort. Unluckily, the trappers and their allies, in searching for the fort, had got scattered, so that Wyeth, and a number of Nez Percés, approached the fort on the northwest side, while others did the same on the opposite quarter. A cross-fire thus took place, which occasionally did mischief to friends as well as foes. An Indian was shot down, close to Wyeth, by a ball which, he was convinced, had been sped from the rifle of a trapper on the other side of the fort.

The number of whites and their Indian allies had by this time so much increased by arrivals from the rendezvous, that the Blackfeet were completely overmatched. They kept doggedly in their fort, however, making no offer of surrender. An occasional firing into the breastwork was kept up during the day. Now and then, one of the Indian allies, in bravado, would rush up to the fort, fire over the ramparts, tear off a buffalo robe or a scarlet blanket, and return with it in triumph to his comrades. Most of the savage garrison that fell, however, were killed in the first part of the attack.

At one time it was resolved to set fire to the fort; and the squaws belonging to the allies were employed to collect combustibles. This however, was abandoned: the Nez Percés being unwilling to destroy the robes and blankets, and other spoils of the enemy, which they felt sure would fall into their hands.

The Indians, when fighting, are prone to taunt and revile each other. During one of the pauses of the battle, the voice of the Blackfeet chief was heard.

"So long," said he, "as we had powder and ball, we fought you in the open field: when those were spent, we retreated here to die with our women and children. You may burn us in our fort; but, stay by our ashes, and you who are so hungry for fighting will soon have enough. There are four hundred lodges of our brethren at hand. They will soon be here — their arms are strong — their hearts are big — they will avenge us!"

This speech was translated two or three times by Nez Percé and creole interpreters. By the time it was rendered into English, the chief was made to say that four hundred lodges of his tribe were attacking the encampment at the other end of the valley. Every one now was for hurrying to the defence of the rendezvous. A party was left to keep watch upon the fort; the rest galloped off to the camp. As night came on, the trappers drew out of the swamp, and remained about the skirts of the wood. By morning, their companions returned from the rendezvous with the report that all was safe. As the day opened, they ventured within the swamp and approached the fort. All was silent. They advanced up to it without opposition. They entered: it had been abandoned in the night, and the Blackfeet had effected their retreat, carrying off their wounded on litters made of branches, leaving bloody traces on the herbage. The bodies of ten Indians were found within the fort; among them the one shot in the eye by Sublette. The Blackfeet afterward reported that they had lost twenty-six warriors in this battle. Thirty-two horses were likewise found killed; among them were some of those recently carried off from Sublette's party, in the night; which showed that these were the very savages that had attacked him. They proved to be an advance party of the main body of Blackfeet, which had been upon the trail of Sublette's party. Five white men and one half-breed were killed, and several wounded. Seven of the Nez Percés were also killed, and six wounded. They had an old chief, who was reputed as invulnerable. In the course of the action he was hit by a spent ball, and threw up blood; but his skin was unbroken. His people were now fully convinced that he was proof against powder and ball.

A striking circumstance is related as having occurred the morning after the battle. As some of the trappers and their Indian allies were approaching the fort through the woods, they beheld an Indian woman, of noble form and features, leaning against a tree. Their surprise at her lingering here alone, to fall into the hands of her enemies, was dispelled, when they saw the corpse of a warrior at her feet. Either she was so lost in grief as not to perceive their approach; or a proud spirit kept her silent and motionless. The Indians set up a yell, on discovering her, and before the trappers could interfere, her mangled body fell upon the corpse which she had refused to abandon. We have heard this anecdote discredited by one of the leaders who had been in the battle: but the fact may have taken place without his seeing it, and been concealed from him. It is an instance of female devotion, even to the death, which we are well disposed to believe and to record.

After the battle, the brigade of Milton Sublette, together with the free trappers, and Wyeth's New England band, remained some days at the rendezvous, to see if the main body of Blackfeet intended to make an attack; nothing of the kind occurring, they once more put themselves in motion, and proceeded on their route toward the southwest. Captain Sublette having distributed his supplies, had intended to set off on his return to St. Louis, taking with him the peltries collected from the trappers and Indians. His wound, however obliged him to postpone his departure ...

That hardy leader, as soon as he could bear the journey, set out on his return to St. Louis, accompanied by Campbell. As they had a number of pack-horses richly laden with peltries to convoy, they chose a different route through the mountains, out of the way, as they hoped, of the lurking bands of Blackfeet. They succeeded in making the frontier in safety. We remember to have seen them with their band, about two or three months afterward, passing through a skirt of woodland in the upper part of Missouri. Their long cavalcade stretched in single file for nearly half a mile. Sublette still wore his arm in a sling. The mountaineers in their rude hunting dresses, armed with rifles and roughly mounted, and leading their pack-horses down a hill of the forest, looked like banditti returning with plunder. On the top of some of the packs were perched several half-breed children, perfect little imps, with wild black eyes glaring from among elf locks. These, I was told, were children of the trappers; pledges of love from their squaw spouses in the wilderness.

The Blackfeet warriors, when they effected their midnight retreat from their wild fastness in Pierre's Hole, fell back into the valley of the Seeds-ke-dee, or Green River where they joined the main body of their band. The whole force amounted to several hundred fighting men, gloomy and exasperated by their late disaster. They had with them their wives and children, which incapacitated them from any bold and extensive enterprise of a warlike nature; but when, in the course of their wanderings they came in sight of the encampment of Fontenelle, who had moved some distance up Green River valley in search of the free trappers, they put up tremendous war-cries, and advanced fiercely as if to attack it. Second thoughts caused them to moderate their fury. They recollected the severe lesson just received, and could not but remark the strength of Fontenelle's position; which had been chosen with great judgment.

A formal talk ensued. The Blackfeet said nothing of the late battle, of which Fontenelle had as yet received no accounts; the latter, however, knew the hostile and perfidious nature of these savages, and took care to inform them of the encampment of Captain Bonneville, that they might know there were more white men in the neighborhood.

The conference ended, Fontenelle sent a Delaware Indian of his party to conduct fifteen of the Blackfeet to the camp of Captain Bonneville. There was at that time two Crow Indians in the captain's camp, who had recently arrived there. They looked with dismay at this deputation from their implacable enemies, and gave the captain a terrible character of them, assuring him that the best thing he could possibly do, was to put those Blackfeet deputies to death on the spot. The captain, however, who had heard nothing of the conflict at Pierre's Hole, declined all compliance with this sage counsel. He treated the grim warriors with his usual urbanity. They passed some little time at the camp; saw, no doubt, that everything was conducted with military skill and vigilance; and that such an enemy was not to be easily surprised, nor to be molested with impunity, and then departed, to report all that they had seen to their comrades.[13]

Robert Campbell

Shortly after the 1832 rendezvous, Robert Campbell became the business partner of William Sublette, transporting supplies to trappers in the Rocky Mountains. He grew to be an influential businessman in St. Louis. From the trappers' gathering in Pierre's Hole, Campbell wrote a letter to his brother, Hugh. He began the letter the day after Milton Sublette led a band of trappers south to prepare for the fall hunt – the day of the battle. His writing was interrupted by the call to arms, then resumed once he came off the battlefield. This is the freshest account of the encounter. In 1870, Campbell dictated a narrative of his life. An excerpt about the battle follows the letter.

Letter to Hugh Campbell

LEWIS' FORK, July 18th, 1832.
<u>*A tributary of Columbia river, foot of the Three Teton*</u>
<u>*Mountains*</u> *[all emphases in original].*

DEAR BROTHER,

– A year has nearly elapsed since we parted, and the Fates, – my wayward disposition, – or both combined, have placed us at a distance of some thousand miles from each other. You, in the enjoyment of peace and security; while I, with a small band of hardy trappers, am in the midst of our old enemies the Black Feet Indians – who if they had a chance would take pleasure in "dancing my scalp." Be that as it may, yours is an enviable lot, when compared with mine. You can retire to rest, without apprehensions of midnight alarms; and can walk forth during the day without fear of an assassin: – whilst I am compelled to recline on the "green sward," with the Heavens for a canopy; my arms by my side – and a strong guard keeping watch over our lives and property.

Such are our different situations, and such must they remain for at least another year, when I fervently hope to be enabled to quit forever, a pursuit which has little besides danger and privation connected with it.

Leaving the boundary line of Missouri, our company, consisting in all of about 60 men, proceeded up the Blue river, which empties into the Kanzas; and from thence up the Platte river. Our trip was more prosperous than usual, having taken every precaution which past experience had taught us to provide for every emergency.

We had two steers and fifteen sheep, besides the usual supplies of bacon, meal, flour, &c. to meet our wants, until we reached the Buffalo. In former letters, I told you that this noble, and (to the hunter and Indian) most useful animal, has been gradually retiring from the haunts of civilized men; and is not met with, at any great distance east of the Black hills. To those, who are not amply provided with supplies, the dreary journey from the boundary line to the Buffalo range, must be attended with great danger and privation.

On 11th June we came in view of the Black hills, and since then have never been out of the sight of snow. Our clothing requires to be as warm as yours in the coldest winter. During the last three weeks we have had frost every night, and have frequently encamped by snow banks; yet such a complaint as a cold is unknown among our men!

19th July. – I was yesterday interrupted in describing our route, by the cry of "Black Feet!" – Instantly I threw down my pen, and hastily preparing for a conflict with those savages, I proceeded in the direction pointed out by the express, in company with my friend S. – In Indian warfare, we do not marshall our forces; nor approach the scene of conflict in any regular order. Each person goes "on his own hook," if I may be allowed the expression; and in this way our party, with the exception of a few left in charge of the camp, proceeded down the ravine at full gallop. Mr. S. and I, without being aware of the cause or nature of the approaching contest, felt convinced we were about entering on a perilous engagement, in which one, or both of us might fall.

We therefore briefly directed each other as to the disposition of our property, or in other words, made our wills, appointing each other sole executor. So far as I have known, (and I have known too many instances,) the utmost respect is paid to the disposal of property in this manner, amongst the hunters; – and I question whether the dying wishes of your fellow citizens, – guarded as they are, by salutary laws, – are better, or more correctly fulfilled, than amongst our mountain traders.

On reaching the party that gave the alarm, we found them debating on the propriety of attacking the enemy, who were strongly fortified in a willow swamp about a mile distant. The information derived from our friends, was given in a few sentences; for at such times "our words are few and full of meaning." No one waits to answer questions, and he who has not a quick ear and ready comprehension, must go to the battle without news. We learned that a small party leaving our encampment on the day previous, had suddenly encountered a band of Black Feet warriors – and, that coming to a halt, a parley ensued; our friends sending two half bred Indians to meet the chief of the Black Feet, who rode out in advance. A few signs (for their languages were unknown to each other) soon satisfied the parties of the irreconcilable enmity existing; an enmity that originated on the part of the Black Feet, with the first visit of Lewis and Clarke to this region and continues, unabated to the present day. This interview took place in sight of both whites and Indians. On a signal given, the latter immediately retired to the swamp where they constructed a fortification of logs, hanging their lodge skins around – by way of masked battery – to conceal their position more effectually. Their number was estimated at 250 warriors.

Our force consisted of from 40 to 50 whites – a few half breeds – and two small bands of friendly Indians, from the <u>Pierced Nose</u> and <u>Flat Head</u> tribes. Mr. S.(brave as a lion) addressed a few words to the whites, telling them that the enemy was near, and that if at the commencement of the season we did not show a bold front, our prospects in the mountains would be blasted. He concluded his brief but energetic address, by remarking "and now boys, here are the Black Feet who have killed so many of your companions; – who have probably been prowling around us for several days, waiting a favorable chance of attacking us, when they believed us unprepared; – and who are at this moment daring the <u>palefaces</u> to the onset. Some of us may fall; but we die in a good cause; for whose life or property will be secure if the foe be encouraged by refusing their challenge?" Addressing my old friends the Flat Heads, I told them our determination to assail their enemies, in their strong hold, and that we knew we should have their assistance. Then raising the <u>war whoop</u>, Mr. S. and myself, with about twenty others, dashed off at full speed towards the willows. Drum, fife and trumpet, are as nothing when compared with the effect of the <u>war whoop</u>. The <u>yell,</u> the <u>action</u>, and their effect, perhaps, in banishing reflection for the time being, prepare us better for entering into battle than all the "pomp and circumstance" of the best martial music. On reaching the willows we fastened our horses in a thicket, a short distance above where the Black Feet were fortified. Our little party was then formed in two divisions; one under Mr. M. S. approached along the creek; while Mr. S. his brother A. four other Americans and myself, kept towards where we knew the Indians were waiting for us. We were soon within a few steps of their rude but formidable breastwork – and here "the boldest held his breath for a time." We approached according to the usage in Indian warfare, on our hands and knees; and while in this attitude Mr. S. and myself a little in advance, – a shot from behind the breastwork mortally wounded a brave fellow named St. Clair, who was within two feet of me. Poor fellow! he had a brother in our company, to whom he was greatly attached, and feeling death approach rapidly, he called to us. "I am shot! – oh God – take me to my brother." These were his last words – and we gave immediate directions that they should be obeyed. A few steps further and another of our men, named Phelps, was wounded in the thigh. One of the men was directed to carry him off, and we were thus left within 10 or 15 steps of the fort with only a party of four effective men, opposed to hundreds!

Perhaps you will call it madness to continue an attack under such circumstances; but you must remember that on entering the thicket we expected our example would be followed by more of our men and by the friendly Indians. Even should our course deserve the name of rashness, a retreat would be attended with greater danger than maintaining our ground; for by crawling cautiously along we more effectually avoided the bullets which were now "hailing" around us, than by exposing our backs to an Indian's aim.

We continued to keep up a steady fire, never rising higher than our knee to take aim, and never losing a shot by firing without an object. While thus engaged on one occasion, with my left heel touching the right knee, and taking deliberate aim at a rascal who was peeping out between the lodge skins, a bullet whistled by so near my leg, as to induce the belief that I was wounded. I soon found it was a false alarm, and am since then grateful that my legs are not larger; – for it requires a <u>centre shot</u> to hit there. In the mean time another brave fellow, quickly, received a bullet in his head – gave one spring from where he stood, leaning against Mr. S. and me and fell down a corpse! Either the same ball, or one fired at the same time, struck Mr. S. on the left arm, fracturing the bone, and passing out under the shoulder blade. He remarked that he was wounded, and continued the attack for a short time, but the loss of blood, and thirst which succeeded, obliged him to call on me for assistance.

By this time the Pierced Nose and Flat Head Indians began to join us, and the fire on the Fort became more formidable and deadly. I assisted Mr. S. from the scene to the creek, where I probed the wound, and dressed it as well as the means within reach admitted of. We then made a litter and carried him back to the encampment, where I am happy to say he seems to be recovering.

To return, however, to the field of battle; our men, and the friendly Indians continued the assault from the time we left (late in the afternoon) until dark, without being able to enter the fortress. The Black Feet defended their position (which was well chosen) with obstinate bravery. During the night our men drew off, and took such stations around the spot as to detect the enemy in case of an attempt to escape. Notwithstanding all their precautions, the Black Feet effected a retreat, so quietly that it was not discovered until this morning. I have just returned from the battle field; – the sight was distressing; – two of our brave men were killed – two more are I fear mortally – and four seriously wounded. Of the friendly Indians I saw the bodies of five braves who –

> *"Could lightly wheel the bright claymore,*
> *And send the whistling arrow far:"* –

dressed and painted for burial; and then laid in one grave. Two or three others I am told have died since morning.

The loss of the enemy I am unable to ascertain. You are aware that it is their custom to carry off the slain, when in their power. We found on examination that we had killed 25 of their horses, which were within the enclosure and conjectured from their <u>trail</u> that there was an equal number in killed and wounded amongst their warriors.

In giving these details of an encounter with savages, while the incidents are yet fresh on my memory. I fear I shall only add to your antipathy of the mode of life that <u>necessity</u> and <u>choice</u> have caused me to adopt. To confess the truth I am sick of it. In the course of a few days I hope to begin my return trip to St. Louis – from whence I may give some further details of "Mountain perils."

Yours, &c. &c.[14]

Campbell Narrative

Campbell's second account resulted from reading Washington Irving's version of the Pierre's Hole battle some years later. Instead of feeling flattered by the story in the *Adventures of Captain Bonneville*, Campbell told William Fayel in 1870 that "the account there given on the Blackfeet fight at Pierre's Hole ... was erroneous, and mixed up with incidents that transpired in other encounters." Campbell averred that he "designed to have that account corrected."[15] This is how Campbell then told the story:

We had nearly got through with the exchange of our wares and merchandise with the trappers and Indians, when the camp was disturbed by an Indian alarm. A trapping party had started out preparatory to the fall hunt, and had fallen in with the Blackfeet that had followed our trail, which had become obliterated by the rains and the length of time that had elapsed since we came in. A halfbreed, Antoine Godin, and a Flathead Indian, discovering they were Blackfeet who were always at war, rode up in advance. They were met by a chief who was unarmed, bearing the pipe of peace.

But Godin, aware of Indian perfidy and suspecting treachery, ordered his Flathead companion to fire on the Blackfoot, as his hand was extended in pretended friendship, and he fell to the ground.

A messenger came back to the main camp and told us they were fighting Blackfeet.

On receiving this information, we started out from camp, leaving a sufficient number of men to guard it. The Indians got into a thicket of willows, at a Beaver dam, forming a masked battery.

They put their horses in there and hung up their lodges to prevent our seeing them.

William Sublette and myself rode out together. We mutually agreed that whoever survived, the survivor should wind up our affairs.

When we came to the fortified place, firing commenced on the Indians and we were satisfied there was a large force of them. They had placed themselves in a position for defence.

We then arranged a place for the wounded to be brought.

A few of us crawled up between the willows. Sublette, myself and Sinclair, (St. Clair) there were two brothers of them. We crawled along on our hands and knees. Sublette was ahead, I second and Sinclair next to me. The Indians saw us and fired upon us, when within ten or fifteen paces of them and killed Sinclair. He was shot through the body. He was a quarter Cherokee. The Indians were concealed behind a breastwork of logs, and well fortified against small arms.

We kept firing upon them. Sublette and myself had a pair of flint-lock pistols. In the lodge which was screened by buffalo skins, one of the Indians peered through a hole.

Sublette fired and plugged him right in the eye.

I was within two steps of Sublette. Just at that time, and he told me, "Watch that place there is a chance for a shot at them." As he said this, three Indians, who were posted in another corner of the fortress fired and shot Sublette in the shoulder, and at the same time a man named Quigley was shot in the right side of the head. Neither shot proved fatal.

A portion of the bone in Sublette's arm was splintered by the shot, and I may anticipate by adding that some months afterwards, pieces of the bone were taken out by Dr. Farrar at St. Louis.

When Sublette told me he was shot, I was watching to get a shot at them in the place he had just designated to me.

As he grew faint from the loss of blood, I bore him out of the thicket, and though disabled, he said, "Bring my gun along, we may get a shot at them yet." We fought on till nearly night. We left the Nez Perces to keep a watch on the enemy. Sublette was conveyed on a litter to our camp, six miles distant from the battle ground. In the battle one of our Nez Perce Chiefs, was shot in the breast. He told us before, that he could not be killed by a bullet.

210

He was hit on the breast bone by a spent ball which dropped to the ground.

It was big medicine that produced the charm, a big thing with the Indians. The chief of the Bannocks had the same belief; that he was invulnerable and could not be killed by a bullet. The Blackfeet fled from their stronghold during the night.

There were three of our party killed in the fight, and the Blackfeet reported seventeen killed on their side. We found twenty-five dead horses, killed in the Blackfeet camp, and among the horses killed were two taken from Fitzpatrick.

In consequence of Sublette's wound we remained in camp for two weeks.

While there, Fitzpatrick joined us in a famished condition. He lost his powder horn, and had nothing to eat for many days.

I then sold out my merchandise to Fallon and Vanderburg, at this rendezvous. Then Sublette, being wounded, I took charge of the party, and made preparations to leave for St. Louis.

At the time the price of beaver rated at $3 per pound, and brought about $5 in St. Louis. There were eighty mules and we had 150 pounds on each mule.

When we hadn't the means of weighing, – 60 beavers were rated at 100 pounds.

When we trapped the first time in the country, they would average more. It would not take 60 beavers to made a hundred pounds, as the old beavers, before they were trapped out, weighed more than young beavers.

The merchandise in demand consisted of blankets, beads, knives, kettles, clothes, etc.

Our party with mules and pack animals, formed a long cavalcade, as we started out.

A man who was shot in the battle, died soon after we started, from mortification.

He got off his horse and died in five minutes.

We then came to St. Louis. On the trip going out we had passed Captain Bonneville and his party on the Blue, and as we were coming back we passed him on the Green river and gave him an account of our fight with the Blackfeet.

Washington Irving passed us in Jackson County, Mo. We did not know him, nor he us.

That winter, after my return to St. Louis, Sublette and myself formed a company partnership.[16]

Warren Ferris

Ferris was a trapper with the American Fur Company brigade that attended the rendezvous; he kept a journal that included a description of the battle. He had been in the mountains since early 1830 and would spend a total of five and a half years in the fur trade. Ferris returned to Pierre's Hole in May 1833, revisiting the scene of the battle. The account of this repeat trip follows his initial journal entry. Ferris also penned an article that appeared in the *Dallas Herald* on January 27, 1873. It is interesting not only because some of the facts changed, but because Ferris' perspective on the Blackfoot seemed to have shifted as well.

Ferris Journal – July 17-August 4, 1832
On the 17th a party of trappers, of the Rocky Mountain Fur Company, having received supplies for the fall hunt, left the company, and passed ten miles up the valley, intending to cross on to Lewis River, near the mouth of Salt River. The following morning they discovered a party of strange Indians near the margin of the stream, some distance above them, and several

of the men immediately departed to ascertain who they were. As they approached, the chief advanced to meet them, armed with nothing but the calumet of peace; but he was recognized to be a Grosventre and in a twinkling was sent to eternity. At the same time the Indians, who perhaps numbered fifty men, besides women and children, entered a grove of cottonwood trees, and without loss of time proceeded to make a breastwork, or pen of trees impenetrable to balls. In the mean time an express was despatched to inform us, and in a few minutes the plains were covered with whites, and friendly Indians, rushing to the field of battle. On their arrival, however, the enemy had completed an impenetrable fort, fifty feet square, within which they had fastened their horses. A general fire was immediately opened upon the fort, and was warmly kept up on both sides until dark. In the mean time a plan was formed by the whites to burn them up in their fort, and quantities of dry wood and brush were collected for that purpose; but the Indians on our side objected to this project, on the ground that all the plunder would be lost, which they thought to appropriate to their own use. At length night came on, and the whites, who were provoked at the Indians, for not consenting to annihilate the enemy at once, departed for their respective camps; the Indians soon followed, and left such of the enemy as survived, at liberty to depart and recount their misfortunes to their friends. We lost in this engagement, two men killed, one mortally wounded, and many others either severely or slightly. The Indians on our side, lost five killed, and many wounded, some supposed to be mortally. The following morning, a large party of both whites and Indians returned to the fort. In it were the dead bodies of three Grosventre Indians, a child, twenty-four horses, and several dogs. Our Indians followed the route of the fugitives several miles, and found their baggage, which they had concealed in divers places, as well as the bodies of five more Indians, and two young women, who were yet unhurt, though their heartless captures sent them to the shades, in pursuit of their relations without remorse. Amongst the dead horses were those lost by Mr. Fitzpatrick some days since; but those stolen from Sublett about the same time, were not among the *number; hence we supposed that a larger party of Indians were yet behind.*

After this period we enjoyed fine weather, and nothing occurred worthy of remembrance, until the 27th. This evening five of seven men who departed for St. Louis, three days since, returned, and informed us that they were attacked yesterday, by a party of Indians in Jackson's Hole, and that two of their number, Moore and Foy, killed. The survivors saved themselves by flight, but one of them was wounded in his thigh.

On the 30th William Sublett departed on his return to St. Louis. He had been detained here much longer than he intended, owing to a wound he had received on the 18th. During the first day's march, Stevens, the person who was wounded in his thigh, several days since, died, and was interred in the southeastern extremity of Pierre's Hole. On the first of August we had a hail storm of one hour's duration. Until this period we had anxiously awaited the appearance of Provenu and Fontenelle; but they came not, and we became apprehensive that they had lost their horses on the way, and were thus prevented from reaching us, according to promise however, Dripps and Vanderburgh resolved to move over to Green River, and learn if possible something definite. We set out on the 2d and reached the head of Pierre's Hole on the 3d. On the 4th we crossed the mountain, and descended into a large prairie valley, called Jackson's Big Hole. It lies due east of the Trois Tetons, and is watered by Lewis River, which leaves the valley through a deep cut in the mountains, impassable for pack horses; hence trappers have to cross the mountains to Pierre's Hole, in order to avoid greater obstacles, which present themselves at any other pass.

Ferris Journal – May 25-26, 1833

We ascended a fork and crossed the mountain, when we arrived at the head of a stream flowing into Pierre's Hole; which we followed down into the plain, four miles; there leaving it, we passed over to the stream which marked the pass to Jackson's

Hole, about two miles, and halted, very much fatigued, about one mile above the battle ground of last summer.

On the succeeding morning, in company with a friend or two, I visited the battle ground which was situate in a grove of aspen trees, several hundred yards in extent. The pen or fort was probably about fifty feet square, was composed of green and dry aspen timber, and though hastily, yet firmly constructed. It had sunk down in some places, however, from decay, below the height of two feet perpendicular. The beseiged had excavated holes or cavities in the earth, within the pen, sufficiently capacious for two or three persons to remain in, quite below the surface of the ground. These holes extended entirely round the pen; and we ascertained that the Indians had fired, in most cases, from small holes at the surface of the ground, beneath the pen or breast work, which circumstance (happily for them) was not observed in the smoke and confusion of the battle, or they would have been annihilated in a few moments. The attack was principally made on the north side, where at every tree, sticks were still seen piled up against the roots, from which the beseigers fought; who had likewise raised a heap of brush and logs, a few paces from the pen or fort, to nearly or quite the same height; and had the Indian allies not objected, in the hope of capturing their arms, ammunition and other equipments, it would have soon been so greatly increased and advanced toward the pen, as to have insured its destruction, if fired, with all its contents and defenders. Parties were also stationed behind trees, and clusters of willows on the other sides of the fort, which was thus entirely surrounded. The trees both within and outside of the pen, were covered with the marks of balls, or of the axes successfully employed by our comrades, to exhume and save them; lead being very valuable in these remote regions, where it is so extremely necessary, both to the purposes of defence and subsistence. Bones, of both men and animals, lay scattered about, in and around the pen, bearing evident indications of having contributed their fleshy covering, to the sustenance of wolves and ravens; who undoubtedly gratified their gastronomical propensities, after a protracted fast, for some days subsequent to the conflict.

215

Excerpt from the Dallas Herald – *January 27, 1873*
Still later a party of these Indians numbering about a hundred and fifty warriors with their women and children, entered Pierre's Hole and had proceeded nearly to the middle of the valley before they discovered the extent of their danger. They however then acted with judgment and discretion.

They immediately sought shelter in a dense grove of aspen trees of which they hurriedly built a very substantial pen large enough to contain themselves and their horses; they also dug a trench around the pen on the inside sufficiently capacious to contain the whole party below the surface of the earth. This enabled them to shoot from the bottom of the pen and gave them a great advantage over their assailants. However, in one hour a thousand guns were constantly discharging at every hole in the pen. The party within it made a gallant resistance, and for a while returned bullet for bullet, but late in the evening resistance had almost ceased, and all parties returned to their several encampments. In the morning we visited the pen which was literally full of dead Indians, squaws, children and horses. It is not probable that any escaped. Two young and rather interesting girls, fourteen or fifteen years of age who were out hunting berries when the fight commenced, concealed themselves, and were found and captured the next morning. The Indians kindly offered to save their lives and treat them kindly, but they said that their friends and relations were all killed and they wished only for death. They were importunate, and earnestly begged for death on their knees until an old warrior finding that he could do nothing with them, released them from the bond of life with his tomahawk. Had any of the white men been present their lives would have been saved unless they had committed suicide, which from their despair was highly probable. The next morning we had sixteen Indians and six white men laid out for interment in our camp. Other parties suffered to the same extent. Many were wounded – some mortally. Subbett was shot in the breast and arm, Dripps had a bullet through his hat that took a lock of hair with it. The Indians, however, being most numerous, suffered the most, and Old Gurgueo had quite a company of wounded men to add to those already in this condition.[17]

Zenas Leonard

Leonard was a free trapper who attended the rendezvous in Pierre's Hole and took part in the battle. He had originally come to the mountains in 1831 with the company of Gantt and Blackwell, and was assigned to the trapping brigade led by Alfred Stephens until the company dissolved. The following year, he was hired as a clerk for Joe Walker's 1833 expedition to California. He kept a journal throughout his years in the Rockies, beginning in spring 1831. When he returned from the mountains, Leonard wrote his story for a local newspaper, which was later published in 1839 in book form though copies are extremely rare. The version presented here was published in 1934, edited by Milo M. Quaife.

August 25th [July 17, 1832].[18] *Every thing necessary for our expedition being ready this morning, we started in a southern direction, but did not go far until we encamped for the night – thinking that if we had neglected any thing which we would stand in need of, we would thus discover it. The next morning finding all things in order, we continued travelling down what is called Pieres hole, or valley. This valley is situated on the river of the same name, and is from 70 to 80 miles in length, with a high mountain on the east and west – each so high that it is impossible to pass over them, and is from eight to ten miles wide. The river runs immediately through the centre, with a beautiful grove of timber along either bank; from this timber to the mountain, a distance of four or five miles, there is nothing but a smooth plain. This meadow or prairie is so perfectly level that a person may look up or down as far as the eye will reach without meeting any thing to obstruct the sight, until the earth and sky appear to meet. After travelling a few miles this morning, some of the men, in taking a view of the country before us, discovered something like people upon horses, who appeared to be coming towards us. After continuing in the same direction for some time we came in view with the naked eye, when we halted. – They advanced towards us displaying a British flag. This we could* not comprehend; but on coming closer discovered them to be hostile Indians. We immediately despatched a messenger back to the rendezvous for reinforcements and prepared ourselves for defence. The Indians commenced building a fort in the timber on the bank of the river; but at the time we were not aware of what they were doing. After waiting here a few hours we were reinforced by 200 whites, 200 Flatheads, and 300 Nez Perces Indians. The Indians with the British flag, on seeing such a number of people galloping down the plain at full speed, immediately retreated within their fort, whither they were hotly pursued. The friendly indians soon discovered them to belong to the Blackfeet tribe, who are decidedly the most numerous and warlike tribe in the mountains, and for this reason are not disposed to have any friendly intercourse with any other nation of an inferior number, unless they are good warriors and well armed with guns, &c. We thought we could rush right on them and drive them out of the brush into the plain and have a decisive battle at once. We advanced with all possible speed, and a full determination of success, until we discovered their fort by receiving a most destructive fire from the enclosure. This throwed our ranks into complete confusion, & we all retreated into the plain, with the loss of 5 whites, 8 Flatheads and 10 Nez Perces Indians killed, besides a large number of whites and Indians wounded. The formation of their fort astonished all hands. We had been within a few hundred yards of them all day and did not discover that they were building it. It was large enough to contain 500 warriors; and built strong enough to resist almost any attempt we might make to force it. After dressing the wounded, and having reconnoitered their fort, our forces were divided into several detachments, and sent in different directions with the intention of surrounding the fort and making them prisoners. This was done under the superintendance of Fitzpatrick, who acted as commander-in-chief.

In a case of this kind any man not evincing the greatest degree of courage, and every symptom of bravery, is treated as a coward; and the person who advances first, furthest and fastest, and makes the greatest display of animal courage, soon rises in the estimation of his companions. *Accordingly with the hope of gaining a little glory while an opportunity offered, though not for any electioneering purpose, as a politician in the States would do – I started into the brush, in company with two acquaintances (Smith and Kean) and two Indians. We made a circuitous route and came towards the fort from a direction which we thought we would be least expected. We advanced closer and closer, crawling upon our hands and knees, with the intention of giving them a select shot; and when within about forty yards of their breast work, one of our Indians was shot dead. At this we all lay still for some time, but Smith's foot happening to shake the weeds as he was laying on his belly, was shot through. I advanced a little further, but finding the balls to pass too quick and close, concluded to retreat. When I turned, I found that my companions had deserted me. In passing by, Smith asked me to carry him out, which met my approbation precisely, for I was glad to get out of this unpleasant situation under any pretext – provided my reputation for courage would not be questioned. After getting him on my back, still crawling on my hands and knees, I came across Kean, lying near where the first Indian fell, who was also mortally wounded and died soon after. I carried Smith to a place of safety and then returned to the siege. A continual fire was kept up, doing more or less execution on both sides until late in the afternoon, when we advanced to close quarters, having nothing but the thickness of their breast work between us, and having them completely surrounded on all sides to prevent any escaping. This position we maintained until sun-set, in the meantime having made preparations to set fire to the fort, which was built principally of old dry logs, as soon as night would set in, and stationed men at the point where we thought they would be most likely to make the first break, for the purpose of taking them on the wing, in their flight. Having made all these preparations, which were to put an end to all further molestation on the part of the Blackfeet, our whole scheme and contemplated victory was frustrated by a most ingenious and well executed device of the enemy. A few minutes before the torch was to be applied, our captives commenced the most tremendous yells and shouts of triumph, and menaces of defiance, which seemed to move heaven and earth. Quick as thought a report spread through all quarters, that the plain was covered with Blackfeet Indians coming to reinforce the besieged. So complete was the consternation in our ranks, created by this stratagem, that in five minutes afterwards, there was not a single white man, Flathead or Nez Perces Indian within a hundred yards of the fort. Every man thought only of his own security, and run for life without ever looking round, which would at once have convinced him of his folly. In a short time it was ascertained that it was only a stratagem, and our men began to collect together where our baggage was. I never shall forget the scene here exhibited. The rage of some was unbounded, and approached to madness. For my own part, although I felt much regret at the result after so much toil and danger, yet I could not but give the savages credit for the skill they displayed in preserving their lives, at the very moment when desperation, as we thought, had seized the mind of each of them.*

By the time we were made sensible of the full extent of our needless alarm, it had began to get dark; and on ascertaining the extent of the injury which we received, (having lost 32 killed, principally Indians,) it was determined not to again attempt to surround the fort, which was a sore disappointment to some of the men who were keen for chastising the Indians for their trick. We then took up our march for the rendezvous; but on starting one of our party of 15 men, who had first started out the day before, could not be found. Search was made, and he was found in the brush, severely wounded. – After carrying him on a litter a few miles he died and was buried in the Indian style: – which is by digging a hole in the ground, wrapping a blanket or skin round the body, placing it in the hole, and covering it with poles and earth. This is the manner of interring the dead in this country both by the Indians and whites, except in the winter season on account of the ground being frozen, when the Indians are in the habit of wrapping their dead in buffaloe robes, and laying them on poles from one tree to another, on which poles the corpse is tied with cords.

The next morning we raised another war party and went back to the battle ground, but no Indians could be found. – They must have left the fort in great haste for we found 42 head of horses, together with Fitzpatrick's which they had taken on the mountain, two warriors and one squaw lying dead inside of their fort, besides a large quantity of their baggage, such as furs, skins, &c. There must have been a great number of them, from the holes they had dug in the ground around their dead horses and the edges of the fort, say from three to four hundred. I learned afterwards that the Nez Perces Indians shortly after found seven more dead Blackfeet, in some brush close by, where they had been secreted to save their scalps, which is the principal object with these Indians, in order to have their women dance. In the afternoon we returned to the rendezvous and presented Mr. Fitzpatrick with his long-lost and highly valued horse, which seemed to compensate for all the sufferings and hardships which he had encountered.

After remaining here a few days a violent dispute arose between Stephens and Fitzpatrick about the price of the horses which the latter was to give to the former for the beaver skins of Gant's which Stephens had sold to Fitzpatrick. No person interfered, for we all knew that it was a dishonest transaction from beginning to end. Fitzpatrick having every thing in his own possession, was therefore contented and as independent as any mean man who had it in his power to make his own terms. Stephens, on the contrary, was in a bad situation – having paid before hand, and not being able to force measures, had to put up with what he could get. Finally he succeeded in hiring four men, and started back to the mouth of the Laramies to secure the fur which he had sold to Fitzpatrick. He had not left many days, however, until he was overtaken by a scouting party of those Indians we had surrounded in the fort. Two of his men were killed, and himself shot through the thigh – having the two mules along, which was the ballance of the original stock, one of which was killed, and the other brought back the wounded Stephens, who died in a few days afterwards from mortification taking place in the wounded leg.

A few days after this occurrence, we were visited by a party belonging to the Nor West, or British trading company, from whom we were enabled to learn the way the Blackfeet Indians had got possession and fought under the British flag. It appeared by their story that these Indians some months previous, had fell on a party belonging to their company – but few of whom escaped to tell the fate of their comrades – and among the spoils which they obtained, was this flag, which they used as a signal to deceive and mislead their enemies, whom they might meet in these extensive plains.[19]

Joseph Meek

After spending eleven years trapping beaver, Meek retired to Oregon in 1840. He was at both rendezvous held in Pierre's Hole, 1829 and 1832, and participated in the battle at the latter rendezvous. Meek recounted his life story to Frances Fuller Victor in 1870, when he was fifty-eight years old. Impressed by this true hero of early Oregon Territory, Mrs. Victor dutifully recorded the tales of Meek's incredible adventures as a first-class mountaineer.

One of the earliest to move was a small party under Milton Sublette, including his constant companion, Meek. With this company, no more than thirty in number, Sublette intended to explore the country to the south-west, then unknown to the fur companies, and to proceed as far as the Humboldt river in that direction. On the 17th of July they set out toward the south end of the valley, and having made but about eight miles the first day, camped that night near a pass in the mountains. Wyeth's party of raw New Englanders, and Sinclair's free trappers, had joined themselves to the company of Milton Sublette, and swelled the number in camp to about sixty men, many of them new to the business of mountain life.

Just as the men were raising camp for a start the next morning, a caravan was observed moving down the mountain pass into the valley. No alarm was at first felt, as an arrival was daily expected of one of the American company's partisans, Mr. Fontenelle, and his company. But on reconnoitering with a glass, Sublette discovered them to be a large party of Blackfeet, consisting of a few mounted men, and many more, men, women, and children, on foot. At the instant they were discovered, they set up the usual yell of defiance, and rushed down like a mountain torrent into the valley, flourishing their weapons, and fluttering their gay blankets and feathers in the wind. There was no doubt as to the warlike intentions of the Blackfeet in general, nor was it for a moment to be supposed that any peaceable overture on their part meant anything more than that they were not prepared to fight at that particular juncture; therefore let not the reader judge too harshly of an act which under ordinary circumstances would have been infamous. In Indian fighting, every man is his own leader, and the bravest take the front rank. On this occasion there were two of Sublette's men, one a half-breed Iroquois, the other a Flathead Indian, who had wrongs of their own to avenge, and they never let slip a chance of killing a Blackfoot. These two men rode forth alone to meet the enemy, as if to hold a "talk" with the principal chief, who advanced to meet them, bearing the pipe of peace. When the chief extended his hand, Antonio Godin, the half-breed, took it, but at the same moment he ordered the Flathead to fire, and the chief fell dead. The two trappers galloped back to camp, Antoine bearing for a trophy the scarlet blanket of his enemy.

This action made it impossible to postpone the battle, as the dead chief had meant to do by peaceful overtures, until the warriors of his nation came up. The Blackfeet immediately betook themselves to a swamp formed by an old beaver dam, and thickly overgrown with cotton-wood and willow, matted together with tough vines. On the edge of this dismal covert the warriors skulked, and shot with their guns and arrows, while in its very midst the women employed themselves in digging a trench and throwing up a breastwork of logs, and whatever came to hand. Such a defence as the thicket afforded was one not easy to attack; its unseen but certain dangers being sufficient to appal the stoutest heart.

Meantime, an express had been sent off to inform Captain Sublette of the battle, and summon assistance. Sinclair and his free trappers, with Milton Sublette's small company, were the *only fighting men at hand. Mr. Wyeth, knowing the inefficiency of his men in an Indian fight, had them entrenched behind their packs, and there left them to take care of themselves, but charged them not to appear in open field. As for the fighting men, they stationed themselves in a ravine, where they could occasionally pick off a Blackfoot, and waited for reinforcements.*

Great was the astonishment of the Blackfeet, who believed they had only Milton Sublette's camp to fight, when they beheld first one party of white men and then another; and not only whites, but Nez Perces and Flatheads came galloping up the valley. If before it had been a battle to destroy the whites, it was now a battle to defend themselves. Previous to the arrival of Captain Sublette, the opposing forces had kept up only a scattering fire, in which nobody on the side of the trappers had been either killed or wounded. But when the impetuous captain arrived on the battle-field, he prepared for less guarded warfare. Stripped as if for the prize-ring, and armed <u>cap-a-pie</u>, he hastened to the scene of action, accompanied by his intimate friend and associate in business, Robert Campbell [emphasis in original].

At sight of the reinforcements, and their vigorous movements, the Indians at the edge of the swamp fell back within their fort. To dislodge them was a dangerous undertaking, but Captain Sublette was determined to make the effort. Finding the trappers generally disinclined to enter the thicket, he set the example, together with Campbell, and thus induced some of the free trappers, with their leader, Sinclair, to emulate his action. However, the others took courage at this, and advanced near the swamp, firing at random at their invisible foe, who, having the advantage of being able to see them, inflicted some wounds on the party.

The few white "braves" who had resolved to enter the swamp, made their wills as they went, feeling that they were upon perilous business. Sublette, Campbell, and Sinclair succeeded in penetrating the thicket without alarming the enemy, and came at length to a more open space from whence they could get a view of the fort. From this they learned that the women and children had retired to the mountains, and that the fort was a slight affair, covered with buffalo robes and blankets to keep out prying eyes. Moving slowly on, some slight accident betrayed their vicinity, and the next moment a shot struck Sinclair, wounding him mortally. He spoke to Campbell, requesting to be taken to his brother. By this time some of the men had come up, and he was given in charge to be taken back to camp. Sublette then pressed forward, and seeing an Indian looking through an aperture, aimed at him with fatal effect. No sooner had he done so, and pointed out the opening to Campbell, than he was struck with a ball in the shoulder, which nearly prostrated him, and turned him so faint that Campbell took him in his arms and carried him, assisted by Meek, out of the swamp. At the same time one of the men received a wound in the head. The battle was now carried on with spirit, although from the difficulty of approaching the fort, the firing was very irregular.

The mountaineers who followed Sublette, took up their station in the woods on one side of the fort, and the Nez Perces, under Wyeth, on the opposite side, which accidental arrangement, though it was fatal to many of the Blackfeet in the fort, was also the occasion of loss to themselves by the cross-fire. The whites being constantly reinforced by fresh arrivals from the rendezvous, were soon able to silence the guns of the enemy, but they were not able to drive them from their fort, where they remained silent and sullen after their ammunition was exhausted.

Seeing that the women of the Nez Perces and Flatheads were gathering up sticks to set fire to their breastwork of logs, an old chief proclaimed in a loud voice from within, the startling intelligence that there were four hundred lodges of his people close at hand, who would soon be there to avenge their deaths, should the whites choose to reduce them to ashes. This harangue, delivered in the usual high-flown style of Indian oratory, either was not clearly understood, or was wrongly interpreted, and the impression got abroad that an attack was being made on the great encampment. This intelligence occasioned a diversion, *and a division of forces; for while a small party was left to watch the fort, the rest galloped in hot haste to the rescue of the main camp. When they arrived, they found it had been a false alarm, but it was too late to return that night, and the several camps remained where they were until the next day.*

Meantime the trappers left to guard the fort remained stationed within the wood all night, firmly believing they had their enemy "corraled," as the horsemen of the plains would say. On the return, in the morning, of their comrades from the main camp, they advanced cautiously up to the breastwork of logs, and behold! not a buffalo skin nor red blanket was to be seen! Through the crevices among the logs was seen an empty fort. On making this discovery there was much chagrin among the white trappers, and much lamentation among the Indian allies, who had abandoned the burning of the fort expressly to save for themselves the fine blankets and other goods of their hereditary foes.

From the reluctance displayed by the trappers, in the beginning of the battle, to engage with the Indians while under cover of the woods, it must not be inferred that they were lacking in courage. They were too well informed in Indian modes of warfare to venture recklessly into the den of death, which a savage ambush was quite sure to be. The very result which attended the impetuosity of their leaders, in the death of Sinclair and the wounding of Captain Sublette, proved them not over cautious.

On entering the fort, the dead bodies of ten Blackfeet were found, besides others dead outside the fort, and over thirty horses, some of which were recognized as those stolen from Sublette's night camp on the other side of the mountains, besides those abandoned by Fitzpatrick. Doubtless the rascals had followed his trail to Pierre's Hole, not thinking, however, to come upon so large a camp as they found at last. The savage garrison which had so cunningly contrived to elude the guard set upon them, carried off some of their wounded, and, perhaps, also some of their dead; for they acknowledged afterwards a much larger loss than appeared at the time. Besides Sinclair, there were five other white men killed, one half-breed, and seven Nez Perces. About the same number of whites and their Indian allies were wounded.

An instance of female devotion is recorded by Bonneville's historian as having occurred at this battle. On the morning following it, as the whites were exploring the thickets about the fort, they discovered a Blackfoot woman leaning silent and motionless against a tree. According to Mr. Irving, whose fine feeling for the sex would incline him to put faith in this bit of romance, "their surprise at her lingering here alone, to fall into the hands of her enemies, was dispelled when they saw the corpse of a warrior at her feet. Either she was so lost in grief as not to perceive their approach, or a proud spirit kept her silent and motionless. The Indians set up a yell on discovering her, and before the trappers could interfere, her mangled body fell upon the corpse which she had refused to abandon." This version is true in the main incidents, but untrue in the sentiment. The woman's leg had been broken by a ball, and she was unable to move from the spot where she leaned. When the trappers approached her, she stretched out her hands supplicatingly, crying out in a wailing voice, "kill me! kill me! O white men, kill me!" – but this the trappers had no disposition to do. While she was entreating them, and they refusing, a ball from some vengeful Nez Perce or Flathead put an end to her sufferings.

Still remembering the threats of the Blackfoot chief, that four hundred lodges of his brethren were advancing on the valley, all the companies returned to rendezvous, and remained for several days, to see whether an attack should take place. But if there had ever been any such intention on the part of the Blackfoot nation, the timely lesson bestowed on their advance guard had warned them to quit the neighborhood of the whites.

Captain Sublette's wound was dressed by Mr. Wyeth's physician, and although it hindered his departure for St. Louis for some time, it did not prevent his making his usual journey later in the season. It was as well, perhaps, that he did not set out earlier, for of a party of seven who started for St. Louis a few days after the battle, three were killed in Jackson's Hole, where they fell in with the four hundred warriors with whom the Blackfoot chief threatened the whites at the battle of Pierre's Hole. From the story of the four survivors who escaped and returned to camp, there could no longer be any doubt that the big village of the Blackfeet had actually been upon the trail of Capt. Sublette, expecting an easy victory when they should overtake him. How they were disappointed by the reception met with by the advance camp, has already been related.[20]

Robert Newell

Robert Newell was a good friend of Joe Meek, both men having come to the mountains at the same time in 1829. They also left for Oregon together in 1840 when opportunities in the fur trade slowed to a halt. Newell, too, was at both of the rendezvous in Pierre's Hole and fought in the battle. His extremely concise memorandum, written sometime after 1836, is typical of his style.

Up Salt River Round to Piers hole Met all hunters of these parts Vanderberg Drips & Co with about 175 men William Sublette arrive with Supplies for our Camp Mr fitzpatrick who was with Sublette left to come to us but was chased by the Indians and Detained and Just escaped death [to] come to us. this is to be Remembered to be the largest party of whites ever Seen together north west or west of the yellow stones mouth or even thare except our American troops (aug 1832) up to the above date[21]   I think our number to exceed 350 but not much but in all whites and indians all sorts and kinds of men about 600, (a [s]crimmage with the Black feet-)

Into Rondezvous   got our Supplies and Scatterd in the following courses to our profession Wm Sublette to the States with the Returns   M. Sublette to the west down Snake River   Mr Fitzpatrick to the north   i wone of that number   from Piers hole to Psalmon River[22]

George Nidever

Nidever began his fur trade career in 1831 with the Bean-Sinclair company, took part in the battle of Pierre's Hole, went to California with Joe Walker, and stayed there to hunt sea otter. His narrative was taken down in 1878 as part of Hubert H. Bancroft's history of California and was finally edited for publication in 1935. Though his dates are a bit off, the information is valid regarding the battle.

> *About the beginning of Aug. the trappers began to leave for their respective hunting grounds. Our party had decided to trap that season on the Marys River, a small stream about South West of Salt Lake. We left Pierre's Hole in company with Frapp and Wyatt, our courses being the same for some distance. Frapp's company was mostly made up of Canadian French half-breeds. Our first camp was about 15 miles from the rendezvous. Frapp's and Wyatt's companies camped together, while we were a short distance in their rear.*

> *The next morning about 8 o'clock we packed up and rode along to Wyatt's and Frapp's camp, only a few hundred yards ahead, and had hardly reached it when Indians were discovered coming towards us in large numbers, and we immediately recognized them as Blackfeet. They belonged to a village of some 400 warriors or more, that with their women, children and camp baggage were moving north. They had discovered us before we did them, no doubt, and had resolved on attacking us. They were riding down on us at full speed and barely gave us time to prepare for them. We hurriedly formed a breastwork of our packs and dispatched a young boy on our fleetest horse back to Pierre's Hole for aid. We saw from their numbers that we would need help, but by holding the Indians in check for two or three hours we knew reinforcements would reach us. As soon as the Indians arrived within range they began shooting, to which we replied. Conspicuous among them was a chief dressed in a bright scarlet coat, and he rode somewhat in advance of his men who began to scatter and surround us upon arriving within shooting distance. On came the chief and out rode one of Wyatt's men, Goddar, a Canadian half-breed, to meet him. Across his saddle Goddar carried a short rifle which the chief did not see until,*

when within 40 or 50 yds. of him Goddar raised it and shot. The chief fell from his saddle dead, and before his companions could come to him his coat was stripped off by Goddar who amidst a heavy fire reached our camp in safety with his trophy. We continued to exchange shots, with a loss to the Indians of one or two killed, and to us of several wounded, until about ten o'clock, when the Indians suddenly took shelter in the heavy narrow belt of woods that lay between us and the river. We soon discovered the cause of this unexpected movement, in the coming of our reinforcements, that began to appear in sight and a few minutes later were among us to the number of about 250. Most of them were without saddles, having lost no time in setting out as soon as our messenger reached them. A council was held and Wm. Sublette was elected as our leader. Many were opposed to attacking them as, being posted in the heavy timber, we would find it difficult to drive them out, and our loss would be considerable. These objections were overruled by Sublette and others, who said we would have to fight them anyway and now that we had them at a disadvantage, we must profit by it.

The plan of attack was formed and the attacking party got into line and advanced, when the firing at once became general. Just after we entered the timber, our captain Alex. Sinclair was shot in the thigh, Phelps, a man who joined us at Pierre's Hole, was wounded in about the same place, and Wm. Sublette was shot in the arm. Our attacking party did not consist of much over 100 men, the rest refusing to join us. As we advanced and drove the Indians toward the river, the wings of our line gradually turned in until they rested on its bank and we had them surrounded.

Upon penetrating into timber we found that the Blackfeet had constructed a fort of logs on the bank of the river in the form of a half moon, the rear opening towards the river. We continued to advance, dodging and crawling from tree to tree and log to log, every foot stubbornly contested by the redskins, until almost sunset. Some of our men had succeeded in getting in the rear of the fort, which, however, afforded its inmates some shelter even on the open side, as it was filled with trees. One of the trappers of Frapp's company got very near the rear of the fort, almost up to it in fact, by crawling flat on the ground and pushing and rolling a large log so as to protect his head.

Several shots struck the log but the trapper got into position and abandoned his log for a tree without being harmed.

Another one of Frapp's men, a Canadian half-breed, tried to distinguish himself by rashly crawling up to the very wall of the fort and then peeping over the top. He paid for his temerity with his life. He had barely raised his head above the breastwork of logs when he received two bullets in his forehead. He was half drunk at the time, liquor having been distributed among the men during the early part of the fight. By sunset we had got so close to the fort that we determined to set it on fire, but before doing so it was agreed to give the Indians a chance to surrender. Accordingly, a renegade Blackfoot who was among Frapp's men was instructed to talk with them and try and induce them to surrender. They refused, however, and answered that, although they would all be killed that day, the next day it would be our turn, as they had sent word to a very large village of their nation, situated only a short distance from there, numbering some 1500 lodges.

It was well known that there was a very large village nearby and that, should they send out all of their force after us, there would be some heavy fighting in which we would in all probability get worsted. Upon hearing the answer of the Indians, Frapp became alarmed and withdrew his men at once and this obliged the rest of us to retire, and those from Pierre's Hole having returned, we travelled on about 9 miles and went into camp with the same companies as the night previous. The next morning several of us went back to the scene of the fight. Within the fort and its immediate vicinity the ground was strewn with dead bodies mostly women and children; but a very few warriors among them.

We counted 50 dead bodies, and inside the fort were the bodies of 20 fine horses. Of the from 300 to 400 Indians which it was calculated the fighting men of the Blackfeet numbered, but very few escaped.

At the beginning of the engagement several got away, many of them being shot in attempting to swim the river. We afterwards learned through the Indians that when we withdrew our men only 6 Indians were left alive in the fort. The dead Indians were thrown into the river to prevent them from falling into our hands.

Many of the women were shot unintentionally as in the timber it was impossible to distinguish the women from men; the children were killed no doubt by stray shots.

The Indians make a very poor fight on foot, their usual mode of fighting being to lay in ambush or to cut off small detached parties with such numbers as to make success sure.

We lost no time in getting out of this neighborhood, pushing forward as rapidly as possible. A few days later we struck buffalo and halted to get meat. We also furnished meat to Wyatt, whose men were mostly green in these matters.[23]

Samuel Parker

The Reverend Samuel Parker was not at the 1832 rendezvous in Pierre's Hole, nor was he at the battle. In August, 1835, on his way to the Pacific Northwest with missionary Marcus Whitman, Parker passed through Pierre' Hole. The party's guide, Jim Bridger, probably told Parker of the encounter that occurred a few years prior and apparently pointed out the battle site. Having read Irving's biography of Bonneville, Parker took exception to some of Irving's apparent literary license in the book's description of the 1832 battle. The reverend's 1835 observations, published in 1838 and tinted with the strong altruism of a New England clergyman, are all the more interesting in light of Robert Campbell's equal desire to set the record straight after reading Irving's book.

On [August] 29th, removed our encampment, and traveled five hours along this valley to the place, where two years before, two fur companies held their rendezvous. Pierre's Hole is an extensive level country, of rich soil, well watered with branches of Lewis's river, and is less frosty than any part we have passed this side of the rocky chain of mountains. The valley is well covered with grass, but like most other places is deficient in woodland, having only a scanty supply of cotton-wood and willows scattered along the streams. It extends around to the north-west, as far as the eye can reach. We expected to have found buffalo here, but saw none. As parties of Blackfeet warriors often range this way, it was probable they had lately been here and frightened them away. Between this and our last encampment, I was shown the place where the men of the fur companies, at the time of their rendezvous two years before, had a battle with the Blackfeet Indians. Of the Blackfeet party there were about sixty men, and more than the same number of women and children; of the white men in the valley, there were some few hundred who could be called into action. From the information given me, it appeared that these Indians were on their way through this valley, and unexpectedly met about forty hunters and trappers going out from the rendezvous to the south-west on their fall and winter hunt. The Indians manifested an unwillingness to fight, and presented tokens of peace; but they were not reciprocated. Those who came forward to stipulate terms of peace were fired upon and killed. When the Indians saw their danger, they fled to the cotton-wood trees and willows which were scattered along the stream of water, and, taking advantage of some fallen trees, constructed as good defenses as time and circumstances would permit. They were poorly provided with guns, and were still more destitute of ammunition. The trappers keeping out of reach of their arrows, and being well armed with the best rifles, made the contest unequal; and still more unequal, when, by an express sent to rendezvous, they were reinforced by veterans in mountain life. The hunters, keeping at a safe distance, in the course of a few hours killed several of the Indians, and almost all their horses, which, in *their situation, could not be protected, while they themselves suffered but small loss. Those killed, on both sides, have been differently stated, but, considering the numbers engaged, and the length of time the skirmishing continued, it could not have been a bloody battle; and not much to the honor of the civilized Americans. The excuses made for forcing the Blackfeet into battle is, that if they had come upon a small party of trappers, they would have butchered them and seized upon the plunder. If heathen Blackfeet would have done so, civilized white men should not. What a noble opportunity was here afforded for our American citizens to have set an example of humanity.*

*When night approached, the hunters retired to their encampment at the place of rendezvous, and the Indians made their escape. Thus, the famous battle of Pierre's Hole began and ended.**

*Since my return, I have seen an account of this battle, written by a graphic hand, in all the fascinating style of romance, representing the Indians as having entrenched themselves in a swamp, so densely wooded as to be almost impenetrable; and there they kept the trappers at bay, until they were reinforced from rendezvous. When the Blackfeet saw the whole valley alive with horsemen rushing to the field of action, they withdrew into the dark tangled wood. When the leaders of the several hunting parties came into the field, they urged their men to enter the swamp, but they hung back in awe of the dismal horrors of the place, regarding it impenetrable and full of danger. But the leaders would not be turned from their purpose – made their wills – appointed their executors – grasped their rifles, and urged their way through the wood. A brisk fire was opened, and the Blackfeet were completely overmatched, but would not leave their fort, nor offer to surrender. The numerous veteran mountaineers, well equipped, did not storm the breastwork, even when the Blackfeet had spent their powder and balls, but only kept up the bloody battle by occasional firing during the day. The Blackfeet in the night effected their retreat; and the

brave mountaineers assembled their forces in the morning, and entered the fort without opposition.

With those who have seen the field of battle, the glowing description, drawn out in long detail, loses its interest; for although I saw it, yet I did not see dense woods, nor a swamp of any magnitude any where near.[24]

Louis Rivet

The information from trapper Rivet comes from notes taken during an interview with William F. Wheeler at Fort Benton, Montana, in 1884. Rivet, eighty-one years of age at the time of the discussion, had never learned to read or write. Rivet had been hired in 1829 by the American Fur Company to take keel boats up the Missouri River. Soon after, he joined Fontenelle's company to trap the Rockies. He attended the 1832 rendezvous in Pierre's Hole and took part in the battle with the Blackfoot. Known as "Revy," he hunted and trapped each winter, well into his eighties.

In the summer of 1832, while the party of trappers to which Mr. Rivet belonged were hunting on a tributary of the Snake river, they discovered a large party of Indians who they found out were Blackfeet coming into the valley where they had their principle camp. They immediately sent messengers to all their friends to come into their rendezvous at once, as they apprehended an attack from the Indians. The messengers were also instructed to give warning to all parties of trappers known to be in the vicinity. In a short time all their own friends and other parties had arrived. He remembered that to their great joy, Sublette and Campbell, leaders of the rival Rocky Mountain Fur Company, were met unexpectedly. The Indians were astonished to find so many white men gathered together so suddenly when they had seen but comparatively few. They therefore immediately fortified themselves in the edge of a swampy wood and awaited the attack of the whites, which was not delayed. The Indians fought bravely from behind their log and brush breastworks, but would not leave it. Their fire was returned with interest by the trappers, and they were so surrounded that it seemed impossible for them to escape, and they would not surrender. Several white men had been killed or wounded. Captain Sublette had been shot through the shoulder. A number of Indians were seen to fall. Some were killed and some wounded. The fight lasted until night, when the whites withdrew into the edge of the woods, determined to renew the attack on the fort in the morning. When they crept through the woods and brush to renew the fight they found the fort deserted and the Indians gone. The fight had been bloody, for blood could be seen in spots all around. A number of dead Indians and horses were found in the enclosure. The wounded had been carried away. Several white men were killed and wounded, as were a number of friendly Indians who joined in the fight. The Blackfeet did not attack the trappers in force again. They would only attack from ambush, or in superior numbers.[25]

William Sublette

William Sublette was an Ashley man and had been in the mountains since 1822. He was the former partner of Jedediah Smith and David Jackson in a fur company of their own. This partnership had sold out in 1830 to five trappers who then formed the Rocky Mountain Fur Company. Sublette subsequently became a supplier of goods and merchandise. He was at both of the rendezvous held in Pierre's Hole, and as reported in most of the previous accounts, took a leadership role in the 1832 incident with the Gros Ventre. Sublette wrote this letter about two months after the event, and upon his return from the mountains, to inform William H. Ashley of the encounter. While Sublette had been busy in the mountains, Ashley had acted as Sublette's agent, buying trade goods and selling furs in New England markets. By this time, Ashley had also been elected as a congressman from Missouri, so Sublette's report to Ashley makes sense on several levels. As the trading license holder, Sublette may have been somewhat guarded in narrating details of the battle. For example, even though he was not present at the beginning of the fight, surely he had heard about Godin's deceit. Yet, Sublette made no mention that trappers may have instigated the entire affair. This letter was published in several newspapers of the day.

Lexington, MO. Sep. 21st 1832

Dear Sir –

I left the settlements on the 13th of May, and on the 2nd of July on the head of the Colorado of the West, a party of Blackfeet Indians endeavored to enter my camp at night, but finding a strong guard around it they thought it dangerous, and, after securing some loose horse and finding they could get no more, they fired on us and immediately ran off. The only injury sustained was two mules slightly wounded.

I arrived on the waters of the Columbia River on the 4th of July and on the 8th at the rendezvous of the Rocky Mtn. Hunters, on the Columbia River, west of the Three Teton Mtns.

On the 18th of July, about 6 miles from my camp, an engagement took place between a small party of whites who had started for their hunting grounds the day before, and a party of Blackfeet Indians. An express was immediately sent to my camp, and I was joined by a considerable number of whites and some friendly Indians of the Pierced-Nose and Flathead Nations to go to the assistance of those engaged. When we arrived at the spot we found the Blackfeet had taken possession of a point of woods surrounded by willows where they had formed a strong fort of fallen timber and had dug holes in the ground inside the fort where they could be secure from our fire. Finding them thus fortified and that we were exposed to their fire on the prairie without being able to injure them, I proposed entering the willows and approaching their fort where we could be on more equal footing. I was joined by 30 whites and as many friendly Indians making our force nearly equal to that of our enemy. We advanced to within 15 paces of their fort and continued firing on them which they vigorously returned for some time. Discovering at length that they were too securely protected against our rifles we determined on burning their fort and when nearly prepared to apply fire to it, one of our friendly Indians who spoke the Blackfeet Language and had held conversation with them during the engagement was told by them they were convinced we could kill them all, but that six or eight hundred warriors of their tribe were momentarily expected there who would give us enough of fighting. Owing to the misconstruction of the interpreter who communicated it to the whites he was understood to say that six or eight hundred warriors were then in the valley attacking our camp; consequently the fight was immediately discontinued and not until we got to the prairie was the matter properly explained. It was then deemed too late to renew the attack.

We lost in the engagement Mr. St. Clair of Arkansas who was killed before we reached the fort. Another man, who too fearlessly ventured up to the fort and fired into it received 2 balls in the head and was instantly killed on the spot, Thomas Quigly of St. Louis was wounded in the head and I understand died on the 8th day afterward. He had started with a trapping party who were about 30 miles from my camp. Miller of Boone Co. in this state was severely wounded in the body which I fear will have proved fatal. Myself and 3 other whites were wounded. Six of the Pierced-nose Indians killed and 2 wounded.

Next morning a party of whites went to the battleground and found the Indians had fled to the mountains in the night, bearing with them their wounded on litters. They left nearly all their baggage and had 9 warriors and 25 horses killed on the ground.

On the 25th of July, 7 men started for Mo. and on the 26th came upon a party of about 20 Blackfeet who killed 2 of them, Moore and Foy, and wounded Alfred K. Stephens of St. Louis supposed at the time not dangerous. The party returned to the camp. The wound of Stephens mortified and he died on the 30th of July.

I left the rendezvous on the 30th of July and the Columbia River on the 3rd of August. On the 4th passed the six or eight hundred warriors which we were told of by the party with whom we had the fight on July 18. I expected an attack from *them daily but for some reason they passed us by. My force was only 60 men. My party arrived here on the 21st of Sept. all in good health.*

The whole number of men killed by the Blackfeet Indians, belonging to the different companies in that country during the last year, amounts to nine, a part of whom were killed after my arrival there.

> *Very respectfully, your obedient servant —*
> *William Sublette*

General W. H. Ashley[26]

John Wyeth

John Wyeth, Nathaniel's cousin, was the youngest member of the expedition, not having attained his twentieth year. He had had enough of the Rocky Mountains and was preparing to head east when the battle in Teton Valley occurred. Mindful of the newsworthy nature of his story, he was quick to get a book into print upon his return to Boston in 1832. Nathaniel would later criticize his young kinsman's tale as "full of white lies," particularly in light of some of John's veiled accusations, but the account of the battle may be considered balanced and reliable. All emphases are in the original.

On the 17th of July, Captain Wyeth and Captain Milton Sublet set out westward with their respective men to go to Salmon river to winter. The former had eleven beside himself: that river they computed at two hundred miles distance. Wyeth accordingly purchased twenty-five horses from the Indians, who had a great number, and those very fine, and high-spirited. Indeed the Western region seems the native and congenial country for horses. They were, however, delayed till the next day. But when they were about moving, they perceived a drove of something, whether buffaloes or men they could not determine with the naked eye; but when aided by the glass, they recognized them for a body of the <u>Black-foot</u> *tribe of Indians, a powerful and warlike nation. As this movement was evidently hostile, Captain Milton Sublet dispatched two men to call on his brother, who was about eight miles off, for assistance;*

when Captain William Sublet ordered every man to get ready immediately. We had about five hundred friendly Indian warriors with us, who expressed their willingness to join in our defence.

As soon as we left Captain Wyeth we joined Captain Sublet, as he said that no white man should be there unless he was to be under his command; and his reason for it was that in case they had to fight the Indians, no one should flinch or sneak out of the battle. It seems that when the Black-foot Indians saw us moving in battle array, they appeared to hesitate; and at length they displayed a white flag as an ensign of peace; but Sublet knew their treacherous character. The chief of the friendly Flat-heads and Antoine rode together, and concerted this savage arrangement; to ride up and accost them in a friendly manner; and when the Black-foot chief should take hold of the Flat-head chief's hand in token of friendship, then the other was to shoot him, which was instantly done! and at that moment the Flat-head chief pulled off the Blackfoot's scarlet robe, and returned with the Captain to our party unhurt. As soon as the Black-foot Indians recovered from their surprise, they displayed a red flag, and the battle began. This was Joab with a vengeance, – Art thou in health, my brother?

The Black-foot chief was a man of consequence in his nation. He not only wore on this occasion a robe of scarlet cloth, probably obtained from a Christian source, but was decorated with beads valued there at sixty dollars. The battle commenced on the Prairie. As soon as the firing began on both sides, the squaws belonging to the Black-foot forces, retreated about fifty yards into a small thicket of wood, and there threw up a ridge of earth by way of entrenchment, having first piled up a number of logs cob-fashion, to which the men at length fell back, and from which they fired upon us, while some of their party with the women were occupied in deepening the trench. Shallow as it was, it afforded a considerable security to an Indian, who will often shoot a man from behind a tree near to its root, while the white man is looking to see his head pop

out at man's height. *This has taught the United States troops,
to load their muskets while lying on their backs, and firing in
an almost supine posture. When the Duke of Saxe-Weimer was
in Cambridge, he noticed this, to him, novel mode of firing,
which he had never before seen, and this was in a volunteer
company of militia. — I do not mean to say that the Indians
fired only in a supine posture; when they had loaded they most
commonly rose up and fired, and then down on the ground
again to re-load. In this action with the formidable Black-foot
tribe, Captain Nathaniel J. Wyeth's party had no concern. He
himself was in it a very short time, but retired from the contest
doubtless for good reasons. After contesting the matter with the
warlike tribe for about six hours, Captain Sublet found it of
little avail to fight them in this way. He therefore determined to
charge them at once, which was accordingly done. He led, and
ordered his men to follow him, and this proved effectual. Six
beside himself first met the savages hand to hand; of these seven,
four were wounded, and one killed. The Captain was wounded
in his arm and shoulder blade. The Indians did not, however,
retreat entirely, so that we kept up a random fire until dark;
the ball and the arrows were striking the trees after we could
see the effects of one and of the other. There was something
terrific to our men in their arrows. The idea of a barbed arrow
sticking in a man's body, as we had observed it in the deer and
other animals, was appalling to us all, and it is no wonder that
some of our men recoiled at it. They regarded a leaden bullet
much less. We may judge from this the terror of the savages on
being met the first time by fire arms, — a sort of thunder and
lightning followed by death without seeing the fatal shot.*

In this battle with the Indians, not one of those who had
belonged to Captain Wyeth's company received any injury.
There were, however, seven white men of Sublet's company
killed, and thirteen wounded. Twenty-five of our Indians were
killed and thirty-five wounded. The next morning a number of
us went back to the Indian fort, so called, where we found one
dead man and two women, and also twenty-five dead horses, a
proof that the Black-foot were brave men. The number of them

was uncertain. We calculated that they amounted to about three hundred. We guessed that the reason the three dead bodies were left at the entrenchment was, that they had not enough left to carry off their dead and wounded. This affair delayed Captain Wyeth three days, and Captain Sublet ten days. The names of those who left Captain Wyeth to return home, were Dr. Jacob Wyeth, John B. Wyeth, his cousin, William Nud, Theophilus Beach, R. L. Wakefield, Hamilton Law, George More, – Lane, and Walter Palmer. The names of those who remained attached to Captain Wyeth, and who went on with him to Salmon river, are J. Woodman, Smith, G. Argent, – Abbot, W. Breck, S. Burditt, – Ball, St. Clair, C. Tibbits, G. Trumbull, and – Whittier.

Several weeks later, on the way east with William Sublette, John Wyeth gave these additional details after an encounter with a different band of Indians:

I would, however, here remark, that the warlike body just mentioned, though of the fierce Black-foot tribe, hunted and fought independently of that troop with which we had a battle in the Rocky Mountains; and were most probably ignorant of that affair, in which a chief was treacherously shot by Antoine, who was half Indian and half French, when bearing a white flag, and with which nefarious deed I believe Captain Sublet had no concern. But of all this I cannot speak with certainty, as I myself was half a mile distant, when the Black-foot chief was shot, and his scarlet robe torn off of him by the mongrel Indian, as a trophy instead of his scalp; for the Indians returned their fire so promptly, and continued fighting so long, even after dark, that there was no time nor opportunity of his securing that evidence of his savage blood and mode of warfare.[27]

Nathaniel Wyeth

Boston ice merchant Nathaniel Wyeth had devised a grand plan for a colony in the Oregon Territory. His enterprise would combine beaver (trapped in the Rocky Mountains and purchased at rendezvous) with salmon from the Columbia River, and would ship these commodities to New England. Vessels sailing into the

Columbia region would bring supplies for both arms of the business. With that in mind, he set out for the West with a small band of men. At the 1832 rendezvous in Pierre's Hole, several disgruntled members of the party, including his brother and cousin, opted to return east.

Besides witnessing the rendezvous and the battle following it, Wyeth wrote a letter to another brother, Leonard, the day after the trappers fought with the Gros Ventres. Wyeth's July 19, 1832 letter is second to Campbell's in terms of proximity to the events (a portion of the actual letter is reproduced in color plate 15).

Rocky Mts July 19th 1832

Bro Leonard

Another skirmish with the Blk-feet has delayed all the Party and give me an opportunity to write you further. I have given to Mr Sublette letters of Introduction to you & Charles   he has assisted me much and I beg you to extend to him as much politeness as you possible can   he is a person of great respectability in this business and has made a fortune in it which is an easy matter for anyone who will follows it provided he meets with no accidents   it is not certain that he will go east with winter but should he my pride is much concerned in his reception. In the skirmish I alluded to above the killed and wounded on our side is about 20   the Black feet were completely defeated leaving about 20 horses dead on the ground and some of their dead (an unusual thing in Indian warfare   they escaped in the night and their trail could be followed by their blood and the dead & dying. among the dead horses were found some of those taken in the first skirmish. they were in a fort which occasioned our severe loss. none of my twelve men were hurt, most of them being on camp guard at the time. we are detained by the wounded. Jacob has enough to do and earns some money by his skill   this battle lasted from 8 oclock in the morning until dark and during the night the miserable remnant of about 100 warriors made their escape. most of them were wounded probably not 20 got away alive. I move down Lewis River on which I know am in Co with 42 men including my own and shall soon be out of the Black foot country say in 200 miles more. Whiskey sells here

*2$ pr pint   flour 2$ rice, sugar the same. Red & Blue cloth
such as you get for 1.50 for $10.00 pr yd. Blankets [account?]
18$ a piece $3. Guns at $40   Traps at 20$ and other
things in proportion and pay in Beaver at $4 pr lb but with all
this chance I have saved only enough to supply myself in Horses
and food for the rout down and subsistence there   I think
of stopping as soon as I get out of the dangerous country and
trapping this fall and next spring in order to get the wherewith
to bottom an order for goods upon $5000 will be a plenty and
I am in hopes to get this by that time barring accidents. please
communicate the contents of this to Charles as I have no time to
spare in writing   give my best respects to your good wife etc*

> *Aff your Bro*
> *Nath'l Wyeth*
> *P.S. Mr Sublette badly wounded*

In his journal as well, Wyeth recorded his experiences of the
battle. He started by telling of the men's departure from the main
rendezvous camp. As with many greenhorns, Wyeth's descriptions
of topography were often wrong.

Journal – *July 17-25, 1832*

*On the 17th we put out and stered S.E. in direction to a pass
through the same mountains by which we entered the valley
these Mts. run E. & W. and the pass I refer to is the next E. of
the one refered to and through it the waters of this valley reach
Lewis River which is on the S. side of this range at night we
encamped within about 8 miles of the commencement of the
pass On the 18th we did not leave camp when near starting
we observed 2 partys of Indians coming out of the pass about
200 in number with but few horses after securing our camp
our riders went out to meet them and soon found them to
be Blackfeet a little skirmish ensued one of the Blackfeet was
killed and his Blankett and robe brought into camp on this the
Indians made for the timber the women and children were seen
flying to the mountains at this time only 42 men being the party
of Mess Milton Sublette & Frapp mine and a few Independent
Hunters were in sight and the Indians were disposed to give us
their usual treatment when they meet us in small bodies but*

while the Indians we[re] making their preparations we sent an express to camp which soon brought out a smart force of Nez Perces Flatheads and whites the Indians finding they were caught fortified themselves in a masterly manner in the wood. We attacked them and continued the attack all day there were probably about 20 of them killed and 32 horses were found dead They decamped during the night leaving most of their utensils lodges &c and many of the dead we have lost 3 whites killed 8 badly wounded among which is Mr Wm. Sublette who was extremely active in the battle about 10 of the Indians were killed or mortally wounded of the Nez Perces and Flatheads in the morning we visited their deserted fort they had dug into the ground to reach water and to secure themselves from our shot It was a sickening scene of confusion and Blood[s]head one of our men who was killed inside their fort we found mutilated in a shocking manner on the 19th we removed back to our former ground to be near our whole force and to recruit the wounded and bury the dead. We think that 400 lodges or about 600 warriors of the Blackfeet are on the other side of the pass and if they come they must be met with our whole force in which case the contest will be a doubtful one. We have mad[e] Horse pens and secured our camp in as good a manner as we can and wait the result this affair will detain us some days. On 24th we again moved out of the valley in the same direction as at first viz about S.E. and encamped at night in the gorge of it during the march I visited the scene of our conflict for the first time since the battle the din of arms was now changed into the noise of the vulture and the howling of masterless dogs the stench was extreme most of the men in the fort must have perished I soon retired from this scene of disgusting butchery On the 25th we proceeded through the pass which is tolerably good and in a direction of about S.W. by S. and encamped 15 miles on Lewis River.[28]

Wyeth traveled through Pierre's Hole again in July 1833 and revisited the battlefield. His journal entries for those days will be discussed later.

Analyzing the Reports

The following summary will try to reconstruct in detail the chain of events that took place at the Battle of Pierre's Hole, taking into account the varying, and often conflicting, reports.

The direction in which the departing trappers traveled – southwest, south or southeast – starts the warped ball rolling. The number of miles traveled from rendezvous – six, eight, ten or fifteen – keeps it spinning. While one account indicates the Indians were first seen through a spyglass, another says the trappers could not tell if the dust in the distance was caused by buffalo, the anticipated AFC caravan or Indians. The Gros Ventres involved in the battle may have numbered sixty, 150 warriors on horseback, or a traveling community of 300 men, women and children. Whether treachery on the part of trappers or Indian aggression (outright or implied) sparked the battle, is open to question. Even the reports of Antoine Godin's ruse differ regarding who was with him, the weapons he carried, whether or not the Blackfoot chief was armed or unarmed, who pulled the trigger and so forth. Was Godin's trophy a scarlet blanket or a red coat? The death toll, for either side, varies notably according to reporter. On the trappers' side, reports were as few as three and as many as a dozen. For the Gros Ventres, estimates ranged from nine to fifty.

Nevertheless, a reasonable synthesis can be created, beginning with the departure of a Rocky Mountain Fur Company brigade led by Milton Sublette on Tuesday, July 17, 1832. Milton was a younger brother of William Sublette and a partner in the RMFC. Andrew, a still younger Sublette brother, was also in the party. Another RMFC partner, Henry Fraeb, accompanied this group. Fraeb, of German descent, was referred to in the journal accounts as "Frapp."

There may have been two RMFC brigades, one led by Milton Sublette, one by Fraeb, that started out together on this date. It seems another party, including Leonard and Nidever, camped a bit in the rear of the RMFC. These groups were headed to south ern Idaho and on to the Wasatch Mountains, some as far as the Humboldt or Salmon rivers, traveling jointly through the common parts of the journey for added protection against unfriendly Indians. Tagging along part of the way for similar reasons, Nathaniel Wyeth and the eleven-man remnant of his party steered for the Columbia

River and Oregon Territory. Heading for the Humboldt River were Alexander Sinclair's party and a few free trappers, making a total of around forty men. A party of friendly Flatheads, returning home from their visit to the rendezvous, accompanied the trappers as well.

The first day's travel was short – between six and fifteen miles according to various accounts, but five writers agree on eight while one reports just six miles and one stretches it to fifteen. The discrepancies in the distance may indicate the separation of starting points, since the location of the various camps was spread over a five-mile radius.

Such a brief jaunt was sometimes referred to as a Hudson's Bay start.[29] It gets the party away from the main event, refocuses the members who may have celebrated their last night at rendezvous a little too much, and allows for early discovery of missing or forgotten equipment. Their direction was up the valley, toward its south end, in order to exit over an unnamed pass that would take them to the Snake River.

While the muddled accounts are difficult to reconcile, it appears the parties encamped within two miles of the entrance to Pine Creek Pass. A good guess puts the camp due west of Victor, Idaho, about where today's Cedron Road crosses Trail Creek, on the south side of the creek with a clear view directly into the pass.

On the morning of July 18, the men were leisurely packing up and preparing to continue their trek. Movement, perhaps a mounted party, was spotted coming down from the pass. At first, the approaching riders were thought to be either buffalo or the long-awaited Lucien Fontenelle and his caravan of AFC trade goods. Nathaniel Wyeth and/or Milton Sublette used a telescope to better identify the newcomers, so they were far enough away that it was difficult to tell Native American from Euro-American with the naked eye. Fontenelle's most likely route would have taken him via Union Pass – Green River – Jackson Hole. The standard approach to Pierre's Hole from that direction would have been Teton Pass, not Pine Creek Pass (for a photograph capturing this view, see color plate 14). It is not likely that Fontenelle was really expected through Pine Creek Pass, and only Bonneville and Meek make this claim. If the approaching riders had been coming from the direction of Teton Pass rather than Pine Creek Pass, the idea of Fontenelle's arrival would have made sense.

Both of these versions were penned by authors other than the mountaineers themselves and Bonneville did not actually see the Battle. Washington Irving, a fiction writer known for novels such as *Rip Van Winkle* and *The Legend of Sleepy Hollow*, embellished battle scenes witnessed by both Robert Campbell and Samuel Parker, who contradicted Irving's report.[30]

Meek's biographer, Frances Victor, much admired Washington Irving and freely admitted Irving's influence on her interpretation of the West.[31] *The River of the West* directly quotes portions of Irving's account of the Battle. Unfortunately, it seems that Irving's embellishment of Bonneville's second-hand story was thereby repeated and reinforced. The two accounts of Fontenelle's approach are too similar in phrasing and pacing to be coincidental, rendering both suspect. The only true difference is in who produced a telescope. Irving wrote:

> *On the following morning, just as they were raising their camp, they observed a long line of people pouring down a defile of the mountains. They at first supposed them to be Fontenelle and his party, whose arrival had been daily expected. Wyeth, however, reconnoitred them with a spy-glass, and soon perceived they were Indians. They were divided into two parties, forming, in the whole, about one hundred and fifty persons, men, women, and children. Some were on horseback, fantastically painted and arrayed, with scarlet blankets fluttering in the wind. The greater part, however, were on foot.*[32]

Victor's version reads:

> *Just as the men were raising camp for a start the next morning, a caravan was observed moving down the mountain pass into the valley. No alarm was at first felt, as an arrival was daily expected of one of the American company's partisans, Mr. Fontenelle, and his company. But on reconnoitering with a glass, Sublette discovered them to be a large party of Blackfeet, consisting of a few mounted men, and many more, men, women, and children, on foot. At the instant they were discovered, they set up the usual yell of defiance, and rushed down like a mountain torrent into the valley, flourishing their*

248

weapons, and fluttering their gay blankets and feathers in the wind.[33]

Since no other primary source mentions the notion that Fontenelle's pack train was looked for on Pine Creek Pass, it is safe to set the idea aside.

The trappers soon discovered that a band of Indians was riding down Little Pine Creek. As explained earlier, the Gros Ventres were returning from a long visit with their cousins, the Arapahoe, in what is now the state of Colorado, and heading for their homeland near the Three Forks of the Missouri River. A route from Colorado, up to Jackson Hole and over the Tetons makes far more sense than coming up Swan Valley and into Pierre's Hole via Pine Creek Pass. From Swan Valley, it would be more reasonable to continue along the Snake River to Henry's Fork, then north, bypassing Pierre's Hole altogether.

But enough evidence points to Pine Creek Pass that the question must be asked – why would the Gros Ventres enter Pierre's Hole from that direction? Based on the various reports, the answer seems to be that the Gros Ventre were following Fitzpatrick. This group had dogged Fitzpatrick's trail and stolen his horses just a few weeks prior. The exact route Fitzpatrick took after separating from Sublette's supply caravan is unknown. Nidever reported going on a short hunt and finding him crossing the Snake River. From Green River, if Fitzpatrick forced his way through the Snake River Canyon to the junction of the Grey's and Salt rivers, then followed the Snake downstream to Pine Creek Pass, these warriors would have been hot on his trail. Taking women and children through such terrain would have been a feat, but not out of the question.

Tracking backward in time, the attack on William Sublette prior to his arrival in Pierre's Hole provides more clues about the Gros Ventres' itinerary. Shortly after crossing South Pass, on the night of July 2, a party of Indians fired on Sublette's camp and made off with a few horses. It was the same band of Gros Ventres who would harass Fitzpatrick and ultimately engage in the Battle of Pierre's Hole. The New Englander Wyeth wrote his brother Charles from the "other side of the Rocky Mountains," telling him of "a most ludicras fight with the Blackfeet, no blood drawn, but I lost 4 horses."[34] To his wife, a similar letter carefully described "a bloodless skirmish."[35]

From this skirmish with Sublette's caravan, the Gros Ventres knew a large party of armed fur traders was on the road through Teton Valley, though Campbell said the track was obliterated by rains and the passage of time since the trappers arrived. Rather than follow such a formidable company and risk injury to the women and children present, perhaps the Gros Ventres crossed westward on a well-traveled trail through the Green River Valley to the Wyoming Range.[36]

Traversing modern McDougal Gap, the Gros Ventres dropped down onto Grey's River and followed it to its junction with the Snake River. Descending the Snake, the party arrived at the mouth of Pine Creek Pass. While this conjecture explains how the Gros Ventre came into Pierre's Hole via Pine Creek Pass, it fails to address why. For that, there appears to be no solid answer and tribal history does not speak to a motive.

Luckily for history, a few Arapahoe families were traveling with the Gros Ventres, and Arapahoe oral tradition retains an account of the incident. An Arapahoe chief, Hanake-baah or Bull Thunder, participated alongside his kinsmen in the fray. Tribal historians confirm the earlier attack on William Sublette, and report that the Arapahoe who had distinguished themselves in this raid were anxious to get home to brag and show off. Becoming impatient, this faction pushed ahead of the main camp. Leaving the heavy baggage and slow horses behind with relatives, parts of two bands struck out for Three Forks ahead of the rest.

The morning of the Battle, these Indians were up and about long before the RMFC, so as the Gros Ventres were descending the pass, they saw the white men still in camp in the valley below. According to the Arapahoe, Gros Ventre chieftain Biahoh knew that Fontenelle's party, with whom he was on good terms, would be in Pierre's Hole around this time. In an ironic twist, Biahoh's first assumption on seeing the trappers was that they must be Fontenelle's group so he rode down to meet them.[37]

The path from Milton Sublette's camp to Pine Creek Pass intersected trails with anyone exiting it. The Indians were heading directly into the RMFC brigade's line of march. The travelers, supposed to be Blackfoot Indians, were assumed to be hostile. There may have been as many as two hundred warriors in two groups, but the party was probably much smaller. The presence of women and children normally would have indicated that war was not the party's intention.

Upon sighting the Indians, RMFC secured its camp. The horses were rounded up, and packs were set up as a barricade. Milton was probably still convalescing from his wound at the hands of the Bannock chief a few weeks prior to rendezvous. Knowing the trappers were outnumbered, Milton sent a dispatch back to the main rendezvous site calling for reinforcements. Fraeb instructed Antoine Godin, the half-breed Iroquois trapper, to take another Indian from the party and meet the approaching Indians to find out what they were up to. This interaction took place as much as a mile from the RMFC camp; the distance surely played a part in the widely divergent views of the event.

Though some sources named Godin's companion as Baptiste Dorian, most reports indicate Godin selected a Flathead man to accompany him.[38] These two soon determined a large party of Blackfoot was coming their way. Both men had reason to hate this

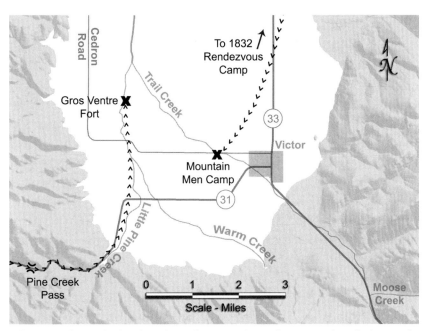

This map shows the landmarks and routes of travel associated with the Battle of Pierre's Hole. For a larger view, see color plate 2. MAP BY CLINT GILCHRIST

251

particular tribe. Just weeks prior to rendezvous, the Flathead and Blackfoot, traditional enemies, had fought in the Lemhi Valley at the Flathead village on the upper waters of Salmon River's East Fork. Twelve Flathead were killed, a thousand head of horses stolen and a half dozen or more tepees were destroyed. Godin's father, Thyery Godin, had been killed by Blackfoot on Big Lost River two years previously. Here was an opportunity for revenge on both men's part.

When the Indians spied the trappers, several scurried back in the direction from which they came. A Gros Ventre representative rode out ahead, apparently unarmed and carrying a peace pipe. Arapahoe historians do not believe Biahoh was contemplating treachery. If he had thought he was facing Fontenelle's competition, he would not have risked his life by advancing with only a peace pipe, especially since the Indians outnumbered the trappers. Nor would he have brought women and children out of the hills and into danger. Some accounts claim the Gros Ventres were "painted and arrayed for war," but Robert Campbell, a credible source, described the chief advancing with a pipe of peace. Arapahoe historians also report the noisy procession as a sign of friendly intentions. A stealthy approach would have been more appropriate for dealing with an enemy.[39]

Leonard stated the Gros Ventres displayed a British flag. Nidever reported "the chief dressed in a bright scarlet coat." Both are examples of the trader practice of "rigging" tribal dignitaries in an attempt to curry favor. A flag was often given to a chief as an emblem of the high regard in which he was held by the trader and the influence that particular man had with the company. Prince Alexander Maximilian recorded an American flag hoisted on a pole in front of a Gros Ventre leader's lodge just a year later. Prominent Indian leaders were also given special clothing, such as a distinctive hat or a "chief's coat," worn by the Native American as a symbol of his ability to provide for his people.[40]

Maximilian described multiple cases of such "rigging" of Gros Ventre and Blackfoot at Fort McKenzie in 1833. He also wrote of an instance in which chiefs coming to trade "delivered up their colours, most of which they had received from English merchants, and which were carried before them on long ensign staffs, quite in military style."[41] But Maximilian also related that this same nation "had entirely demolished a fort, on the frontiers of Canada, two years before, killed a clerk, and eighteen other persons, besides murdering several other white people in those parts."[42]

Since the Gros Ventre band that descended into Pierre's Hole had been in Colorado for the past few years, it was probably not the same aggressive group Maximilian described.[43] It seems more probable their British flag was awarded them by HBC traders prior to embarking on their family reunion.

Zenas Leonard was convinced the Gros Ventres had stolen the British flag from a Northwest Company party they had recently ambushed. Since the Northwest Company merged with HBC several years prior, Leonard likely meant a Hudson's Bay brigade, but there is no record of such a defeat in company records. Nor does any other primary source document an HBC party coming to the Pierre's Hole rendezvous or anywhere near it.[44]

Deserved or not, suspicion ran high as the chief held out his hand in apparent friendship. Any discussion would have likely been between Godin and Biahoh due to the hostility existing between the Flathead and Gros Ventre. Campbell wrote that "a few signs (for their languages were unknown to each other) soon satisfied the parties of the irreconcilable enmity existing." Rather, from all accounts, it appears this "enmity" did not allow for peaceful discourse.[45]

As the trappers rode up, they had concocted a treacherous plan. Meeting the chief halfway from the trappers, Godin grabbed the outstretched hand and the Flathead shot the warrior, by some accounts with a concealed, shortened rifle. Godin then snatched up the enemy's red blanket and galloped about a mile back to the RMFC camp. Several accounts omit this duplicitous act but there is ample evidence that it occurred; due to this one impetuous act, history will never know whether the Gros Ventres approached in peace.

As the murder of Biahoh, the Gros Ventre leader, registered in the minds of trapper and Indian, the two sides began shooting at each other.[46] Wyeth's men, new to the mountains, stayed primarily out of the battle, crouched behind the bales of equipment thrown up as defense for the camp. The contingent of Gros Ventres may also have divided in two at this stage of the confrontation as some reports indicate a second group of Indians. Some of the Gros Ventre women slipped back into the trees along the creek and began constructing their own defensive fortification.

In 1832, the Gros Ventres were a strong nation. The tribe boasted 430 lodges early the following year when George Catlin recorded a tribal census.[47] In 1833, the same year as Catlin's survey, Prince Maximilian noted the Gros Ventres were fairly wealthy even though they had fought at Pierre's Hole and been attacked frequently by the Crow. He also stated these Indians had been very poor at one time, but could now supply their wants through trade. According to the prince, the Gros Ventres counted 400 to 500 warriors just one year after the battle.[48] Facing Milton Sublette and his handful of mountaineers, the Gros Ventres likely thought the odds were in their favor. As many as one hundred warriors against about forty trappers would have boosted their confidence in a quick victory.

However, when the thundering hooves of reinforcements from the main camp were heard at about ten o'clock that morning, the notion of an easy conquest was abandoned. The Gros Ventre warriors retreated into the cottonwoods to assist the women in building an impromptu log fort. The Gros Ventres draped lodge covers and buffalo hides over their breastwork to shield themselves from the trappers' view. Many of their horses were brought within the enclosure as well. Furrows were scooped in the ground for some degree of cover and perhaps a water pit, according to Nathaniel Wyeth. Anticipating a lengthy siege, the Indians recognized the potential thirst ahead, though given the damp surroundings, they probably did not have to dig very deep to find moisture.

Riding hard to the scene were William Sublette and Robert Campbell, leading a large force of mountaineers and friendly Indians. Nidever put the number of reinforcements at 250. Campbell told his brother that all the trappers "with the exception of a few left in charge of camp" came to assist. Sublette, however, indicated "only 30 whites and as many friendly Indians" joined the attack. Most of these new arrivals rode bareback, not wasting the time to saddle their mounts before rushing to the aid of their comrades. Along the way, Sublette and Campbell arranged with each other for the care of their respective estates should one or the other be killed in the ensuing engagement. On the field, Sublette harangued the RMFC men, telling them they would have to fight the Blackfoot sooner or later – it might as well be sooner.

The main mountaineer assault was launched from the north. Some of the trappers found a ravine for cover and blasted away at the enemy while others maneuvered to surround the opponent's defenses. Sublette and Campbell were first to enter the woods, slipping in close enough to spot Gros Ventres aiming between the logs of the fortification. William Sublette shot one of them between the eyes and told Campbell to watch for a similar opportunity. Nearby, Alexander Sinclair was fatally wounded. Shortly after, Sublette took a bone-splintering ball in the arm that exited through his shoulder blade, and Campbell had to carry him to safety.

The fighting went on all day with little true effect. Many of the Gros Ventre women, children and elderly were believed to have slipped back up toward Pine Creek Pass when the shooting began. As evening approached, the trappers proposed burning the log structure, but the Flatheads argued against the idea because it would have ruined the plunder they had set their hearts on obtaining from the adversary they planned to defeat.

During this debate, one of the Gros Ventres was heard to announce that an even larger party of their people would soon arrive to avenge their deaths should they be wiped out. This was misinterpreted as a warning that the greater force was already attacking the main rendezvous, now poorly manned, with all the trappers at the battle scene in the south end of the valley. A mad rush back to the primary camp ensued, only to find it was a false alarm. Nidever says this was a nine-mile ride.

Nidever also blamed the bungled translation on a "renegade Blackfoot who was among Frapp's men" who had been instructed to negotiate a Gros Ventre surrender. This Indian may have been a Blackfoot chief mentioned in John Townsend's 1834 journal as having earlier killed a rival tribe member, and who joined his traditional enemies in order to escape punishment.[49] Regardless of the intention or the translation, the Gros Ventre message could not have worked better as a ruse.

Too late to take up the attack again, the fur companies prepared for night, setting additional guards as a precaution. When daylight came, the trappers returned to the battle ground to find the Gros

Ventres had stolen away under cover of darkness. Alexander Sinclair had died of his wounds during the night and was buried in the horse pen where the ground was so trodden his body would not be found. Several of the trappers spent the morning chopping as much spent lead as they could from the logs of the Gros Ventre fortress and the surrounding tree trunks. Lead was a valuable commodity in the Rocky Mountains and the quantity they recently purchased at rendezvous had to last them all year.

Several trappers and their Indian allies examined the hastily-built fortress. The body of one trapper, probably Thomas Quigley, was found mutilated within the barricade. A handful of dead warriors were also found inside and as many as ten scalps may have been taken. A few women and children died in the skirmish, probably by accident rather than being targeted, but given the recent Flathead defeat in the Lemhi Valley, Godin may not have been the only one with a "take no prisoners" attitude. Several dead horse carcasses also lay within the Gros Ventre stronghold.

The rather sensational anecdote about the Indian woman who, lost in grief and devotion to her fallen mate, begged for death after the battle is told in slightly different versions by both Irving and Victor. It is tempting to discount the entire event, except that Warren Ferris echoes it eerily with his story of two young women who "without remorse" were struck down in the battle's aftermath. There may have been several wounded Gros Ventres who were quickly dispatched upon discovery.

Even if it were possible to declare a victor in the Battle of Pierre's Hole, it would serve little purpose. Not surprisingly, though, several trappers wrote accounts proclaiming themselves the winners. Andrew Drips claimed in a letter to John B. Sarpy, written soon after the conflict:

> *We had a fight with the Black Feet Indians four or five days ago. There were several killed & wounded on both sides but we got the best of the fight. Wm. Sublette is severely wounded. If he lives to get down he will give the particulars of it.*[50]

Simply from a body count basis, the trapper side seemed to have killed more of its opponents.

Yet, Campbell declared the Gros Ventre defended their well-chosen position "with obstinate bravery" before effecting an undetected retreat. Leonard did not hesitate to "give the savages credit for the skill they displayed in preserving their lives" and seemed to appreciate the "most ingenious and well executed device" used by their foe to clear the battlefield. Rivet insisted the Gros Ventres "fought bravely from behind their log and brush breastwork," and "they would not surrender." Perhaps designating the winner depends on how "victory" is defined.

Based on the varied reports then, there may have been seven or eight mountain men who lost their lives in the fray, but only four are named. Confirmed deaths on the trapper side included Thomas Quigley and Alexander Sinclair, whose brother, Prewett, survived the battle. A trapper whom Zenas Leonard named only as Kean was also killed. This Kean was probably the person Sublette referred to as "another man." William Sublette named "Miller of Boone Co." as being "wounded severely in the body which I fear will have proved fatal." Ferris learned of Miller's death when his AFC brigade met up with an RMFC team in early October, affirming the young man died a month after the battle and was buried in Cota's Defile, today's Birch Creek in modern Lemhi County, Idaho.[51]

Leonard told of a missing man who, after a search, was found in the brush, severely wounded. They carried him on a litter back toward the main camp, but he died after a few miles and they buried him "Indian style." Nidever described a "Canadian half-breed" who had had a bit too much to drink, then brazenly attempted to storm the fort, only to be killed by a shot to the head. This raises the question of how liquor may have contributed to casualties in general.

Several of the mountaineers experienced close calls. Andrew Drips was shot in the hat, losing a lock of hair though he fails to mention this near escape in his letter to Sarpy.[52] John (Jack) Robertson, was "shot through the shirt, just above the heart."[53] Two other men, identified only as "Smith" and "Phelps" were wounded and dragged to safety.

Not all the wounds may have been from Gros Ventre weapons. According to Irving and Victor, Wyeth was convinced an Indian ally near him was shot by friendly fire from the other side of the fortifications. In their fervor to kill their enemy, mountain men wound up on both sides of the fort. Bonneville, echoed by Meek, said "A cross-fire thus took place, which occasionally did mischief to friend as well as foes."

Surviving trappers who were specifically named in the accounts as participants in the battle included William Sublette, Milton Sublette, Andrew Sublette, Robert Campbell, Nathaniel Wyeth, Zenas Leonard, Andrew Drips, Henry Fraeb, Antoine Godin, Prewett Sinclair, Warren Ferris, Thomas Fitzpatrick, George Nidever, Joe Meek, John Robertson, Smith and Phelps. There were numerous others, between sixty and as many as 250, whose identity can only be speculation.

A Nez Perce chief, Ta-kin-shwai-tish, was wounded in the stomach during the battle. As this injury festered, he earned the name Rotten Belly, though he is not to be confused with Arapooish, the Crow chieftain with the same nickname.[54] No Crow were present at the Pierre's Hole rendezvous.

On June 18, 1834, the Nez Perce Rotten Belly met up with William Sublette while staying on the Green River, just before that year's rendezvous. William M. Anderson recorded,

Mr. Sublette has met here an old acquaintance and friend in Rotten-belly, a tall, commanding-looking fellow, who was wounded in the same Blackfoot fight where the former received a ball in his arm and side. The bread-basket of the Nes Perce was so seriously damaged that he has ever since borne a name indicative of the fact. It was curious to see how those two iron men enjoyed their wounds. For a short time the scene was uproarious. Shouting, laughing, slapping and joking with each other, then winding up by cursing the Blackfeet with a hearty and vicious eloquence.[55]

Rotten Belly's wound later healed completely.

Hallalhotsoot, another Nez Perce leader, was wounded in the hip during the fray and never completely mended. This man was known to trappers as "The Lawyer" due to his talent for argument and debate. Some accounts name him "The Talker." He may have been part Nez Perce and part Flathead for his Indian name derived from the Flathead, or Salish, tongue. His father was Twisted Hair, who met Lewis and Clark in 1805 during their expedition. The Lawyer met many noted Euro-Americans and by 1835, had learned enough English to serve as an interpreter.[56]

Campbell imparted the curious report of a Nez Perce chief who was hit in the chest with a spent ball. This old head-man believed he was invulnerable and could not be killed by a bullet. When the flagging lead hit his breast bone and dropped to the ground, it caused quite a commotion, convincing his people he was bullet proof. Though he spit up some blood, it was "big medicine."

Three Gros Ventre chiefs may have been killed in the encounter.[57] Jim Bridger later reported, "The loss of the Gros Ventres was never fully known. They left nine killed, with twenty-five horses and all their baggage, and admitted a loss of twenty-six warriors."[58] At least two women were killed and several dead children were found in the fort.

Two dozen or more Gros Ventre horses were also killed. Among them were animals William Sublette recognized as those stolen when his party had been attacked while camped on Green River. Both mounts of Thomas Fitzpatrick's were found alive and returned to him. When the dust settled, John Wyeth witnessed Indian first-aid.

After the battle at Pierre's Valley, I had an opportunity of seeing a specimen of Indian surgery in treating a wound. An Indian squaw first sucked the wound perfectly dry, so that it appeared white as chalk; and then she bound it up with a piece of dry buck-skin as soft as woollen cloth, and by this treatment the wound began to heal, and soon closed up, and the part became sound again. The sucking of it so effectually may have been from an apprehension of a poisoned arrow. But who taught the savage Indian that a person may take poison into his mouth without any risk, as the poison of a rattlesnake without harm, provided there be no scratch or wound in the mouth, so as to admit it into the blood?[59]

The battle was big news in the Rocky Mountains. An example of how fast news traveled in the 1830s West occurred on September 12, less than two months after the Battle of Pierre's Hole. A Cayuse Indian entered the HBC camp of John Work in what is today Morrow County, Oregon. "Just arrived from the plains," the Indian informed Work of "two great battles fought with the Blackfeet by the Nezperces & F. Heads and again by these joined by the Americans." The Pierre's Hole battle was a headliner![60]

Other observations emerged later in works of fiction. William Drummond Stewart did not come to the mountains until 1833, so he did not witness the Battle of Pierre's Hole, but he did write two novels about life in the Far West, and some interesting tidbits about the battle are embedded in them.[61] One passage in *Altowan* hints that Stewart was quite familiar with the lore surrounding the Battle:

> *When did a Blackfoot break his word or offer the hand of peace with a heart of evil until taught to do so by them [the whites]? Who fired at my brother, while giving the hand of friendship? ... Who but a half-breed, taught by the whites, gave his hand to a Blackfoot chief, while he told his companion to shoot him? His blood was spilled by a dog in the sight of the Great Spirit.*[62]

A backward glance at Godin's duplicitous act also takes in a story told by John Townsend about its later consequences. On May 22, 1836, a Gros Ventre band showed up at Fort Hall, which had been established just two years prior by Nathaniel Wyeth. Camped across the Portneuf River from the fort, the Indians signaled for someone to come across and trade with them. The person sent to barter was Antoine Godin. A man named James Bird, an adopted member of the tribe, acted as interpreter and may have been the leader of the Indian delegation. They all sat down to smoke the pipe, a prefatory act to trading, and as Godin received the pipe, the Gros Ventres shot him. Before he died, they scalped him and Bird carved the initials "N.J.W." into his forehead. Historians believe this act was retribution for Godin's deceit at the Pierre's Hole fight. There is no evidence Bird was present at the battle, but he would have heard the tales from his adopted kinsmen.[63]

Exactly how Wyeth's initials figure in the retaliation is unclear since Wyeth was not, in any way commanding the trappers during the battle at Pierre's Hole. Historian John Jackson suggests Bird's action was more political. It may have been an attempt to intimidate the Americans into vacating Fort Hall, at the time an unwelcome inconvenience for the HBC, with whom the Gros Ventres were on relatively good terms.[64]

This tale is corroborated by F. A. Wislizenus, M.D., who visited Fort Hall in 1839:

Near the fort were some graves. In one of them rested Antoine Godin, an adventurous mountaineer and a bitter foe of the Blackfeet. It was he who brought on in 1832 the bloody fight with the Blackfeet at Pierre's Hole, related in W. Irving's "Rocky Mountains," by treacherously grasping the hand of their leader, while another shot him. The Blackfeet after that harbored the bitterest enmity for him. Some years later a band of Blackfeet appeared near Fort Hall, on the right bank of the Snake River. Through signs they made it known that they were peaceably disposed and wished to trade with the fort. Some white men – among them Godin, who chanced to be there – crossed the river, and smoked the pipe of peace with them. While they were thus employed, a Blackfoot shot Godin from behind, and so avenged the death of their leader through similar treachery. Such occurrences are here, unfortunately, not uncommon; and the first provocation is given ordinarily by the whites rather than by the Indians.[65]

William Drummond Stewart spiced up his second novel, *Edward Warren*, with an account of the death of Godin, whom he named Goddard. Stewart aptly concluded: "the taste of blood and revenge might be too sweet to be withstood."[66] Had any other man besides Godin been sent forward to treat with the Gros Ventre chief at Pierre's Hole, the battle might have been delayed or avoided altogether. A bit of tobacco for the pipe carried by the head man and perhaps a few inconsequential gifts may have opened a peaceful trade. In any case, Godin's ultimate fate casts a backward-shining light on the battle itself.

There is a roadside marker, not especially visible, on Highway 33 in Teton County, just south of Driggs, Idaho that describes the rendezvous and the battle. Unfortunately, some of the trappers listed in the text as participants were not at the rendezvous and battle. Kit Carson was never in Pierre's Hole in 1832.[67] Jim Bridger does not appear in any of the primary accounts of the rendezvous or the battle at its end. Bridger was assuredly at Pierre's Hole, however, because both Bonneville and Meek indicate that Bridger and Fitzpatrick led a trapping brigade north out of Teton Valley once the rendezvous wound to a close.[68] "D. Sinclair" is included in the monument's list of attendees, but only Alexander Sinclair and his brother Prewett have ever been recorded at the 1832 event. A more accurate and visible historic marker would better serve the community and visitors alike.

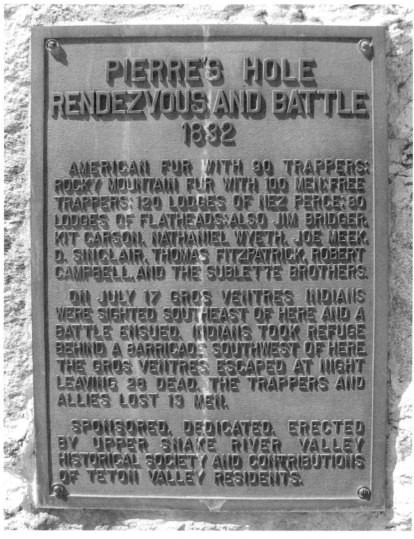

This marker, at the south edge of Driggs, Idaho, reports the Battle of Pierre's Hole but names trappers who were not at the rendezvous or the battle.
JIM HARDEE PHOTO

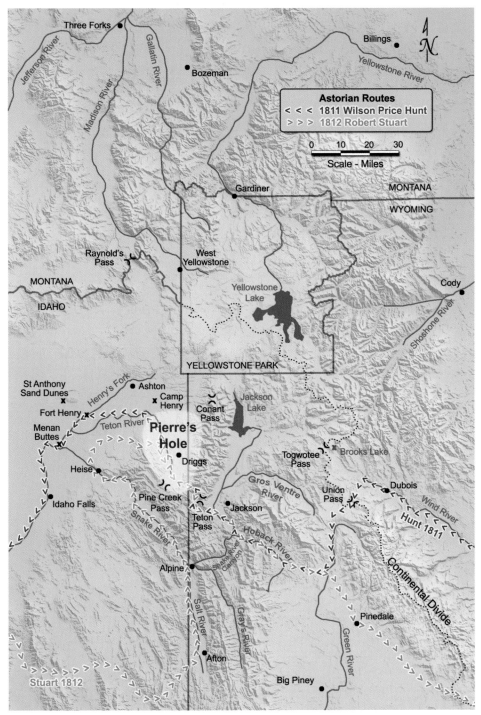

Plate 1. *Map of the region. Pierre's Hole is located in one of the most active areas of the Rocky Mountain fur trade. This map demonstrates how Teton Valley is linked to many other fur trade sites mentioned in the book. It also shows a broader view of the trails taken by Astorians Wilson Price Hunt in 1811 (westward) and Robert Stuart in 1812 (eastward). Modern towns are shown to orient the reader.* MAP BY CLINT GILCHRIST

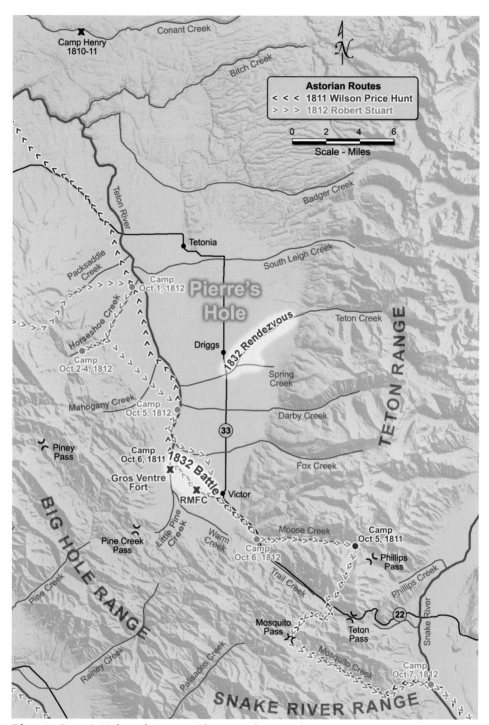

Plate 2. *Pierre's Hole and vicinity. This map places modern towns in Teton Valley in relationship to historic landmarks mentioned throughout the text. Mountain passes around the valley are marked, as are the routes of Wilson Price Hunt and Robert Stuart. The general area of the 1832 rendezvous and the site of the Battle of Pierre's Hole are also indicated. For greater detail on the Battle site, see map on page 251.* MAP BY CLINT GILCHRIST

Plate 3. *Beaver Pond in Trail Creek.* JIM HARDEE PHOTO

Plate 4. *John F. Clymer illustrated the story of Colter's long trek from Fort Remon in John Colter Visits the Crow – 1807.*

Plate 5. *A summer evening in Pierre's Hole.* JIM HARDEE PHOTO

Plate 6. *The approximate location of Fort Henry is on the bench of land in the center of the photograph. Note the Tetons visible in the background.* JIM HARDEE PHOTO

Plate 7. *Camp Henry is situated in the meadow below the tallest clump of cottonwood trees, just left of center. The small hut was built by the Boy Scouts of America to shelter the inscribed stones discussed on pages 78-80.* JIM HARDEE PHOTO

Plate 8. *These artifacts were found in the Snake River, near the Cauldron Linn, and are believed to be some of the equipment lost by Hunt's party when canoes capsized.* IDAHO STATE HISTORICAL MUSEUM

Plate 9. *Robert Stuart's party rafted this section of the Snake River on September 27, 1812. About eight miles downriver from this point, they left their rafts and started overland.* BRUCE BELASON PHOTO

Plate 10. *John F. Clymer's* Trader at Pierre's Hole *is an artist's conception of a scene at one of the Pierre's Hole rendezvous "under the three Teton mountain."* COURTESY OF DAVID J. CLYMER AND THE CLYMER MUSEUM OF ART

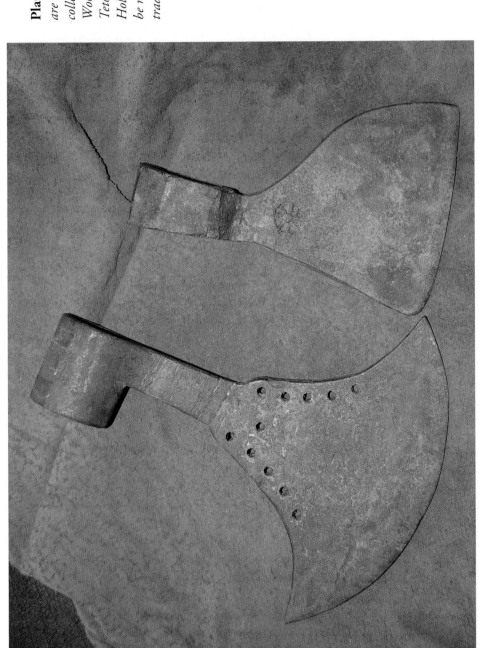

Plate 11. *These axe heads are some of the artifacts collected by Jim and Debbie Wood of Rigby, Idaho along Teton Creek in Pierre's Hole. They are believed to be remnants of rendezvous trade goods.* JIM HARDEE PHOTO

Plates 12 and 13.
(this and facing page)
An amazing variety
of trade beads has
been discovered along
Teton Creek where
trappers camped
during rendezvous.
The labels were
attached to note the
location of each find.
JIM HARDEE PHOTOS

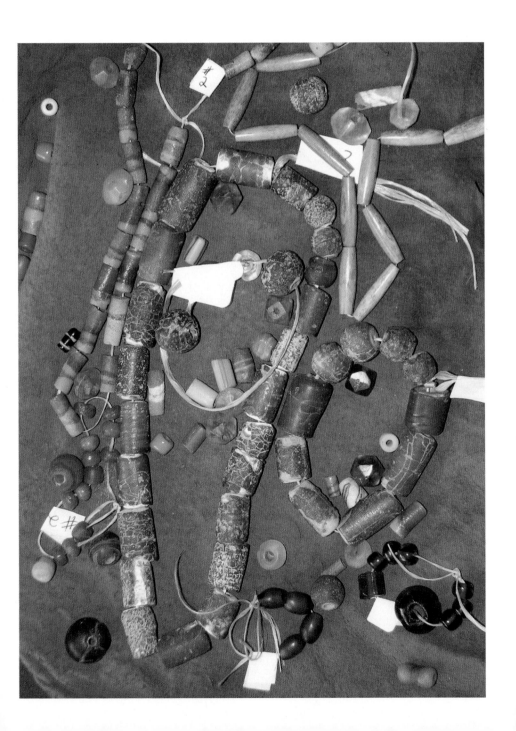

Plate 14. *This is the view from the proposed campsite of Milton Sublette's brigade as it left the 1832 rendezvous. The site is near the junction of Cedron Road and Trail Creek, west of Victor, Idaho. The view is toward Pine Creek Pass, about two miles away. The tree line that crosses the center of the photo, above the structures, is Little Pine Creek. The red arrow indicates the exit from the pass; the blue arrow shows a heavily treed area, similar to what the Gros Ventres used for their fortification. The encounter between Biahoh and Godin which sparked the Battle of Pierre's Hole likely occurred within the light band across the middle ground.* JIM HARDEE PHOTO

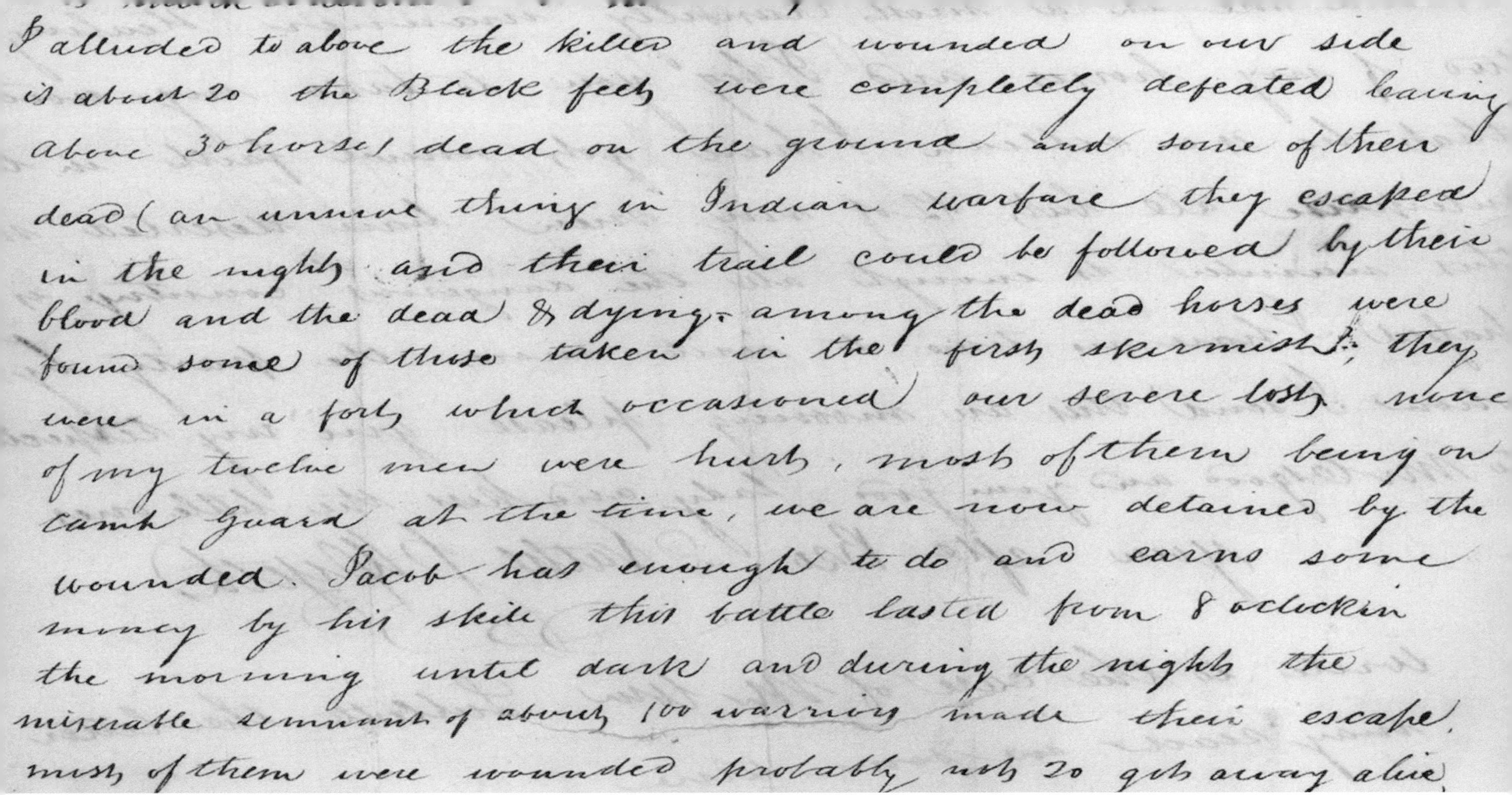

I alluded to above the killed and wounded on our side
is about 20 the Black feet were completely defeated leaving
above 30 horses dead on the ground and some of their
dead (an unusual thing in Indian warfare they escaped
in the night) and their trail could be followed by their
blood and the dead & dying among the dead horses were
found some of these taken in the first skirmish they
were in a fort which occasioned our severe loss were
of my twelve men were hurt, most of them being in
rank guard at the time, we are now detained by the
wounded Jacob has enough to do and earns some
wounded by his side this battle lasted from 8 oclock
the morning untill dark and during the night the
miserable remnant of about 100 warriors made their escape,
most of them were wounded probably not 20 got away alive

Plate 15. *Nathaniel Wyeth wrote to his brother Leonard on July 19, 1832, giving an account of the Battle of Pierre's Hole. The entire letter is transcribed on pages 243–244.* SUBLETTE COUNTY FUR TRADE PAPERS, MUSEUM OF THE MOUNTAIN MAN, PINEDALE, WYOMING

Plate 16. *In the painting* Sublette and Campbell – 1832, *John F. Clymer shows the fur company's pack train heading up the Gros Ventre River out of Jackson Hole after the Battle of Pierre's Hole. Sublette's arm is still in a sling due to the wound he sustained during the fight.*

15
LOCATING THE BATTLE SITE

Conflicting information has led to confusion regarding the actual site of the Battle of Pierre's Hole. Misinterpretation of trapper statements, coupled with misguided oral histories, has made determining where the battle actually took place a difficult proposition. Attempts to determine the site of the RMFC campground after that company departed rendezvous and the ensuing battle site have proved as fractured as the accounts of the battle itself. Nor has the field of battle yet been confirmed by the archeological record.

Milton Sublette and his men traveled south, up the valley, toward one of two exits at that end of Pierre's Hole. Which pass did they intend to cross? It appears the next day was slated for a fairly long pull that would take the trappers to the Snake River, as much as twenty-five miles of travel. They had camped, according to reports, near or in front of the mouth of a pass. The options for the location of this camp depend on whether they planned to go into Jackson Hole or Swan Valley.

If their destination was to be Jackson Hole via Teton Pass, they were likely camped near the mouth of Moose Creek, where the well-used trail would take them east over the mountain. Alternatively, a Swan Valley objective would place the encampment closer to where Little Pine Creek exits the mountains. They would then travel southwest over Pine Creek Pass to the Snake River.

It is also possible that the camp was located more centrally in the basin, between the trail to Teton Pass and the path to Pine Creek Pass. A location flanked by these two passes would have allowed a view of both, thus riders could have been seen entering the valley floor from either direction. The view into Teton Pass from a more centrally located camp would have been somewhat obstructed, so anyone coming from the east would have been less visible than persons descending from Pine Creek Pass.

Several journal accounts indicate a southwesterly direction of travel from the main encampment. From a rendezvous located up Teton Creek, following a line essentially along the base of the Teton

Range provides a compass bearing to the west of south. This allows either of the preceding options for an exit route. Ferris indicated the RMFC brigades intended "to cross on to Lewis River, near the mouth of Salt River." This lends credence to a Pine Creek Pass departure from Pierre's Hole and a campsite closer to the west side of the basin. Since Milton Sublette was headed to Salmon River and Nidever's group aimed for the Humboldt, Pine Creek would also be the logical choice.

Samuel Parker crossed from Jackson Hole into Teton Valley a couple of years later on his way to the Pacific Northwest. The reverend's description of a stream that "commences and increases from springs and rivulets to considerable magnitude, and winds its way through the valley of Pierre's Hole" suggests the Parker group came through Teton Pass and Moose Creek.[1] The travelers descended from the mountain and made camp almost immediately. The next day they traveled down the valley for five hours to the old rendezvous grounds. Along the way, Parker was shown the battle site. It is not clear he detoured from his line of travel. His informant, likely Jim Bridger, may have simply pointed to the vicinity. From this information, it would seem Milton Sublette's 1832 post-rendezvous camp must have been closer to the center of the upper end of the valley near its southern border.

Nathaniel Wyeth attempted to differentiate between the pass for which their course was directed after rendezvous and the pass through which they had entered Teton Valley ten days earlier:

On the 17th we put out and stered S.E. in direction to a pass through the same mountains by which we entered the valley these Mts. run E. & W. and the pass I refer to is the next E. of the one refered to and through it the waters of this valley reach Lewis River which is on the S. side of this range at night we encamped within about 8 miles of the commencement of the pass.[2]

Though Wyeth's description is somewhat confusing, it appears the group was headed for a pass (Pine Creek Pass) which crossed the same range the (Teton Mountains) the men traversed when they arrived (via Teton Pass) in Pierre's Hole. Teton Pass is the pass east of Pine Creek Pass. Placing Wyeth's and Milton Sublette's men in a camp somewhere along Trail Creek, eight miles from the commencement of Teton Pass, fits Wyeth's journal entry if the junction of Moose Creek and Mesquite Creek is considered as its starting place. The trail from the valley floor up Moose Creek is relatively level until it turns up Mesquite Creek. But the waters of Teton Valley do not reach the Snake River through any pass at the south end of the basin so Wyeth was mistaken in that regard.

Therefore, Milton Sublette was most likely taking the party over Pine Creek Pass. This possibility is further strengthened by a statement Wyeth made regarding his party's route on July 25, about a week after the battle:

We proceeded through the pass which is tolerably good and in a direction of about S.W. by S. and encamped 15 miles on Lewis River (here concentrated into one rapid stream) and about 30 miles S. of where we crossed it in going into the valley.[3]

The distance traveled from the Teton Valley side of Pine Creek Pass to the Snake River is approximately fifteen miles. In Swan Valley the river is one convergent flow rather than the divided bottom of eight rapid streams described by Wyeth on the Jackson Hole side of the Tetons, where they forded it on July 6.[4] However, it is nearly sixty miles, rather than Wyeth's thirty miles, to where he forded the Snake earlier in the month. Since a route through Snake River Canyon between the Hoback Junction and modern Alpine, Wyoming was seldom if ever used at this time, the discrepancy might be explained by unfamiliarity.

Oral histories of settlers living in Teton Valley in the 1920s place the battle site just off modern Highway 33, on property then owned by William H. Woolstenhulme. This was about three miles south of the modern town of Driggs and on the south side of Darby Creek. B. W. Driggs recorded that:

Bill Spears established a homestead at the location of this battlefield, among the early settlers in this vicinity, and Richard Leigh, who had traversed this valley with Indians from 1840 to the time of its early settlement, had the battlefield pointed out to him by the Indians who knew of its location, and made the statement to D. O. Walton that this claim of Bill Spears' was a historic spot where the battle occurred that Captain Bonneville told about.

The only man now living that we are aware of that knows its location is John F. Carnes, one of the first pioneers of Jackson Hole, living at the time he was interviewed in 1925, near Fort Hall. He is now about 90 years of age. He had this battle ground pointed out to him by an Indian woman of the Shoshone tribe, whom Bridger's trappers called Mary Ann, who was one of the friendly Indians here at the time of the battle. The writer made a map of the valley from Teton Creek to Trail Creek, showing the various streams and the swamp, and had Mr. Carnes mark on the map his cross to denote where the location of the battle was, as pointed out to him by Mary Ann, and his designation was apparently but a few rods from where we had estimated the barricade was constructed.

In addition to all this evidence, Indian skulls have been found in this vicinity, after people began to clear the land of its timber and brush. These skulls and bones had lain under the debris until the clearing fires uncovered them. One skull was found near the river to which they had fled during the night with their wounded.

Arrowheads have also been found here, and an old Queen Ann musket bayonet, similar to those used by the Hudson Bay people, which the Indians had no doubt secured from that source. Then, too, in the early days of white settlement there was a large grove of cottonwood and aspens, as well as dense willows, vines, etc. that made the "thicket of tanglewood" mentioned, at this place where the barricade was constructed, and while most of the timber has been removed and the land cleared in places for meadows and pastures, yet the embankment in a sort of long semicircle, the place where they dug down to water, still remains.

We have evidence and good reason to believe these Indians came over the hills from Moose Creek and thence down the long ridge south of Fox Canyon. This hill was their long noted point of observation, called "Bald Hill," where the stone fort was located, as heretofore mentioned. From this point there has always been a well defined trail leading over to Moose Creek,

266

the beginning of the steep ascent over Teton Pass. This route over the hills was traveled to avoid the heavy growth of brush and timber in the canyon, and no doubt in order to be on high ground where they could observe any lurking enemy.[5]

However, there are several problems with this scenario. First and foremost, it does not line up with the primary documentation. This site is little more than three miles from the proposed main rendezvous camp; nearly every first-hand account of the battle places the location six or more miles farther south. Second, many of those reports indicate the Gros Ventres were coming from a "pass" which would not have been the case if they had somehow entered Teton Valley via Darby Canyon. Finally, had Bald Hill been a Gros Ventre point of observation on this trek, it seems certain the Gros Ventres would have seen and reconnoitered the substantial encampment of trappers in Pierre's Hole prior to descending to the valley floor.

In his 1963 book on Fort Hall, Frank C. Robertson reminisced about walking over the supposed battlefield on property owned by his brother Chauncey. Coincidentally, he said this was in 1932, one hundred years after the battle. Robertson wrote of seeing "the marks of Blackfoot trenches" still visible on the acreage along Darby Creek. He had been told it was still possible to pick up relics of the fight, such as flint arrowheads, but he had no luck.[6] Teton County land records indicate Chauncey Robertson had bought the Woolstenhulme property that had been proposed by B. W. Driggs as the battle site.[7]

If not the Pierre's Hole battlefield, what occurred on the Darby Creek site to leave behind so much apparent and compelling evidence? A plausible explanation is provided by Warren Ferris. Vanderburgh had sent the trapper to speak with some Flatheads about the upcoming 1832 rendezvous. This band was led by Guigneo, whose name Ferris spelled a variety of ways throughout his journal and translated as "French for bad-luck:"

Guigneo assembled his warriors in council to learn the nature of my embassy. I was instructed to offer them a liberal present of ammunition, blankets, and tobacco if they would meet us at the rendezvous in Pierre's Hole. My arrival proved to be auspicious; the day before they had had a severe fight with the

Blackfeet Indians, that lasted all day, and when the parties withdrew from the field of battle, the Flatheads had not a single load of powder and ball left for half of their number, and had the Blackfeet known this, the Flatheads would in all probability have been exterminated. The council at once determined to comply with our wishes, but old Guigueo said he would be compelled to make short and easy marches on account of the forty-odd wounded Indians in his village. Many of his braves had been killed, and some of the severely wounded were dying daily. On the following morning we set out, returning by the same route we had already followed. The wounded Indians were conveyed on litters consisting of two lodge poles fastened on either side of a packhorse with skins stretched on cross bars so as to form a bed for each of the sufferers.[8]

After the Pierre's Hole fight, Ferris wrote tellingly of the Flathead casualties: "The Indians, however, being the most numerous, suffered the most, and Old Gurgueo had quite a company of wounded men to add to those already in this condition."[9]

It is plausible that the Flathead camp, under Guigneo, set up on Darby Creek within relative proximity to the trader's tents. This band of the Salish stayed at rendezvous for six weeks.[10] If men wounded prior to rendezvous "were dying daily," it would not be unexpected to find the skeletal remains described by B. W. Driggs. Furthermore, an encampment of that duration would easily have left other relics to be discovered by modern treasure hunters.

Another possible origin of the Darby Creek artifacts may well have been major activity during the 1829 rendezvous. There are a few reminiscences of the first rendezvous in Pierre's Hole, though none hint at its site. Ultimately, the Battle of Pierre's Hole was not fought on Darby Creek.

Many historians have written that Milton Sublette's party was bound for Teton Pass and that the Gros Ventres entered Teton Valley from there. One of the best examinations of the Battle of Pierre's Hole was done by Willard C. Hayden for the *Idaho Yesterdays* quarterly. Hayden used many of the available primary sources, yet still cited Teton Pass as Sublette's destination and the Indians' entrance point.

Hayden also indicated Fontenelle's caravan arrived in Pierre's Hole too late to sell its wares. Thus, a "cache was made during the hours of darkness in the horse corral of their camp so the hoofprints would obliterate any sign of digging."[11] A romantic notion, no doubt, except according to Ferris, Fontenelle and the AFC supplies never made it to Pierre's Hole. The company men were forced to track the supply train down, and found it near the Green River. What few goods they bought from Campbell would be needed immediately to outfit the crew with essentials, and not cached.

Hayden came close to pinpointing the location of the battlefield, yet misinterpreted a vital clue provided by Warren Ferris. The AFC party to which Ferris was attached had returned to Pierre's Hole on May 25, 1833, nearly a year after the battle.[12] Ferris recorded that they entered the valley by way of Pine Creek Pass and followed Little Pine Creek onto the valley floor for about four miles. The AFC brigade then "passed over to the stream which marks the pass to Jackson Hole, about two miles and halted," which Hayden construed to mean the trappers stopped two miles from the pass. This places the AFC camp too far east on Trail Creek, thus Hayden's proposed battle site was farther upstream than Ferris intended. Rather, Ferris indicated they traveled two more miles east from Little Pine Creek to the stream that exits Teton Pass – Trail Creek – where the men stopped about one mile above the battle ground. At about that distance downstream from where Ferris camped on Trail Creek, that stream and Little Pine Creek merge, becoming the headwaters of Teton River.

Just prior to the Battle of Pierre's Hole, Milton Sublette's party was camped near where Cedron Road crosses Trail Creek, in the same general area described by Ferris. From there, the trappers had a clear view of Pine Creek Pass and parties coming into the valley from there. Riders departing Pine Creek Pass, headed north, would be on a collision course with this proposed site of Sublette's camp. As the Gros Ventre chief rode to meet Antoine Godin and his lone ally, the remaining Indians could have moved into any copse of trees along Little Pine Creek probably just beyond its junction with Warm Creek. Even today, "woods surrounded by willows" along the stream's bank, as William Sublette described, are found in this vicinity. If the downed logs used to construct the Gros

Ventre fortifications were to turn bullets, they would have been several inches in diameter and fairly abundant. With as much modern farming and ranching as occurs in this area, it is doubtful any evidence remains of the battle-ground, but based on the facts presented here, the site was along Little Pine Creek near its junction with Trail Creek, close to the headwaters of Teton River.

Bernard DeVoto's *Across the Wide Missouri* is a popular book on the fur trade. DeVoto visited Teton Valley, attempting to determine the location of the battle. He placed the rendezvous site at the south end of Pierre's Hole, and consequently suggested the battle may have taken place "well out of the Basin" – speculation that should be discounted.[13]

The power of oral history was hard at work when the location of the Battle of Pierre's Hole was nominated for the National Register of Historic Places. The designation was granted in September 1984, erroneously naming the site south of Driggs along Darby Creek. Oddly, although the nomination forms cite Hayden's information and map which so closely acknowledges the actual site, that data was ignored in favor of oral history traditions. B. W. Driggs' history of the valley was not even listed as a source.

In 1972, well before the battleground was nominated for the National Register, the editor of the *Upper Snake River Historical Society Quarterly*, Louis Clement, wrote:

> *Locating the area of the Battle proved to be a chore with many problems. There are almost as many different locations of the battlefield as there are persons interested in finding it ... Until recently, [B. W. Driggs'] explanation was unchallenged, at least by researched sources, although some privately expressed opinions suggested other areas for possible sites of the battle ... Although residents of the Valley tend to scoff at any new proposals it is the opinion of the editor that Hayden's proposals should be given careful study.*[14]

Clement announced the formation of expeditions with metal detectors, bent on locating the actual site. No follow-up articles appear in the Quarterly so if the expeditions occurred, they were apparently unsuccessful.

16

After the Battle of Pierre's Hole

With the enemy gone from the field, the battle was over. The wounded were tended so that the business of concluding rendezvous could resume. Several key events would occur in and around the valley before the fur companies cleared out of Pierre's Hole for the summer, although the valley would see trapping parties return before the year was out.

William Sublette's badly wounded shoulder was treated by Dr. Jacob Wyeth, brother of Nathaniel Wyeth and physician for that expedition. Months later, pieces of bone would be removed from Sublette's splintered shoulder by Dr. Bernard Farrar of St. Louis.[1] Meanwhile, the wound kept Sublette in Pierre's Hole to recuperate before riding for St. Louis with the summer's take of beaver.

Nine men had opted to withdraw from Nathaniel Wyeth's brigade. Three of these, Wakefield, Nud and Lane, signed on with Milton Sublette in the trapping business so traveled westward with Wyeth for a time. The remaining six New Englanders had chosen to return east with William Sublette, so they, too, were obliged to cool their heels while their new captain convalesced. This may have been seen by some as a welcome delay, allowing the Gros Ventres to clear out of the area.

The day after the battle a blessed event further solemnized the occasion – the first recorded birth in Pierre's Hole. Macompemay, the Otoe wife of Andrew Drips (known more commonly as Margaret or Mary) brought the couple's fourth child into the world. The proud parents named her Catherine. This little girl became a favorite pet of trapper Jacques Fournaise, also known as Old Pino, who happily exhibited her around to the trapper camps calling her *"ma petite Catherine."*[2]

Arapahoe historians report the fleeing Gros Ventres made it back to the main camp on the Snake River. Their story greatly fired up their relatives. At a chief's council, further attack on the trappers was debated. Those whose kin had died in Pierre's Hole were eager to avenge their deaths. Both Fontenelle's and Bonneville's parties were in the Green River Valley and several Gros Ventres were in favor of launching an assault on them, even though these men had had nothing to do with the Pierre's Hole fight. A handful of the White Clay people started off at once for the Green River.[3]

As the 1832 rendezvous wound down, Thomas Fitzpatrick and Jim Bridger prepared their brigade for travel. They departed northward out of Pierre's Hole around July 22 intent on trapping the headwaters of the Missouri River. Robert Newell would later remember they went from Pierre's Hole to Salmon River, crossed the mountains to the Three Forks and headed up the banks of the "galiton fork."[4] About the time the brigade was mounting up, Alfred Stephens determined he had been cheated by Fitzpatrick on the Laramie River in June, when Stephens had sold him Gantt and Blackwell's furs. A violent dispute erupted between Fitzpatrick and Stephens before Fitzpatrick cleared out of Teton Valley.[5]

Then Stephens had an epiphany: he would make a dash to the Laramie River and retrieve the cached furs before Fitzpatrick could claim them. On July 24, Alfred Stephens and six men departed Pierre's Hole, headed east on their ill-fated mission. Stephens had recruited George More (also reported as Joseph More) formerly of Wyeth's Boston party, Mississippian John Foy of the Bean-Sinclair party, "two grandsons of the celebrated Daniel Boone," and two others who are not identified.[6]

Which two of Boone's grandsons were in this party? Albert Gallatin Boone went up the Missouri in 1824 with Ashley's crew at the age of 18. He even later named his first-born son William Ashley Boone. In 1828, Albert returned to the mountains and is believed to have trapped the waters of the Columbia in 1832. It is likely that Albert was one of these "grandsons of the celebrated Daniel Boone" traveling with Stephens but the other Boone is not identifiable.[7]

Stephens and his six followers crossed the Tetons, passed through Jackson Hole and began negotiating the canyon of the Hoback River. As the trappers descended a hill, they were ambushed by the party of Gros Ventres headed for Green River. More, who was in front, had ridden to within about twenty yards of the Indians when they sprang up and fired. His horse wheeled around in fright, dumping the young Bostonian to the ground. The greenhorn tried to scramble across the side of the hill, but with a screaming horde of as many as two dozen warriors bearing down on him, he froze, paralyzed in fear. John Wyeth later reported

> As the Indians knew that More could not get away from them, they passed him, and about twenty Indians were coming up the hill where they were. Eight or ten Indians followed up while only five trappers had gained the hill. They were considering how to save George More, when one of them shot him through the head, which was a better fate than if they had taken him alive, as they would have tortured him to death.[8]

More's comrades fled back up the hill but two of them, Foy and Stephens, had seen the danger More was in. They turned back and dismounted to go to his aid. Foy was instantly shot and killed. Stephens was severely wounded in the thigh but managed to get back on his horse. One of the party's extra mules was killed as well. Stephens and the others hightailed it out of Hoback Canyon, leaving the bodies of More and Foy where they lay. From Wyeth's wording, it is not clear just who shot More, perhaps an Indian, perhaps one of his companions. The five survivors returned to Pierre's Hole on the evening of July 27th, bearing tidings of the disaster.[9] Stephens would become the final casualty a few days later.

Meanwhile, on July 25, the day after Stephens had left for the Laramie River, Milton Sublette and Fraeb finally led their brigade out of the valley, heading for fall trapping in parts west.[10] Nathaniel Wyeth and his eleven remaining Oregon-bound men tagged along. They crossed out of the valley by way of Pine Creek Pass and fell on the Snake River in Swan Valley. Here, they killed enough buffalo and antelope to make bullboats from the hides and crossed the river on the 26th without incident.[11] Continuing west, Wyeth noted two days later they "took the bearing of the Trois Tetons which was N.E. by E. and I think 75 miles."[12] They were a few miles north of present day Idaho Falls, Idaho. Wyeth continued on a westerly heading to the HBC post, Fort Vancouver, in Oregon Territory.

Also on July 25, the AFC captains, tired of waiting for Fontenelle, and perhaps fearful their supplies would never arrive at all, gave in and purchased equipment from Robert Campbell's independent venture meant to provide capital for his impending partnership with William Sublette. Among the many records of

Campbell's 1832 transactions is a statement of their business deal. The list provides a clear picture of the equipment used by the men and the trade articles this brigade carried with it on the trail, as well as the hefty cost charged for goods in the mountains.

Invoice of goods sold to O'Fallon and Vandeburgh by Robert Campbell on the Teton Fork of the Columbia River and under the three Teton mountain July 25th 1832

5	c	Gun Flints @	2$	$10.00	
6		Flannel Shirts	3$	18.00	
1		3 pt Blanket		10.00	
1		2 1/2 pt Do		8.00	
1		wrapper Do		3.00	
3	doz	Knives @	9$	27.00	
1		Cacheing Hoe	2.00	78.00	
10		Trap Springs	1$	10.00	
18		Blk Silk Hdkf	150	27.00	
2	pr	Russia sheeting pantaloons	3$	6.00	
57	cakes	shaving soap	25c	14.25	
11		combs (long dressing)	50 cts	5.50	
21		fine combs	50c	10.50	
1		3 pt Blanket		10.00	
1		wrapper		3.00	86.25
Amount Carried forward					$164.25

Amt brought forward					164.25
2		Surcingles	@1.50	3.00	
2		Green Blankets	10$	20.00	
12	pr	Goggles	4$	48.00	
2	doz	files (flat & 3 square)	12$	24.00	
2	"	Looking Glasses	6.00	12.00	107.00
6	papers	Vermillion	3$	18.00	
1	pr	Green Blankets		20.00	
1		wrapper Do		3.00	
1		Cappo 2 1/2 pt		10.00	
19		Flannel Shirts	3$	57.00	108.00

2		surcingles	150c	3.00	
1	pr	2 1/2 pt Blankets		16.00	
2		Indian axes	3$	6.00	
1	pr	3 pt Blankets		20.00	
1		wrapper		3.00	
2		surcingles	150	3.00	
1	pr	2 1/2 pt Blankets		16.00	73.00

Amt carried forward $452.25

Amt brought forward $452.25

2		axes	3$	6.00	
1	pr	3 pt Blankets		20.00	
1		wrapper		3.00	
5	@	pepper	125	6.25	
7/12	doz	Knives	9$	5.25	
3		Blue Blankets	10	30.00	70.50
33	doz	Hawk Bells	50c	16.50	
1		wrapper Blanket		3.00	
2		Surcingles	150	3.00	
6		Fancy bells	150	9.00	
9	doz	Knives	9$	81.00	112.50
4		Gun Locks	5$	20.00	
17	yds	Scarlet cloth	5$	85.00	
13½	yds	Blue Do	5$	67.50	
1		wrapper Blanket		3.00	
2		Surcingles		3.00	
10	Doz	Knives	9$	90.00	
12		Razors in Cases	24	24.00	
20	Gro	Awl Blades	6$	12.00	304.50

Amt carried forward $939.75

Amt brought forward 939.75

16½	yds	Scarlet Cloth	5$	82.50
9½	"	Blue Do	5$	47.50
1		wrapper		3.00
6		Combs	50c	3.00
27	Bunches	Seed Beads	1$	27.00

275

28	Bunches	Cut Glass	2$	<u>56.00</u>	219.00
9½	@	Small pound Beads	3	28.50	
173	@	Tobacco	125	216.25	
100	@	powder	125	125.00	
246	@	Lead	125c	307.50	
3		Kettles (Small tin)		<u>4.00</u>	681.25
5		Tin pans	75 cts	3.75	
10	Gallons	Liquor	16$	160.00	
1		belt & Scabbard		1.50	
1		Bridle		1.50	
2		Flannel Shirts	3$	6.00	
2	pr	Socks	1$	2.00	
1	@	Soap		<u>1.25</u>	<u>176.00</u>

Amt carried forward $2016.00

Amt brought forward 2016.00

36		Beaver Traps	10$	360.00	
50	@	Sugar	125	62.50	
1½	@	Thread	1	1.50	
2		Bridle Bitts	1$	2.00	
8	pr	Horse Shoes	3$	24.00	
1	sett	Shoeing tools		<u>7.50</u>	507.50
		Clinching Hammer Chisels &c		5.00	
1	pr	Steelyards		3.00	
1	pr	Pistols & Holsters		40.00	
4		Blank Books		4.75	
5	slips	paper	50c	2.50	
1		Tomohawk		3.00	
2		Iron Kettles		<u>5.00</u>	63.25
5		Rifle Guns of men	30$	150.00	
9		Horses & rigging	80	720.00	
1	pr	Suspenders (To Henry)		<u>1.00</u>	<u>871.00</u>
					3457.75
2	Gro	Awl Blades	6	12	

Amt carried forward $3469.75

Amt brought forward 3469.75

Amt due by Wm Fallon.. 13.50
5 .... @ .... powder............................... 125............................ 6.25
3489.50
Something else which I have forgotten..2.00
$3491.50

By Wm H Vanderburgh's draft as agent for with Amn Co. in the mountains or P Chouteau Esq. agt. Amn. Furr Co. St Louis for three thousand four hundred and ninety one Dollars fifty cents in payment of above

> *dated July 25th, 1832*
> *Robert Campbell*[13]

The final cryptic entry reflects the informal, sometimes unprofessional methods used in the mountains, even between competitors. Other items of note include the razors and shaving soap, horse shoes and related tools, and the steelyard – a balance or scale with which to determine weight. An interesting variety of clothing articles is found among these items as well. Horses and an assortment of tack were also purchased, including rigging, bridle bits, and surcingles (wide leather straps that pass over a saddle to help secure it to the animal).

Yet another notable event of July 25 was that five of the laborers who had accompanied William Sublette with the incoming supply train signed on as trappers with the Rocky Mountain Fur Company. Christian Shotts, Alfred R. Shute, William M. Price, John A. Mytinger and John C. Hawkins enlisted to remain in the mountains until the fall of 1833 at the rate of fourteen dollars per month for the first four months, presumably while they learned the trapping trade, then sixteen dollars per month for the latter months. Sublette had paid several men's wages through July 10, including these five, a week earlier. They had apparently been unemployed for the past two weeks, though RMFC was now responsible for their support.[14]

William Sublette, impatient over the delay caused by his wounds, was finally strong enough to start toward home on Monday, July 30.[15] The long cavalcade was made up of eighty pack animals, each laden with 150 pounds of fur. Robert Campbell reported, "At that time, beaver was rated at $3 per pound and brought about $5 each in St. Louis. When we hadn't the means of weighing – 60 beavers were rated at 100 pounds."[16] All Sublette had to do was get his nearly $60,000 worth of pelts across 1,400 miles of wilderness to civilization (see color plate 16).

William Sublette's mail pouch was full of letters home from various trappers, as well as assorted business documents. Stuffed inside the leather bag was his newly signed contract, heavily weighted in his favor, to supply the Rocky Mountain Fur Company at next summer's rendezvous, giving him a stranglehold on a big part of the mountain trade. He also had a statement from Robert Campbell and a second witness that they had weighed and marked beaver fur and other items raised from caches that RMFC had made earlier on the Sweetwater and Platte rivers. As the sole agent for the Rocky Mountain Fur Company, Sublette would profit through markup on the goods he carried to future rendezvous, as well as the higher prices he would realize when he sold the fur he brought back. Additionally, Sublette would be paid to transport that peltry to market while earning 8 percent interest on several RMFC unpaid notes.

The correspondence Sublette carried included letters to the friends and families of Nathaniel Wyeth and John Ball, among others. Trapper John Robertson too had composed a letter to his father, two weeks before the mail left the valley:

Rocky Mountains
Pierre's Hole, July 15, 1832

My dear Father: I write these lines to let you know that I am enjoying good health at this time. I am now about to make a fall hunt having bought horses and traps which has taken all the money I had made; and if I have success catching beaver … I have got a little spending money but it is not a thousand dollars, still afloat and plenty of friends. I should have come down this fall but Sublette and Fitzpatric persuaded me to stay out this year, and besides I got to be lazy and do not believe I could go to work. I have sent down $100 by Mr. Sublette …

You must look out for yourselves, I can't always be with you. We are poor in this country but I am trying to make a living and want you to do the same.

John Robertson[17]

Robertson had hired on with Fitzpatrick in 1831 and had accompanied him on the trip to Santa Fe, following Smith, Sublette and Jackson on a quest for RMFC supplies. Robertson would become the first permanent settler in southwestern Wyoming, having built a cabin in the Black's Fork bottoms, a short distance below where Fort Bridger would be built.

Before the rendezvous in Pierre's Hole ended, Fitzpatrick had given an order on W. L. Sublette:

To pay John Robinson or order on arrival of the beaver now on hand, at St. Louis, the sum of $100. Charge same to account of

Rocky Mountain Fur Co., Thos Fitzpatrick
Teton fork, Columbia river
July 24, 1832[18]

William Sublette carried this draft along with many other notes payable against the RMFC. A large number of them are preserved in the Sublette Collection at the Missouri History Museum. These drafts provide the names of many obscure trappers who worked the Rocky Mountain streams catching beaver.[19]

The wounded Alfred Stephens departed Pierre's Hole on July 30 with William Sublette's party. Toward the end of first day's march, Stephens got off his horse and, about five minutes later, collapsed dead. Gangrene, or what the trappers called "mortification," had developed in the severe leg wound. He was buried in the southeastern extremity of Pierre's Hole that evening.[20]

The men who had separated from Nathaniel Wyeth's Pacific Trading Company now accompanied William Sublette for safety on the trip back to New England. After crossing the Tetons and entering Jackson Hole, John Wyeth commented on the goods that had been cached on their way into Pierre's Hole almost a month previous: "I have my doubts whether they who hid the goods will ever return to dig up their hidden treasure. We did not meddle with it on our return with Captain Sublette."[21]

Avoiding Hoback Canyon due to the earlier attack on the Stephens party, Sublette ascended the Gros Ventre River east out of Jackson Hole instead. This led him across Union Pass. Soon after, on August 4, the caravan ran into the Indians they had detoured to avoid. Sublette estimated six to eight hundred warriors – the band the trappers had been warned of during the Battle of Pierre's Hole. Sublette presented the leaders with twenty-five pounds of tobacco and they proceeded on, unmolested.[22] The pack train descended the Wind River, picked up the Sweetwater, and followed it to the Platte, ultimately reaching Independence, Missouri about September 18.[23]

Drips, Vanderburgh and the men of the American Fur Company stayed in Teton Valley, still hoping to meet Fontenelle's supply caravan and at least know its fate. On August 1, they huddled under tarps to wait out a hail storm that lasted about an hour.[24] Fearing Fontenelle and Provost had run into trouble, AFC captains Drips and Vanderburgh decided to go look for them. Everyone packed up and left the rendezvous site the following day, reaching the south end of Pierre's Hole on August 3.[25] At some point, John Grey and a small party of his own separated from the main AFC brigade to once again trap independently.[26]

The next morning, the main AFC brigade crossed the Tetons, forded the Snake River, and passed down Jackson Hole. On August 5, choosing to brave Hoback Canyon, Warren Ferris reported that hunters from the party saw the bones of two men and supposed them to be those of More and Foy.[27] The trail along the Hoback River zigged and zagged through a deep defile along an almost perpendicular mountain side. At times there was scarcely enough room for the feet of the horses, so they dismounted and led the animals over the most dangerous places. Still, three of the mounts lost their footing and fell sixty to seventy feet into the river below. Two were but slightly injured; one was killed instantly.[28]

The party found a buffalo herd and obtained fresh meat which they had not had since leaving Pierre's Hole. They also saw signs of a large Indian encampment, five to six days old, which they presumed had been left by the Gros Ventres involved in the rendezvous battle. Finally reaching the Green River, they stumbled onto Benjamin

Bonneville and his newly-constructed fort. Bonneville was able to point the trappers in the direction of Fontenelle's latest camp. Nevertheless, when the jumpy AFC men saw a party of horsemen, they initially feared they had caught up with the Gros Ventres, whom they suspected were not too far ahead of them. It turned out, however, to be the long-awaited Fontenelle supply train.

Concluding the customary transactions, Fontenelle departed for Fort Union on August 12, carrying the furs from the AFC trappers.[29] Vanderburgh and Drips lined out their mountaineers to begin the fall hunt. Being relative newcomers to this region of the Rocky Mountain trade, they planned to shadow the RMFC to learn the best beaver country. So, they backtracked to Pierre's Hole once more.

On August 16, 1832, at the head of Teton Valley, the AFC brigade found the bones of several Indians.[30] These they supposed had been killed during the fight the previous month and had been carried here, several miles from the battlefield, by their relations. Vanderburgh and Drips soon found the trail of Bridger, Fitzpatrick and the RMFC force passing out the north end of the valley, and made haste to catch up. Before that November was over, this ploy would get Vanderburgh killed by the Blackfoot.[31]

Benjamin L. E. Bonneville, another newcomer to the mountains, was on an ambitious trek that would take him through Teton Valley and beyond to a winter camp on the Salmon River. Bonneville was an officer in the U.S. Army and had taken leave from military service to try his hand in the fur trade. While evidence is lacking, some propose that he may have been on official duty, traveling throughout the West on confidential reconnaissance.[32] His caravan left Fort Osage, Missouri in May 1832 with 110 men and twenty wagons of goods.[33] Bonneville was not the first to use wagons to transport supplies to the Rocky Mountains, but he was the first to take them over South Pass and onto the Green River.[34] Arriving on the Green in late July, he originally figured on wintering there, and lost no time in the construction of a fortified camp.

Many trappers felt the location of Bonneville's post was poorly chosen due to its exposed surroundings and dubbed it "Fort Nonsense" and "Bonneville's Folly." Be that as it may, of the sixteen Rocky Mountain fur trade rendezvous, six of the final eight summer gatherings were held in this same vicinity in the coming years.[35]

Bonneville crossed paths earlier with Fontenelle (still trudging along toward Pierre's Hole) in the Green River Valley not long before the supplier encountered his AFC customers. The two men spent a great deal of time discussing the fur trade and what lay ahead for the West Point graduate. A group of free trappers camped in the valley also shared valuable information. From all that he gleaned, Bonneville concocted plans to winter on the Salmon River in what is now central Idaho where the weather would not be as harsh as it was reported to be on the Green. Regrettably, Bonneville's education included the discovery that Fontenelle had recruited a small but valuable band of Delaware Indians away from his company.

Bonneville dug caches, then secreted away most of his supplies and the wagons – none of which would be necessary in the winter ahead.[36] Before he could get his horses loaded and on the trail, the AFC men arrived from the Pierre's Hole rendezvous in search of their supplier. Bonneville informed them they would find Fontenelle camped across the Green River a few miles further on.

Neither Bonneville nor Fontenelle was ever attacked by the Gros Ventres, though both interacted with the tribe as they passed through the Green River neighborhood that summer. The Gros Ventres whose relatives had not suffered in the Battle of Pierre's Hole were anxious to stay on solid ground with the trappers, according to Arapahoe accounts, since they did not wish to isolate themselves from McKenzie's trade goods at Fort Union. Finally reaching a compromise in council, the chiefs had opted to leave the trappers alone and go against another long-time rival, the Crow. As the Gros Ventres moved up the Wind River later that summer, Crow scouts saw them coming and arranged an ambush, killing forty of the band.[37]

Bonneville broke camp on August 22, setting out for the Salmon.[38] Three or four days into his route brought him through Hoback Canyon where he, too, reported finding the bones of More and Foy. Irving wrote, "The feelings of the Captain were shocked at beholding the bones of these unfortunate young men bleaching among the rocks; and he caused them to be decently interred."[39] Oddly, Wyeth would say nearly a year later, in both his journal and a letter to Francis Ermatinger, that he saw the bones even after Bonneville was said to have buried them.[40] Warren Ferris wrote in his journal that on August 14, his AFC party collected the bones and deposited them in a small stream flowing into the Hoback River.[41] Exactly what transpired regarding these bones is not clear.

Bonneville and his men crossed the pass from Jackson Hole into Teton Valley on September 3, 1832.

> *[He] arrived at the summit of a mountain which commanded a full view of the eventful valley of Pierre's Hole; whence he could trace the winding of the stream through green meadows and forests of cottonwood and have a prospect, between distant mountains, of the lava plains of Snake River, dimly spread forth like a sleeping ocean below.[42]*

There are occasional spots along Teton Pass that "command" a full view of the valley. But another of Bonneville's biographers, Edith Lovell, has pointed out that to see the plains of Snake River, one must be farther south. Bonneville may have continued westward from Mosquito Pass following the later sheep trails over Fogg Hill before descending to Pierre's Hole.[43]

Once on the valley floor, he visited the scene of the summer's conflict with the Gros Ventres and saw "the remains of the rude log fortress in the swamp, shattered by rifle shot, and strewed with the mingled bones of savages and horses."[44]

Indications abounded of the multitude that had occupied Pierre's Hole just a few months prior. Traces of trappers' camps and Indian lodges were easily spotted, though the people "had all dispersed to different points of wilderness, and the valley had relapsed into its pristine solitude and silence."[45] That night, the captain encamped on the battleground. The next day his toilsome trip through the mountains resumed, the group exiting Pierre's Hole probably to the north, and eventually reaching the Salmon River on September 19.[46]

On display at the Teton County Museum is a pack saddle allegedly found by Bonneville in 1832. While documentation is sorely lacking, the exhibit indicates Bonneville found the saddle cached in a cave somewhere in Bull Elk Canyon. The saddle was donated to the museum by Samuel Swanners, the first probate judge for Teton County, who gained possession of it in 1887 from an unknown source. Bull Elk Creek can be found to the northeast of today's Tetonia, Idaho. If Bonneville had found this cache in

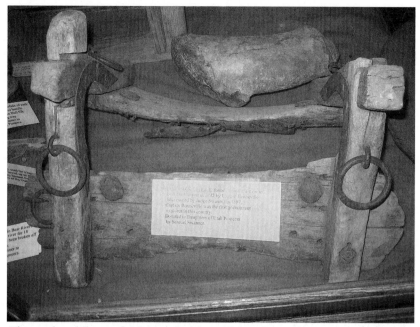

This pack saddle, on display at the Teton County Museum, is purported to have been found by Benjamin Bonneville in Teton Valley in 1832, though documentation is lacking. BRUCE BELASON PHOTO

1832, there was no mention of it in Irving's writings which were based largely on the captain's journals. The saddle's construction incorporates nuts and bolts, and strap metal that appears to be riveted on. While these features could have been added at a later time, they were not common in pack saddles of the period.

Records of other free trappers or parties visiting Pierre's Hole in the latter months of 1832 have not been found. The level of activity in the Teton Basin for this year would never be equaled in the future of the fur trade because the demand for beaver soon began to decline. For the time being, Teton Valley was quiet.

17

THE WANING YEARS OF THE FUR TRADE: 1833-1840

1833

On March 24, 1833, Andrew Drips, left winter camp at the junction of Henry's Fork and the Snake, shadowed by the Menan Buttes, to begin what turned out to be a successful spring hunt. No longer accompanied by Vanderburgh, who had been killed by the Blackfoot near modern Montana's Ennis Pass the previous fall, Drips and his AFC brigade trapped its way through a busy season, then moved on to the rendezvous site on the Green River via Pierre's Hole. Arriving at the mouth of Horse Creek on June 7, Drips was among the first outfits to set up camp for rendezvous.[1]

Many of the trappers in the mountains had plied their trade west of the Continental Divide that year but none are recorded as having worked in Teton Valley. Of the several brigades that traversed Pierre's Hole on their way to rendezvous, the first to hit the basin that spring was the aforementioned Drips/AFC party.

With Vanderburgh dead, Drips had about sixty men under his lone command. They had hunted and trapped their way up the Snake, over into Grey's Hole, then descended the Salt River and retraced their earlier route back down the Snake. They had crossed over the Snake River Mountains, via Pine Creek Pass, and by late May, Drips was in Pierre's Hole.

The brigade started up Pine Creek from the west side on May 23 and camped in the mountains near the summit of the pass. Ferris commented on how thick the forest was:

Our road, in many places was almost impassable, in consequence of the thick dense growth of aspen, through which we were obliged to force our way, to the no small detriment of our clothing, and in great danger of losing our eyes, or being at least severely bruised by the numerous branches, which were continually flying back from a strained position, caused by the pack horses forcing themselves through; and which frequently coming against us with no gentle force, in their efforts to regain their natural position, seemed determined to give us a practical lesson on the elasticity of that species of timber.[2]

May 24 was a sunny and pleasant day. They continued their ride, following Little Pine Creek down the mountain and about four miles into Pierre's Hole. A couple of more miles east, on to Trail Creek, the exhausted AFC brigade camped. According to Ferris, it was about a mile upstream from the site of the previous summer's Indian battle. The next day, Ferris and a fellow trapper were sent in search of several horses the party had lost in crossing the mountains the day before. The two men backtracked all the way to the Snake River before finding the missing steeds feeding in a ravine. They returned "at a round pace" and got to camp sometime in the evening.[3]

On the succeeding morning, Ferris and some friends did a bit of sightseeing.[4] When the companions returned to the camp on Trail Creek, they learned one of the men had been attacked and severely wounded by a grizzly bear. Several trappers hunting buffalo had discovered the bruin near a willow grove along a stream. They shot and wounded it, but the bear managed to crawl off into the brush. Not wanting to let it get away, the unlucky mountaineer scrambled into the thicket after it. The enraged animal sprang on him and threw him to the ground. His comrades were afraid to shoot for fear of hitting man rather than bear. Finally, "a one eyed Spaniard by the name of Manuel, a famous hunter ... threw his gun to his eye, and fired."[5] The ball was well-aimed and the beast fell lifeless beside the prostrate body of their friend. The man lived, but was so badly bitten in the hand, arm and thigh as to be unfit for duty for several weeks.

The AFC brigade took its time crossing the mountains to Jackson Hole, ascending Teton Pass on May 31. The men rode by immense banks of snow but managed to get over the pass without incident. Adding to an arduous day, an evening rain shower drenched them, which, Ferris related with a touch of cynicism, "did not, in any degree contribute to our comfort or complacency."[6] From Jackson Hole, Drips aimed his men up the Gros Ventre Fork, skirting Union Pass to Kinky Creek and down onto the headwaters of Green River. From there, they dropped into the site of the rendezvous.

286

Nathaniel Wyeth, having wintered with the HBC while scouting future business prospects in the Oregon Territory, also headed east in the spring of 1833. Before leaving Boston the prior year, he had sent the brig *Sultana* around the Horn with supplies. The vessel shipwrecked, which scuttled most of his other plans for the year as well. By now, all of his men had left him, but he managed to rehire two of them, John Woodman and Wiggin Abbott, for the return journey. The HBC Snake Country Expedition, led that year by Francis Ermatinger, provided escort for the three eastbound travelers.

Along the way, they met up with Benjamin Bonneville and forty men returning from winter camp on Salmon River. The two American parties joined forces for the remainder of the trip to rendezvous, while the HBC trappers split off to hunt beaver. For the next several days, Wyeth's journal demonstrated the use of the Tetons as true Pilot Knobs, like Wilson Price Hunt's original name. Wyeth's entry for June 5, 1833 proclaimed, "Saw the three Butes come in sight one by one and then the Trois Tetons the Butes S.E. by S 20 miles distant." Then, on the 7th, he indicated seeing, "the Trois Tetons bearing E. perhaps 90 miles distant over a level and dry plain." After being camped for several days, Wyeth wrote on June 16, "Trois Tetons bear E. S. E." On the 20th, "Trois Tetons bear E. S. E. I should think about 80 miles distant."[7]

Continuing toward rendezvous, Bonneville maintained military-like precautions, setting round-the-clock sentries for fear there might be Blackfoot in the neighborhood. However, no disasters occurred.

On July 7, 1833, near Henry's Fork, Wyeth recorded passing "low hills of pure sand with not the least appearance of vegetation."[8] These are the St. Anthony Sand Dunes – 11,000 acres of mounded sand about eight miles west of modern St. Anthony, Idaho. These dunes play an intriguing role in Shoshone/Bannock lore. While grappling with the Blackfoot over possession of the region, some of the bloodiest battles between the two factions took place here. Legend says one day as the sun was setting in the west, the great dunes arose and engulfed the warring Indian parties. Not a single warrior escaped from either side. Their families fled to avoid extinction. It is said that every evening as the sun sets, the spirits of the dead warriors chant and moan the tortured cry of the vanquished.[9]

Warren Ferris mentioned the same dunes in his journal, as well as in an 1872 *Dallas Herald* article:

> *A few miles west of Henry's Fork with the Snake River, we find the "Sand Mountain." This is a lone mountain some thousand feet high, constituted of pure white sand. Like the Butes it has a desolate appearance from the want of vegetation. Its snowy whiteness redeems if from the forbidding aspect of the Butes. Around the mother mountain are thousands of conical hillocks of the same pure whiteness, that have been licked in to shape by whirlwinds that prevail here. Like the plains near the Butes, all is dry and arid, no water being found for many miles around. The peculiarity or singularity of this mountain consists in this, that there is nothing to be found in the whole range of the Rocky Mountains that has any resemblance to it or is constituted of similar materials for two miles away from the base of this mountain, and white sand is about as scarce as white sugar in these regions.*[10]

Clearly the dunes made a big impression on Ferris (not least because his horses sank to their knees while crossing them): he included the dunes on his *Map of the Northwest Fur Country – 1836*. This valuable document provides a single mountain man's grasp of the geography of the fur trade West and is a unique and unparalleled primary source document. It locates Pierre's Hole, Pierre's Fork, the "3 Buttes of Snake R." and many landmarks familiar to those who live in Teton Valley. It displays the remarkable amount of data gained in Ferris's five and one-half years in the mountains. The map contains a few geographical errors, for example Ferris showed Henry's Fork passing between the Menan Buttes, which he designated as "mounds," but it is a significant cartographic work, nonetheless.

As Wyeth and Bonneville approached the junction of Henry's Fork with the Snake River, mosquitoes plagued the travelers. Wyeth believed the two rivers joined about fifteen miles below their camp, "near two butes but some say not until you get as low as Three Butes."[11] This is a reference to the Menan Buttes and the Three Buttes that rise from the Snake River Plains between the modern towns of Arco and Blackfoot, Idaho.

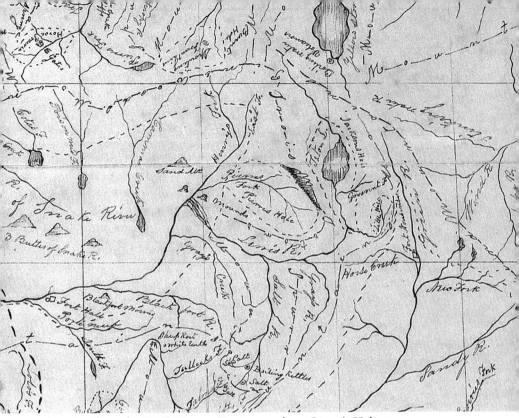

A section from the 1836 Warren Ferris map shows Pierre's Hole at center, and the Sand Dunes slightly left, just across Henry's Fork.

Wyeth also pointed out the narrow-leafed cottonwood trees, *populus angustifolia*, on his route. This information was important to trappers who depended on cottonwood bark to feed their livestock in winter months. Horses would eat only the broad, round-leafed or "sweet" variety, *populus angulata*.[12]

On July 9, the Americans turned due east for a little over twenty-two miles toward the Trois Tetons. Wyeth recorded striking a "small creek with cut banks running N.W. and to the river last crossed," likely Canyon Creek. Cutting the foot of the Big Hole Mountains, the combined party entered Pierre's Hole from the northwest. A few miles into the basin, they made camp, possibly along Pack Saddle or Horseshoe creeks, where they found buffalo.[13] The next day, they moved twelve miles southeast, and forged their way across a swamp, likely the region a few miles west of Victor, Idaho where Trail Creek and Little Pine Creek merge. In his journal, Wyeth remarked on one of the typical summer plagues of the Teton

Basin even today: "a great quantity of grasshoppers for several days past so much so as to discolor the ground in many places."[14]

They stopped that night about two miles beyond the prior summer's battle ground, a site that seems to be a natural camping spot and, in all probability, was the same place Wyeth camped with Milton Sublette just before the Battle of Pierre's Hole. On the morning of July 11, they got an early start, traveled three miles to the foot of the mountains at Moose Creek, then on up the trail toward the summit. The livestock was troubled by horseflies while crossing into Jackson Hole. One mule was lost along the way and the man sent to find it did not return until the following morning, having gone all the way back to their last camp in Pierre's Hole before locating the animal. As his young cousin predicted, Wyeth made no mention of recovering the items left cached in Jackson Hole last summer.[15] Perhaps that cache is still to be discovered.

Twenty-six years later, additional evidence of this expedition was discovered by the exploring party led by General William F. Raynolds, which crossed from Jackson Hole into Pierre's Hole on June 18, 1860, following the same trail. Besides providing an excellent description of the difficulties of Teton Pass, in his official "Report on the Exploration of the Yellowstone River," Raynolds wrote of finding a pine tree on the summit with a curious inscription. It read "J.M. July 7th, 1832" and "July 11, 1833."[16]

These are the same two dates on which Nathaniel Wyeth crossed the pass on his way to the Pacific and back, almost exactly one year apart. The returning group consisted of only Wyeth, John Woodman, and Wiggin Abbott – the only three men who passed in both directions. Since no one in either of Wyeth's parties had the initials "J.M.," one likely explanation is that John Woodman used his knife on the tree and, as the tree attempted to heal the scar over time, the "W" came to look more and more like an "M." It is also suggested Wyeth scribed his own "N.J.W." and the tree healing from both sides of the cut obscured parts of the letters making it look like "J.M." instead.

At least one author has surmised the "J.M." was carved by Joe Meek.[17] However, in 1832, Meek was in Pierre's Hole well before July 7 and in 1833, he was already at rendezvous on the Green River by the date of the carving. In spring 1833, Meek trapped regions of

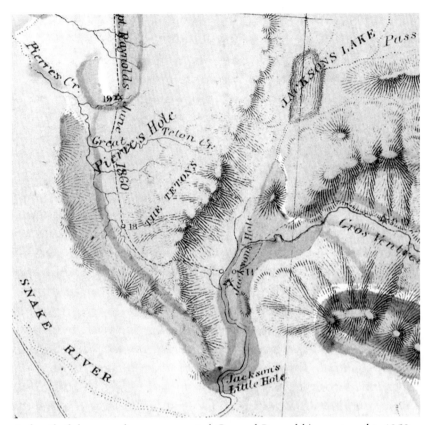

A detail of the map that accompanied General Raynolds' report on his 1859-1860 western expedition shows the trail over the Tetons. LIBRARY OF CONGRESS, GEOGRAPHY AND MAP DIVISION

the Snake River and farther south, around Salt Lake. Being that far south, it is doubtful he had to cross the Tetons to get to rendezvous. Thus, Meek was not present on the pass at either date so the initials are not those of Meek.[18]

Irving reported a curious topographical feature noted by Bonneville while crossing the Tetons:

> *No accident of a disastrous kind occurred , excepting the loss of a horse, which, in passing along the giddy edge of the precipice, called the Cornice, a dangerous pass between Jackson's and Pierre's Hole, fell over the brink and dashed to pieces.*[19]

This is the only mention of the "Cornice" as a landmark in the Tetons that appears in trapper journals of the period. However, in a letter to General Alexander McComb, written from the Wind River on July 29, 1833, Bonneville himself wrote:

> *From the Forks of Horse Creek of the Colorado to the head of Salmon River, the route lays generally through a country easily passed, with the exception of two Mountains which must be gone over – One is low, the other must be passed on the river, and upon a cornice of the Mountain from which horses fell from every party, descent perpendicular 270 feet high.*[20]

Irving may have made "cornice" into a proper noun for better dramatic effect; he may also have mistaken a description of Hoback Canyon for a section of the trail over the Tetons. The details suit both locations. Geographic mistakes are not uncommon by authors who, not having been on the ground in the region about which they attempt to write, try to identify landmarks using only maps.

The account of General Raynolds, crossing the Tetons in the same general area in 1860 makes an interesting comparison to Bonneville's 1833 experience. Jim Bridger led the Raynolds expedition over an old Indian trail that wound around the mountainside, then based on their map apparently followed Trail Creek instead of Moose Creek about eight miles before entering the valley. This may be the earliest documented use of the Trail Creek route on the Pierre's Hole side of the Tetons.

> *In ascending the Teton range we took advantage of the valley of a mountain stream flowing down its side, following a narrow bridle-path, skirting the foot of a precipice upon one hand and the bank of the dashing brook upon the other. Towards the last the slope became quite steep, but the road was far from bad for a pack-train. We passed across the summit of the range without difficulty, but upon coming to the western slope found our descent seriously obstructed by immense snow-banks, completely blocking up the Indian trail which we were following.*[21]

This brief detour into the future demonstrates the difficulty that every trapping party encountered in crossing these mountains, yet the trail between Jackson and Pierre's Holes was heavily traveled. Mountaineers anticipated a rugged Teton traverse. Still, Bonneville's loss of a horse may have been a singular event if it happened here.

Further along the trail now, Wyeth wrote in his journal about traveling through Hoback Canyon. Wyeth mentioned passing the place where More and Foy had been killed the summer before. Bonneville must have told Wyeth what little he knew, which seemed to be the first Wyeth had heard of the fight for he wrote, "I am apprehensive that More, a sick man whom I left in charge of Stevens, must be one of them."[22] Bonneville also told him the bones were "laying about the valley" the previous year. If Bonneville had indeed buried them, as Irving told, it was not remarked in Wyeth's diary.[23]

A final scrap of information regarding the death of More turned up while Wyeth was at Fort Union on his way east after the 1833 rendezvous. Wyeth noted:

> *A Mr. Patten shewed me a powder flask which he traded from the Blkft. I immediately knew it to be one of mine and on examination found No. 4 H. G. O. M. graven with a point on it. It was Mores flask who was killed in Little Jackson Hole last year on his return home after rendezvous.*[24]

Interestingly, Wyeth is not mentioned during the trip from Henry's Fork to the Green River in Irving's tale of Bonneville's adventures. But Wyeth did cite Bonneville's presence, so it is clear the two parties traveled together.

As Bonneville and Wyeth approached the Green River Valley for the rendezvous of 1833, parties of mountain men were also drifting in. On July 5, the RMFC supply caravan under Robert Campbell arrived.[25] Among the greenhorns who assisted with the mule train was a twenty-six-year-old man who would play a large role in the fur trade of future years – Charles Larpenteur. The impressionable Larpenteur had been in St. Louis when Sublette arrived out of the wilderness with the caravan of furs from the 1832 rendezvous. Larpenteur's 1872 memoir recaptured his response to that scene:

> *It is impossible to describe my feelings at the sight of all that beaver – all those mountain men unloading their mules, in their strange mountain costume – most of their garments of buckskin and buffalo hide, but all so well greased and worn that it took close examination to tell what they were made of. To see the mules rolling and dusting is interesting and shocking at the same time; most of them, having carried their burdens of 200 pounds'*

weight for about 2,000 miles, return with scarcely any skin on their backs; they are peeled from withers to tail, raw underneath from use of the surcingle, and many are also lame.

The sight of all this made me determined to take a trip of the same kind. The journey to the Rocky Mountains at that early period was considered very hard, and dangerous on account of the Pawnees and Blackfeet. While trapping that summer William Sublette had been badly wounded in the shoulder in a fight with the Blackfeet. But not all this danger, and the hardships to be endured on such a trip, could prevent me from engaging, in the spring of 1833.[26]

Now arrived at the 1833 rendezvous, Larpenteur recorded in his journal, "on the 8th [July, 1833] they was a party of 18 men which went for a cache of Beaver which was cashed near Pierre hole, and on the 15th they returned."[27] Larpenteur's 1872 autobiography expanded this brief statement:

The day after we reached the rendezvous Mr. Campbell, with ten men, started to raise a beaver cache at a place called by the French Trou á Pierre, which means Peter's Hole ... After seven or eight days Mr. Campbell returned with ten packs of beaver.[28]

This notation described Robert Campbell's week-long dash from Green River to Pierre's Hole and back to recover ten packs of beaver. Campbell's group, perhaps concerned it would miss some of the typical rendezvous festivities, certainly did not dally. There is no record of who had made this cache or when, but it indicates additional trapping activity in Teton Basin.

At the end of the rendezvous, Warren Ferris and Robert Newell took a small party and some trade goods north, destined for the Flathead people. Besides Newell and Ferris, the outfit consisted of six engagès with pack horses and five armed Indians. This group of thirteen men was one of the first to leave the Green River rendezvous, pulling out on July 20, 1833.[29]

It was late in the day before they got away, but Ferris and Newell managed to press on fifteen miles before making camp on a spring in the highlands near Jackson's Little Hole. That first evening they killed a "fine" buffalo bull. Over the next several days, the troop passed through Hoback Canyon, cut the south corner of Jackson's Big Hole, and ascended the mountain, bound for Pierre's Hole.

From the top of Teton Pass, Ferris left a description of the view seen by many tourists and all of those in modern times who commute from Teton Valley to Jackson on a regular basis. For a rough and tumble mountain man, Ferris waxed quite eloquent:

> *Gazing down, in the direction of Jackson's Hole, from our elevated position one of the most beautiful scenes imaginable, was presented to our view. It seemed quite filled with large bright clouds, resembling immense banks of snow, piled on each other in massy numbers, of the purest white; wreathing their ample folds in various forms and devious convolutions, and mingling in one vast embrace their shadowy substance. – Sublime creations! emblems apt of the first glittering imaginings of human life! like them redolent of happiness, and smiling in the fancied tranquil security of repose; like them, liable to contamination by intercourse with baser things, and like them, dissipated by the blasts of adversity, which sooner or later are sure to arrest and annihilate them. Alike evanescent are the dreamy anticipations of youth, and the aerial collections of vapor. Such the reflections suggested by this lovely scene, which, though often on the mountains, I have never before seen below me. Clouds of this pure snow-white appearance, are, however, by no means uncommon; but those usually observed beneath us, when on the mountains, have a dark and lowering aspect.*[30]

The men must have paused for some time to look in awe upon the natural beauty, because Ferris next wrote, "Turning in reluctance to things of a more terrestrial nature, we pursued our way down into Pierre's Hole."[31] Once in the valley, they again killed a solitary buffalo, the only such animal they had seen since their first night's camp ten days prior.

1834

That winter, Ferris left the employ of the AFC to become a trader. He joined forces with Nicholas Montour, bought supplies from HBC's Flathead Post and the two men set out to make it on their own.[32] Of the motley assortment of people they assembled, Ferris recorded:

> *Our party was composed of Mr. Montour, his son, two "engages," two Nez-perces, four Pend'orielles, one Cotena [Kootenai], one boy, four women and two or three small children. From the number of dialect in our camp, I am convinced, that a stranger would have been greatly puzzled to determine, which of the five languages continually spoken there, was predominant. However, we understood each other sufficiently well, to prevent mistakes; and the Indians comprehended one another, though they cannot be induced to convey their ideas in any tongue except their own. This custom would in a great measure prevent a proper understanding in many instances, were it not for their numerous signs, which constitute a kind of universal communication, not to say language, at once understood by all the various Indians in the mountains. These signs are made with their hands or fingers, in different positions, with rapidity; and are so extremely simple, that a person entirely unacquainted with them, will readily conceive a great portion of what may be expressed by them.[33]*

In May 1834, on his way to another rendezvous on the Green River from what is now Montana, the Ferris/Montour party used a route that crossed Medicine Lodge Pass. This gap was also known as Bannock Pass or Pioneer Pass at various times and sits on the Continental Divide along the border of Montana and Idaho. Climbing a "bold hill," Ferris reported they "came in view of the plains of Snake river, and the 'Trois Titons,' which bore nearly East." They saw "immense herds of buffalo in the plains below, which were covered in every direction by them, as far as the eye could distinguish." He also remarked on the "Sand Mountain in the distance."[34]

Having heard rumors while at an earlier rendezvous of boiling springs on the headwaters of the Madison River, Ferris and two Indians made a detour "at a round pace" into the region that is now Yellowstone National Park. Here he discovered "the half was not told me," as he explored the geysers, mud pots and other natural phenomenon found in the area.[35]

When Ferris got back to Henry's Fork, he found Montour and

the others had gone on, intending to return to the Green River Valley in time for the 1834 rendezvous. On May 21, Ferris reached the vicinity of Pierre's Hole "where the country assumes a rolling appearance, and is dotted with an occasional grove of aspen trees," much as it is today along Highway 33 approaching the basin through the dry farms from the northwest.[36]

Entering the valley, Ferris and his band paralleled the Teton River until they eventually found the main party's trail. Following the track at a rapid pace, they overtook Montour after about three miles, arriving just as camp was setting up for the evening. Suffocating clouds of dust rising from their horses' feet had filled their lungs and gouged their eyes, causing a great deal of discomfort along the trail. Meat was aplenty, for the hunters had killed several bulls, a bald eagle and a goose.

The small brigade stayed in Pierre's Hole an extra day to dry and pack meat for the trail. Their jerky was sufficiently dehydrated by evening so the next morning, May 23, they pursued their journey, passing southeastward through the Teton Basin. They halted part way up the mountain, on the trail leading over it, and encamped. During the day's march, they had killed five more buffalo and an antelope. One of the Indians had found a pair of boots and a few articles of clothing in Pierre's Hole. These appeared to have been there for some time, doubtless lost by a trapper, perhaps two years back at the 1832 rendezvous.[37]

Ferris wrote that they made their way over the mountains on May 24, crossing an enormous snow bank with extreme difficulty. When the party got down to the Snake River, the water was so high at the ford that the travelers were obliged to swim the horses across. The next day, Ferris passed through "the tortuous windings, abrupt elevations, and precipitous descents" of Hoback Canyon, which he called the Narrows.[38] "We now directed our course to 'Bonnyville's Folly,' or 'Fort Nonsense,' as it was more frequently called," before getting directed to the camp of Andrew Drips by two Indians attached to the AFC brigade.[39] A hard march of forty miles brought them to Drips' camp on Fremont Lake in the Wind River Mountains, northeast of modern Pinedale, Wyoming.

In the meantime, Nathaniel Wyeth had not been idle. At the end of the 1833 rendezvous, he had contracted with the RMFC to bring supplies to the 1834 gathering. Returning to Cambridge, Massachusetts, Wyeth busied himself with the necessary preparations for such an undertaking, in addition to proceeding with his business plan for Oregon Territory. He organized the Columbia Fishing and Trading Company, outfitted and dispatched the brig *May Dacre* to meet him on the Columbia, recruited men, then set out with a caravan of supplies for the RMFC in early May 1834. Milton Sublette accompanied Wyeth initially, but soon turned back to St. Louis due to health-related issues.

The RMFC had reorganized the previous summer with the addition of a new partner, Edmund Christy. The company was officially known as the Rocky Mountain Fur Company and Christy, as of July 20, 1833.[40] It was this new outfit that Wyeth had contracted to supply, and which would forfeit its earnest money if it failed to meet its end of the agreement with Wyeth.

William Sublette, not wanting to lose the RMFC business himself, had heard about Wyeth's contract and was determined to beat him to rendezvous – and to the sales opportunity. The race was on; but it was a race in which ill fortune seemed to continually dog Wyeth. Sublette even stopped part way along and began construction of Fort William (later to be renamed Fort Laramie), yet still managed to reach the rendezvous several days ahead of the Bostonian.

"Much to my astonishment," Wyeth wrote in his diary with a touch of bitter sarcasm, "the goods which I had contracted to bring up to the Rocky Mountain fur Co. were refused by those honorable gentlemen."[41] The enterprise of RMFC & Christy dissolved June 20, 1834, a fact the company used to justify refusing Wyeth's contract.[42] Yet another new partnership rose phoenix-like from the remains, consisting only of Fitzpatrick, Bridger and Milton Sublette. This company continued to do business with Milton's brother, William. The latter two partners, Bridger and Milton Sublette, were not even present at the rendezvous when all this took place.[43]

To say Wyeth was disappointed would be an understatement. A key component of this second journey was the fulfillment of the contract which Wyeth had made the previous August with Milton Sublette and Thomas Fitzpatrick to supply the Rocky Mountain Fur Company at the 1834 Ham's Fork rendezvous. This agreement called for Wyeth to provide $3,000 worth of trade goods, for which he would receive $3,521 above cost, paid in beaver pelts at $4.00 a pound. Wyeth was willing to accept the 175 percent mark-up on goods at rendezvous – a figure far less than that charged by most merchants supplying the mountain trade.

As it turned out, Milton's brother had every intention of supplying the 1834 rendezvous in spite of Wyeth. William got to the rendezvous two days ahead of Wyeth and convinced the fur company partners to do business with him and cancel Wyeth's contract. This involved paying a $500 penalty fee for reneging on the deal. Had Milton been able to stay with Wyeth all the way to the rendezvous, a confrontation with his brother may have led to a remarkably different outcome for Wyeth's enterprise.

A letter from Edward M. Samuels, Wyeth's agent in Liberty, Missouri, to Wyeth's New England financial backers adds insight to the results of Wyeth's business at the rendezvous. It reported that William Sublette paid the $500 forfeit and afterward bought goods from Wyeth at 300 percent profit – quite a bit higher than what Wyeth had contracted with Milton. According to Samuel's report, Wyeth may have "done as well or better than if he had filled the contract himself."

Wyeth sent drafts totaling $1866.93 to St. Louis. These drafts, drawn on the firm of Sublette and Campbell, represented the proceeds of the $500 default, repayment of an advance to Milton Sublette of about $500 and the sale of what Wyeth termed "a few goods at low prices." An undisclosed amount for the payment of Wyeth's men who returned east after the rendezvous had already been deducted from the amount of the drafts. These men had been hired at $13.89 per month.

Wyeth also sold $514 worth of goods to Henry Fraeb and Jean-Baptiste Gervias, probably with similar profit margins as charged to Sublette and Campbell. Thus, Wyeth had recouped nearly $2,400 – over half of the original contract – about $1,000 of which did not involve the sale of goods. On top of that, the bulk of his men's wages had been paid. In a July 1 letter to his Boston supporters, Wyeth indicated the "amount due for wages is trifling." It seems the men spent their money as fast as they earned it "in goods at about 500 per ct. on the original cost." Expenses for the year, Wyeth predicted, would be very small.

With the large portion of unsold goods still on hand, Wyeth's new strategy aimed to increase competition in the mountains. Following the rendezvous, he traveled about 150 miles west to the Portneuf River. There, he built and supplied Fort Hall without first having to go to the Columbia River to arrange for merchandise that arrived on the *May Dacre* from Boston to be shipped to the new trading post.[44]

Plans to build a fort along the Snake River had been on Wyeth's mind since his 1832 expedition. In November 1833, he had told his backers that, in the event the RMFC reneged on its contract, he would

> proceed to a safe country on the Columbia [Snake] River where some furs may be traded and there leave them with a few men ... leaving some men and a trusty person to keep them and trade as many more as he can.[45]

Apparently, Wyeth had already selected the place for such a trading post. The day after being rebuffed by the trapping company, Wyeth wrote that his plan was to

> build a fort on Lewis River about a hundred and fifty miles west of this which is in Latt. 45 deg. 15 min. Long 112 deg. 15 min. and there deposit my goods for sale when there is Beaver to pay for them.[46]

These bearings likely referred to an area near his campsite of August 13, 1832.

Now, with nearly a full load of supplies, Wyeth determined to build this trading post and compete head-on with William Sublette. He would sell goods to trappers and Indians and procure beaver hides as well. Finding his way to the Bear River, Wyeth stopped on the Fourth of July for a small celebration. His journal revealed his melancholy: "I gave the men too much alcohol for peace took a pretty hearty spree myself."[47] Another member of his party provided an amusing vignette:

> This being a memorable day, the liquor kegs were opened, and the men allowed an abundance. We, therefore, soon had a renewal of the coarse and brutal scenes of the rendezvous. Some of the bacchanals called for a volley in honor of the day, and

*in obedience to the order, some twenty or thirty "happy" ones
reeled into line with their muzzles pointed to every point of the
compass, and when the word "fire" was given, we who were not
"happy" had to lie flat upon the ground to avoid the bullets,
which were careering through the camp.*[48]

From Bear River, Wyeth traveled north through the area of
Soda Springs, eventually striking the Portneuf River. Here, on July
15, Wyeth and his men began construction of Fort Hall, named
for Henry Hall, one of his chief financiers. This post was destined
to play a key role in the coming western migration on the Oregon
Trail, but for the next few years, it would serve Wyeth's business
plan for the Pacific Northwest.[49]

Several erroneous points regarding Wyeth's 1834 expedition
crop up in a passage of B. W. Driggs' Teton Valley history:

*All these assembled at the rendezvous in Pierre's Hole. We do
not know of any religious service held while they were here; but
by this time the fur company had changed leaders, and Milton
Sublette, Bridger, Fitzpatrick, Frapp and Jervais, the new
co-partners, refused to purchase Wyeth's goods; he therefore, on
July 12 left this noted rendezvous, going southwest over what
is now called Piney Pass. On the thirteenth, their first Sunday
out, they found the fish so plentiful where they encamped that
they rested and fished the day away. When they reached near
the junction of the Portneuf and Snake Rivers, they selected a
site for a fort, where they commenced building the next day,
and named it Fort Hall in honor of Henry Hall, who had
financed the expedition.*[50]

To set the record straight, the 1834 rendezvous was held in the
Green River Valley, not in Teton Valley. Wyeth left the rendezvous
on June 20th but never went to Pierre's Hole, thus did not cross
Piney Pass. Wyeth did not mention fishing but another member of
his party, naturalist John Townsend, recorded that, while stopped
for their little Fourth of July soiree, one of the "sober" men caught
upwards of thirty pounds of trout, averaging fifteen or sixteen inches
in length, each weighing three-quarters of a pound or more.[51] While
camped on the Blackfoot River, Townsend also reported seeing

"three remarkable conic summits known by the name of the 'Three Butes' or 'Tetons.'"[52] This reference is to the three buttes rising from the Snake River Plains, not the mountains of the Teton Range.

In relating 1834 events in the Basin, B. W. Driggs also wrote of a battle between trappers and Blackfoot in the fall. He placed it in the "northern part of Pierre's Hole, from which the mountaineers started for their trapping fields via a northern route."[53] Joe Meek described the same battle, almost to the letter, including a list of men who participated in the fight. However, Meek reported that his company trapped the "country lying east of the mountains and upon the head-waters and tributaries of the Missouri."[54] Meek indicated the confrontation occurred on a branch of the Gallatin River – far from Pierre's Hole – this battle is thus not part of Teton Valley's story at all.

1835

In the latter part of April 1835, Jim Bridger took a brigade through Teton Valley on the spring hunt. All that is known comes from Isaac Rose, who indicated:

> *His route was by what was then known as the Tetons' Pass. The Tetons are three lofty peaks in the mountains, whose tops are nearly always hid in the clouds. These peaks serve as a good land-mark for the trappers for many miles around. On the last of April, Bridger, with the most of his company, started for the Tetons' Pass.*[55]

Bridger and the other Rocky Mountain trappers surely knew of the new trading post, Fort Hall, which was also the center of trapping operations for Nathaniel Wyeth's Columbia River Fishing and Trading Company. From there, trapping parties outfitted for their sorties against the beaver populations and at least one such expedition found its way to Pierre's Hole. On June 15, 1835, Joseph Gale led a twenty-four-man brigade of fourteen trappers and ten camp keepers. The party's chronicler was twenty-one-year-old trapper Osborne Russell, whose journal, along with that of Warren Ferris, even now provides so much valuable information about the day-to-day operations of the Rocky Mountain fur trade.

According to Russell, Gale's men planned to trap in the vicinity of Yellowstone Lake. With that destination in mind, they headed east from Fort Hall, then climbed over a mountainous region and into Grey's Hole. From there, they followed Grey's Creek down to the Snake River and up Swan Valley. Abraham Patterson, a twenty-three-year-old recruit from the HBC, drowned in the Snake River on June 22, after only twelve days with his new employer. The brigade ascended the Snake River Mountains and camped in an area "thickly covered with tall pines intermingled with fallen timbers."[56] Crossing Pine Creek Pass nine days into their journey put them in Teton Valley. Russell wrote:

> *24th Crossed the mountain 12 mls. East course and descended into the South W. extremity of a valley called Pierre's hole where we staid the next day. This valley lies north & South in an oblong form abt. 90 mls long and 10 wide surrounded except on the Nth. by wild and rugged Mountains: the East range resembles Mountains piled on Mountains and capped with three spiral peaks which pierce the cloud. These peaks bear the French name of Tetons or Teats – The Snake Indians call them the hoary headed Fathers. This is a beautiful valley consisting of a Smooth plain intersected by small streams and thickly clothed with grass and herbage and abounds with Buffaloe Elk Deer antelope etc 27th We travelled to the north end of the valley and encamped on one of the numerous branches which unite at the Northern extremity and forms a stream called Pierre's fork which discharges its waters into Henry's fork of Snake River. The stream on which we encamped flows directly from the central Teton and is narrowly skirted with Cottonwood trees closely intermingled with underbrush, on both sides. We were encamped on the South Side in a place partially clear of brush under the shade of the large Cottonwoods.[57]*

Gale's brigade camped on June 24 near the base of Pine Creek Pass, likely along the eponymous stream. Russell gave no account of June 26, but the men were without doubt busily trapping the many streams that are still abundant in the south end of the valley. They relocated to the east side of the valley, down to Teton Creek and camped on its south shore amongst the many cottonwoods along its banks.

On the morning of June 28, at about nine o'clock, Gale's camp was attacked by Piegan Indians. Though no primary account actually names this conflict, it is almost certainly what some Teton Valley locals refer to as the "Battle of Teton Creek." Here is Russell's description of the encounter:

AM we were arouse by an alarm of "Indians" we ran to our horses, All was confusion – each one trying to catch his horses. We succeeded in driving them into Camp where we caught all but 6 which escaped into the prarie: in the meantime the Indians appeared before our camp to the number of 60 of which 15 or 20 were mounted on horse back & the remainder on foot – all being entirely naked armed with fusees, bows, arrows etc They immediately caught the horses which had escaped from us and commenced riding to and fro within gunshot of our Camp with all the speed their horses were capable of producing without shooting a single gun for about 20 minutes brandishing their war weapons and yelling at the top of their voices; Some had Scalps suspended on small poles which they waved in the air. Others had pieces of scarlet cloth with one end fastened round head while the other trailed after them. After Securing my horses I took my gun examined the priming set the breech on the ground and hand on the Muzzle with my arms folded gazing at the novelty of this scene for some minutes quite unconscious of danger until the whistling of balls about my ears gave me to understand that these were something more than mere pictures of imagination and gave me assurance that these living Centaurs were a little more dangerous than those I had been accustomed to see portrayed on canvass –

The first gun was fired by one of our party which was taken as a signal for attack on both sides but the well directed fire from our Rifles soon compelled them to retire from the front and take to the brush behind us: where they had the advantage until 7 or 8 of our men glided into the brush and concealing themselves until their left wing approached within about 30 ft of them before they shot a gun they then raised and attacked them in the flank the Indians did not stop to return the fire, but retreated thro. the brush as fast as possible dragging their wounded along with them and leaving their dead on the spot. In the meantime myself and the remainder of our party were closely engaged with the centre and right. I took the advantage of a large tree which stood near the edge of the brush between the Indians and our horses: They approached until the smoke of our guns met. I kept a large German horse pistol loaded by me in case they should make a charge when my gun was empty. When I first stationed myself at the tree I placed a hat on some twigs which grew at the foot of it and would put it in motion by Kicking the twig with my foot in order that they might shoot at the hat and give me a better chance at their heads but I soon found this sport was no joke for the poor horses behind me were killed and wounded by the balls intended for me. The Indians stood the fight for about 2 hours then retreated thro the brush with a dismal lamentation. We then began to look about to find what damage they had done us: One of our comrades was found under the side of an old root wounded by balls in 3 places in the right and one in the left leg below the knee no bones having been broken. another had received a slight wound in the groin. We lost 3 horses killed on the spot and several more wounded but not so bad as to be unable to travel.[58]

Later that evening, some of the trappers followed down the creek toward the river about a mile and found a place where the retreating warriors had stopped. Blood stained the earth in a large circle where the injured had been laid on the ground. There were nine pools of congealing blood where wounds were likely dressed as best could be. A few months later, in September, Gale and his men would run into this same band of Piegans and learn that four Indians had been killed on the spot, while eight more had died of their wounds on the way to their village.[59]

Gale kept his men at the same camp that night and the next day, unafraid of further attack by the band whom he thought had probably left the valley. On June 30, they moved ten miles south, up the Teton River toward the head of Pierre's Hole. The next day, Gale's brigade camped at the southeast extremity of the valley.[60]

The wounded man, Richard Owens, suffered from all the motion of travelling, though Russell claims "everything was done which lay in our power to ease his sufferings."[61] The best-gaited horse in their herd had been selected for him to ride and a pallet was made on its saddle. Owen rode gingerly while another lead the animal.

Having finished their trapping in Pierre's Hole, Gale's brigade crossed the Tetons the following day. The ascent was described as very steep and rugged, covered with tall pines, but the descent was somewhat smoother, probably along Mosquito Creek. They dropped onto the Snake River, then turned north toward their goal, Yellowstone Lake.

Reverend Samuel Parker told of a journey he took in August 1835 in which Jim Bridger led the group from rendezvous on the Green River into the Teton Basin. Dr. Marcus Whitman had been a part of this missionary journey since St. Louis and at this particular rendezvous, he famously removed an arrowhead from Jim Bridger's back. Fascinated by the doctor's surgical skill, several Flathead and Nez Perce leaders had been drawn into discussions of religion with the missionaries. Encouraged by the inquisitiveness shown by these Indians, when the AFC caravan headed east on August 22, Whitman opted to return to the States with them to recruit associates for a mission among these people. Reverend Parker continued on to the Pacific Northwest.

August 23, being a Sabbath, the group took an opportunity to rest and partake of "devotional exercises" while they were in Jackson's Little Hole.[62] That afternoon, public worship was held for those of the company who understood English. The reverend recorded that "The men conducted with great propriety, and listened with attention."[63] Joseph Meek made the sermon out to be a little less successful. Meek declared, "in the midst of the discourse, a band of buffalo appeared in the valley, when the congregation incontinently broke up, without staying for the benediction," as every man excitedly joined in the hunt.[64]

They rose early and Bridger led them northwest along the Hoback on August 24. The travelers spent three days in Jackson Hole recruiting the livestock. While there, Parker

> *took an Indian and went up to the top of a very high mountain to take a view of the scenery around. The prospect was as extensive as the eye could reach ... The Trois Tetons were in full view, and not very far distant at the north. They are a cluster*

*of very high pointed mountains, not less than ten thousand feet,
rising almost perpendicularly, and covered with snow; five in
number, but only three of them are so very high as to be seen at
a great distance, and therefore take the above name.*[65]

Finally, on August 28, Parker's group resumed its journey and
crossed over Teton Pass. Parker described a "mountain so high,
that banks of snow were but a short distance from the trail."[66] And
this in August! When they had ascended two-thirds of the way, a
number of buffalo, which were being pursued by Indians from their
party, crashed down the mountainside through the midst of the
company. One bison ran over a horse with a child on its back and
the unfortunate youngster was thrown "far down the descent, but
providentially was not materially injured."[67] Parker continued:

*Our descent was through woods more dense than those on
the other side, and the most so of any since we left the waters
of the Missouri. Many parts of the descent were of almost
impassable steepness; and part of the way down a rough, deep
ravine, in which a stream of water commences and increases
from springs and rivulets to considerable magnitude, and
winds its way through the valley of Pierre's Hole; in the upper
part of which we made our encampment among the willows
in the prairie vale.*[68]

On August 29, Parker's group moved camp, traveling for five
hours along the valley to "the place, where ... two fur companies
held their rendezvous."[69] Though they expected to find bison in
Pierre's Hole, Parker reported they found none and chalked it up
to parties of Blackfoot that often ranged the basin. On the trail
between camps, Parker said he was shown the place where the men
of the fur companies battled the Blackfoot in 1832.

While in Pierre's Hole, Parker conducted a worship service
on the evening of August 30, 1835, with as many chiefs as could
assemble in one lodge. He explained the Ten Commandments,
attempted to show them "their sins by the transgression of God's
holy law, pointed them to the Savior, and endeavored to make
them understand the way they can be saved."[70] This was the first
Christian observance recorded in Teton Valley.

At Pierre's Hole, Parker separated from Bridger and his party. Parker and some Nez Perce and Flathead Indians turned their faces toward the Salmon River, while the trappers continued northwest into the mountains, heading for their hunting grounds.

1836

No activity in Pierre's Hole is recorded for the early months of 1836. The varied excitements of the summer's rendezvous having been exhausted, trapper brigades departed the confluence of Horse Creek and the Green River in order to commence their work. In the latter years of the Rocky Mountain fur trade, fur companies and leadership changed quickly from one season to the next. A company of nearly three hundred men left rendezvous under Bridger and Fontenelle, who both now worked for the same company.[71] From the valley of the Green, Bridger's command proceeded west to the Salt River, on to Snake River, and then camped in Pierre's Hole. Joe Meek, a member of this brigade, reported:

Pierre's Hole, notwithstanding its beauties, had some repulsive features, or rather perhaps one repulsive feature, which was, its great numbers of rattlesnakes. Meek relates that being once caught in a very violent thunder storm, he dismounted, and holding his horse, a fine one, by the bridle, himself took shelter under a narrow shelf of rock projecting from a precipitous bluff. Directly he observed an enormous rattlesnake hastening close by him to its den in the mountain. Congratulating himself on his snakeship's haste to get out of the storm and his vicinity, he had only time to have one rejoicing thought when two or three others followed the trail of the first one. They were seeking the same rocky den, of whose proximity Meek now felt uncomfortably assured. Before these were out of sight, there came instead of twos and threes, tens and twenties, and then hundreds, and finally Meek believes thousands, the ground being literally alive with them. Not daring to stir after he discovered the nature of his situation, he was obliged to remain and endure the disgusting and frightful scene, while he exerted himself to keep his horse quiet, lest the reptiles should attack him. By and by, when there were no more to come, but all were safe in their holes

*in the rock, Meek hastily mounted and galloped in the face of
the tempest in preference to remaining longer in so unpleasant
a neighborhood.*[72]

Rattlesnakes were apparently a relatively common nuisance in
the Teton Basin. Meek related the story of an old Frenchman in his
brigade who used to charm rattlers. To the disgust of the men in
camp, this snake handler would

*place them in his bosom, or allow them to wind about his arms,
several at a time, their flat heads extending in all directions,
and their bodies waving in the air, in the most snaky and
nerve-shaking manner.*[73]

Meek told that, on laying down to sleep, trappers often found
it necessary to encircle their beds with a hair rope, thus effectually
fencing out the reptiles, which are "too fastidious and sensitive of
touch to crawl over a hair rope."[74]

Moving on, Bridger left Pierre's Hole for the headwaters of the
Yellowstone. The brigade probably rode north, using Conant Pass to
access Jackson Hole, then crossed Two Ocean Pass to reach its fall
trapping grounds.

1837

Information related to trapping activities in Pierre's Hole is
extremely scarce in these final few years of the beaver trade. Existing
data are often garbled by historians' attempts to make sense of what
few records there are. One hint of mountain men in the valley
comes from Matthew Field, writing well after the fact. Although it
is not absolutely clear these events actually occurred in Teton Valley,
Field related an interesting incident:

*In '37 Mark [Head] was making his way to trap in Piere's
Hole – 7 men – at daylight they were fired on – none hurt
– they rushed to the brush for concealment, and while Mark
was crawling to get a shot at an Indian, when he received a
ball in the flesh of the knee, running up, and lodging in the
thigh, where it remains to this day – he couldn't walk for a
month.*[75]

1838

Sometime in the spring of 1838, Joe Meek left Fort Hall, heading north. Meek and his brigade were at the Cross Creeks of the Yellowstone River by May 14, 1838.[76] The men encountered a bear and also had several skirmishes with Indians before moving west to Henry's Lake. From there, they crossed into Pierre's Hole on their way to exploit the tributaries of the upper Snake River.

Meanwhile, Osborne Russell was no longer trapping under Gale but had accompanied Bridger's brigade that spring. He wrote that on June 8, 1838

we commenced our March thro. the pine woods by the lower track which runs South nearly parallel with the course of Henry's fork of the Snake and on the 11th we emerged from the pine woods onto the plains of Snake River where we stopped and trapped until the 14th. From thence we went to Pierre's Hole where we found a party of 10 trappers who had left the Camp at 25 yard river they had been defeated by the Blackfeet lost most of their horses and one man was wounded in the thigh by a fusee ball.[77]

In Teton Valley Joe Meek fell in with Bridger and the main company. Meek did not stay with the company long, but took off with seven other trappers under John Larison to trap the Salmon River. Meanwhile, the main outfit, Bridger in the lead, left Pierre's Hole on June 18 and trapped its way into Jackson Hole. From there, Russell and another trapper took off on a short trapping excursion of their own, then went south, expecting to find the rendezvous in the Green River Valley.

Robert Newell offered, "We are at this time on Snake River June 12th 1838 3 men left this morning for to hunt the flat head village."[78] From the brevity of Newell's information that "3 men left this morning," he may well have referred to the side trip by Osborne Russell since it is so close in date. In the same breath, Newell described a route for Bridger's brigade, to which he was attached, "from pier's hole to Jacksons hole Lewis fork, June 17 No buffalow: warm and pleasant."[79] Bridger and his cadre of trappers worked along the established route toward Green River, the rendezvous on their minds as well.

310

Unbeknownst to them, the site of the 1838 conclave had been moved to the Popo Agie River on the east side of South Pass. AFC was reluctant to have HBC brigades crash its party so, while the location had earlier been announced as Green River, it was secretly changed to the Popo Agie. The new location was on the Atlantic side of the Continental Divide and, according to the Joint Occupancy agreement between the United States and Great Britain regarding the Oregon Territory, HBC was not allowed to conduct commerce in this zone.[80] It was hoped that moving to the east of South Pass would be inconvenient enough to prevent the British company from attending.

Yet another missionary, Cushing Eells, who had already found his way to the trappers' trade fair, recorded:

Some one ... who had learned of the rendezvous of the American Fur Company, had with charcoal written on the old storehouse door, come to Poposua on wind River and you will find plenty trade, whiskey, and white women.[81]

This message spilled the beans and Francis Ermatinger's HBC brigade showed up anyway.[82]

Rumors flew at the summer's rendezvous that there would be no more such annual gatherings. Some reported that only 2,000 pelts had been brought in by the 125 trappers present.[83] The beaver trade was indeed winding down, though it may also have indicated the impact Fort Hall was having on rendezvous as an alternative and timelier place to sell furs and obtain supplies.

At the conclusion of the 1838 gathering of trappers and traders in mid-July, Jim Bridger guided sixty AFC men under the command of Andrew Drips.[84] The group included Newell. Russell eventually joined this brigade in Jackson Hole after a few days of trapping with an unidentified colleague on the Wind and Gros Ventre rivers. Newell started out with Bridger, "up wind river in to Jackons hole on to piers hole," but had struck out on his own by August 5: "left for the hudsons bay Co on Snake river with my woman and two little boys."[85] Fort Hall, Newell's destination, had been sold and was at that time owned by the HBC.[86]

Russell's elusive sidekick on the Wind and Gros Ventre rivers is never identified in these portions of Russell's diary, but in late January

1839, Russell refers to Elbridge Trask as "my old comrade."[87] It might be safe to assume this is the same man. Trask had come to the Columbia River on board the *May Dacre* in 1834 as an employee of Nathaniel Wyeth. Russell also began his career working for Wyeth, having come overland that same year. Only a year apart in age, these two young men appear to have hit it off. They may have known each other before, but had certainly met by rendezvous of 1838 when both signed on with Drips.[88]

By August 4, Bridger led Drips' company into Pierre's Hole. While Newell steered his path for Fort Hall, Russell and presumably Trask separated from the larger party to trap the streams running from the Tetons. In the middle of the afternoon, as they were "winding down a steep declevity which overhung a precipice of rocks nearly 200 ft perpendicular my horse slipped fell headlong down and was dashed to pieces."[89] Exactly where this occurred is impossible to identify based on the scant information provided, but cliffs to the north of Teton Valley, especially near the confluence of Teton River and Bitch Creek, are rugged enough to fit so sparse a description.

Down to one horse for two men, Russell and Trask spent the night where they were, then returned to Drips' camp in the valley on August 6. Here Russell acquired a fresh horse and made another start with this same partner the next day. They left camp, according to Russell, "in a SW direction across the valley," but given the itinerary laid out in Russell's journal for the next few days, this must be in error.[90] Only by traveling in a north east direction from the camp could the next week's passages be possible. North east is 180° from south west, the exact opposite direction, so perhaps Russell merely looked at his compass upside down.

Leaving before dawn, the two men traveled over the "low hills covered with pines" at the north end of Pierre's Hole until the sun was about an hour high.[91] At that point, they stopped and began setting their traps in the many streams to the northeast of present Tetonia, Idaho including Spring, Leigh and Badger creeks. Russell related:

> On the 8th we travelled down the stream about 3 Mls and then ascended a left hand branch in a NE direction After traveling about 10 Mls we fell into a Valley surrounded by high mountains except on the S.W. Side This Valley is about 4 Mls

long and one wide whilst the huge piles of rocks reaching above
the clouds seemed to overhang the place on the North and East
sides. We stopped here on the 9th and on the 10th returned to
hunt the Camp When leaving the Valley we took up the valley
in a west direction and from thence travelled a NW course
thro. dense forests of pine about 15 Mls. when we struck the
trail of the Camp going North.[92]

From a camp in what appears to be the vicinity of Badger Creek,
Russell worked his way upstream. Aubrey Haines, who edited the
trapper's journal, indicates Russell's references to "right" or "left"
hand of a stream are always made as though looking upstream.[93] This
is the opposite of accepted practice which calls for facing downstream
to determine the stream bank. Thus, South Badger Creek would
likely be the fork up which the two hunters traveled. Ten miles up
this creek brought them to the canyon at the head of South Badger
Creek which fits Russell's account pretty well.

Meanwhile, Newell did not stay at Fort Hall for long. Sometime
in the fall of 1838, he wrote, "I then left fort hall and Joined Mr
Drips in piers hole went from thare [to] the head of Green River
commen[ced] winter quarters with 8 men and verry Cold."[94] No
further record relays the travels of Drips, thus his brigade may have
stayed in or around Pierre's Hole since arriving in early August,
until joined by Newell that autumn.

1839

March 1839 found Meek at Fort Hall, after wintering with the
Nez Perce and acquiring yet another wife, whom he called Virginia.
Leaving Virginia at Fort Hall, Meek went trapping with a partner
named Allen.[95] They traveled up the Salmon River to Godin's River,
along Henry's Fork and into Pierre's Hole. From "Pierre's Fork,"
today's Teton River, Meek and Allen went to Lewis' Fork, today's
Snake, and made camp. They were on the west side of the Big Hole
Mountains, and "set their traps on a little stream that runs out of
the pass which leads to Pierre's Hole" (Pine Creek).[96]

Leaving their camp one morning to take up their traps they
were discovered and attacked by a party of Blackfeet just as
they came near the trapping ground. The only refuge at hand

was a thicket of willows on the opposite side of the creek, and towards this the trappers directed their flight. Meek, who was in advance, succeeded in gaining the thicket without being seen; but Allen stumbled and fell in crossing the stream, and wet his gun. He quickly recovered his footing and crossed over; but the Blackfeet had seen him enter the thicket, and came up to within a short distance, yet not approaching too near the place where they knew he was concealed. Unfortunately Allen, in his anxiety to be ready for defense, commenced snapping caps on his gun to dry it.[97] The quick ears of the savages caught the sound, and understood the meaning of it. Knowing him to be defenceless, they plunged into the thicket after him, shooting him almost immediately and dragging him out still breathing to a small prairie about two rods away.

And now commenced a scene which Meek was compelled to witness, and which he declares nearly made him insane through sympathy, fear, horror, and suspense as to his own fate. Those devils incarnate deliberately cut up their still palpitating victim into a hundred pieces, each taking a piece; accompanying the horrible and inhuman butchery with every conceivable gesture of contempt for the victim, and of hellish delight in their own acts.

Meek, who was only concealed by the small patch of willows, and a pit in the sand hastily scooped out with his knife until it was deep enough to lie in, was in a state of the most fearful excitement. All day long he had to endure the horrors of his position. Every moment seemed an hour, every hour a day, until when night came, and the Indians left the place, he was in a high state of fever.

About nine o'clock that night he ventured to creep to the edge of the little prairie, where he lay and listened a long time, without hearing anything but the squirrels running over the dry leaves; but which he constantly feared was the stealthy approach of the enemy. At last, however, he summoned courage to crawl out on to the open ground, and gradually to work his way to a wooded bluff not far distant. The next day he found two of his horses, and with these set out alone for Green River, where the American Company was to rendezvous. After twenty-six days of solitary and cautious travel he reached the appointed place in safety, having suffered fearfully from the recollection of the tragic scene he had witnessed in the death of his friend, and also from solitude and want of food.[98]

Late August 1839 found Osborne Russell and a few companions in a bad fix as well.[99] The four mountaineers had been trapping within the region of what is now Yellowstone National Park. While camped at the mouth of Pelican Creek, near the outlet of Yellowstone Lake, they too were attacked by Blackfoot. Only Russell and a man named White were in camp when the assault came. White, still sleeping at the time, jumped up from his blankets and escaped wearing only his hat and shirt. He caught an arrow in the hip but managed to limp away. Russell was hit by an arrow in the right hip and another in the right leg above the knee. Both men hobbled and hopped along, and as incredible as it seems, successfully eluded their pursuers.

The four trappers reunited at their campsite later in the afternoon only to find all their belongings gone. Russell found one sack of salt but everything else had been carried away or cut to pieces. White made some crutches for Russell, enabling him to get along slowly, but White had to carry his partner's rifle for him. They cobbled together a rough shelter of logs and slash, but in the night, it caught fire and the ensuing blaze "ran to the tops of the trees."[100]

In the morning, one man went to hunt while Russell bathed his wounds in "salt water and made a salve of Beaver's Oil and Castoreum" which "eased the pain and drew out the swelling in a great measure."[101] Though quite stiff, "bent considerably and swelled," Russell could bear half his weight on the lame leg. The mountaineers slowly hiked south, finding little game and virtually nothing to eat. Russell wrote:

We had passed up the left hand fork on the 9th of July on horse back in good health and spirits, and came down by the right on the 31st of Aug. on foot with weary limbs and sorrowful countenances.[102]

At night, even though they built a fire, Russell could only sleep fifteen to twenty minutes at a time due to cold temperatures. They made moccasins of raw elk hide and eventually found themselves camped on the west side of Jackson Lake. They limped their way up Owl Creek to the west. On September 2, 1839, Russell recorded:

> *We then had the Teton mountain to cross which looked like a laborious undertaking as it was steep and the top covered with snow. We arrived at the summit however with a great deal of difficulty before sunset and after resting a few moments travelled down about a mile on the other side and stopped for the night.*[103]

They had crossed Conant Pass and were now on the Pierre's Hole side of the Tetons, in the far northern sector of the valley. After another cold and tedious night, they descended the mountain through the pines at daylight. The next day, they staggered down to Henry's Fork via Fall River. Three days later, they arrived at Fort Hall. This was Osborne Russell's last foray into the Pierre's Hole area.

Allegedly, Meek's Nez Perce wife Virginia bore him a son on December 7, 1839 – in Pierre's Hole. The happy couple named their infant Courtney Walker Meek, after the factor in charge of Fort Hall at the time.[104] If true, this would be the second recorded birth in the valley. However, on a pension application filled out in 1878, Courtney Meek told T. A. Wood he was born in December 1838, "at what is now Bingham County of ... Idaho ... State of Oregon."[105]

The difference in year is due to Courtney Meek's enlistment to fight in Oregon's Yakima Wars, as well as voting illegally in November 1860 – he would have been one month too young.[106] Meek's application information has other complications, as well. First, Idaho's Bingham County was not created by the legislature until 1885. Second, even at that time it included all of present Bannock, Bonneville, Clark, Caribou, Fremont, Madison, Teton, and Bingham counties.[107] So, while that vast region embraces Pierre's Hole, it leaves a host of other possibilities, not to mention Fort Hall itself, for Courtney's birthplace. Another account states Courtney was born in Brown's Hole.[108]

1840

The year 1840, and the last of the trappers' rendezvous, is often considered the end of the beaver trade in the Rocky Mountains. In June, Joe Meek set out on what would prove to be his final trapping expedition before emigrating to the Oregon Territory. Along with a Frenchman named Mattileau, Meek visited the old trapping grounds that included Pierre's Fork, "Lewis' Lake," "Jackson's River," Jackson's Hole and Salt River, "but beaver were scarce."[109]

The best chronicler of that year's few glimpses of Teton Basin is another missionary – the Jesuit priest Father Pierre Jean De Smet. He accompanied the American Fur Company's final expedition to the mountains for a rendezvous, leaving Westport, Missouri on April 30, 1840.[110] The supply train was guided by Andrew Drips who had also shepherded several other Protestant missionaries on their journeys west. Following the rendezvous, De Smet and his Flathead escort left the Green River Valley on July 4, 1840. He wrote:

> *Three days we ascended Green River, and on the 8th we crossed it ... On the 10th, after crossing lofty mountains, we arrived upon the banks of Henry's Fork [Snake River], one of the principal tributaries of the Snake river ... The next day we had another high mountain to climb [Teton Pass] through a thick pine forest, and at the top we found snow, which had fallen in the night to the depth of two feet ... In descending into the great valley known as Pierre's Hole, we found the trail very steep and slippery.*[111]

De Smet's description of Teton Valley is quite simple, but vivid:

> *This valley is situated at the foot of the three Tetons, sharp peaked mountains of a prodigious height, rising almost perpendicularly more than 10,000 feet, and covered with perpetual snow. There are five of them but only three can be seen at any great distance.*[112]

Having arrived in Teton Valley, De Smet reported:

> *One day's travel in the great valley of Pierre's Hole brought us to the camp of the Flatheads and the Pend d'Oreilles. The poles were already up for my lodge, and at my approach men, women and*

children came all together to meet me and shake hands and bid me welcome; the number of them was about 1,600. The elders wept with joy, while the young men expressed their satisfaction by leaps and shouts of happiness. These good savages led me to the lodge of the old chief, called in his language Big Face.[113]

De Smet did not leave Teton Valley until July 16.[114] The priest spent the days teaching and preaching to "the Flat Heads and Ponderas assembled, to the number of sixteen hundred, in the beautiful Peter's Valley," and baptized 600 Indians before he left.[115] De Smet celebrated the first recorded Catholic mass in the basin on Sunday, July 12, 1840.

No other available primary records reveal mountaineer activity in Teton Valley for 1840. The beaver trade was all but over.

18
EPILOGUE

Trapping had been dwindling in Pierre's Hole and rapidly declined after 1840. However, the impact of mountaineers on the environment, commerce and eventual settlement in the Rocky Mountains was felt for many years to come. Joseph Meek and his French friend Mattileau appear to have been the last two recorded men to trap Pierre's Hole during the heyday of the Rocky Mountain fur trade. This last expedition was in the late spring of 1840. The final rendezvous would be held that summer on the Seedskeedee Agie, the Shoshone name for Green River. Trappers had begun taking their furs to such places as Fort Hall, Fort Crockett or Fort Robidoux to obtain supplies and to dispose of their beaver.[1]

Fashion had changed from felted beaver hats to toppers made from silk. The nutria, imported at far less expense from South America, possessed fur with similar qualities to the beaver and made felt equal in quality. The price of prime beaver fell from a high of about six dollars per pound to less than three dollars per pound.[2]

Regarding that final rendezvous, Robert Newell stated with a touch of melancholy:

I went to the American randezvous Mr Drips Feab & Bridger from St Louis with goods   but times was certainly hard no beaver and every thing dull some Missionaries came along with them for the Columbia.[3]

Victor's biography of Meek supplied Newell with a motivational speech:

"Come," said Newell to Meek, "We are done with this life in the mountains — done with wading in beaver-dams, and freezing or starving alternately — done with Indian trading and Indian fighting. The fur trade is dead in the Rocky Mountains, and is no place for us now, if ever it was. We are young yet, and have life before us. We cannot waste it here; we cannot or will not return to the States. Let us go down to the Wallamet and take farms ... What do you say, Meek? Shall we turn American settlers?"[4]

In November 1841, Russell wrote about the area along Idaho's Portneuf River, but he could have just as easily described nearby Pierre's Hole:

> *In the year 1836 large bands of Buffaloe could be seen in almost every little Valley on the small branches of this Stream at this time the only traces which could be seen of them were the scattered bones of those that had been killed. Their trails which had been made in former years deeply indented in the earth were over grown with grass and weeds The trappers often remarked to each other as they rode over these lovely plains that it was time for the White man to leave the mountains as Beaver and game had nearly disappeared.*[5]

By the end of the golden age of the fur trade, mountain men had picked clean the prime trapping and hunting grounds. Once numbering an estimated two hundred million in North America, beaver were trapped to near extinction in many regions. Today, the beaver has repopulated much of its original habitat, recovering to an estimated population of over two million.

Buffalo, which once ranged most of the Great Plains and in many quarters of the Rockies, were thought to have been as numerous as sixty million at one time. With the decline of the beaver trade, many former trappers turned to the buffalo hide trade. A vigorous market in bison robes opened after 1840. By 1900, fewer than six hundred of these animals were thought to exist. Today, bison continue to recover from the slaughter of earlier times.[6]

Rather than trade in buffalo hides, a few fur men became guides along the Oregon-California Trail. Still others went to work as scouts for U.S. Army patrols. Some returned to city life, only to dream of the beauty of Pierre's Hole. Joe Meek, at age 30, and Robert Newell, just turned 33, settled in Oregon country, having been the first to take wagons into that region. Both took active roles in the growing territory. Other trappers turned settler, too, expanding American populations in regions such as California and the Pacific Northwest.

From 1840 until 1860, there seems to be no recorded history of the valley. In 1860, when Captain W. F. Raynolds and Jim Bridger explored the Yellowstone Country, they spent some time in and around Pierre's Hole. A number of other exploring and surveying parties followed Raynolds. Sometime in the late 1860s, Richard "Beaver Dick" Leigh settled in the valley for a while. Cattle rustlers and horse thieves soon found the isolation of Pierre's Hole ideal for their needs. Finally, in the late 1880s, Mormon settlers followed the old trapper trails into the valley, bringing their families and settling throughout the basin.

The pursuit of beaver had introduced many people to Pierre's Hole and to what would become the state of Idaho. The first rendezvous held in the Teton Basin, in 1829, had been attended by a young man named William Craig. He returned for the big event in 1832 as well – the only two such gatherings held in Idaho. Craig went to California with Joe Walker's 1833-1834 expedition and helped establish Fort Davy Crockett in Colorado in 1836. Departing from the 1840 rendezvous, he guided a missionary party to Fort Hall, then on to the Whitman mission at Walla Walla, Washington.

In November 1846, Craig and his Nez Perce wife Isabel settled in Lapwai Valley, a region claimed by Isabel's people, located just east of modern Lewiston, Idaho. Though he would became a thorn in the side of missionary Henry Spalding, former mountain man William Craig and his wife were the first permanent settlers and developed the first cultivated farm in modern Idaho.[7] Several landmarks bear his name – the town of Craigmont, Idaho; Craig Mountain near Lewiston, Idaho; and Craig Crossing on the Salmon River, to name a few.[8]

In a romantic and perhaps apocryphal tale, it is said that famed poet Joaquin Miller, known as the "Byron of the Rockies," credited William Craig with the origin of the name "Idaho." Miller said he and his friend Craig were riding in the Rocky Mountains one morning, facing east, when the rising sun popped over the horizon. Miller commented on the stunningly beautiful sight before them. Craig then offered the Shoshone term for the scene as "e-dah-hoe," meaning "light coming over the mountains."[9] The fur trade had brought William Craig to Pierre's Hole; but Idaho made him stay.

NOTES

Introduction

1 Contact the Teton Valley Chamber of Commerce for further demographics on the valley at PO Box 250, 29 N. Main St. Driggs, ID 83422. (208) 354-2500. (www.tetonvalleychamber.com) See also: U.S. Census Bureau "Quick facts" for Teton County, Idaho (http://quickfacts.census.gov/qfd/states/16/16081.html)

2 Ongoing correspondence between the author and naturalist Carol Kuhn, K & K Environmental, Leavenworth, KS.

3 E-mail correspondence between the author and Dr. Robert Van Kirk, California State University - Humboldt, August 3-28, 2009. Many of Dr. Van Kirk's publications and technical reports can be found on the Internet, as of the time of this writing, at: http://www.isu.edu/~vankrobe.

4 For example, see *Men's Journal* magazine, March 2002, which ranked Driggs as No. 1 on its list of the "50 Best Places to Live." *Men's Journal* magazine, August 1996, listed Driggs as one of America's "coolest mountain towns." National Geographic's *Adventure* magazine showed Teton County among the "top ten summer sports Meccas" in 2001 and listed Driggs as one of the 10 best outdoor recreation destinations in the U.S.

5 For information on Manuel Lisa and his fur company, see Oglesby, *Manuel Lisa*, 65-98.

6 Lindsley, *Major Andrew Henry*, 8.

7 Hunt, *Overland Diary*, 33-34.

8 A concise account of these British trapping excursions is found in Morgan, *Jedediah Smith*, 117-130.

9 De Smet, "Letters and Sketches," 170.

10 The story of Beaver Dick is found in Edith Thompson and William Thompson, *Beaver Dick* (Laramie, WY: Jelm Mountain Press, 1982).

11 Benjamin W. Driggs, *History of Teton Valley Idaho* (Caldwell, ID: The Caxton Printers, Ltd., 1926).

12 Nolie Mumey, *The Teton Mountains, Their History and Tradition* (Denver: The Artcraft Press, 1947); Margaret Sanborn, *The Grand Tetons: The Story of the Men Who Tamed the Western Wilderness* (New York: G.P. Putnam's Sons, 1978); Benjamin W. Driggs, *History of Teton Valley, Idaho*, eds. Louis J. Clements and Harold S. Forbush (Rexburg, ID: Eastern Idaho Publishing Company, 1970).

Chapter 1:
The Mountains

1   *Eighth Biennial Report of the Board of Trustees of the State Historical Society of Idaho for the Year 1921-1922* (Boise, ID: Idaho State Historical Society, 1922), 58-59, references traveling from Victor over "scenic Piney Pass" to Swan Valley and Irwin, Idaho. Also, Driggs, *History of Teton Valley,* 86.

2   Further information regarding the geology of the Teton Range is found in Fritiof Fryxell, *The Tetons* (Berkeley, CA: University of California Press, 1946). Fryxell, a geologist, was the first naturalist in Grand Teton National Park.

3   An interesting and fact-filled book about Grand Teton National Park is Orrin H. and Lorraine G. Bonney, *Bonney's Guide: Jackson's Hole and Grand Teton National Park* (Houston, TX: by the authors, 1961).

4   Boone, *Idaho Place Names,* 369. The name is often seen as Tyghee or Tahgee along with various other spellings. The man is deemed to be Shoshone rather than Bannock by some writers.

5   Information provided by Driggs, *History of Teton Valley,* 48, regarding Jedediah Smith is wrong. His sketch of Smith's death, outside of the wrong date, is roughly acceptable. The section to be addressed begins: "[Smith] stood out a marked figure in all his rough trapper life, because he would invoke a blessing on his meat and kneel and pray beside his blanket every evening, and carried a Bible with him ... It is a wonder how Smith did so much, especially after amputation of his leg. It was while he was operating in the vicinity of Pierre's Hole that his horse stepped in a badger hole and Smith's leg was broken. He, however, managed to get to his lodge where he and his Indian wife made a saw from a hunting knife, and the two managed to saw off the broken leg ... After the leg was healed Smith made himself a wooden leg, and ever after that he went by the name of 'Pegleg Smith.'"

     Unfortunately, there is no evidence Smith ever blessed his food or carried a Bible, even though that is a common tradition that has followed Smith since about 1880. See Auld, "The Legend of Jedediah Smith," 1-9.

     There is no record of Jedediah Smith ever breaking a leg, much less amputating one. He never married, be it an Indian woman or otherwise, and he never went by the nickname of "Pegleg." There was, however, another trapper named Thomas L. Smith who lost a leg and went by that moniker, though the details surrounding his ordeal are dramatically different from the description offered by Driggs, who likely confused these two Smiths. For the story of the real Pegleg Smith, see Templeton, *The Lame Captain,* 73-78.

6   Daugherty, *A Place Called Jackson Hole,* 31.

7   Driggs, *History of Teton Valley,* 13.

8   Lightner, *Roads Through Time,* 11.

9   Daugherty, *A Place Called Jackson Hole,* 35-39.

10 L. and O. Bonney, *Guide to Jackson's Hole,* 35, 112; Platts, *The Pass,* 12-14; Driggs, *History of Teton Valley,* 69, 110.

11 Russell, *Journal of a Trapper,* 15.

12 Mattes, *Jackson Hole, Crossroads,* 15; Lightner, *Roads Through Time,* 6.

13 Mumey, *Teton Mountains,* 5.

14 Ross, *Fur Hunters,* 250. This passage indicates the buttes of the Snake River Plains, near Arco, Idaho, were named "Trois Tetons."

15 Bruce Blevins, *A.K.A. the Tetons* (Powell, WY: WIM Marketing, 1999).

16 Ibid., 8-12, 23.

17 Ibid., 8. Also Ross, *Fur Hunters,* 249.

18 Blevins, *A.K.A. the Tetons,* 9.

19 Ferris, *Map of the Northwest Fur Country – 1836.* Also Blevins, *A.K.A. the Tetons,* 13. The journal of Warren Ferris was originally published as a series of monographs in a newspaper from 1842 through 1844. This is the earliest documented source for the Trois Tetons at their modern location, presuming the designation was not changed by the publisher to reflect contemporary usage. The map was not published until 104 years later.

20 Blevins, *A.K.A. the Tetons,* 14.

21 Irving, *Astoria,* 257.

22 Washington Irving, *The Adventures of Captain Bonneville, U.S.A., in the Rocky Mountains and the Far West,* ed. Edgeley Todd (Norman, OK: University of Oklahoma Press, 1961).

23 Peter Skene Ogden, *Peter Skene Ogden's Snake Country Journals 1824-25 and 1825-26,* ed. E. E. Rich (London: The Hudson's Bay Record Society, 1950).

24 Mumey, *Teton Mountains,* 5-6. In the years 1871 through 1877, the first formal, scientific expeditions visited southeastern Idaho. Overall, this project was known as the Geological and Geographical Survey of the Territories, popularly called the Hayden Survey. Ferdinand V. Hayden led an assemblage of geologists, paleontologists, mineralogists, topographers, artists, and photographers in exploring, mapping, and documenting this part of the West, and effectively put Yellowstone on the map. See Charles A. White, "Memoir of Ferdinand Vandiveer Hayden, 1839-1887," *Biographical Memoirs of the National Academy of Sciences,* 3 (1895): 402-403.

Chapter 2:
The Shoshone – First People in the Valley

1 Driggs, *History of Teton Valley,* 13.

2 These tribal names reflect common Euro-American titles for these nations, not necessarily what these people called themselves. There are three primary bands of the Blackfeet, including Siksika (Blackfoot), Piikani (Piegan) and Kainai (Blood). The Crow call themselves Apsáalooke, the Flathead go by Salish and the Nez Perce are the Nimíipuu. Bannock people referred to themselves as Banate. All of these names are seen in a variety of spellings.

"Blackfoot" can be confusing as this designation is applied to many tribes in fur trade documents. "Blackfoot" is the English translation of the word *siksika*. Some Blackfoot people are annoyed by the plural "Blackfeet," an Anglicized version, but most Blackfoot people seem to accept either name. "Blackfoot" is more commonly used in Canada; "Blackfeet" is more commonly used in the United States. Some authorities indicate "Blackfeet" represents the Confederacy of the assorted bands while "Blackfoot" represents the Siksika band. The word is not plural in the Blackfoot language, thus that is the version opted for use throughout this book unless it is used in another form within a quoted passage. The Uto-Aztecan relationship of Bannock and Shoshone may be found in Lowie, *Indians of the Plains*, 7.

3 Mann, *Sacajawea's People*, nn. 192-193. The legally incorporated name of the modern tribe uses "Shoshone" so that is the spelling predominately used throughout this book unless it is used in a different form within a quoted passage.

4 http://www.shoshoneindian.com/

5 Ross, *Fur Hunters*, 166.

6 Sanborn, *The Grand Tetons*, 42. Unfortunately, Sanborn does not provide a source. LaVerendrye reported hearing of *gens du serpent* as early as 1742, found in Morgan, *Shoshonean Peoples and the Overland Trail*, 43.

7 Madsen, *Northern Shoshoni*, 18.

8 Merkley, *The Shoshone-Bannock and Old Fort Hall*, 1; Boone, *Idaho Place Names*, 348.

9 Ross, *Fur Hunters*, 167.

10 Mann, *Sacajawea's People*, 11.

11 Moulton, *Journals*, 5: 91. Entry for Aug. 14, 1805 by Lewis.

12 The majority of the information in the next few pages comes from the following sources: Madsen, *Northern Shoshoni*; Mann, *Sacajawea's People*; Merkely, *The Shoshone-Bannock of Old Fort Hall*; Sanborn, *The Grand Tetons*; and Stamm, *People of the Wind River*.

13 Boone, *Idaho Place Names*, 251.

14 Moulton, *Journals*, 5: 119-141, 148-164. Lewis and Clark recorded many ethnographic notes regarding the Shoshone in journal entries for August 19-21 and 23-24, 1805.

15 Sanborn, *The Grand Tetons*, 43.

16 Stamm, *People of the Wind River*, 6.

17 Madsen, *Northern Shoshoni*, 18.

18 Janetski, *Indians in Yellowstone*, 37-39; Sanborn, *The Grand Tetons*, 45-46.

19 Madsen, *Northern Shoshoni*, 18.

20 For an account of the Hidatsa capture of Sacagawea, see Moulton, *Journals*, 5: 9. A summary of the event can be found in Saindon, "The Abduction of Sacagawea," 383-387. For the quote from Cameahwait, see Moulton, *Journals*, 5: 91.

21 Madsen, *Northern Shoshoni*, 18-19; Merkley, *The Shoshone-Bannock of Old Fort Hall*, 1, 4, 38.

22 Urbanek, *Wyoming Place Names*, 211. The name "Washakie" has been given several meanings: "Shoots Straight," "Shoots-on-the-Fly," "Sure Shot," and "Gambler's Gourd." The name is generally accepted as coming from a word meaning "rawhide rattle." According to later reports, Washakie supposedly saved the pate of the first buffalo he ever killed, dried it, blew it up like a bladder, and put stones in it so they would rattle. He would ride amongst enemy warriors shaking this rattle, scaring their horses, so he was called "The Rattler." Hebard, *Washakie*, 50-51. "Togwotee" means "Lance Thrower," according to Urbanek, *Wyoming Place Names*, 211.

23 The official name of the Hudson's Bay Company, chartered in 1670, was the Governor and Company of Adventurers of England Trading into Hudson's Bay. Newman, *Company of Adventurers,* 1.

24 Morgan, *Jedediah Smith*, 271-72.

25 Madsen, *Northern Shoshoni*, 23-26.

26 Ibid., 25.

27 J. Wyeth, *Oregon*, 81.

28 Madsen, *Northern Shoshoni,* 25.

29 Liljeblad, *The Idaho Indians in Transition*, 20-21.

30 Idaho Historical Society Reference Series, "Snake River." No. 38, Feb. 1964. Robert Stuart's journal entry for August 12, 1812 indicates the river was known "by the generality of whites, [as] the Snake River." Stuart, *On the Oregon Trail*, 74-75.

31 Ross, *Adventures of the First Settlers*, 234.

32 Irving, *Astoria*, 305.

33 The Works Progress Administration, *Idaho, A Guide in Word and Pictures*, 412.

34 Moulton, *Journals,* 3: 104-145. Lewis and Clark recorded consistent contact with the Teton Sioux from September 23-October 5, 1804.

35 Driggs, *History of Teton Valley*, 107-08.

36 Ibid., 106.

37 Hanson, "The Trapper's Last Shot," 2-3.

Chapter 3:
The "Hole" Story

1 The Big Hole in Montana bears no relation to the Big Hole Mountains which border the western edge of Pierre's Hole. When Lewis and Clark entered today's Big Hole Valley in Montana, they named the river flowing through it the Wisdom River. Trappers later coined the term "Big Hole" in reference to the expansive valley through which the river flowed. The same connotation likely applies to the Big Hole Mountains.

2 Victor, *River of the West*, 58.

3 Ferris, *Life in the Rocky Mountains*, 224.

4   Campbell, *Narrative of Colonel Robert Campbell's Experiences*, 17.

5   Victor, *River of the West*, 84, 92.

6   Mattes, *Jackson Hole Crossroads*, 36.

7   Tobie, *No Man Like Joe*, 11.

8   For a complete study of each annual rendezvous, see Gowans, *Rocky Mountain Rendezvous*.

9   Wells, "Ignace Hatchiorauquasha (John Grey)," 162.

10   Driggs, *History of Teton Valley*, 13.

11   Chittenden, *The American Fur Trade of the Far West*, 747.

12   Coutant, *History of Wyoming*, 134. This early record contains a lot of information now known to be in error. It is likely Driggs used Coutant as a source for a great deal of the particulars in *History of Teton Valley*.

13   Ferris, *Life in the Rocky Mountains*, 219. It is easy to understand how some writers could interpret "receives its name from" to mean "was named by." A recent example of this confusion can be found in Barbour, *Jedediah Smith, No Ordinary Mountain Man*, 67. "A veteran trapper, 'Old Pierre' discovered and named Pierre's Hole in Idaho."

14   Larpenteur, *Forty Years a Fur Trader*, 32.

15   De Smet, *Early Western Travels 1748-1846*, 27: 170.

16   Larpenteur, *Forty Years a Fur Trader*, nn. 32-33.

17   Mumey, *The Teton Mountains*, 205. According to Beal, *A History of Southeastern Idaho*, n. 416, "Teton Valley" became the new name on October 31, 1897.

18   Idaho Transportation Department, Historical Marker #139 at milepost 144 on Highway 33, south of Driggs, Idaho.

Chapter 4:
Pierre Tevanitagon

1   Driggs, *History of Teton Valley*, 13. Mumey, *Teton Mountains*, n. 185.

2   George Washington assigned Sullivan to neutralize the Iroquois, who were then allied with the British, and to destroy what Indian villages could be found, capturing as many prisoners as possible in the process. In all, Sullivan burned over forty villages. Thrapp, *Encyclopedia of Frontier Biography*, 3: 1387-1388.

3   Irving, *Captain Bonneville*, 87.

4   Jackson, *Children of the Fur Trade*, 20.

5   Masson, *Les Bourgeois de la Compagnie du Nord-ouest*, 413.

6   Morgan, *The West of William Ashley*, 291.

7   Wells, "Old Pierre," 351.

8   Karamanski, "The Iroquois and the Fur Trade," 6.

9   Ross, *Fur Hunters*, 109.

10   Driggs, *History of Teton Valley*, 13, 33. Compare with Ross, *Fur Hunters*, 284-285. Driggs provided no primary source citation for this information.

11   Ross, *Fur Hunters*, 136.

12 Wells, "Old Pierre," 352.

13 Morgan, *Jedediah Smith*, 120-121. Jackson, *Children of the Fur Trade*, 25.

14 Wells, "Old Pierre," 353.

15 Ibid. Wells took the quote from The Minutes of Council: Northern Department of Rupert Land, 1821-1831.

16 Ross, *Journal of Alexander Ross*, 375.

17 Ibid., 377.

18 Ross, *Fur Hunters*, 243-244.

19 Ibid., 245.

20 Wells, "Old Pierre," 354.

21 This episode is covered in greater detail in chapter ten. For a thorough version, see also Morgan, *Jedediah Smith*, 127-130.

22 Ott, "'Ruining' the Rivers in the Snake Country," 177.

23 Ogden, *Snake Country Journals, 1824-26,* 2-3.

24 Ibid., 39.

25 Ibid., 163.

26 Ibid., 147, 163.

27 For a thorough discussion of the incident between Peter Ogden and Johnson Gardner, see Reid, *Contested Empire,* 101-134.

28 Ibid., 234.

29 The following information regarding Pierre Tevanitagon's 1825 rendezvous account comes from Morgan, *The West of William Ashley,* 119-120, 122-123.

30 Ogden, *Snake Country Journals, 1824-26,* 154.

31 Ibid.

32 Campbell, *A Narrative of Colonel Robert Campbell's Experiences,* 29.

33 Morgan, *The West of William Ashley,* 186.

34 Morgan, *Jedediah Smith,* 341.

35 Ogden, *Snake Country Journals, 1827-29,* 63.

36 Campbell, *A Narrative of Colonel Robert Campbell's Experiences,* 30.

37 Morgan, *The West of William Ashley,* n. 314.

38 Ogden, *Snake Country Journals 1827-29,* 63.

39 Campbell, *A Narrative of Colonel Robert Campbell's Experiences,* 30.

40 Ferris, *Life in the Rocky Mountains,* 219.

41 Irving, *Captain Bonneville,* 87.

Chapter 5:
John Colter and Pierre's Hole

1 For the journal entries Meriwether Lewis recorded describing these events, see Moulton, *Journals,* 5: 73-84.

2 Moulton, *Journals,* 8: 302.

3 Morris, *The Fate of the Corps,* 39, n. 220.

4 Irving, *Astoria,* 176.

5 This post has variously been known as Fort Remon, Fort Raymond, Fort Ramon, Fort Lisa, Lisa's Fort and Fort Manuel. The name was given in

honor of Lisa's first son, Remon, reportedly as written by Lisa. Douglas, *Manuel Lisa*, 66. On the baptismal record, the priest spelled the name Raimond.

6   Morris, *The Fate of the Corps,* 40-41.

7   Letter from Reuben Lewis to Meriwether Lewis, April 21, 1810. Meriwether Lewis Papers, Missouri History Museum, St. Louis, MO.

8   Lowie, *The Crow Indians,* 3. LeForge spent most of his life living with the Crow and was often referred to as a "White Crow Indian." Many sources relating to the origin of the Crow Nation are available on the Internet, for example: http://www.crowtribe.com/about.htm.

9   Brackenridge, *Views of Louisiana,* 91.

10 The imaginative account of Colter's route written by Driggs, which includes finding a Crow village in Teton Valley and Colter giving them a feast, should be skipped altogether. Driggs, *History of Teton Valley,* 21-25.

11 Paul Allen and Nicholas Biddle, eds., *History of the Expedition Under the Commands of Captains Lewis and Clark* (Philadelphia: Bradford and Inskeep, 1814). Biddle was responsible for editing the journals and the development of the narrative contained in two volumes. Paul Allen prepared them for publication when Biddle became overburdened with other tasks. How much Allen actually contributed to the narrative is debated by historians. Though Biddle's name does not appear in the edition, it is often attributed to him. For more information, see Paul Cutright, *A History of the Lewis and Clark Journals* (Norman, OK: University of Oklahoma Press, 1976).

12 Harris, *John Colter,* 104.

13 Dr. J. L. Allen, e-mail to author, Oct. 20, 2009.

14 Wheat, *Mapping the Transmississippi West,* 94, 233. Vandermaelen's monumental map was composed of seventy-six separate sheets in four volumes.

15 Chittenden, *Yellowstone National Park,* 174-175, 177.

16 For an in-depth discussion of the identity of Lake Biddle see, Blevins, *A.K.A. Jackson Lake.*

17 Ferris, *Life in the Rocky Mountains,* 224.

18 Vinton, *John Colter,* 59.

19 All of these various theories regarding Colter's route are thoroughly explored in Mattes, "Behind the Legend of Colter's Hell," 251-282.

20 Mattes, *Colter's Hell & Jackson's Hole,* 14-15.

21 Potts, *John Colter, The Discovery of Jackson Hole and the Yellowstone,* 7.

22 Harris, *John Colter,* 97-98.

23 John L. Allen, "William Clark 1812: Redux." (Paper presented at the annual meeting of the Lewis and Clark Heritage Trail Foundation in Great Falls, MT, August 2008.) A secondary presentation of this paper, titled "A New Look at the Route of John Colter," can be found in the Wyoming State Museum Lecture Series, accessed on-line at http://odeo.com/episodes/23644856-A-New-Look-at-the-Route-of-John-Colter.

24   A complete discussion of the location of Colter's Hell is found in Mattes, *Colter's Hell and Jackson's Hole.*

25   Colter's rifle was decidedly not the Hawken portrayed by some inventive writers. It may have been the same weapon he carried on the Lewis and Clark Expedition. During his famous "Race for Life" his gun was confiscated by the Indians who had captured him. These Indians later traded at HBC's Edmonton House in October 1808 reporting they killed two trappers. They displayed a heavy rifle that belonged to one of the trappers which may have been Colter's military rifle. The Indians considered it heavy and difficult to load: of no use to a buffalo running hunter. Jackson, "Revisiting the Colter Legend," 10.

26   Moulton, *Journals,* 8: 209-211.

27   Ewers, *The Blackfeet,* 49.

28   Beckwourth, *Life and Adventures,* 24-25.

29   Moulton, *Journals,* 3: 271.

30   Brackenridge is quoted in Chittenden, *A History of the American Fur Trade,* 715.

31   Allen, "William Clark 1812: Redux."

32   Moulton, *Journals,* 7: 106.

33   Driggs, *History of Teton Valley,* 23.

34   James, *Three Years Among the Indians,* 52-54. The actual number of Blackfoot participants in this battle may well have been far less. British Alexander Henry's 1808 census suggests the Siksika, Kainai and Piikani combined only counted for 650 tents in all – not much over 1400 warriors total. See discussion in Jackson, "Revisiting the Colter Legend," 8.

35   Grand Teton National Park, Collections Accession File, "The Colter Stone," Accession File 63, 2 folders, F.M. Fryxell to National Park Service Director Arno Cammerer, May 8, 1934.

36   Several sample signatures and a listing of Colter's estate appear in Colter-Frick, *Courageous Colter,* 148-154, 506-507.

37   Lawrence, *John Colter Journey of Discovery,* 13-14.

38   Department of the Interior, National Park Service, September 4, 1936; October 6, 1936 and June 5, 1937; Grand Teton National Park Files.

39   A document places Colter at Fort Remon on December 31, 1809. Shortly afterward, he led Andrew Henry and a party to the Three Forks. That is a fairly small window in the middle of winter in which to carve but this stone might be authentic. Colter-Frick, *Courageous Colter,* 98-99.

40   Colter biographer Ruth Colter-Frick found historical documents with the surname spelled COLTER, COULTER, and COALTER. Many times the L and the T were both crossed and COLTER appeared as COTTER. However, all existing examples of Colter's signature are spelled COLTER. Colter-Frick, *Courageous Colter,* 134, 506-507.

41   Daugherty, *A Place Called Jackson Hole,* 47.

42   *Idaho Register,* Idaho Falls, ID for September 12, 1911, and March 12 and 24, 1912; Abraham, "Here Before Lewis and Clark," 28-30; Lovell,

"The Clark Stone," 19. Lovell indicates the stone's inscription bears no resemblance to Clark's carving on Pompey's Pillar in Montana and surmises the "0" in the date may actually be a "9." Joseph Clark, who surveyed the area, apparently liked the Swan Valley region, thus Lovell surmises he may have carved the inscription.

43 Vinton, *John Colter*, 61-62.

44 It seems this John Coulter was fishing along the banks of the creek when he had a face-to-face encounter with a bear, causing him to jump into the water. Daugherty, *A Place Called Jackson Hole*, 47.

45 Calkins, *Jackson Hole*, 43-44.

46 Myths surrounding Colter are examined in Jackson, "Revisiting the Colter Legend," 1-19.

47 Colter-Frick, *Courageous Colter*, 147-148. Many historians have stated the date of death as November 26, 1813 but that is the date the estate was opened. His date of birth is unknown but is thought to be sometime in 1774.

Chapter 6:
Andrew Henry and the St. Louis Missouri Fur Company

1 Oglesby, *Manuel Lisa*, 68-69. A copy of the Articles of Agreement are found in Appendix III of the same book, 202-208.

2 Morgan, *Jedediah Smith*, n. 396. Courter's death is reported in David Thompson's journal in February 1810. There is potential evidence of a fort in the Three Forks region that predates the stockade built by the Missouri Fur Company. Morgan posits Courter was associated with Jeremy Pinch who entered the area as early as 1807. See note 5 below.

3 Hayden, *From Trapper to Tourist in Jackson Hole*, 9. A review of multiple books on British guns by historian Scott Walker showed several early gun barrels marked "London" but none with date stamps. Some barrels had proof stamps while locks were often dated. Thus, this story may be more hearsay that fact.

4 James, *Three Years Among the Indians*, 9.

5 Henry may not have been the first to establish a post in the vicinity of Three Forks. Finan McDonald, the red-whiskered Scot, wrote a letter in 1824 describing a fort he had previously seen on the Missouri River. His writing style provides a good example of the challenge presented by some diarists: "I Sa the Musasourey Last fall down as far is the falls in that Part of the Cuntre is ruint of Corta is old Fort it is fine river all long and about the size of the N Parsey [Snake] River." This passage, according to historian Dale Morgan, "provides evidence of an American fort in the Three Forks Country antedating the stockade the Missouri Fur Company built in the spring of 1810 between the Jefferson and the Madison ... most probably associated with the mysterious Jeremy Pinch, who penetrated into this country as early as the summer of 1807." From this scanty evidence, it is

difficult to establish with any confidence that American trappers, beyond Lisa's company, constructed a post as early as 1807. Morgan, *Jedediah Smith,* 123, n. 396. For more information regarding these early forays by Americans into the Rocky Mountains, see Morris, "The Mysterious Charles Courtin," 21-39.

6   A map, entitled "Sketch of part of the Missouri & Yellowstone Rivers with a description of the country, &c" is filed with the Records of the Office of the Quartermaster General, Record Group 92, Map 281, National Archives, College Park, Maryland. The map was published in the National Archives' journal, *Prologue,* in the fall of 1971. It is often referred to as "the Dougherty map." The narrative on the reverse discloses facts pertaining to the 1809-1810 St. Louis Missouri Fur Company expedition.

7   James, *Three Years Among the Indians,* 68.

8   Ibid., 72.

9   Ibid., 66.

10   Ibid., 87.

11   Letter, William Clark to William Eustis, July 20, 1810, in William Clark Papers, Missouri History Museum, St. Louis, MO. Harris, *John Colter,* 150, indicates the group could not have been much more than nine men. A newspaper report in the *Louisiana Gazette,* January 16, 1811, reports a doubtful 140 men in Henry's party.

12   Clements, "Andrew Henry," 177.

13   See note 11.

14   Letter, Reuben Lewis to Meriwether Lewis, April 21, 1810, in Meriwether Lewis Papers, Missouri History Museum, St. Louis, MO.

15   See note 11.

16   See note 6.

17   Mark Kelly, Unpublished manuscript on the life of John Dougherty. Ongoing correspondence with the author.

18   Upstream, the Big Horn becomes the Wind River, though exactly when that change in verbiage took place is difficult to determine. General W. F. Raynolds led an exploration of that country in the late 1850s and reported, "Here I desire to state a fact of some importance with reference to the nomenclature of the Big Horn and its branches. The river which last summer we descended under the name of the Big Horn is formed by the junction of the Popo-Agie and the Wind River at this point, and should properly be called the Big Horn below the site of our present camp. By the trappers, however, it is always spoken of as the Wind River until it enters the cañon some 30 miles below here. There is no good reason for this arbitrary distinction, whereby the same stream passes into the mountains under one name and emerges with another, and it is necessary that these facts be known to avoid confusion." Raynolds, *Report on the Exploration of the Yellowstone River,* 82.

19   Driggs, *History of Teton Valley,* 26. Interestingly, Driggs brings Henry south through modern Yellowstone National Park into Jackson Hole,

before crossing the Tetons – a route for which there is no historical documentation.

20 Clements, "Where Was Fort Henry?" 53; and Clements, "Upper Snake River to 1840."

21 Hunt, *Overland Diary,* 34.

22 Driggs, *History of Teton Valley,* 26.

23 Beal, *History of Southeastern Idaho,* n. 397. Ore, *Andrew Henry,* 78-79.

24 Ibid., 27. There was never a sixteen-star United States flag. The number of stars jumped from fifteen to twenty in 1818. While this is pure conjecture, the sixteenth state, Tennessee, joined the Union on June 1, 1796. Perhaps this is some sort of State Militia device struck after June 1, 1796 but before February 19, 1803 when Ohio became a state.

25 Beal, *History of Southeastern Idaho,* nn. 397-398.

26 Driggs, *History of Teton Valley,* 106. Driggs gives the following inscriptions: 1810 - A. Henry, Reznor, J. Day, W. Weir; 1827 - J. Gardner, Stullock, A. Godin, H. Godin, Louis La Valle; 1828 - Henry Fraeb, M. Harris, B. Gervaise, W. L. Sublette, Meek, D.E. Jackson, J. S. Smith, T. Fitzpatrick, Robt. Newell; 1831-1832 - J. Beckworth, J. L. Meek. Frayor. There are inherent problems with several of the names and the alleged dates.

Yet, these names are corroborated by a letter dated October 3, 1935 from J. A. Harrington of Boise, Idaho to J. Neilson Barry of Portland, Oregon. Harrington includes additional inscriptions near the Menan Buttes: J. E. B. Bonneville 1832; De Smet 1840; Jos. Gale 1834; Newell 1829; V. Pierre 1819; J. Hoback, Jacob Reznor, Edw. Robinson 1810; and Kit Carson 1832; S. Parker 1835. Other names without dates include: Michael Immel, J. Dougherty, Arch Pelton, W. D. Stewart, Jas. Bridger, Frapp, Jarvais, Smith, Stephens, Grant, Leonard, Blackwell and Sinclaire. Barry speculated that some of the young members of the survey parties of Hayden, Wheeler or King who were in the area in the 1860s and 1870s might have carved rocks with inscriptions of names they knew from accounts such as Washington Irving's *Astoria*. Still, there is no hard evidence these names were forged.

The location of these inscriptions has been elusive and a search is ongoing. One source believes the 1976 Teton Dam Flood may have washed the rock into the rushing waters of the Snake River. Another source believes they can still be seen, but only by boat from the river when the water is low.

27 Hayden, *Trapper to Tourist in Jackson Hole,* 10-11.

28 Lindsley, *Major Andrew Henry in Idaho,* 7-12.

29 Ibid., 21.

30 Keith Nyborg, a former owner of the Conant Creek site, reported to Ned Eddins that when Nyborg was a boy, shallow caves were visible along the creek bank. It is not inconceivable to believe Henry's men dug shelters in the hillside. Ned Eddins, e-mail messages to author, January 1-4, 2010.

31 Clements and Forbush, *Pioneering in the Snake River Fork Country,* 12.

32 Letter, Thomas Biddle to Col. Henry Atkinson, October 29, 1819, American State Papers, 1789-1838, Indian Affairs, Vols. 1-2.

33 Boone, *Idaho Place Names,*123.

34 *Louisiana Gazette,* October 26, 1811.

35 In August 1832, Nathaniel Wyeth traveled through the area between modern Idaho Falls and American Falls, Idaho. He observed in his journal, "the Pawnacks [Bannocks] come here to winter often on account of the Buffaloe." N. Wyeth, *Journal,* 163.

36 Hunt, *Overland Diary,* 35.

37 Franchère, *Adventure at Astoria,* 67.

38 Cox, *The Columbia River,* 60-61.

39 *Louisiana Gazette,* August 8, 1811.

40 Ibid., October 26, 1811.

Chapter 7:
Wilson Price Hunt and the Pacific Fur Company

1 Madsen, *America's First Multimillionaire,* 22-34. In 1845, *The New York Sun* placed Astor on the top of the city's wealthiest people with $25 million to his credit.

2 Ibid., 166-167, 244-252. See also Haeger, *John Jacob Astor,* 37, 174-175.

3 Both Pierre Dorion Sr. and Jr. appear in the late August, 1804 journals of the Lewis and Clark expedition while among the Yankton Sioux. The older Dorion's involvement with the expedition was more extensive, but the younger son is mentioned several times. For example, see Moulton, *Journals,* 3: 21-24.

4 Irving, *Astoria,* 151.

5 Even though the two companies competed against one another, Lisa recognized the advantage of traveling together up the Missouri River for safety. Lisa also feared Hunt might incite tribes along the route to attack the Missouri Fur Company boats. Pushing off on April 2, 1811, Lisa overtook Hunt on June 2. Oglesby, *Manuel Lisa,* 109-114.

6 Ibid., 215.

7 Hunt, *Overland Diary,* 30.

8 Irving, *Astoria,* 257. Irving is writing this in 1836 so he can say the "peaks were known as the Tetons," but these mountains were unknown to Hunt by anything other than Pilot Knobs.

9 Ibid., xviii-xxxii. Washington Irving met John Jacob Astor in Paris in 1821 and the two became friends. The rich businessman commissioned Irving to write *Astoria* as a token of that friendship. Astor provided a variety of documents for Irving's use in preparing the manuscript, including Hunt's original diary, which had been sent to Paris around 1820 and translated into French. The original is thought to be lost, although it may still lie

buried in the Paris archives. Irving was able to collect additional details for the book from oral interviews with participants in the adventure, such as Ramsay Crooks, and from other writers who were present such as Gabriel Franchère and Ross Cox. Irving published *Astoria, or Anecdotes of an Enterprise Beyond the Rocky Mountains*, in 1836. A somewhat romanticized work of non-fiction, *Astoria* described the terrain, people and activities of the Rocky Mountain West in vivid prose.

10 Hunt, *Overland Diary*, 32.
11 Urbanek, *Wyoming Place Names,* 102.
12 Hunt, *Overland Diary*, 33.
13 Ibid.
14 Ibid., 32.
15 Ibid., 33.
16 Bradbury, *Travels in the Interior of America*, 230.
17 Davis and Davis, *Jackson Hole From A to Z*, 87. The pass became known as Teton Pass in 1900.
18 Hunt, *Overland Diary*, 33-34.
19 Boone, *Idaho Place Names*, 34.
20 Townsend, *Narrative of a Journey*, 249, 267-268.
21 http://www.greencanyonhotspring.com/history/#indians
22 Hunt, *Overland Diary*, 34.
23 Ibid.
24 Irving, *Astoria*, 271.
25 Ibid.
26 Hunt, *Overland Diary*, 35. There is no evidence these caches were ever accessed again. Further, there seems to have been no plan to return to the area so leaving the horses in charge of the Shoshone men makes little sense. Additionally, it seems a bit questionable for Hunt to reveal the location of the cache to these Indians without imagining they would dig them up if none of Hunt's men returned after some length of time.
27 Irving, *Astoria,* 269.
28 Ore, Andrew Henry, 78-79, 80. Beal, *History of Southeastern Idaho*, n. 397; J. Neilson Barry, *The Problem of the Stone Lasts*, 76; and http://www.nps.gov/history/history/online_books/grte2/hrs3.htm.
29 Hunt, *Overland Diary*, 36.
30 Ibid.
31 Lovell, *Captain Bonneville's County*, 249; Beal, *History of Southeastern Idaho*, 217-218.
32 Hunt, *Overland Diary*, 36.
33 Irving, *Astoria*, 273.
34 Hunt, Overland Diary, 52.
35 Ibid., 63.
36 Brandon, "Wilson Price Hunt," 204.

Chapter 8:
Robert Stuart

1   After delivering the Pacific Fur Company, the *Tonquin* continued up the coast trading for furs. Dropping anchor on the northwest end of Vancouver Island, Captain Jonathon Thorn managed to so anger the natives that they attacked the vessel. Crew members, seeing their inevitable defeat, stowed away in the powder magazine and blew up the ship along with its assailants. See Ronda, *Astoria and Empire*, 235-237; Irving, *Astoria*, 108-116.

2   South Pass soon became a primary route over the Rocky Mountains, increasing the number of trappers making their way into Pierre's Hole. Eventually, the Oregon Trail would arise from the path used by mountaineers but it effectively bypassed Pierre's Hole, taking many immigrants to the region of Fort Hall.

3   Irving, *Astoria*, 355.

4   Information for Williams may be found in an article written by Frederic Voelker in Vol. 9 of the Hafen series, which rightfully declares most of the sources regarding this trapper as "unsatisfactory." Williams apparently always operated as a free trapper, beginning as early as 1807.

5   Stoller, "Alexander Carson," 44-45.

6   Stuart, *The Discovery of the Oregon Trail*, xcvi.

7   Holmes, "John Day," 117-122.

8   Carter, "Robert McClellan," 221-228.

9   Carter, "Ramsay Crooks," 125-132.

10   Several books examine the returning Astorians including: Robert Stuart, *On the Oregon Trail*; *Robert Stuart's Journey of Discovery*, ed. Kenneth A. Spaulding (Norman, OK: University of Oklahoma Press, 1953); Robert Stuart, *The Discovery of the Oregon Trail – Robert Stuart's Narratives*, ed. Phillip A. Rollins (New York: Charles Scribner's Sons, 1935); and Laton McCartney, *Across the Great Divide: Robert Stuart and the Discovery of the Oregon Trail* (New York: Free Press, 2003).

11   Stuart, *On The Oregon Trail*, 29-31.

12   Stuart, *The Discovery of the Oregon Trail*, 82.

13   Ibid., 83.

14   Irving, *Astoria*, 368-369.

15   Stuart, *The Discovery of the Oregon Trail*, 84.

16   Ibid., 86.

17   Ibid. Martin Cass disappeared from the records at this point. Robinson told John Reed a somewhat different version of these events than what was related to Stuart, saying Cass had been killed in the affray with the Arapahoe. According to Irving, this discrepancy "concurred with other circumstances, to occasion afterwards some mysterious speculations and dark surmises as to the real fate of Cass." Irving, *Astoria*, 439-440. Such wording has led some to think perhaps Cass was eaten by his comrades.

18   Irving, *Astoria*, 372.

19 Stuart, *The Discovery of the Oregon Trail*, 86.

20 Ibid.

21 Ibid. This estimated 950 miles must have included all of the mileage Hoback's party traveled since leaving Fort Henry the prior year, not just the distance from their furthest eastern point until they met up with Stuart. The latter distance would only be about 600 miles. If it was truly 950 miles they traveled from somewhere in central Wyoming, they were almost as close to St. Louis, Missouri. Also to be considered is why this band did not return to Fort Henry. They knew a cache had been established there but did not know about Hunt's caches farther east. Plus, there was the chance Hunt's horses might still be at Henry's abandoned post.

22 Irving, *Astoria*, 372.

23 Stuart, The Discovery of the Oregon Trail, 113.

24 Ibid., 132; Irving, *Astoria*, 380.

25 Irving, *Astoria*, 378.

26 Stuart, *The Discovery of the Oregon Trail*, 131.

27 Ibid., 132.

28 Ibid., 133. The "spur of the mountains" is without doubt the Teton Range, and the "party who came across the continent last year" is obviously that led by Wilson Price Hunt.

29 Ferris, *Life in the Rocky Mountains,* 224.

30 Russell, *Journal of Trapper*, 90.

31 Stuart, *The Discovery of the Oregon Trail,* 134.

32 Ibid., 133.

33 Ibid., 135.

34 Ibid., 136.

35 Stuart, *On the Oregon Trail*, 103.

36 Stuart, *The Discovery of the Oregon Trail*, 136.

37 Ibid. Locations of Stuart's camps are approximate. The construction of Palisades Dam and reservoir in 1957 only complicates the matter. Editors of Stuart's journals, Phillip A. Rollins and Kenneth A. Spaulding, came up with their own differing conclusions, as well.

38 Ibid., 136.

39 Ibid., 137.

40 Stuart, *On the Oregon Trail*, 105.

41 Stuart, *The Discovery of the Oregon Trail*, 138-139.

42 Ibid., 150-151.

43 Ibid., 150.

44 Ibid., 151, 168.

45 They probably descended Packsaddle Creek out of the Big Holes, but that watercourse trends to the north once it reaches the valley floor, contrary to their desired route of travel. Horseshoe Creek runs into Teton River to the south of Packsaddle Creek.

46 Ibid., 151.

47 Ibid., 152.

48 Ibid.

49 Prior editors of Stuart's journals fail to recognize that Stuart differentiates between "river" and his use of "fork" in this passage, thus they send Stuart down the Teton River rather than up the creek. Horseshoe Creek is the only stream in the northern portion of the valley with anything resembling a southern flow at its junction with the Teton River. Moving the party up the Teton River on this date actually foils the remaining itinerary in Teton Valley.

50 Ibid., 153.

51 Ibid.

52 Ibid.

53 Ibid. Instead of the right hand fork, Moose Creek, editors of his journal would have Stuart suddenly veer from a generally satisfactory geography and use Trail Creek, the left hand fork, likely because the modern highway follows Trail Creek to Teton Pass.

54 Ibid., 153. Proper determination of the right and left side of a stream is made while facing downstream. Several editors conclude this day's route was up Trail Creek, based on a misinterpretation of right/left side and thinking the road to the pass was up Trail Creek as it is today. Facing downstream from the camp "on nearly equal branches," the "right hand Fork" is unquestionably Moose Creek.

55 Ibid., 154. Having gone up Horse Creek (not to be confused with Horse Creek on the Green River), Stuart avoided the restricted flow of the Snake River where the Gros Ventre and Snake River ranges nearly meet. He strikes the Hoback River six miles upstream from its junction with the Snake – the point the party would have reached if they had found a way through the Snake River Canyon back on September 17. See also chapter 11, note 13.

56 Ibid. How many other men with Andrew Henry or in the Wilson Hunt party whose names were "Henry" is unknown.

57 Ibid.

58 Ibid., 155.

59 Ibid., 156.

60 Ibid., 157.

61 Ibid., 158.

62 Ibid., 164.

63 Ibid., 239, 249.

64 McCartney, *Across the Great Divide*, 268.

65 Ibid., 274; Dolin, *Fur, Fortune and Empire*, 214.

66 For details of the story, see: Hardee, "The Ordeal of Marie Dorion," 46-49.

Chapter 9:
The Snake Country Expeditions

1 Mumey, *The Teton Mountains*, 89.

2 Morgan, *Jedediah Smith*, 117-118.

3   Barbour, *Jedediah Smith, No Ordinary Mountain Man,* 60.

4   Ross, *Fur Hunters,* 187.

5   Ibid., 125.

6   Ibid., 177.

7   Mattes, *Jackson Hole, Crossroads,* 26.

8   Mackenzie, *Donald Mackenzie, King of the Northwest,* 121. An unpublished
     paper by H. Lloyd Keith, "Traders' Tales of 'Big' Donald Mackenzie:
     Myths and Myth Making in the Pacific Northwest Fur Trade," examines
     Mackenzie's 1819 route. Keith points out that Black Bears' Lake is not
     modern Bear Lake on the Idaho/Utah border, but he also indicates
     Mackenzie is no closer to Pierre's Hole than south of Craters of the Moon
     National Monument.

9   Mattes, "Behind the Legend of Colter's Hell," 263-264 and Hayden, *From
     Trapper to Tourist in Jackson Hole,* 15.

10   Chittenden, *Yellowstone National Park,* 38.

11   Ross, *Fur Hunters,* 142; Ogden, *Snake Country Journals, 1824-26,* xxxiii.

12   Driggs, *History of Teton Valley,* 13.

13   Wells, "Michel Bourdon," 58.

14   Morgan, *Jedediah Smith,* 124.

15   Ibid., 122-123.

16   Ross, *Fur Hunters,* 211.

17   Ibid.

18   Ibid., 212.

19   Ibid., 224.

20   Ibid., 225.

21   Ibid., 234.

22   Ibid., 245.

23   Ibid., 249.

24   Ibid., 250.

25   Ibid., 251-252.

26   Ibid., 284; Morgan, *Jedediah Smith,* 128-129.

27   Sullivan, *Jedediah Smith, Trader and Trail Breaker,* 59.

28   Ross, *Fur Hunters,* 284-285.

29   Ibid., 285.

30   Ibid.

31   Morgan, *Jedediah Smith,* 129.

32   Ibid.

33   Ross, *Fur Hunters,* 293.

34   Women increased the efficiency of these expeditions. In addition to
     mundane daily tasks, women were assigned to dress the pelts – a job that
     would slow the pace of the trappers. The fastest a beaver could be skinned,
     cleaned and stretched, according to one source, was one-half hour. On May
     12, 1825, the traps produced fifty-two beaver while on the Little Bear River.
     It would have taken the women at least twenty-six hours of labor to process
     the pelts before the next day's catch was brought to camp. In the absence

of women, the impact of the fur desert might have been far different. Ott, "'Ruining' the Rivers in the Snake Country," 177-178.

35 Morgan, *Jedediah Smith,* 271-272. Also, the HBC was resigned to the inevitable loss of areas west of the Divide when Joint Occupation finally ran its course. They focused trapping on the area south and east of the Columbia River, to which they believed British claim would disappear. Meanwhile, they tried to improve British claims north of the river by building and enlarging forts to increase British presence. Ott, "'Ruining' the Rivers in the Snake Country," 167-173.

36 Ogden, *Snake Country Journals, 1824-26,* 54.

37 Ibid., 57.

38 Ibid., 59.

39 Ibid., 60.

40 Ibid.

41 Ogden, *Snake Country Journals, 1827-29,* 26.

42 Reid, *Contested Empire,* 180-185.

43 Ibid., 83.

44 Ott, "'Ruining' the Rivers in the Snake Country," 173.

45 Ibid., 189.

46 Ott provides a succinct summary of the many environmental effects of the fur desert policy on the Snake River Country in "'Ruining' the Rivers in the Snake Country," 184-191.

Chapter 10:
The Henry-Ashley and Ashley-Smith Companies

1 A good biography of Ashley can be found in Richard M. Clokey, *William H. Ashley, Enterprise and Politics in the Trans-Mississippi West* (Norman, OK: University of Oklahoma, 1980).

2 Gowans and White, "Traders to Trappers, Andrew Henry and the Rocky Mountain Fur Trade, Part 2," 56.

3 These early rendezvous are discussed in Podruchny, *Making the Voyageur World,* 165-200.

4 Pond, *The Narrative of Peter Pond,* 47.

5 Further discussion of the rendezvous not being totally the idea of Henry and Ashley can be found in Clokey, *William H. Ashley,* 158-159 and Terrell, *The Six Turnings,* 176- 179.

6 Berry, *A Majority of Scoundrels,* 105, 110.

7 Townsend, *Narrative of a Journey Across the Rocky Mountains,* 226; Mathews, *A Dictionary of Americanisms, On Historical Principles,* credits George Ruxton for first using the phrase in 1848. Ruxton, *Life in the Far West,* 6.

8 Morgan, *The West of William Ashley,* 70.

9 For an examination of Ashley's difficulties with the Arikara, see William R. Nester, *The Arikara War, the First Plains Indian War: 1823* (Missoula, MT: Mountain Press Publishing Company, 2001).

10 Edward Rose was a member of Smith's party. Rose had wintered with the Crows as a part of Manuel Lisa's earlier expedition so it is likely Rose had a hand in arranging winter quarters for all the Henry-Ashley men. See Morgan, *Jedediah Smith*, 80-89.

11 Hafen, *Broken Hand*, 339. John S. Robb, writing under the pseudonym of "Solitaire," penned the article "Major Fitzpatrick, the Discoverer of South Pass," in 1847. The idea of beaver in the Green River Valley being so plentiful that traps were unnecessary derives from that writing. The article is printed in its entirety in Hafen's book.

12 Smith was not the first Euro-American to reach the Green River Valley for "John Colter may have traversed its remote headwaters as early as 1807 on the great circuit he made into the wilderness south and west of Manuel Lisa's post on the Big Horn. Andrew Henry's men almost certainly saw something of the upper valley in the spring of 1811, and the Astorians crossed and recrossed it that year and the next. Donald Mackenzie trapped the valley from the west at the head of a brigade of Nor'Westers in 1820-1821, and another British brigade made a rich haul on the Green as late as the summer of 1823." Morgan, *Jedediah Smith*, 93.

13 Fitzpatrick and Clyman arrived at the rendezvous early so Clyman went to explore the Sweetwater River, hoping to find it a navigable method of getting furs to St. Louis. In a mix-up of timing, Smith found one of Clyman's camps with a lot of Indian sign about but no Clyman. Smith wrongly presumed Clyman had been killed. Meanwhile, Clyman had gone farther downstream, as far as the Platte, to evade the Indians who had come upon him as he was about to strike a fire. When he felt safe enough to go back to the rendezvous site, Smith and the others were gone. After waiting twelve days, Clyman walked eastward by himself, all the way to Fort Atkinson – a journey of 700 miles. Camp, *James Clyman*, 241-242.

14 Dale, *Ashley-Smith Explorations*, 93.

15 Mattes, *Jackson Hole, Crossroads*, 30.

16 Hood drew this map while stationed on the Missouri frontier. Rather than travel to the region of Teton Valley, he plagiarized an 1834 map by Aaron Arrowsmith. Hood claimed to have derived data from "frequent conversations with two highly intelligent trappers, William A. Walker of Virginia, and Mr. Coates of Missouri who belonged originally to Captain Bonneville's party, but subsequently continued to roam the mountains as free trappers during six consecutive years." Washington Hood, "Map Exhibiting the Practicable Passes of the Rocky Mountains," Cartographic Records Section, National Archives. Quoted in Goetzmann, *Army Exploration in the American West*, 56.

17 Kittson, *Journal of Occurrences in a Trapping Expedition to and from the Snake Country in the Years 1824 and 1825*, published as an addendum to Ogden, *Snake Country Journals, 1824-26*, 209.

18 Dale, *Ashley-Smith Explorations*, 96-97. Apparently, Dale does not consider the Hunt and Stuart parties traveling through Pierre's Hole as an effort to "explore" the area.

19   Clokey, *William H. Ashley*, 139.

20   Morgan, *The West of William Ashley*, 100, 106.

21   Ibid., 106.

22   Gowans, *Rocky Mountain Rendezvous*, 17-18.

23   Mattes, *Jackson Hole, Crossroads*, 32.

24   Ibid.

25   Mattes credits Coutant, *History of Wyoming*, 126, for this tidbit regarding Fitzpatrick and Bridger's whereabouts. Coutant failed to provide sources for many of the statements in his history of Wyoming.

26   Gowans, *Rocky Mountain Rendezvous*, 21.

27   Clokey, *William H. Ashley*, 161-162.

28   Morgan, *Jedediah Smith*, 176.

29   Ibid., 176-177.

30   Ogden, *Snake Country Journals, 1824-26*, 168-169. Ogden reported from Salmon Falls Creek in late May that "a party of Americans about 30 in number had descended this Stream on their return from Salt Lake without beaver."

31   Dale L. Morgan, *The West of William Ashley* (Denver: Old West Publishing Co., 1964).

32   Ibid., n. 302.

33   Campbell, *A Narrative of Colonel Robert Campbell's Experiences*, 18-21. Also excerpted in Morgan, *The West of William Ashley*, 143.

34   Beckwourth, *Life and Adventures*, 23.

35   Ibid., 37.

36   Two of these newspaper announcements are published in Morgan, *The West of William Ashley*, 141-142.

37   Morgan's original report regarding Smith provides the only reference in the secondary source historical records to trappers in the vicinity of the Tetons during the period between the first rendezvous in 1825 and its follow up event, held in Willow Valley, now known as Cache Valley, Utah, in 1826. However, Campbell and Beckwourth's memoirs, combined with newspaper stories of Ashley's supply train, effectively negate that version along with any visit to Teton Valley. The larger problem comes from later historians who use Morgan's testimony recorded in the Smith biography apparently without knowledge of the newer information contained in Morgan's work on Ashley.

38   Beckwourth, *Life and Adventures*, 96.

39   Ferris, *Life in the Rocky Mountains*, 123-124.

40   Driggs, *History of Teton Valley*, 190.

Chapter 11:
The Smith, Jackson and Sublette Fur Company

1   Campbell, *A Narrative of Colonel Robert Campbell's Experiences*, 24. Even though Campbell says Smith was headed to Colorado, it was, in fact, California. Both regions were in Mexican territory at the time and the

Colorado River being in Smith's path is likely what led Campbell to choose his wording.

2   Letter, Daniel T. Potts to Robert T. Potts, July 8, 1827 in Gowans, *Travels of Daniel T. Potts*, letter 3, page 1. See also, Bagley, *The First Known Man in Yellowstone*, 148-149, 280.

3   Letter, Daniel T. Potts to Thomas Cochlen, July 7, 1824 in Gowans, *Travels of Daniel T. Potts*, letter 1, page 1.

4   Beckwourth, *Life and Adventures*, 126.

5   Ibid., 138.

6   Mattes, *Jackson Hole, Crossroads*, 33.

7   Gowans, *Travels of Daniel T. Potts*, letter 3, 1n.

8   Morgan, *Jedediah Smith*, 216.

9   Mattes, *Jackson Hole, Crossroads*, 34.

10 In 1830-1831, Jedediah Smith prepared a map of his travels though it has never been found. George Gibbs made notations on an 1845 map that are believed to derive from Smith's map. Gibbs dubbed Yellowstone Lake as Sublette's Lake but David Burr's 1839 map changed it to Yellowstone. See Hays, "David E. Jackson," 224-225. Some historians credit David Jackson with christening the lake after Sublette. The story goes that in 1826 Sublette named Jackson Lake after his partner, who reciprocated the following year by so naming the larger lake to the north. Jackson, *Shadow on the Tetons*, 99, 114.

11 Beckwourth, *Life and Adventures*, nn. 554-555.

12 Berry, *A Majority of Scoundrels*, 207.

13 Lovell, *Bonneville*, 65, suggests the trail through Hoback Canyon left Hoback River at Camp Creek, crossed northwest over the foothills, and rejoined the Snake River at Game Creek before entering Jackson Hole. Other sources indicate the trail descended into Jackson Hole via Horse Creek. See Lightner, *Roads Through Time*, 166. Either route avoided the steep canyon walls of the Snake River in the southern end of Jackson Hole, shaving a mile or more off the trip.

14 Simpson, *Fur Trade and Empire*, 289.

15 Rich, *The Letters of John McLoughlin*, 36.

16 Dale, *Ashley-Smith Explorations*, 292.

17 Berry, *Majority of Scoundrels*, 207. Historian Berry, who readily admits a penchant for conjecture, surmises Campbell's brigade was "probably working slightly to the north of Bill Sublette."

18 Morgan, *Jedediah Smith*, 269, 287-290. Unlike many HBC partisans, John McLoughlin, the man in charge at Fort Vancouver when Jedediah Smith arrived, granted assistance to virtually every American who came to the post. He has been called "the father of Oregon" due to his open-handed and benevolent treatment of people who came to the territory.

19 Victor, *River of the West*, 58.

20 Newell, *Robert Newell's Memoranda*, 31.

21 Ebberts, *A Trapper's Life in the Rocky Mountains*, 6.

22 Letter, Jedediah Smith to William Clark, quoted in Morgan, *Jedediah Smith*, 306.

23 Newell, *Robert Newell's Memoranda*, n. 40. Jackson, *Shadow on the Tetons*, 155, n. 223.

24 Victor, *River of the West*, 49-50.

25 Ibid., 48-49.

26 Ibid., 58-59.

27 Irving, *Captain Bonneville*, 56.

28 Raynolds, *Report on the Exploration of the Yellowstone River*, 96.

29 Victor, *River of the West*, 60.

30 Gowans, *Rocky Mountain Rendezvous*, 48-49. Castoreum is an oily secretion from the castor glands under a beaver's tail that is used by trappers for bait. It is also a key ingredient in many perfumes. See Sandoz, *The Beaver Men, Spearheads of Empire*, 47. A detailed description of castoreum was recorded by Meriwether Lewis while at Fort Clatsop in January 1806. See Moulton, *Journals*, 6: 174-175.

31 Victor, *River of the West*, 60.

32 Berry, *Majority of Scoundrels*, 226.

33 Morgan, *Jedediah Smith*, 315.

34 Munnick, "Jean-Baptiste Gervais," 123.

35 Driggs, *History of Teton Valley*, 44.

36 Ibid.

37 Victor, *River of the West*, 69-70.

Chapter 12:
The Rocky Mountain Fur Company

1 B. W. Driggs made a statement in *The History of Teton Valley*, 47, that requires correction and clarification. He said: "At the rendezvous in Pierre's Hole on August 4, 1830, an important change took place. The three copartners, Smith Sublette and Jackson, sold out to Milton Sublette, James Bridger, Thomas Fitzpatrick, Henry Frapp and John Baptiste Jervais. Not only this document but many others were dated at 'Pierre's Hole under the three Teton Mountains,' the then noted place of designation for headquarters of the Rocky Mountain Fur Company."

Only two rendezvous were ever held in Pierre's Hole; one in 1829 and one in 1832. The rendezvous of 1830 was unmistakably not held there. That year's summer gathering was on Wind River, near modern Riverton, Wyoming. Second, to clarify, Driggs has misspelled two of the soon-to-become partners' names. While many contemporaries also misspelled the names, it was Henry Fraeb and Jean-Baptiste Gervais who joined William Sublette's brother Milton, Jim Bridger and Thomas Fitzpatrick in the formation of the Rocky Mountain Fur Company (RMFC). Third, the documents for this transaction do not exist, thus nothing from the 1830 business transfer says anything about "Pierre's Hole, under the three

Teton Mountains," as charming as the phrase sounds. However, there are documents from 1832 containing a similar inscription which will be discussed in the pages ahead. It is likely B. W. Driggs confused these contracts. Finally, RMFC never officially designated Pierre's Hole as its headquarters.

Noley Mumey's book, *The Teton Mountains,* 89, also errs in the statement, "The Rendezvous of 1831 at Pierre's Hole, in which the American Fur Company and the Rocky Mountain Fur Company met, furthered the fur trade in the area." The 1831 rendezvous was not in Pierre's Hole but was in Willow Valley, which would soon get its name changed to Cache Valley, in what is now Utah. These two fur companies met in the spring of the year 1830. At that time, AFC offered the first true competition, not to the RMFC but to the Smith, Jackson and Sublette enterprise before they sold out.

2   Wilhelm, *Travels in North America,* xxii, and Colby, *Sacagawea's Child,* 112.

3   Dyer and Sachsen-Altenburg, *Duke Paul of Wuerttemberg on the Missouri Frontier,* 83. Hafen, "Jean-Baptiste Charbonneau," 211.

4   This information is obtained from the request for a passport written by William Clark to Secretary of War John Eaton. The letter, dated December 23, 1829, is reproduced in its entirety in Hebard, *Sacajawea,* 101. Dyer also reports Charbonneau's departure with the Duke and appears to quote the Missouri Intelligencer edition for January 29, 1830 which indicated Wilhelm was accompanied by "Shirly" and "Mr. John Baptist." Dyer, *Duke Paul of Wuerttemberg,* 84.

5   Dyer, *Duke Paul of Wuerttemberg,* 241. Sanborn, *The Grand Tetons,* 136.

6   Ibid. The idea of Charbonneau accompanying Wilhelm from St. Louis to the rendezvous seems unique to Sanborn. Most writers place Charbonneau in Robidoux's AFC brigade (see note 2). Sanborn's is an intriguing and plausible notion for Wilhelm met Robidoux during his 1823 trip west. Robidoux treated Wilhelm kindly and provided a lot of assistance. Wilhelm could have arranged, through Robidoux, for Charbonneau to accompany him until rendezvous, after which Charbonneau would assume his duties as an AFC trapper. Mattes, "Joseph Robidoux," 296-297.

7   Dyer, *Duke Paul of Wuerttemberg,* 84; Ferris, *Life in the Rocky Mountains,* 138. Ferris stated simply "Mr. Robidoux" so it could have been Joseph, Francois or Michel; though most historians agree it was probably Joseph. Mattes, "Joseph Robidoux," 302.

8   Wilhem, "Account of Adventures in the Great American Desert," 210.

9   Sanborn, *The Grand Tetons,* 136.

10   Dyer, *Duke Paul of Wuerttemberg,* 205; Wilhem, *Travels in North America,* xxiii.

11   For a description of the natural history contents of the Duke's journal, see Jason Fridley, "The Flora and Fauna of Duke Paul's Missouri: A Natural Landscape in Transition," reprinted in Dyer, *Duke Paul of Wuerttemberg,* 219-236.

12 The number of writers who speak of Henry-Ashley, Ashley-Smith, and Smith, Jackson and Sublette companies as the Rocky Mountain Fur Company is astounding. It may be splitting hairs, for these firms were fur companies in the Rocky Mountains, so each could be referred to as a Rocky Mountain fur company, but not until August 1830 did a business entity called the Rocky Mountain Fur Company come into existence.

13 Victor, *River of the West*, 98.

14 Ferris, *Life in the Rocky Mountains,* 193.

15 Gowans, *Rocky Mountain Rendezvous*, 62.

16 Meek reported the Indian was a "Rockaway Chief, named Gray," which most sources interpret as being a Bannock Indian. However, it is more likely this was the Iroquois John Gray. Wells, "Ignace Hatchiorauquasha (John Grey)," 169.

17 Newell, *Robert Newell's Memoranda,* 32.

18 Hawken guns are too frequently portrayed as the favorite weapon of mountain men, often with no evidence to support the presence of the popular gun maker's product. In this case, Campbell had recently purchased a new rifle made by P. Carmer for $17, then spent $30 for two Hawken pistols. Campbell Ledgerbook, April 1832, Campbell Papers, Mercantile Library Association.

19 Nester, *From Mountain Man to Millionaire,* 60-61.

20 Ibid., 61.

Chapter 13:
Rendezvous 1832

1 Benjamin Bonneville was not at the rendezvous but got enough second-hand information for his biographer, Washington Irving, to weigh in on the events of that summer.

2 N. Wyeth, *Journal*, 158-159.

3 J. Wyeth, *Oregon,* 60-63, 68.

4 N. Wyeth, *Journal*, 159.

5 Ball, *Autobiography of John Ball*, 74.

6 J. Wyeth, *Oregon*, 57.

7 Ibid., 64.

8 Ferris, *Life in the Rocky Mountains*, 219-222.

9 John Colter, who was discussed in Chapter 5, had a narrow escape from the Blackfoot in the fall of 1808. He was stripped naked and chased for five miles by Indians. Reaching the Madison River, he dove in and concealed himself in a log jam while the Blackfoot searched diligently. At nightfall, he escaped and made his way 250 miles to Lisa's fort at the mouth of the Big Horn River after eleven lonely days of travel. Burton Harris, *John Colter* (New York: Charles Scribner's Sons, 1952), is Colter's primary biography.

Hugh Glass was attacked and severely mauled by a grizzly bear in the summer of 1823. As Glass clung to life, two volunteers, said to be young

Jim Bridger and John Fitzgerald, were left behind to bury him while Andrew Henry moved the party on. Fearful of Indians in the area, the two companions abandoned Glass a few days later, claiming he was dead and buried. Glass recovered sufficiently to crawl nearly 300 miles from the Grand River to Fort Kiowa, near the confluence of the White and Missouri rivers, driven by thoughts of revenge. Once recuperated, he sought out the two "friends." John Meyers Myers, *Pirate, Pawnee and Mountain Man* is a biography of Glass.

10   The Gantt and Blackwell Company left St. Louis for the Rocky Mountains on April 24, 1831. At the Laramie River, they divided into three trapping parties while Blackwell returned east for more supplies. They encountered Fitzpatrick, who was on his way to the States, reporting him to be guarded and distant. Blackwell traveled on to St. Louis with Fitzpatrick. The following spring, then on his way to rendezvous, Fitzpatrick ran across one of the three Gantt and Blackwell brigades still in the vicinity of the Laramie. Fitzpatrick declared the company insolvent, though it appears he may have only done so in order to recruit the trappers for the Rocky Mountain Fur Company. Having lost his horses over the winter, Gantt was on Green River at that very moment, returning from Santa Fe where he had gone to procure more horses. His trappers, who had not heard from him since they separated the previous summer, found a note from Gantt in September 1832, telling them Blackwell had returned with supplies and they now planned to establish a trading post on the Arkansas River. It appears that Fitzpatrick blatantly lied to decrease competition in the field. These events are summarized in Carter, "John Gantt," 104-107.

11   Nidever, *Life and Adventures*, 24.

12   De Voto, *Across the Wide Missouri*, 55-56. While De Voto describes trapper acceptance of Delaware people, the same can also be said of Iroquois, Shawnee and a few other tribes.

13   Nidever, *Life and Adventures*, 24. The man with O'Felon is John Harris, not "Black" Harris.

14   Peltier, *Black Harris*, 79, n. 135.

15   Victor, *River of the West*, 103-104.

16   Ball, *Autobiography of John Ball*, 74-75.

17   Victor, *River of the West,* 110-111.

18   Letter, John Ball to Nathaniel Ball, July 13, 1832, from Pierre's Hole, published in Quaife, "The Letters of John Ball," 457.

19   Nidever, *Life and Adventures*, 24-26.

20   J. Wyeth, *Oregon*, 64-68.

21   N. Wyeth, *Journal*, 159.

22   Leonard, *Narrative of the Adventures of Zenas Leonard,* 68-69.

23   Newell, *Robert Newell's Memoranda*, 32.

24   One other account of the Pierre's Hole rendezvous was left by Benjamin Bonneville. He was not at the 1832 rendezvous, though some historians have placed him there. Bonneville was in the Green River valley busily

constructing a fort at the time of the rendezvous. He had contact with many men who attended and later reported: "In this valley was congregated the motley populace connected with the fur trade. Here the two rival companies had their encampments, with their retainers of all kinds: traders, trappers, hunters, and half-breeds, assembled from all quarters, awaiting their yearly supplies, and their orders to start off in new directions. Here, also, the savage tribes connected with the trade, the Nez Perces or Chopunnish Indians, and Flatheads, had pitched their lodges beside the streams, and with their squaws, awaited the distribution of goods and finery. There was, moreover, a band of fifteen free trappers, commanded by a gallant leader from Arkansas, named Sinclair, who held their encampment a little apart from the rest. Such was the wild and heterogeneous assemblage, amounting to several hundred men, civilized and savage, distributed in tents and lodges in the several camps.

"The arrival of Captain Sublette with supplies put the Rocky Mountain Fur Company in full activity. The wares and merchandise were quickly opened, and as quickly disposed of to trappers and Indians; the usual excitement and revelry took place, after which all hands began to disperse to their several destinations." Irving, *Captain Bonneville,* 56-57.

25 Victor, *River of the West,* 110.

26 Driggs, *History of Teton Valley,* 111.

27 Ibid., 50.

28 Hayden, "The Battle of Pierre's Hole," 4.

29 For 1828, see Gray, "Young Fur Trapper, Phillip Covington," 20. For 1838, see Gowans, *Rocky Mountain Rendezvous,* 179.

30 Letter, John Ball to Nathaniel Ball, July 13, 1832, from Pierre's Hole, Quaife, "The Letters of John Ball," 459.

31 Trottman, "Lucien Fontenelle," 90.

32 Ferris, *Life in the Rocky Mountains,* 224. This conflicts with Hayden who said: "Fontenelle's caravan arrived too late to get any of the Indian or free trapper trade, the trade surplus had to be secretly cached before the trappers started out on their fall hunt. This cache was made during the hours of darkness in the horse corral of their camp so that the hoofprints would obliterate any sign of digging. The railroad siding called Cache is nearby." See Hayden, "The Battle of Pierre's Hole," 4.

This never happened. As Ferris described, the AFC men left Pierre's Hole to hunt down Fontenelle and met up with him on the Green River, near where Bonneville was constructing a fort. There is no record of any cache being dug by the AFC in Pierre's Hole and they would not have had any extra supplies to put in it if they did.

33 There is not enough information to be certain, but this may be the wife and son of Pierre Tevanitagon.

34 The identity of this person in unknown. It is likely a misspelling of Narcisse, a common French name, and Prevost or Provost, both common French surnames.

35 Selected pages from Papers of the St. Louis Fur Trade, Part 3: Robert Campbell Family Collection, from the St. Louis Mercantile Library Association.

36 The bulk of the agreement can be found in Hafen, *Broken Hand,* 116.

37 That fall, Sublette and Robert Campbell formed a partnership that would not only supply the 1833 rendezvous but become a profitable business entity for years to come. Sunder, *Bill Sublette,* 115.

38 For additional reading on the whiskey trade, see William Unrau, *White Man's Wicked Water: the Alcohol Trade and Prohibition in Indian Country, 1802-1892* (Lawrence, KS: University Press of Kansas, 1996).

39 Ibid., 113.

40 Gowans, *Rocky Mountain Rendezvous,* 78; Hafen, *Broken Hand*, 118-120.

Chapter 14:
The Battle of Pierre's Hole

1 For a few examples of these diverse, synthesized accounts, see Berry, *Majority of Scoundrels*, 266-269; Chittenden, *A History of the Fur Trade of the Far West*, 658-664; and De Voto, *Across the Wide Missouri*, 80-86.

2 The number of skirmishes that trappers had with this tribe is astounding. More often than not, when mountaineers described clashes with "Blackfeet," they were referring to Gros Ventres. See Chittenden, *A History of the American Fur Trade*, 851-853.

3 Wishart, *Encyclopedia of the Great Plains Indians*, 76.

4 Clark, *The Indian Sign Language*, 197-198. Schilz, "The Gros Ventres and the Upper Missouri Fur Trade," 25.

5 Schilz, "The Gros Ventres and the Upper Missouri Fur Trade," 24, and Curtis, *The North American Indian*, 105.

6 Gregg, Commerce of the Prairies, 228, 231, 239. It was on this same trip to Santa Fe that Jedediah Smith was killed, presumably by Commanches, while searching for water.

7 Terry Brockie, Gros Ventre historian, telephone conversation and e-mail message to the author, on various dates in September 2009.

8 W. L. Sublette to W. H. Ashley, September 21, 1832, Sublette Family Papers, Missouri History Museum and quoted in Sunder, Bill Sublette, 106-107.

9 Gowans, *Tragedy at Pierre's Hole,* 1-5.

10 Letter, John Ball to Dr. T. C. Brinsmade, January 1, 1833 written from Fort Vancouver, Quaife, "Letters of John Ball," 463-464.

11 Ball, *Autobiography of John Ball,* 76-79.

12 Irving said Bonneville provided him with a "mass of manuscript ... to fit for publication. That manuscript has formed the staple of the following work. I have occasionally interwoven facts and details, gathered from various sources, especially from the conversations and journals of some of the captain's contemporaries, who were actors in the scenes he describes. I have

also given it a tone and coloring drawn from my own observation…however the work is substantially the narrative of the worthy captain, and many of its most graphic passages are but little varied from his own language." Irving, *Captain Bonneville*, liii. Though this author disagrees, Chittenden considered Irving's account of the battle as the best, for "he evidently digested his account from information derived from all available sources." Chittenden, *A History of the American Fur Trade*, 664.

13 Irving, *Captain Bonneville*, 57-68.

14 Letter, Robert Campbell to Hugh Campbell, July 18, 1832. Eberstadt, *The Rocky Mountain Letters of Robert Campbell*, 7-11.

15 Campbell, *A Narrative of Colonel Robert Campbell's Experiences*, 14.

16 Ibid., 39-42.

17 Ferris, *Life in the Rocky Mountains*, 222-224, 269-271, 412-413.

18 Here, as in many places in Leonard's narrative, the date is wrong. The brigade left the rendezvous five weeks earlier than Leonard recorded – on July 17 – and the battle occurred the next day.

19 Leonard, *Narrative of Adventures*, 68-77.

20 Victor, *River of the West*, 111-118.

21 Newell, *Robert Newell's Memoranda*, 32. According to editor Dorothy Johansen, Newell is probably referring to the 1100 soldiers and trappers who were involved in the Leavenworth Arikara campaign in 1823, not 1832. Oddly, in this same footnote, Johansen references Pierre's Hotel rather than Pierre's Hole – hopefully just a misprint.

22 Ibid.; see also 25-26.

23 Nidever, *Life and Adventures*, 26-30.

24 Parker, *Journal of an Exploring Tour*, 87-90.

25 William F. Wheeler, "Personal Interview with Louis Rivet," 252.

26 Letter, William Sublette to William Ashley, September 21, 1832. Published in *St. Louis Beacon*, October 11, 1832.

27 J. Wyeth, *Oregon*, 69-74, 88.

28 N. Wyeth, *Journal*, 159-160. It is possible that Wyeth's transcriber misread Wyeth's cursive penmanship and mistook "sw" for "se" since the direction of travel over the same pass is reported as "s.w. by s" in a later journal entry.

29 Bakeless, *Journals of Lewis and Clark*, 26 n. 2.

30 Irving, *Captain Bonneville*, 64. Edgeley Todd, editor of *Captain Bonneville, U.S.A.*, makes a valiant effort to defend the veracity of Irving's version from Parker's attack but ignores Campbell's assault on Irving, thus failing to make a solid case.

31 Victor, *River of the West*, iii. Victor's fascination with Irving is made clear in the first line of her introduction to Meek's life story: "When the author of this book has been absorbed in the elegant narratives of Washington Irving, reading and musing over *Astoria* and *Bonneville*, in the cozy quiet of a New York study, no prescient motion of the mind ever gave prophetic indication of that personal acquaintance which has since been formed with the scenes and even with some of the characters which figure in the works just referred to."

32 Irving, *Captain Bonneville*, 57.

33 Victor, *River of the West*, 112.

34 Letter from Nathaniel Wyeth to Charles Wyeth, dated July 14, 1832. Private collection.

35 Letter from Nathaniel Wyeth to Elizabeth Wyeth dated July 14, 1832. Sublette County Fur Trade Papers, Museum of the Mountain Man, Pinedale, Wyoming.

36 This proposed route roughly parallels what would become a portion of the Oregon Trail's Lander Cut Off in future years.

37 Vestal, *Mountain Men*, 111-112. Kenneth McKenzie, the AFC partisan in command at Fort Union, had told the Gros Ventres to be on the lookout for his clerk, Fontenelle, who would be in the region. Nearly all of the Blackfoot were on good terms with McKenzie and the AFC. The biggest quandary with this explanation is the timing of McKenzie's information since the Gros Ventres were in Colorado for several years prior to 1832.

38 Haines, "Antoine Godin," 177.

39 Vestal, *Mountain Men*, 113.

40 Fowler, *Shared Customs, Contested Meaning*, 35.

41 Maximilian, *Travels in the Interior of North America*, 126-127.

42 Ibid., 73.

43 Smith, "Battle of Pierre's Hole," 49.

44 McLoughlin, *McLoughlin's Fort Vancouver Letters*, 100-106. In McLoughlin's report to superiors dated October 28, 1832, the only Blackfoot confrontations are those experienced by Work.

The closest HBC brigade at the time was that year's Snake River Brigade led by John Work. At the end of January 1832, Work's party was attacked by a large band of Indians, described as "chiefly Blood Indians and Big Bellies." This battle sounds much smaller than the one Leonard reported: one man was killed and a handful wounded. Moreover, the attack occurred far to the north of Teton Valley in Montana, nowhere near the Gros Ventres who participated in the Battle of Pierre's Hole. Furthermore, Work's brigade did not travel close to Pierre's Hole. The Salmon River was about as near as it got and that is about two hundred miles west. Four men separated from the main brigade, of which two drowned. It is conceivable, but doubtful that they veered east to the Teton Basin. Work was back at the HBC Fort Walla Walla by July 19, the day after the Battle of Pierre's Hole, and learned the two survivors had already reached the fort. The HBC party Leonard mentioned did not reach the rendezvous until closer to the end of the month. Other trappers splintered off Work's main brigade throughout the spring, but they were all accounted for by July 21, according to Work's journal. See Work, *The Journal of John Work*, 127-129, 140, 174-175.

One other intriguing hint derives from additional HBC letters. McLoughlin wrote to Edward Ermatinger that his brother Francis, had been "trading in the Snake Country" in 1832. In an 1833 letter, Francis Ermatinger told Edward he "made a trip last summer and collected about

400 skins." It is conceivable Ermatinger found his way to Pierre's Hole. See McLoughlin, *The Letters of John McLoughlin*, xcvii and Ermatinger, *The Fur Trade Letters of Francis Ermatinger*, 161.

45 Campbell laid the blame for this ongoing hostility between Blackfoot and Americans at the feet of Lewis and Clark due to their clash in late July 1806. On the Expedition's return trip, Lewis and a small contingent of men fought with a band of young Piegan on the Two Medicine River in modern Montana, killing two of them. Washington Irving pegged this encounter as the cause of resentment between the two cultures in his book *Astoria*, 101. Others have charged John Colter with instigating this aggression by allying with the Crow in a battle against the Blackfoot. Some writers accuse Hudson's Bay Company traders of stirring animosity against American rivals, including HBC gun sales to Blackfoot in the mix. A thorough discussion of the root of such enduring resentment is found in Ewers, *The Blackfeet*, 45-57, and Large, "Riled-up Blackfeet: Did Meriwether Lewis Do It?" 614-623.

46 Vestal, *Mountain Men*, 111; Smith, "Battle of Pierre's Hole," 48. Smith appears to have taken the name "Biahoh" from Vestal's account of Arapahoe oral traditions.

47 Catlin, *Letters and Notes*, 95.

48 Maximilian, *Travels in the Interior of North America*, 75-76.

49 Townsend, *Narrative of a Journey*, 196. Townsend, a naturalist, came west with Nathaniel Wyeth in 1834.

50 Letter from Andrew Drips to John B. Sarpy, dated July 27, 1832, from Pierre's Hole, Rocky Mountains. This letter is in the Drips Papers, Missouri History Museum, St. Louis. Drips does not mention his near escape.

51 Ferris, *Life in the Rocky Mountains*, 235. Vestal mistook Miller for a member of the AFC brigade based on a misinterpretation of Ferris. See Vestal, *Mountain Men*, 126. In 1843, Matthew Field also reported that Miller was killed in the battle so Sublette's fears seem to be realized. See Field, *Prairie and Mountain Sketches*, 154.

52 Carter, "Andrew Drips," 147.

53 Field, *Prairie and Mountain Sketches*, 156.

54 Josephy, *The Nez Perce*, 77. The Crow chief Rotten Belly was killed in the summer of 1836.

55 Anderson, *The Rocky Mountain Journals of William Marshall Anderson*, 136-137, 351-353.

56 Ibid., 232, 352. Josephy, *The Nez Perce*, 94. There is much additional information regarding The Lawyer in Josephy's book.

57 Bryan, *Montana's Indians: Yesterday and Today*, 30. Unfortunately, Bryan provides no source for this information.

58 Dodge, *Biographical Sketch of James Bridger*, 10. Irving, *Captain Bonneville*, 62, also reported this number of Gros Ventre casualties and may be Grenville's source.

59 J. Wyeth, *Oregon*, 78.

60 Work, *Fur Brigade to the Bonaventura*, 4.

61 Davenport and Porter, *Scotsman in Buckskin*, 35.

62 Stewart, *Altowan*, 107.

63 Townsend, *Narrative of a Journey*, 353-354. See also, Jackson, *Jemmy Jock Bird*, 86-87.

64 Jackson, *Jemmy Jock Bird*, 87.

65 Wislizenus, *A Journey to the Rocky Mountains in the Year 1829,* 116-117.

66 Stewart, *Edward Warren*, 253-254.

67 Carter, *Dear Old Kit,* 52-52. Carson, in his own words, said, "In April [1832], we commenced our hunt again ... They told me that Capt. Gaunt was in the New Park ... I wished to join his party. Four of us left the party and struck out in search of Gaunt. In ten days, we found him and party at the New Park. We remained trapping in the Park for some time ... We trapped on the waters of the Arkansas until the river began to freeze, and then went into winter quarters on the main stream."

68 Irving, *Captain Bonneville*, 74-75; Victor, *River of the West*, 130.

Chapter 15:
Locating the Battle Site

1 Parker, *Journal of an Exploring Tour*, 88.

2 N. Wyeth, *Journal,* 159.

3 Ibid., 160.

4 Ibid., 158.

5 Driggs, *History of Teton Valley*, 68-70.

6 Robertson, *Fort Hall, Gateway to the Oregon Country,* 78.

7 Teton County Land Records, Quit Claim Deed, Instrument 26571, dated May 21, 1934.

8 Ferris, *Life in the Rocky Mountains*, 182, 410-412.

9 Ibid., 413.

10 Ibid.

11 Hayden, "The Battle of Pierre's Hole," 4.

12 Ferris, *Life in the Rocky Mountains,* 269-271.

13 De Voto, *Across the Wide Missouri,* 80, n. 422.

14 Clement, "Battle of Pierre's Hole," 27.

Chapter 16:
After the Battle of Pierre's Hole

1 Campbell, *A Narrative of Colonel Robert Campbell's Experiences*, 40.

2 Carter, "Andrew Drips," 144-145n and Voelker, "Jacques (Old Pino) Fournaise," 179. Carter gives the date of July 12 rather than 18, and spells the baby's name Katherine. This child, as an adult, was responsible for preserving a trunk full of her father's papers.

3 Vestal, *Mountain Men,* 124.

4   Newell, *Robert Newell's Memoranda*, 32.

5   Alfred Stephens, of the Gantt and Blackwell Company, had met Thomas
    Fitzpatrick on the Laramie River back in June 1832, well before the Pierre's
    Hole rendezvous. Zenas Leonard, a trapper assigned to Stephen's party
    wrote about this encounter in his journal: "Mr. Fitzpatrick and a company
    of 115 men, came to our camp. He was on his way to join his company on
    the west side of the mountains, on the Columbia river, and to supply them
    with merchandize, ammunition, horses, &c. This company informed us
    that the firm of Gant & Blackwell had become insolvent. At this news we
    all became discouraged; and finally Mr. Stephens and the whole company
    agreed to join in with Fitzpatrick and go with him to his rendezvous,
    where we were to make arrangements as to hiring, purchasing equipments,
    &c. Mr. Stephens took 120 beaver skins, which belonged to Captain
    Gant, and sold them to Fitzpatrick, which he secreted in the ground,
    with the intention of raising them when on his return to Missouri – in
    consideration of which, he was to furnish him with horses and such other
    equipments as he might want." See Leonard, *Narrative of the Adventures of
    Zenas Leonard*, 46.

    Stephens made a remarkable trek from the Laramie Fork to Pierre's
    Hole, covering almost four hundred miles in twenty some odd days.
    Leonard's calendar is skewed but they seemed to have averaged almost
    twenty miles each day.

6   Irving, *Captain Bonneville*, 65.

7   Hardeman, "Albert Gallatin Boone," 33-35.

8   J. Wyeth, *Oregon*, 73-74.

9   Ferris, *Life in the Rocky Mountains*, 223.

10 N. Wyeth, *Journal*, 160.

11 Ibid.

12 Ibid., 161.

13 A selection of Campbell's 1832 business records are found in Papers of the
    St. Louis Fur Trade, Part 3: Robert Campbell Family Collection from the
    St. Louis Mercantile Library Association and, at the time of this writing,
    on-line at http://www.xmission.com/~drudy/mtman/html/campacct.
    html#13.

14 G. Scott and J. Scott, "John Christian Hawken," 4-5. The list of men paid
    by Sublette included an Alfred Quigley, but whether this is any relation to
    Thomas Quigley, or is the same man, is not clear. Two men with as unusual
    a surname as Quigley seems too coincidental for them to be unrelated.

15 Gowans, *Rocky Mountain Rendezvous*, 78.

16 Campbell, *A Narrative of Colonel Robert Campbell's Experiences*, 42.

17 Hafen, "John Robertson ('Jack Robinson')," 248.

18 Ibid.

19 The names in these records, and the amounts to be credited to most of
    them, can be found in Hafen, *Broken Hand*, nn. 118-119. This documented
    list of men known to have been at the 1832 rendezvous includes Poliet

Dejurdy, Miller Francis, George Ennis, Strother Coleman, Louis Vasquez, Rud D. Lewis, Francis Lajones, Joseph Wash, Isaac Lyonsa, L. Underwood, Julian Lacont, David Carson, Louis Clermo, Baptist Lapage, William C. Hutton, Charles Dufon, Jefferson Smith, Joseph Pilkey, Tessant Demet, Robert Campbell, "a Spaniard (on Bent and Savory)," Charles Adams, James White, John Robinson, Thomas Eddie, Christian Shotts, Alfred R. Shute, William M. Price, John A. Mytinger, John C. Hawkins, Antoine Janice, Fuller P. Sinclair, Jacob Foreman, Thomas "Fitchpaterick," S. H. Everitt and Joshua Palen.

20 Campbell, *A Narrative of Colonel Robert Campbell's Experiences*, 42; Ferris, *Life in the Rocky Mountains*, 223-224.

21 J. Wyeth, *Oregon*, 62.

22 Ibid., 86.

23 Sunder, *Bill Sublette*, 112-113. However, Campbell says they met Bonneville on Green River which means the caravan descended from Union Pass to the south, probably via Kinky Creek, then crossed South Pass to the Sweetwater. See Campbell, *A Narrative of Robert Campbell's Experiences*, 42.

24 Ferris, *Life in the Rocky Mountains*, 224.

25 Ibid.

26 Wells, "Ignace Hatchiorauquasha (John Grey)," 170.

27 Ferris, *Life in the Rocky Mountains*, 224-225.

28 Ibid.

29 Ibid., 226.

30 Ibid., 227. One wonders how they missed these bones on the way out of Pierre's Hole.

31 Ibid., 242-243.

32 For a concise discussion of Bonneville as a spy, see Goetzman, *Exploration and Empire*, 147-150.

33 Irving, *Captain Bonneville*, 13-16.

34 Ibid., n. 116.

35 Ibid., nn. 49-50.

36 Ibid., 73.

37 Vestal, *Mountain Men*, 124-125. The Crow claim they were greatly superior in numbers and the Gros Ventres were so overcome by the first day's fighting that they fled in the night, leaving most of their camp supplies. Crow warriors would have exterminated the Gros Ventres that day but for the bravery of one man, Iron Robe, who fought with such fury that no Crow could stand before him. See Curtis, *The North American Indian*, 106.

38 Ibid., 76.

39 Ibid., 77.

40 N. Wyeth, *Journal*, 69, 204.

41 Ferris, *Life in the Rocky Mountains*, 226.

42 Irving, *Captain Bonneville*, 77.

43 Lovell, *Benjamin Bonneville*, 189, 260.

44 Irving, *Captain Bonneville*, 78.

45 Ibid.
46 Ibid.

Chapter 17:
The Waning Years of the Fur Trade

1   Carter, "Andrew Drips," 148.
2   Ferris, *Life in the Rocky Mountains,* 269.
3   Ibid., 269-270.
4   The description of what Ferris saw in May 1833 was included earlier in journal entries about the Battle of Pierre's Hole.
5   Ibid., 271-272.
6   Ibid., 272.
7   N. Wyeth, *Journal,* 199, 200.
8   Ibid., 203.
9   *The Rexburg Standard Journal,* June 19, 1997.
10 Ferris, *Life in the Rocky Mountains,* 218, 227, 289-290, 326; *Dallas Herald,* December 28, 1872, found in Ferris, *Life in the Rocky Mountains,* n. 251.
11 N. Wyeth, *Journal,* 203.
12 Numerous trapper journals indicated the use of cottonwood bark as fodder. William Ashley mentioned implementing this feed on numerous occasions in his lengthy narrative to General Henry Atkinson, dated November 3, 1824 and reproduced in Dale, *Ashley-Smith Explorations,* 134-135, referencing both cottonwood varieties.
13 N. Wyeth, *Journal,* 204.
14 Ibid. *The New York Times* August 24, 1873 edition reported the Hayden Survey, while in Teton Valley, found "At certain seasons of the year, usually in August and September, the air filled to a great height with grasshoppers flying in every direction. They sometimes rise to the height of several thousand feet."
15 Wyeth had hidden goods in several caches prior to reaching his ultimate destination on the Columbia River. Before returning east from Fort Vancouver, letters home had declared Wyeth's intentions to recover "deposits." He told HBC's George Simpson he had goods in deposits that "will probably be lost to me." In his 1834 expedition journal, on Nov. 19, Wyeth spoke of raising a deposit on the Walla Walla River, but no mention is ever made regarding the cache dug on the east flank of the Tetons in 1832. N. Wyeth, *Journal,* 55-57, 235-236.
16 Raynolds, *Report on the Exploration of the Yellowstone River,* 96.
17 Hayden, *From Trapper to Tourist in Jackson Hole,* 23.
18 Victor, River of the West, 107-108, 142.
19 Irving, *Captain Bonneville,* 149.
20 Ibid., 388.
21 Raynolds, *Report on the Exploration of the Yellowstone River,* 95-96.
22 N. Wyeth, *Journal,* 204.

23 Ibid.

24 N. Wyeth, *Journal*, 213.

25 Gowans, *Rocky Mountain Rendezvous*, 81.

26 Larpenteur, *Forty Years a Fur Trader*, 7-8.

27 Larpenteur, *The Original Journal of Charles Larpenteur*, 3.

28 Larpenteur, *Forty Years a Fur Trader*, 32, 34.

29 Ferris, *Life in the Rocky Mountains*, 283.

30 Ibid., 283-284.

31 Ibid., 284.

32 Ibid., 320. For an in-depth discussion of the experience Ferris had as a trader, see Scott Walker, "Warren Ferris, The Hudson's Bay Company, and the Rendezvous of 1834," *The Rocky Mountain Fur Trade Journal*, 4 (2010): 80-107.

33 Ibid., 323-324.

34 Ibid., 326. The identification of Medicine Lodge Pass is found on **333n.**

35 Ibid., 327.

36 Ibid., 337.

37 Ibid.

38 Ibid., 338.

39 Ibid.

40 Gowans, *Rocky Mountain Rendezvous*, 96.

41 N. Wyeth, *Journal*, 225.

42 Gowans, *Rocky Mountain Rendezvous*, 109.

43 Ibid., 110.

44 The financial information in the preceding paragraphs is found in Cole, "Failure on the Columbia," 276, letter from Edward Samuel to "Gentlemen," dated Sept 24, 1834; Sublette County Fur Trade Papers, Museum of the Mountain Man, Pinedale, Wyoming; Nathaniel Wyeth, *Journal*, 124, 130, 138-139).

45 N. Wyeth, *Journal*, 77.

46 Ibid., 134.

47 Ibid., 225.

48 Townsend, *Narrative of a Journey Across the Rocky Mountains*, 198.

49 Ibid., 227.

50 Driggs, *History of Teton Valley*, 86.

51 Townsend, *Narrative of a Journey Across the Rocky Mountains*, 198.

52 Ibid., 208.

53 Driggs, *History of Teton Valley*, 88.

54 Victor, *River of the West*, 166.

55 Marsh, *Four Years in the Rocky Mountains*, 77.

56 Russell, *Journal of a Trapper*, 14-15.

57 Ibid., 15-16.

58 Russell, *Journal of a Trapper*, 16-17.

59 Ibid., 32.

60 Ibid., 17.

61 Ibid.

62 Parker, *Journal of an Exploring Tour,* 83.

63 Ibid.

64 Victor, *River of the West,* 187.

65 Ibid., 86-87.

66 Ibid., 87.

67 Ibid., 88.

68 Ibid.

69 Ibid.

70 Ibid., 90.

71 Victor, *River of the West,* 214.

72 Ibid., 214-215.

73 Ibid., 215.

74 Ibid.

75 Field, *Prairie and Mountain Sketches,* 154.

76 Tobie, *No Man Like Joe,* 69. Meek placed these events in 1836 though Harvey, basing his summation on Newell and Russell, is convinced Meek's calendar was skewed.

77 Russell, *Journal of a Trapper,* 89.

78 Newell, *Robert Newell's' Memoranda,* 37.

79 Ibid.

80 Reid, *Contested Empire,* 3-6 contains a good discussion of the Joint Occupancy treaty.

81 Gowans, *Rocky Mountain Rendezvous,* 183.

82 Ibid., 183-184. Cushing Eells surmised it might have been Robert Newell, Black Harris or another free trapper who left the message announcing the site change.

83 Gowans, *Rocky Mountain Rendezvous,* 180.

84 In 1838, The American Fur Company transformed from Pratte, Chouteau and Company to Pierre Chouteau, Jr. and Company, though it was still more often called the American Fur Company. Andrew Drips was a primary field captain and Jim Bridger now worked under Drips.

85 Newell, *Robert Newell's' Memoranda,* 37.

86 The sale of Fort Hall to HBC was completed on December 16, 1837. See Grant, "Fort Hall Under the Hudson's Bay Company," n. 35.

87 Russell, *Journal of a Trapper,* 94.

88 Tuthill, "Elbridge Trask," 369-372.

89 Russell, *Journal of a Trapper,* 91.

90 Ibid.

91 Ibid.

92 Ibid., 91-92.

93 Ibid., n. 171.

94 Newell, *Robert Newell's Memoranda,* 38.

95 Victor, *River of the West,* 253, 256.

96 Ibid., 253.

97 This muzzle loading gun had a percussion lock. For this type of ignition system, a small cap containing a minute charge of black powder is placed on a hollow tube, often called a nipple, which leads to the main powder charge. Pulling the trigger allowed the hammer to fall on this small cap, exploding the small amount of powder and sending a spark down the tube to ignite the main charge. In this instance, Allen tries to dry his wet weapon's ignition system by "snapping caps" multiple times on the tube in hopes the resulting heat of repeated sparks would dry the tube enough to allow the gun to fire.

98 Ibid., 254-255.

99 A common belief that trappers did not take fur in the summer is false. In warmer months, the hide may not have been as valuable due to the shedding of thicker, winter peltry, but the skins were still worth money. Trapper journals reference trapping in virtually all months of the year. These hides were traded and priced by the pound – for the hair, not the leather. A winter hide had more hair and was heavier. Though more trapping may have been done in colder months, any beaver hide taken at any time of the year was sold to traders.

100 Russell, *Journal of a Trapper,* 101-105.

101 Ibid.

102 Ibid., 107.

103 Ibid.

104 Tobie, *No Man Like Joe,* 82.

105 Ibid., n. 291.

106 Ibid.

107 Lovell, *Captain Bonneville's County,* 220.

108 Tobie, "Joseph L. Meek," 323-324.

109 Victor, *River of the West,* 262-263. Lewis Lake is probably today's Jackson Lake and Jackson River is today's Snake River.

110 Gowans, *Rocky Mountain Rendezvous,* 194.

111 De Smet, "Life, Letters, and Travels," 221-223.

112 Ibid., 228.

113 Ibid., 223.

114 Driggs wrote that Father De Smet held a religious service in Pierre's Hole on Sunday, July 5, 1840 and that a feast was held in his honor at which the chief's three best dogs were served up as the main course. But De Smet did not reach the Teton Basin until July 11. The place at which De Smet celebrated the mass of July 5 is now called "The Prairie of the Mass," located a little southeast of today's Daniel, Wyoming in the Green River Valley. As for the feast mentioned by Driggs, it occurred, but not in Pierre's Hole and not with the Flathead. When the AFC expedition, led by Drips and accompanied by De Smet, had reached the Cheyenne village in early June 1840, that chief feted the "minister of the Great Spirit." De Smet said the chief told him, "As soon as I was appraised of your coming, I ordered my great kettle to be filled, and in your honor, I commanded that my three

fattest dogs should be served up." See De Smet, "Life, Letters, and Travels," 136, 222; and Olson, *Landmarks of the Rocky Mountain Fur Trade*, 31, 56.

115 De Smet, "Life, Letters, and Travels," 170.

Chapter 18:
Epilogue

1 Gowans, *Rocky Mountains Rendezvous*, 197.

2 For an examination of factors leading to the end of rendezvous see, Hanson, "The Myth of the Silk Hat and the End of the Rendezvous," 2-11.

3 Newell, *Robert Newell's Memoranda*, 39.

4 Victor, *River of the West*, 264-265.

5 Russell, *Journal of a Trapper*, 123.

6 Daugherty, *A Place Called Jackson Hole*, 62.

7 Mark, "William Craig," 110-116. Craig's father-in-law was the Nez Perce chief called James. Spaulding had virtually eliminated the chief's authority over his Lapwai band prior to Craig's arrival. Spaulding was quick to blame Craig for any of his troubles.

8 Ibid., 115-116.

9 Ibid., 115. See also Ware, "William Craig, Mountain Man and Homesteader," 17-18, and Brosnan, *History of the State of Idaho*, 183-184. There seems to be some controversy regarding the veracity of the term "e-dah-hoe" and whether it is truly of Native American origin. This is discussed thoroughly in John E. Rees, "Idaho – Its Meaning, Origin and Application," *Quarterly of the Oregon Historical Society*, 28-2 (June 1917): 83-92.

BIBLIOGRAPHY

Abraham, Terry. "Here Before Lewis and Clark." *Idaho Yesterdays*, 34-2 (Summer 1990): 28-30.

Allen, W. A. *The Sheep Eaters*. Fairfield, WA: Ye Galleon Press, 1997.

Alter, J. Cecil. *Jim Bridger*. Norman, OK: University of Oklahoma Press, 1950.

Allen, John L. "William Clark 1812: Redux." A paper presented at the annual meeting of the Lewis and Clark Heritage Trail Foundation in Great Falls, MT, August 2008.

Allen, Paul and Biddle, Nicholas, eds. *The History of the Expedition Under the Commands of Captains Lewis and Clark*. Philadelphia: Bradford and Inskeep, 1814.

Anderson, William M. *The Rocky Mountain Journals of William Marshall Anderson – The West in 1834*. Edited by Eleanor T. Harris and Dale L. Morgan. San Marino, CA: The Huntington Library, 1967.

Auld, James. "The Legend of Jedediah Smith: Fact, Fantasy and Opinion." *The Rocky Mountain Fur Trade Journal*. 2 (2008): 1-13.

Bagley, Jerry. *The First Known Man in Yellowstone*. Rigby, ID: Old Faithful Eye-Witness Publishing, 2000.

Bakeless, John. *The Journals of Lewis and Clark*. New York: Penguin Books USA, Inc., 1964.

Ball, John. *Autobiography of John Ball*. Glendale, CA: The Arthur H. Clark Company, 1925.

———. "Letters of John Ball 1832-1833." *Mississippi Valley Historical Review*. Edited by Milo Quaife. 5-4 (March 1919): 450-468.

Barbour, Barton H. *Jedediah Smith, No Ordinary Mountain Man*. Norman, OK: University of Oklahoma Press, 2009.

Barry, J. Neilson "The Problem of the Stone Lasts." *Washington Historical Quarterly*, 25 (1934): 276-277.

Beal, Merrill D. *A History of Southeastern Idaho*. Caldwell, ID: Caxton Printers, Ltd., 1942.

———. *The Story of Man in Yellowstone*. Caldwell, ID: Caxton Printers, Ltd., 1949.

Beckwourth, James P. *The Life and Adventures of James P. Beckwourth*. Edited by Delmont R. Oswald. Lincoln, NE: University of Nebraska Press, 1972.

Bell, C. R. "Indian Fights of the Fur Trade After 1830." *The Journal of America's Military Past*. 27- 2 (Fall 2000): 74-84.

Berry, Don. *A Majority of Scoundrels*. New York: Harper & Brothers, 1961.

Betts, Robert B. *Along the Ramparts of the Tetons, the Saga of Jackson Hole, Wyoming*. Boulder, CO: Colorado Associated University Press, 1978.

Binns, Archie. *Peter Skene Ogden, Fur Trader*. Portland: Binfords & Mort, Publisher, 1967.

Blevins, Bruce H. *A.K.A. Jackson Lake*. Powell, WY: WIMM, Inc., 1998.

———. *A.K.A. the Tetons*. Powell, WY: Wim Marketing, 1999.

Bonney, Orrin H. and Lorraine G. *Bonney's Guide – Grand Teton National Park and Jackson's Hole*. Houston, TX: Authors, 1961.

———. *Guide to the Wyoming Mountains and Wilderness Areas*. Denver: Sage Books, 1960.

Boone, Lalia. *Idaho Place Names*. Moscow, ID: University of Idaho Press, 1988.

Boyle, Stanley M. *Narrative History of Teton Valley, Idaho*. Logan, UT: Unpublished paper, Utah State University, 1957.

Bradbury, John. *Travels in the Interior of America*. Chester, VT: Readex Microprint Corporation, 1966.

———. "Travels in the Interior of America," *Early Western Travels*. Vol. 5. Edited by Reuben Thwaites. New York: AMS Press, Inc., 1966.

Brandon, William, "Wilson Price Hunt," *The Mountain Men and the Fur Trade of the Far West*. Vol. 6. Edited by Leroy R. Hafen. Glendale, CA: The Arthur H. Clark Company, 1968.

Brackenridge, Henry M. *Views of Louisiana Together with a Journal of a Voyage up the Missouri River in 1811*. Pittsburgh: Cramer, Spear and Eichbaum, 1814.

Brooks, Charles E. *The Henry's Fork*. New York: Nick Lyons Books, 1986.

Brosnan, C. J. *History of the State of Idaho*. New York: Charles Scribner's Sons, 1935.

Brown, Jennie B. *Fort Hall on the Oregon Trail*. Caldwell, ID: Caxton Printers, Ltd., 1932.

Bryan, William L. *Montana's Indians: Yesterday and Today*. Helena, MT: American & World Geographic Publishing, 1996.

Burger, Carl. *Beaver Skins and Mountain Men*. New York: E. P. Dutton & Co., 1968.

Burkes, Glenn R. "History of Teton County." *Annals of Wyoming*. 44-1, 2 (Spring, Fall 1972): 73–106, 241–267.

Calkins, Frank. *Jackson Hole*. New York: Alfred A. Knopf, 1973.

Camp, Charles. "James Clyman." *The Mountain Men and the Fur Trade of the Far West*. Vol. 1. Edited by Leroy R. Hafen. Glendale, CA: The Arthur H. Clark Company, 1965.

Campbell, Robert. *A Narrative of Colonel Robert Campbell's Experiences in the Rocky Mountain Fur Trade From 1825 to 1835*. Edited by Drew A. Holloway. Fairfield, WA: Ye Galleon Press, 1991.

———. *The Rocky Mountain Letters of Robert Campbell*. Edited by Charles Eberstadt. Printed for Frederick W. Beinecke, 1955. Originally published in *The National Atlas and Tuesday Morning Mail* (Philadelphia, PA), Vol. 1, nos. 14-19 (Nov. 1 - Dec. 6, 1836).

Carter, Harvey L. "Andrew Drips." *The Mountain Men and the Fur Trade of the Far West*. Vol. 8. Edited by Leroy R. Hafen. Glendale, CA: The Arthur H. Clark Company, 1972.

———. *Dear Old Kit, the Historical Christopher Carson.* Norman, OK: University of Oklahoma Press, 1968.

———. "John Gantt," *The Mountain Men and the Fur Trade of the Far West.* Vol. 5. Edited by Leroy R. Hafen. Glendale, CA: The Arthur H. Clark Company, 1968.

———. "Ramsay Crooks." The Mountain Men and the Fur Trade of the Far West. Vol. 9. Edited by Leroy R. Hafen. Glendale, CA: The Arthur H. Clark Company, 1972.

———. "Robert McClellan." *The Mountain Men and the Fur Trade of the Far West.* Vol. 8. Edited by Leroy R. Hafen. Glendale, CA: The Arthur H. Clark Company, 1971.

Catlin, George. *Letters and Notes on the Manners, Customs, and Conditions of the North American Indians.* Philadelphia: Willis P. Hazard, 1857.

Chittenden, Hiram M. *A History of the American Fur Trade of the Far West.* Stanford, CA: Academic Reprints, 1954.

———. *The Yellowstone National Park.* Edited by Richard A. Bartlett. Norman, OK: University of Oklahoma Press, 1964.

Clark, William. *The Indian Sign Language.* Lincoln, NE: University of Nebraska Press, 1982.

Clements, Louis J. "Andrew Henry." *The Mountain Men and the Fur Trade of the Far West.* Vol. 6. Edited by Leroy R. Hafen. Glendale, CA: The Arthur H. Clark Company, 1968.

———. "Battle of Pierre's Hole." *The Upper Snake River Valley Historical Society Quarterly.* 2-2 (Fall 1972): 25-29.

———. "Upper Snake River to 1840." *Snake River Echoes.* 27-1 (June 1998): 27-32.

———. "Where Was Fort Henry?" *Snake River Echoes.* 3-3 (Spring 1974):52-54.

Clements, Louis J. and Forbush, Harold S. *Pioneering in the Snake River Fork Country.* Rexburg, ID: Eastern Idaho Publishing Co., 1972.

Cline, Gloria G. *Peter Skene Ogden and the Hudson's Bay Company.* Norman, OK: University of Oklahoma Press, 1974.

Clokey, Richard M. *William H. Ashley, Enterprise and Politics in the Trans-Mississippi West.* Norman, OK: University of Oklahoma Press, 1980.

Colby, Susan. *Sacagawea's Child, The Life and Times of Jean-Baptiste (Pomp) Charbonneau.* Spokane, WA: The Arthur H. Clark Company, 2005.

Cole, Bradford. "Failure on the Columbia: Nathaniel Wyeth's Columbia River Fishing and Trading Company." *The Fur Trade Revisited.* Edited by Jennifer S. H. Brown, W. J. Eccles, and Donald P. Heldman. Lansing, MI: Michigan State University Press, 1994.

Colter-Frick, L. R. *Courageous Colter and Companions.* Washington, MO: Author, 1997.

Coutant, Charles G. *The History of Wyoming.* Laramie, WY: Chaplin, Spafford & Mathison, Printers. 1899.

Cox, Ross. *The Columbia River.* Edited by Edgar I. and Jane R. Stewart. Norman, OK: University of Oklahoma Press, 1957.

Curtis, Edward S. *The North American Indian*. Cambridge, MA: The University Press, 1909.

Cutright, Paul. *A History of the Lewis and Clark Journals*. Norman, OK: University of Oklahoma Press, 1976.

Dale, Harrison C. *The Ashley-Smith Explorations and the Discovery of a Central Route to the Pacific, 1822-1829*. Glendale, CA: The Arthur H. Clark Company, 1941.

Daugherty, John. *A Place Called Jackson Hole*. Moose, WY: Grand Teton National Park, 1999.

Davenport, Odessa and Porter, Mae Reed. *Scotsman in Buckskin, Sir William Drummond Stewart and the Rocky Mountain Fur Trade*. New York: Hastings House Publishers, 1963.

Davis, Lynne and Davis, Meade. *Jackson Hole from A to Z*. Cheyenne, WY: Pioneer Printing, 1979.

De Smet, Pierre J. "Letters and Sketches with a Narrative of a Year's Residency among the Indian Tribes of the Rocky Mountains." *Early Western Travels*. Vol. 27. Edited by Reuben Thwaites. New York: AMS Press, Inc., 1966.

———. *Life, Letters, and Travels of Father Pierre Jean De Smet*. Edited by Hiram M. Chittenden. New York: Francis P. Harper, 1905.

DeVoto, Bernard. *Across the Wide Missouri*. Boston: Houghton Mifflin Co., 1947.

Dodge, Grenville. *Biographical Sketch of James Bridger, Mountaineer, Trapper and Guide*. New York: Unz and Company, 1905.

Dolin, Eric J. *Fur, Fortune and Empire*. New York: W. W. Norton & Company, 2010.

Douglas, Walter B. *Manuel Lisa*. Nasatir, Abraham, ed. New York: Argosy-Antiquarian Ltd., 1964.

Driggs, Benjamin W. *History of Teton Valley*. Caldwell, ID: The Caxton Printers, Ltd., 1926.

Driggs, B. W. *History of Teton Valley*. Edited by Louis J. Clements and Harold S. Forbush. Rexburg, ID: Eastern Idaho Publishing Company, 1970.

Dyer, Robert L. *Duke Paul of Wuerttemberg on the Missouri Frontier, 1823, 1830, and 1851*. Booneville, MO: Pekitanoui Publications, 1998.

Ebberts, George W. *A Trapper's Life in the Rocky Mountains and Oregon From 1829 to 1839*. Bancroft, Hubert H. comp. Berkeley, CA: unpublished manuscript, Bancroft Library, University of California.

Ehrenberg, Ralph E. "Sketch of Part of the Missouri & Yellowstone Rivers with a Description of the Country &c." *Prologue, Quarterly of the National Archives*. 3 (Fall 1971): 73-78.

Ermatinger, Francis. *Fur Trade Letters of Francis Ermatinger*. Edited by Lois Halliday McDonald. Glendale, CA: The Arthur H. Clark Company, 1980.

Ewers, John C. *The Blackfeet, Raiders on the Northwestern Plains*. Norman, OK: University of Oklahoma Press, 1958.

———. "Iroquois Indians in the Far West." *Montana, the Magazine of Western History*. 13-2 (April 1963): 2-10.

Ferris, Warren A. *Life in the Rocky Mountains*. Edited by Leroy R. Hafen. Denver: The Old West Publishing Co., 1983. First published in a series in the *Western Literary Messenger,* Buffalo, NY, July 13, 1842 to May 4, 1844.
———. *Map of the Northwest Fur Country, 1836*. Orem, UT: Mountain Grizzly Publications, 2000.

Fetter, Richard. *Mountain Men of Wyoming*. Boulder, CO: Johnson Books, 1982.

Field, Matthew C. *Prairie and Mountain Sketches*. Edited by Kate L. Gregg and John F. McDermott. Norman, OK: University of Oklahoma Press, 1957.

Fowler, Loretta. *Shared Customs, Contested Meaning: Gros Ventre Culture and History, 1798-1984*. Ithaca, NY: Cornell University Press, 1987.

Franchére, Gabriel. *Adventure at Astoria, 1810-1814*. Translated and edited by Hoyt Franchére. Norman, OK: University of Oklahoma Press, 1967.

Frost, Donald M. *Notes on General Ashley, The Overland Trail and South Pass*. Barre, MA: Barre Gazette, 1960.

Fryxell, Fritiof. *The Tetons, Interpretations of a Mountain Landscape*. Berkeley, CA: University of California Press, 1946.

Gates, Charles M., ed. *Five Fur Traders of the Northwest*. St. Paul: Minnesota Historical Society, 1965.

Gilbert, Bil. *Westering Man, The Life of Joseph Walker, Master of the Frontier*. New York: Atheneum, 1983.

Goetzman, William H. *Army Exploration in the American West*. New Haven, CT: Yale University Press, 1959.
———. *Exploration and Empire*. New York: Alfred A. Knopf, 1967.

Gowans, Fred. *A Fur Trade History of Yellowstone Park*. Orem, UT: Mountain Grizzly Publications, 1989.
———. *Rocky Mountain Rendezvous*. Layton, UT: Gibbs M. Smith, Inc., 1985.
———. *The Mystery Trail*. Orem, UT: Mountain Grizzly Publications, 2008.
———. *Tragedy at Pierre's Hole*. Orem, UT: Mountain Grizzly Publications, 2004.
———. *Travels of Daniel T. Potts*. Orem, UT: Mountain Grizzly Publications, 2006.

Gowans, Fred R. and Oman, Kerry R. *Trails & Passes of the Great Divide*. Orem, UT: Mountain Grizzly Publications, 2001.

Gowans, Fred. R. and White, Linda Harper. "Traders to Trappers, Andrew Henry and the Rocky Mountain Fur Trade. Part 2." *Montana, the Magazine of Western History*. 43-3 (Summer 1993): 54-63.

Grant, Louis S. "Fort Hall Under the Hudson's Bay Company, 1837-1856." *Oregon Historical Quarterly*. 41-1 (March 1940): 34-39.

Graustein, Jeannette E. *Thomas Nuttall, Naturalist*. Cambridge, MA: Harvard University Press, 1967.

Gray, John S., ed. "Young Fur Trapper, Phillip Covington Travels to the Rockies with William Sublette," *Colorado Heritage*, 1 (1982): 10-25.

Gregg, Josiah. "Commerce of the Prairies," *Early Western Travels*. Vol. 19. Edited by Reuben Thwaites. New York: AMS Press, Inc., 1966.

Haeger, John Denis. *John Jacob Astor, Business and Finance in the Early Republic.* Detroit: Wayne State University Press, 1991.

Hafen, Ann W. "Jean-Baptiste Charbonneau." *The Mountain Men and the Fur Trade of the Far West.* Vol. 1. Edited by Leroy R. Hafen. Glendale, CA: The Arthur H. Clark Company, 1965.

Hafen, Leroy R. "The Bean-Sinclair Party." *The Colorado Magazine.* 31- 3 (July 1954): 161-171.

———. *Broken Hand, The Life of Thomas Fitzpatrick.* Denver: The Old West Publishing Co., 1973.

———. *The Mountain Men and the Fur Trade of the Far West.* 10 Vols. Glendale, CA: The Arthur H. Clark Company, 1965-1972.

Haines, Aubrey L. *Yellowstone National Park, Its Exploration and Establishment.* Washington, D.C.: National Park Service, 1974.

Haines, Aubrey L. "Antoine Godin." *The Mountain Men and the Fur Trade of the Far West.* Vol. 2. Edited by Leroy R. Hafen. Glendale, CA: The Arthur H. Clark Company, 1965.

Hanson, Charles Jr. "The Trapper's Last Shot." *Museum of the Fur Trade Quarterly.* 20-1 (Spring 1984): 2-3.

Hanson, James A. "The Myth of the Silk Hat and the End of the Rendezvous." *The Museum of the Fur Trade Quarterly.* 36-1 (Spring 2000): 2-11.

Hardee, Jim. "The Ordeal of Marie Dorion." *True West Magazine.* 38-10 (October 1991): 46-49.

Hardeman, Nicholas P. "Albert Gallatin Boone." *The Mountain Men and the Fur Trade of the Far West.* Vol. 8. Edited by Leroy R. Hafen. Glendale, CA: The Arthur H. Clark Company, 1971.

Harris, Burton. *John Colter, His Years in the Rockies.* New York: Charles Scribner's Sons, 1952.

Hayden, Elizabeth W. *From Trapper to Tourist in Jackson Hole.* Moose, WY: Grand Teton Natural History Association, 1992.

Hayden, Willard C. "The Battle of Pierre's Hole." *Idaho Yesterdays.* 16-2 (Summer 1972): 2-11.

Hays, Carl D. W. "David E. Jackson," *The Mountain Men and the Fur Trade of the Far West.* Vol. 9. Edited by Leroy R. Hafen. Glendale, CA: The Arthur H. Clark Company, 1972.

Hebard, Grace. *Sacajawea.* Mansfield Centre, CT: Overland Trails Press, 1999.

———. *Washakie.* Cleveland: The Arthur H. Clark Company, 1930.

Holmes, Kenneth. "John Day," *The Mountain Men and the Fur Trade of the Far West.* Vol. 2. Edited by Leroy R. Hafen. Glendale, CA: The Arthur H. Clark Company, 1965.

Holmes, Reuben. "The Five Scalps." *Glimpses of the Past,* 5-1, 2, 3 (January-March 1938): 3-54.

Hunt, Wilson P. *The Overland Diary of Wilson Price Hunt.* Edited by Hoyt Franchére. Ashland, OR: The Oregon Book Society, 1973.

Innis, Harold A. *The Fur Trade in Canada.* Toronto, ON: University of Toronto Press, 1973.

Irving, Washington. *The Adventures of Captain Bonneville, USA.* Edited by
   Edgeley W. Todd. Norman, OK: University of Oklahoma Press, 1961.
   First published Philadelphia, PA: Carey, Lea, and Blanchard, 1837.

———. *Astoria or Anecdotes of an Enterprise Beyond the Rocky Mountains.* Edited
   by Edgeley W. Todd. Norman, OK: University of Oklahoma Press, 1964.

Jackson, John C. *Children of the Fur Trade.* Missoula, MT: Mountain Press
   Publishing Co., 1995.

———. *Jemmy Jock Bird, Marginal Man on the Blackfoot Frontier.* Calgary, AB:
   University of Calgary Press, 2003.

———. *Piikani Blackfeet, A Culture Under Siege.* Missoula, MT: Mountain
   Press Publishing, 2000.

———. "Revisiting the Colter Legend." *The Rocky Mountain Fur Trade Journal.*
   3 (2009): 1-19.

———. *Shadow on the Tetons, David E. Jackson and the Claiming of the
   American West.* Missoula, MT: Mountain Press Publishing Co., 1993.

James, Thomas. *Three Years Among the Indians and Mexicans.* Edited by Milo
   Quaife. New York: The Citadel Press, 1966.

Janetski, Joel C. *Indians in Yellowstone National Park.* Salt Lake City: University
   of Utah Press, 2002.

Johnson, Olga W. *Flathead and Kootenay.* Glendale, CA: Arthur H. Clark
   Company, 1969.

Josephy, Alvin M. *The Nez Perce Indians and the Opening of the Northwest.* New
   Haven, CT: Yale University Press, 1965.

Judge, Bill. "The Battle of Pierre's Hole." *True West Magazine,* 11-6 (July-August
   1964): 10-12.

Karamanski, Theodore J. "The Iroquois and the Fur Trade of the Far West." *The
   Beaver, Magazine of the North.* Spring 1982: 4-13.

Keith, H. Lloyd. *Traders' Tales of 'Big' Donald Mackenzie: Myths and Myth
   Making in the Pacific Northwest Fur Trade.* Unpublished manuscript.

Kelly, Mark W. *Life of John Dougherty.* Unpublished manuscript.

Large, Arlen. "Riled-Up Blackfeet: Did Meriwether Lewis Do It?" Edited by
   Robert Saindon. *Explorations into the World of Lewis and Clark.* Vol. 2.
   Great Falls, MT: Lewis and Clark Heritage Trail Foundation, Inc., 2003.

Larpenteur, Charles. *The Original Journal of Charles Larpenteur.* Edited by
   Michael M. Casler. Chadron, NE: The Museum Association of the
   American Frontier, 2007.

———. *The Personal Narrative of Charles Larpenteur.* Edited by Elliot Coues.
   Minneapolis: Ross & Haines, Inc., 1962.

Lavender, David. *The Rockies.* New York: Harper and Row Publishers, 1968.

———. *The Big Divide.* Garden City, NY: Doubleday and Co., 1948.

Lawrence, Paul. *Hiking the Teton Backcountry.* San Francisco: Sierra Club Books,
   1979.

———. *John Colter: Journey of Discovery.* Jackson, WY: Uinta Pioneer Press,
   1978.

Leonard, Zenas. *Narrative of the Adventures of Zenas Leonard.* Edited by Milo Quaife. Chicago: The Lakeside Press, R. R. Donnelley & Sons Co., 1934.

Lightner, Sam. *Roads Through Time: A Roadside History of Jackson Hole.* Jackson, WY: Exotic Rock Publishing, 2009.

Liljblad, Sven. *The Idaho Indians in Transition: 1805-1960.* Pocatello, ID: Idaho State University Museum, 1972.

Lindsley, Margaret H. *Major Andrew Henry in Idaho.* Idaho Falls, ID: Author, 1985.

Lovell, Edith H. *Benjamin Bonneville, Soldier of the American Frontier.* Bountiful, UT: Horizon Publishers, 1992.

————. *Captain Bonneville's County.* Idaho Falls, ID: The Eastern Idaho Farmer, 1963.

————. "The Clark Stone." *Snake River Echoes.* 5-1 (1976): 18-20.

Lowie, Robert H. *The Crow Indians.* Lincoln, NE: University of Nebraska Press, 1983.

————. *Indians of the Plains.* Lincoln, NE: University of Nebraska Press, 1954.

Luttig, John C. *Journal of a Fur-Trading Expedition on the Upper Missouri, 1812-1813.* Edited by Stella M. Drumm. St. Louis: Missouri Historical Society, 1920.

Mackenzie, Cecil W. *Donald Mackenzie – King of the Northwest.* Los Angeles: Ivan Deach, Jr. Publisher, 1937.

Madsen, Axel. *America's First Multimillionaire, John Jacob Astor.* New York: John Willey & Sons, Inc., 2001.

Madsen, Brigham D. *The Bannock of Idaho.* Caldwell, ID: Caxton Printers, Ltd., 1958.

————. *The Northern Shoshoni.* Caldwell, ID: Caxton Printers, Ltd., 1980.

Mann, John W. *Sacajawea's People: The Lemhi Shoshones and the Salmon River Country.* Lincoln, NE: University of Nebraska Press, 2004.

Mark, Frederick A. "William Craig." *The Mountain Men and the Fur Trade of the Far West.* Vol. 2. Edited by Leroy R. Hafen. Glendale, CA: The Arthur H. Clark Company, 1965.

Marsh, James B. *Four Years in the Rockies: The Adventures of Isaac P. Rose.* Newcastle, PA: W. B. Thomas, 1884.

Masson, L. R. *Les Bourgeois de la Compagnie Nord-Ouest.* New York: Antiquarian Press Ltd., 1960.

Mathews, Mitford M. *A Dictionary of Americanisms: On Historical Principles.* Chicago: University of Chicago Press, 1951.

Mattes, Merrill J. "Behind the Legend of Colter's Hell: The Early Exploration of Yellowstone National Park." *The Mississippi Valley Historical Review,* 36-2 (September 1949): 251-282.

————. *Colter's Hell & Jackson's Hole: The Fur Trappers' Explorations of the Yellowstone and Grand Teton National Park Region.* Moose, WY: Yellowstone Library and Museum Association, 1962.

————. *Jackson Hole, Crossroads of the Western Fur Trade, 1807-1840.* Jackson, WY: Jackson Hole Museum and Teton County Historical Society, 1994.

————. "Joseph Robidoux." *The Mountain Men and the Fur Trade of the Far West*. Vol. 8. Edited by Leroy R. Hafen. Glendale, CA: The Arthur H. Clark Company, 1971.

Maximilian, Alexander. "Travels in the Interior of North America." *Early Western Travels*. Vol. 23. Edited by Reuben Thwaites. New York: AMS Press, Inc., 1966.

McCartney, Laton. *Across the Great Divide – Robert Stuart and the Discovery of the Oregon Trail*. New York: Free Press, 2003.

McDonald, Lois H. *Fur Trade Letters of Francis Ermatinger*. Glendale, CA: The Arthur H. Clark Company, 1980.

McLoughlin, John. *Letters of Dr. John McLoughlin*. Edited by Burt B. Barker. Portland: Binfords & Mort, 1948.

————. *The Letters of John McLoughlin*. Edited by E. E. Rich. London: The Hudson's Bay Record Society, 1941.

Merkley, Anne. *The Shoshone-Bannock of Old Fort Hall*. Pocatello, ID: Copy Graphics, 1993.

Meyers Myers, John. *Pirate, Pawnee and Mountain Man*. Boston: Little, Brown and Company, 1963.

Morgan, Dale. *Jedediah Smith and the Opening of the West*. New York: Bobbs-Merrill Co., 1953.

————. *Shoshonean Peoples and the Overland Trail: Frontiers of the Utah Superintendency of Indian Affairs, 1849-1869*. Logan, UT: Utah State University Press, 2007.

————. *The West of William Ashley*. Denver: The Old West Publishing Co., 1964.

Morgan, Dale L. & Wheat, Carl I. *Jedediah Smith and his Maps of the American West*. San Francisco: California Historical Society, 1954.

Morris, Larry E. *The Fate of the Corps, What Became of the Lewis and Clark Explorers After the Expedition*. New Haven, CT: Yale University Press, 2004.

————. "The Mysterious Charles Courtin and the Early Missouri Fur Trade." *Missouri Historical Review*, 104-1 (October 2009): 21-39.

Moulton, Gary E., ed. *The Journals of the Lewis and Clark Expedition*. 13 vols. Lincoln, NE: University of Nebraska Press, 1983-2001.

Mumey, Nolie. *The Teton Mountains, Their History and Tradition*. Denver: Artcraft Press, 1947.

Munnick, Harriet D. "Jean-Baptiste Gervais." *The Mountain Men and the Fur Trade of the Far West*. Vol. 7. Edited by Leroy R. Hafen. Glendale, CA: The Arthur H. Clark Company, 1969.

Nelson, Fern K. *Mountain Men of Jackson's Hole*. Jackson, WY: Jackson Hole Museum, 1989.

Nester, William R. *From Mountain Man to Millionaire: The Bold and Dashing Life of Robert Campbell*. Columbia, MO: University of Missouri Press, 1999.

————. *The Arikara War, the First Plains Indian War: 1823*. Missoula, MT: Mountain Press Publishing Company, 2001.

Newell, Robert. *Robert Newell's Memoranda*. Portland, OR: Champoeg Press, 1959.

Newman, Peter C. *Company of Adventurers*. Markham, ON: Penguin Books, 1985.

Nidever, George. *The Life and Adventures of George Nidever*. Edited by William Ellison. Berkeley, CA: University of California Press, 1937.

Nunnis, Doyce B. *Andrew Sublette, Rocky Mountain Prince, 1808-1853*. Los Angeles: Dawson Book Shop, 1960.

Ogden, Peter S. *Peter Skene Ogden's Snake Country Journals, 1824-25 and 1825-26*. Edited by E. E. Rich. London: The Hudson's Bay Record Society, 1950.

———. *Peter Skene Ogden's Snake Country Journals, 1826-27*. Edited by K. G. Davies. London: The Hudson's Bay Record Society, 1961.

———. *Peter Skene Ogden's Snake Country Journals, 1827-28 and 1828-29*. Edited by Glyndwr Williams. London: The Hudson's Bay Record Society, 1971.

Oglesby, Richard E. *Manuel Lisa and the Opening of the Missouri Fur Trade*. Norman, OK: University of Oklahoma Press, 1963.

Olson, Pierce. *Landmarks of the Rocky Mountain Fur Trade*. Jackson, WY: Jackson Hole Historical Society and Museum, 1997.

Ore, Lois H. *Andrew Henry and his Contribution to the Western Fur Trade*. Unpublished Masters thesis. Idaho State University, 1964.

Ott, Jennifer. "'Ruining' the Rivers in the Snake Country: the Hudson's Bay Company's Fur Desert Policy." *Oregon Historical Society Quarterly*, 104-2 (June 2003): 166-195.

Parker, Samuel. *Parker's Exploring Tour Beyond the Rocky Mountains*. Minneapolis: Ross & Haines, 1967. First published Ithaca, NY: Mack, Andrus, and Woodruff, Printers, 1840.

Patterson, Bradley H. *Great Western Indian Fights*. Garden City, NY: Doubleday & Co., 1960.

Peltier, Jerome. *Black Harris*. Fairfield, WA: Ye Galleon Press, 1986.

Platts, Doris B. *The Pass, Historic Teton Pass and Wilson, Wyoming*. Jackson, WY: Bearprint Press, 1988.

Podruchny, Carolyn. *Making the Voyageur World, Travelers and Traders in the North American Fur Trade*. Lincoln, NE: University of Nebraska Press, 2006.

Pond, Peter. "The Narrative of Peter Pond." *Five Fur Traders of the Northwest*. Edited by Charles M. Gates. St. Paul, MN: Minnesota Historical Society, 1965.

Potts, Merlin K. "John Colter, The Discovery of Jackson Hole and the Yellowstone." *Campfire Tales of Jackson Hole*. Moose, WY: Grand Teton Natural History Association, 1960.

Raynolds, W. F. *Report on the Exploration of the Yellowstone River*. Washington, D.C.: Government Printing Office, 1868.

Rees, John E. "Idaho: Meaning and Origin," *Quarterly of the Oregon Historical Society*, 28-2 (June 1917): 83-92.

Reid, John P. *Contested Empire, Peter Skene Ogden and the Snake River Expeditions.* Norman, OK: University of Oklahoma Press, 2002.

Robertson, Frank C. *Fort Hall, Gateway to the Oregon Country.* New York: Hastings House Publishers, 1963.

Ronda, James P. *Astoria and Empire.* Lincoln, NE: University of Nebraska Press, 1990.

Ross, Alexander. *Adventures of the First Settlers on the Oregon or Columbia River.* Edited by Milo Quaife. New York: The Citadel Press, 1969.

———. *The Fur Hunters of the Far West.* Edited by Kenneth A. Spaulding. Norman, OK: University of Oklahoma Press, 1956.

———. "Journal of Alexander Ross - Snake Country Expedition, 1824." Edited by T. C. Elliot. *Quarterly of the Oregon Historical Society,* 14-4 (Dec. 1913): 366-385.

Russell, Osborne. *Journal of a Trapper.* Edited by Aubrey L. Haines. Portland: Oregon Historical Society, 1955. First published Boise, ID: Syms-York, 1914. Edited by L. A. York.

Ruxton, George F. *Life in the Far West.* Edited by Leroy R. Hafen. Norman, OK: University of Oklahoma Press, 1964.

Sabin, Edwin L. *Kit Carson Days.* New York: Press of the Pioneers, 1935.

Saindon, Robert A. "The Abduction of Sacagawea." *Explorations Into the World of Lewis & Clark.* Vol.1. Edited by Robert A. Saindon. Great Falls, MT. Lewis and Clark Heritage Trail Foundation, 2003.

Sanborn, Margaret. *The Grand Tetons: The Story of the Men Who Tamed the Western Wilderness.* New York: G.P. Putnam's Sons, 1978.

Sandoz, Mari. *The Beaver Men, Spearheads of Empire.* New York: Hastings House Publishers, 1964.

Saylor, David. *Jackson Hole, In the Shadow of the Tetons.* Norman, OK: University of Oklahoma Press, 1970.

Schilz, Thomas F. "The Gros Ventres and the Upper Missouri Fur Trade, 1806-1835," *Annals of Wyoming,* 56-2 (Fall 1984): 21-28.

Scott, Glenn R. and Juanita M. "John Christian Hawken – Fur Trapper and Rifle Maker." *The Museum of the Fur Trade Quarterly,* 28-2/3 (Summer/Fall 1992): 1-20.

Simpson, George. *Fur Trade and Empire, George Simpson's Journal, 1824-25.* Edited by Frederick Merk. Cambridge, MA: Belknap Press of Harvard University Press, 1968.

Smith, Robert B. "Battle of Pierre's Hole." *Wild West Magazine,* 5-1 (June 1992): 46: 52.

Sprague, Marshall. *The Great Gates, the Story of the Rocky Mountain Passes.* Boston: Little, Brown & Co., 1964.

Stamm, Henry E. *People of the Wind River: The Eastern Shoshones, 1825-1900.* Norman, OK: University of Oklahoma Press, 1999.

Stewart, William D. *Altowan.* New York: Harper and Brothers Publishers, 1846.

———. *Edward Warren.* Edited by Bart Barbour. Missoula, MT. Mountain Press Publishing Company, 1986.

Stoller, Ruth, "Alexander Carson." *The Mountain Men and the Fur Trade of the Far West*. Vol. 9. Edited by Leroy R. Hafen. Glendale, CA: The Arthur H. Clark Company, 1972.

Stuart, Robert. *On the Oregon Trail, Robert Stuart's Journey of Discovery, 1812-1813*. Edited by Kenneth A. Spaulding. Norman, OK: University of Oklahoma Press, 1953.

————. *The Discovery of the Oregon Trail – Robert Stuart's Narratives*. Edited by Phillip A. Rollins. New York: Charles Scribner's Sons, 1935.

Sullivan, Maurice. *Jedediah Smith, Trader & Trailbreaker*. New York: Press of the Pioneers, 1936.

————. *The Travels of Jedediah Smith*. Santa Anna, CA: The Fine Arts Press, 1934.

Sunder, John E. *Bill Sublette – Mountain Man*. Norman, OK: University of Oklahoma Press, 1959.

Talbot, Vivian L. *David E. Jackson, Field Captain of the Rocky Mountain Fur Trade*. Jackson, WY: Jackson Hole Historical Society and Museum, 1996.

Templeton, Sardis W. *The Lame Captain, The Life and Adventures of Pegleg Smith*. Los Angeles: Westernlore Press, 1964.

Terrell, John. *The Six Turnings, Major Changes in the American West, 1806-1834*. Glendale, CA: The Arthur H. Clark Company, 1968.

Thompson, Edith M. S. & William L. *Beaver Dick, The Honor and the Heartbreak*. Laramie, WY: Jelm Mountain Press, 1982.

Thrapp, Dan L., ed. *Encyclopedia of Frontier Biography*. Spokane, WA: The Arthur H. Clark Company, 1990.

Thwaites, Reuben, G. *Early Western Travels, 1748-1846*. 32 vols. New York: AMS Press, Inc., 1966.

Tobie, Harvey E. "Joseph L. Meek." *The Mountain Men and the Fur Trade of the Far West*. Vol. 1. Edited by Leroy R. Hafen. Glendale, CA: The Arthur H. Clark Company, 1965.

————. *No Man Like Joe*. Portland: Binfords & Mort, 1949.

Townsend, John K. *Narrative of a Journey Across the Rocky Mountains to the Columbia River*. Fairfield, WA: Ye Galleon Press, 1970.

Trottman, Alan C. "Lucien Fontenelle." *The Mountain Men and the Fur Trade of the Far West*. Vol. 5. Edited by Leroy R. Hafen. Glendale, CA: The Arthur H. Clark Company, 1968.

Tuthill, Jo. "Elbridge Trask." *The Mountain Men and the Fur Trade of the Far West*. Vol. 4. Edited by Leroy R. Hafen. Glendale, CA: The Arthur H. Clark Company, 1966.

Tykal, Jack B. *Etienne Provost, Man of the Mountains*. Liberty, UT: Eagle's View Publishing, 1989.

Unrau, William E. *White Man's Wicked Water, the Alcohol Trade and Prohibition in Indian Country, 1802-1892*. Lawrence, KS: University Press of Kansas, 1996.

Urbanek, Mae. *Wyoming Place Names*. Boulder, CO: Johnson Publishing Co., 1974.

Utley, Robert M. *A Life Wild and Perilous*. New York: Henry Holt and Co., 1997.

Voelker, Frederic. "Ezekiel Williams." *The Mountain Men and the Fur Trade of the Far West*. Vol. 9. Edited by Leroy R. Hafen. Glendale, CA: The Arthur H. Clark Company, 1966.

———. "Jacques (Old Pino) Fournaise." *The Mountain Men and the Fur Trade of the Far West*. Vol. 8. Edited by Leroy R. Hafen. Glendale, CA: The Arthur H. Clark Company, 1971.

Vestal, Stanley. *Joe Meek*. Caldwell, ID: Caxton Printers, Ltd., 1952.

———. *Mountain Men*. Boston: Houghton Mifflin Company, 1937.

Victor, Frances F. *The River of the West*. Hartford, CT: R. W. Bliss Co., 1870.

Vinton, Stallo. *John Colter, Discoverer of Yellowstone*. New York: Edward Eberstadt, 1926.

Walker, Scott, "Warren Ferris, The Hudson's Bay Company, and the Rendezvous of 1834." *The Rocky Mountain Fur Trade Journal*, 4 (2010): 80-107.

Ware, Marcus J. "William Craig, Mountain Man and Homesteader." *Museum of the Fur Trade Quarterly*, 41-3 (Fall 2005): 13-18.

Wells, Merle. "Michel Bourdon." *The Mountain Men and the Fur Trade of the Far West*. Vol. 2. Edited by Leroy R. Hafen. Glendale, CA: The Arthur H. Clark Company, 1966.

———. "Ignace Hatchiorauquasha (John Grey)." *The Mountain Men and the Fur Trade of the Far West*. Vol. 7. Edited by Leroy R. Hafen. Glendale, CA: The Arthur H. Clark Company, 1971.

West, G. Derek. "The Battle of Pierre's Hole." *American History Illustrated Magazine*, 3-1 (April 1968): 10-17.

Wheat, Carl I. *Mapping the Transmississippi West*. San Francisco: The Institute of Historical Cartography, 1958.

Wheeler, William F. "Personal Interview with Louis Rivet, Fort Benton, Montana, 1884." *Contributions to the Historical Society of Montana*. Vol. 10. Boston: J.S. Canner and Company Inc., 1966. Portion reproduced by permission.

Wilhem, Paul, Duke of Württenberg. "An Account of Adventures in the Great American Desert." Translated by Louis C. Butscher. *New Mexico Historical Review*, 17-3, 4 (July October 1942): 181-225.

———. *Travels in North America 1822-1824*. Edited by Robert W. Nitske, Translated by Savoie Lottinville. Norman, OK: University of Oklahoma Press, 1973.

Wilson, Elinor. *Jim Beckwourth*. Norman, OK: University of Oklahoma Press, 1972.

Wishart, David J., ed. *Encyclopedia of the Great Plains Indians*. Lincoln, NE: University of Nebraska Press, 2007.

Wislizenus, F. A. *A Journey to the Rocky Mountains in the Year 1839*. Fairfield, WA: Ye Galleon Press, 1989.

Work, John. *Fur Brigade to the Bonaventura, John Work's California Expedition, 1832-1833*. Edited by Alice B. Mahoney. San Francisco: California Historical Society, 1945.

———. *The Journal of John Work*. Edited by William S. Lewis and Paul C. Phillips. Cleveland: Arthur H. Clark Company, 1923.

———. *The Snake Country Expedition of 1830-1831, John Work's Field Journal*. Edited by Francis D. Haines. Norman, OK: University of Oklahoma Press, 1971.

Work Progress Administration. *Idaho, A Guide in Word and Pictures*. Caldwell, ID: Caxton Printers, Ltd., 1937.

Wyeth, John B. *Oregon; or a Short History of a Long Journey*. Edited by Reuben Thwaites. Fairfield, WA: Ye Galleon Press, 1970. First published Cambridge, MA: printed for John B. Wyeth, 1833.

Wyeth, Nathaniel J. *The Correspondence and Journals of Captain Nathaniel J. Wyeth, 1831-36*. Edited by F. G. Young. Eugene, OR: Oregon Historical Society, University Press, 1899.

INDEX

Nonsense 281, 297
Osage 281
Remon *47*, 48, 57, 58, 60, 61, 64,
    68, 69, 71, 328, 330
Riley 141
Robidoux 319
Smith 5
Spokane House 34, 120
Three Forks 71, 72, 81, 82, 331
Union 154, 157, 182, 281, 282,
    293, 351
Vancouver 145, 147, 191, 273,
    343, 349, 351, 356
Walla Walla 118, 351
    See also Fort Nez Perces
William 298
    See also Fort Laramie
William, on Thunder Bay
    (NWC) 32, 132, 133
Fournaise, Jacques (Old Pino) 271,
    354
Fox Canyon 9, 266
Foy, John 214, 238, 272, 273, 280,
    282, 293
Fraeb, Henry 153, 156, 157, 184,
    185, 246, 251, 258, 273, 299,
    333, 344
    See also Frapp, Henry
Franchère, Gabriel 81, 335
Francis, Miller 355
Frapp, Henry 163, 173, 191, 192,
    229, 231, 244, 246, 255, 301,
    333, 344
    See also Fraeb, Henry
Fremont Lake 297
Fryxell, Fritiof 62, 323, 330

G

Gale, Joseph 302, 303-306, 310, 333
Gallatin, Albert 18, 19
Gallatin River 60, 61, 73, 302
Game Hill 112
Gantt and Blackwell Company 168,
    177, 178, 217, 272, 347, 354
Gantt, John 168, 177, 178, 217,

272, 347, 354
Gardner, Johnson 26, 38, 40, 41,
    126, 328, 333
Garns Mountain 8
Gervais, Jean-Baptiste 153, 156, 344
Gibbon Pass 121
Glass, Hugh 167, 347
Glineau, Nicholas 72
Godin
    Antoine 195, 209, 246, 251, 258,
        260, 261, 269, 351
    Thyery 124, 252
Godin's River 124, 313
Gormer Canyon 106
Gowans, Dr. Fred 144, 327, 340,
    342-344, 346, 348, 349, 355,
    357-360
Graham Hollow 107
Grand Portage 132
Grand Teton National Park 8, 9, 56,
    62, 63, 323, 330
Granite Creek 77, 112
Gravois Creek 98
Great Basin 18, 119, 146
Great Britain 38, 116, 125, 311
Great Lakes 31
Great Salt Lake 140
Green Canyon Hot Springs 91, 107,
    108
Green River 26, 29, 34, 39, 57, 74,
    86, 91, 101, 104, 112, 121,
    131, 135, 138, 139, 144, 145,
    156, 157, 172, 173, 188, 194,
    202, 214, 247, 249, 250, 258,
    259, 269, 272, 280-282, 285,
    286, 290, 293, 294, 296, 297,
    301, 306, 308, 310, 311, 313,
    315, 317, 319, 338, 341, 347,
    348, 355, 360
    Rio del Norte 57, 74, 166
    Seeds-ke-dee 202
    Seedskeedee Agie 319
    Seedskerdie 184
Green River valley 86, 104, 112, 135,
    139, 202, 250, 272, 282, 293,